BLEAK & BLUE

22 Years at the Manchester Academy of Football Farce

Craig Winstanley

Published by Sigma Leisure – an imprint of
Sigma Press, 1 South Oak Lane, Wilmslow, Cheshire SK9 6AR, England.

British Library Cataloguing in Publication Data
A CIP record for this book is available from the British Library.

ISBN: 1-85058-678-0

Typesetting and Design by: Sigma Press, Wilmslow, Cheshire.

Cover Design: MFP Design & Print

Cover photograph: Craig Winstanley

Text photographs: by permission, Manchester Evening News

Printed by: MFP Design & Print

Preface

'farce (färs) *noun*

   1. a. A light dramatic work in which highly improbable plot situations, exaggerated characters, and often slapstick elements are used for humorous effect. **b.** The broad or spirited humour characteristic of such works.

   2. A ludicrous, empty show; a mockery: *The election was a farce, for it was fixed.*

   3. A seasoned stuffing, as for roasted turkey.'

Microsoft Bookshelf '95 – Dictionary.

I was a premature baby, but not sufficiently premature to make my appearance whilst 'Blue Moon' by The Marcels was number one in the hit parade. I missed it by a week.

Nevertheless, this cosmic coincidence must have exerted a profound influence on my development. I was a blue baby. As far as the simple game called football is concerned, this blue baby grew up to be a disillusioned and hardened cynic, a fatalist of the most negative disposition, completely paranoid, jaundiced, bitter, peevish and unreasonable. I wasn't always like this. According to my mother I was a quite happy little thing at school. My personality has become inextricably linked with Manchester City Football Club, a giant not so much sleeping as languishing in a persistent vegetative state.

In 1976 Manchester City were a force to be reckoned with. Then I bought a season ticket, or to be more precise, I had one bought for me. The consequences for all concerned have been devastating.

Bleak and Blue is a highly personal account of more than two decades of emotional investment in Manchester City Football Club; an investment that has proven to be singularly unrewarding. It is 22 years since Manchester City last won a trophy, a barren spell coinciding precisely with my time as a season ticket holder. During that period, my beloved club has contrived to slump from the third-biggest in the country and perennial contenders for serious silverware, to a pitiful laughing stock struggling to lay claim to being the fifth-best team in Greater Manchester, and condemned to the English third division for the first time in their history.

Still, looking on the bright side, the Maine Road undersoil heating has performed splendidly throughout, the pitch is always well turned out, and following Manchester City has rarely been an uneventful obsession. The tale involves 16 managers, four relegations, two Cup Finals, two promotions, European nights, pies, bananas, comedy own goals and countless alleged footballers of varying ability; from Francis Lee to Ged Brannan.

The drama of each season from 1975/76 to the present day is recounted, with personal experiences and gratuitous references to music and hair thrown in, in a more or less random fashion. The story of my obsession with this football club is one of almost incessant failure, incompetence, catastrophe, calamity and misadventure. There is no happy ending, and the only moral is that just when you think it can't get any worse, it always does.

The story begins a long time ago ....

Dedication

This book is dedicated to my dad, as the longest sufferer from my football obsession, and to all those others who have been forced to put up with football-induced sulks and moods, particularly my mum and Barbara. It is also dedicated to all other fellow-sufferers who have had the dubious pleasure of my company at matches (especially Jon, Richard and Patrick), including the many who will vehemently disagree with most of my opinions.

Some of the characters in this book bear little or no resemblance to proper footballers living or dead, unfortunately.

Contents

Part Three: A TEMPORARY RESPITE

Part Four: THE NIGHTMARE NINETIES

Why Manchester City?

Once upon a time, there was a happy land where governments were inclined to change every few years without inflicting too much irreversible damage. People had the expectation of secure employment, the Eurovision Song Contest and Jimmy Saville were both taken seriously, Chicory Tip were considered innovative, mobile phones did not exist, the pavements were littered with gold and Manchester City had a good football team. For the younger ones amongst you, there was a deliberate lie hidden in there. Did you spot it?

Wrong! Manchester City did once have a good football team. There were truly great players in that team, genuine Manchester City icons, heroes worthy of the jealousy of other supporters. There were players such as Francis Lee, an endearingly chubby, baby-faced scamp of a forward, who possessed a terrific ability for 'inducing' penalty kicks, and packing the kind of shot that sent the goalkeeper either into the net or into orbit along with the ball, should he be daft enough to get in the way. Colin Bell was an elegant, athletic and influential midfield player, with a knack of arriving at precisely the crucial moment to finish off something that he had himself started. Mike Summerbee, yes, Mike Summerbee, was an old-fashioned winger with an eye for a goal and a talent that does not appear to be genetically inheritable. These three were the famous City trio, capturing most of the headlines, but there were quality players throughout the side built by Joe Mercer, with Malcolm Allison as his lieutenant. In 1968, City won the League Championship in dramatic fashion, with a last-match 4-3 win at Newcastle. The records state that there were two goals scored by Neil Young and one each by Mike Summerbee and Francis Lee, as City finished two points clear of their bitter rivals, *The Nation's Team*. Back in those days men were men (only with longer sideburns), women were women, transvestites were quiet and two points really were two points. In 1969, City won the FA Cup. This was followed by the League Cup and the European Cup Winners Cup in the same season. There were more cups than at a chimps' tea party. You could hardly see the front row in the team photograph for cups. Joe Mercer was manager, Malcolm Allison was coach and all was well with the world.

Regrettably, I don't actually recall any of those triumphs, apart from a vague awareness of the League Cup Final result, but I do believe that they really happened because I have the Manchester City Football Books to prove it. I can remember men bouncing about on the moon, Ali fighting Frazier, and that fantastic 1970 Brazilian World Cup team, but the obviously far more momentous 1969 FA Cup Final has failed to leave a permanent deposit in my memory bank. Even worse, I can clearly remember Chelsea's 1970 FA Cup win, but not City's Cup Winner's Cup triumph. My mind seems to have utterly blanked out City's most inspiring period.

In the 1969 Manchester City Football Book (Stanley Paul, London) there is a whole chapter by Francis Lee, entitled 'The Soccer Tycoon', in which he revealed his ambition, 'to open a woman's club-cum-boutique in Bolton. In this I envisage sauna baths, hairdressing salons, scope for every kind of beauty treatment, one or two shops and relaxation rooms, and a dining room.' This was clearly an ambitious man. Lee was already big in waste paper at the time. Some might say that his considerable experience with rubbish stood him in good stead later on.

Now it's time for a confession. This is where I might lose a few fellow-sufferers from the affliction of Manchester City fandom, but it's best out in the open. Here it is. I don't come from Manchester! This is a crucial flaw in my credibility, but I shall attempt a defence. As soon as possible I moved to Manchester, and I've been trying ever since that happy situation ended (involuntarily) to get back there. There are hidden forces conspiring to prevent this from happening, and therefore my successes in that particular quest have been limited, even though many of my friends remain in the great city. I did say that I was paranoid.

For the uninitiated, it should be explained that Mancunian status is important for a true Manchester City believer because without it there is little ammunition left to attack *The Nation's Team* and their followers: more of them later. My confession over, let's go back to the beginning.

I come from a town called Chorley, about 20 miles north of Manchester, where there is a football club, albeit a non-league one. Chorley FC used to be in the Northern Premier League, then slumped to the Cheshire League, and have since spent seasons in leagues with strange names of the *Ogden's Fish Fingers Always Crisp and Fresh Buy Six Get Two Free League* variety. The nearest Chorley have come to football fame was in 1878, when the second ever 'illuminated' match should have taken place there on 25 October, 11 days after the first-ever floodlit match, at Bramall Lane, Sheffield. Unfortunately, a rainstorm led to cancellation for safety reasons. So near to greatness, and yet so far.

My first experiences of live football involved visits to Victory Park to watch The Magpies – the *real* Magpies. Any visitor to Chorley must understand two peculiarities specific to the town: Chorley Football Club are the real Magpies and the *Chorley Guardian* is the real Guardian. If you ask for *The Guardian* in Chorley, you will receive a newspaper where feminism, advertisements for villas in Tuscany, special feature articles on Damien Hirst or double-page spreads entitled 'Twenty Inspiring Things to do with Tarragon' are conspicuous by their absence. The lead story is much more likely to contain details of the latest roundabout in Chorley town centre – they appear to collect roundabouts in Chorley. There may be articles concerning people who cut up dead animals, but in Chorley they call them butchers not artists. If you engage a local in conversation about the big Magpies game, you will find yourself discussing a replay against Droylsden in an obscure cup competition, rather than Alan Shearer's latest goal or the merits of the Kevin Keegan regime.

Between 1970 and 1972, I was in regular attendance at the home of Chorley FC, the optimistically named Victory Park. For a while, I even had my own season ticket entitling me to enter the Main Stand (well, the only proper stand, actually), where I could observe matters from a seated position, if I so desired. I seldom availed myself of the opportunity, preferring instead to stand, leaning on the iron railing which surrounded the pitch, but provided only a token barrier from it. From that position it was possible to follow the constant stream of sarcasm and abuse aimed at the hapless, balding, overweight linesman who waddled by, at times no more than a yard or so away from his tormentors. Linesmen, or referee's assistants as we are now supposed to call them, are figures inviting ridicule. They seem incapable of both observing the moment at which a ball is kicked and the position of a forward player at the same time. Since their only useful function is to judge offside decisions, this basic inability, demonstrated *ad nauseum* at all levels of the game, renders them worse than useless. As far as I can see, they are mainly decorative. Indeed the main role of a linesman appears to be as a target at which fans can direct their bile. There is something distinctly odd about grown men, dotted around the edge of the pitch, eagerly awaiting those moments when the match official passes within range to trigger one of a very limited repertoire of juvenile utterances. I sometimes joined in with comments questioning the linesman's requirement for spectacles. I used to think that was very amusing. I was only 10 or 11.

There are fully grown men who think themselves terribly amusing for much less. Often a loud expletive is considered the height of wit and repartee. The abuse received by match officials back at Victory Park was fairly subdued by modern standards, but it still puzzled me why no linesman ever confronted any of their ageing detractors. Maybe they recognised the inalienable right of all football fans to hurl abuse at the men (or women) in black, green or pastel shades, whatever the current fashion.

At Victory Park it was possible to change ends with the teams at half-time, but I rarely did so because that would have meant relinquishing the benefits of the area reserved for season ticket holders, such as losing optimum position for the on-site catering facilities. The pies and pasties were to be highly recommended, especially when washed down with a hot, coffee-like substance on a freezing cold night, as Chorley battled with the mighty Atherton Collieries in one of numerous cup competitions. Chorley took part in so many cup competitions that the chances of winning something must have been pretty high. I don't actually recall them winning anything, but I'm sure that they must have. The Magpies (notice the 'pies' in that nickname) did reach the semi-final of the Lancashire County Cup in 1972, losing to *The Nation's Team* after a replay. I attended both matches. It was my first visit to *The Swamp*. By then the official programme, *Magpie Review*, had risen in cost to five new pence, a scandalous doubling in price from the previous year. My first-ever away match as a Chorley fan was in far more salubrious surroundings, the Magpies winning 4-2 on Horwich RMI's sloping pitch. I can't recall how the pies compared to Chorley's, but I bet that they weren't so good.

The trip to Victory Park involved a brisk five-minute walk from our house, past the recreation ground, where many an evening I played football until it went dark; past Duke Street Primary School, my school; down a narrow dark alleyway and up to the turnstiles. These, if you had a season ticket, you could bypass disdainfully. I don't suppose such a walk in the dark for a young boy on his own would be encouraged these days, but I thought nothing of it. To the left of the turnstiles was the Social Club, which I did not frequent back then, but discovered subsequently is the hub of the whole operation and a good place to get a cheap pint, albeit not as cheap as some other social clubs in the locality.

Chorley had some great players in the early seventies. Well actually, they didn't, it's just that all footballers seem great to a 10-year-old. There was outside-right Ian Humphries, outside-left Colin Trussell who was rumoured to wear contact lenses, big centre forward Ron Pickering, and my favourite, Mickey Worswick, whose position, described as inside-forward, doesn't appear to exist any longer. The only well-known player I did see was Paul Mariner, who used to play in midfield for Chorley before advancing via Plymouth Argyle to nationwide prominence, playing for Ipswich Town. He even featured for England, receiving a number of international caps as a striker. Mariner's transfers kept the Chorley finances in good order for quite some time. Unfortunately for them, he was a one-off.

It was my regular habit to invade the pitch at the end of a match and thrust my autograph book under the nose of some unsuspecting, sweaty and knackered part-time footballer. On the whole, they were surprisingly obliging. Chorley's biggest grudge match of that era was against Wigan Athletic, giants of the non-league circuit. Chorley went on to have some memorable victories. Well, maybe memorable isn't the correct word, since I can't remember any of them, although I can confirm that I witnessed a 2-0 win over Wigan on 28 September 1971. For all I know, they may still be talking about that one. Several years later, Chorley beat Wimbledon in the FA Trophy, only to lose to Dagenham in the quarter-final, but by then I'd moved on. Astonishingly, the *Magpie Review* for the Dagenham game in 1977 still cost five pence.

On 16 September 1969, Manchester City sent a team to play Chorley in the first round of the LFA County Challenge Cup. I was eight years old, and this was my first sight of a Manchester City téam. It was probably only a third or fourth team, but there were one or two players whose names and faces I knew. Tony Coleman, a prominent member of the all-conquering Joe Mercer side, was one of them. I've no idea why he was playing. Maybe he was recovering from injury and needed a match for fitness purposes; maybe City just knew that a crack squad would be required for this prominent fixture. Every time he went past I squealed out, 'Go on TC.' It must have made him cringe. There he was, reduced to playing with the youngsters at some godforsaken place, and every time he went down the left wing a youthful voice chirped out encouragement using a stupid nickname. I was already a Manchester City fan and I wanted to demonstrate it. I aspired to Maine Road. It was just easier to get to Victory Park. The programme for that match cost six old pennies, and on the front page was the Chorley FC crest containing the word 'beware'. There's no indication of what or whom you should beware; just a helpful call to general wariness.

I think, looking back, that it was a mixture of my dad, Francis Lee and sheer bloody-mindedness that turned me into a Manchester City fan. However, I can only speculate because as far as I can recall, I always was one. My dad had been an admirer of Franny Lee, and when Lee went from Bolton to City for a massive £60,000, my dad's inclinations went with him. My bedroom was a shrine to two heroes: Francis Lee and Marc Bolan. Not Marc Bolan the silky-skilled, nimble midfielder with an 'educated' left foot, but Marc Bolan the curly-haired writer of strange songs who fronted T-Rex. At this point I will gratuitously place on record the fact that my first-ever LP record was 'Electric Warrior' by T-Rex in 1971. I think that's pretty damn good, all things considered. I'm not as keen to mention my first single, which was either 'Julie Do Ya Love

Me' by The White Plains or 'Chirpy, Chirpy, Cheep, Cheep' by Middle of the Road. I think it's best that I keep quiet about those.

Picture the scene: massive posters of Marc Bolan, including one of the man himself posing seated, legs astride a toy tank, the phallic significance of which was lost on me at such a tender age, and a noticeboard crammed full of pennants, rosettes and photographs of the Manchester City team and, in particular, Francis Lee. Throw in the Thunderbirds wallpaper and that was my bedroom, circa early 1970s. I also had Thunderbirds pyjamas, but that isn't really integral to the plot.

The other reason why it had to be Manchester City was because nobody else at school supported them. Well, maybe nobody is an exaggeration, but they were certainly not amongst the popular choices. Boys always have to support somebody. You must have an answer to the question, 'Who do you support?' It is absolutely compulsory in the playground. Some would say Bolton or Blackburn, others would say Leeds or Chelsea, just because they were successful and on television a lot around that time, but most, and especially those who knew nothing about it, would opt for *The Nation's Team*. They were the default team.

This was the case throughout my school days, and probably remains the case now. Few claimed support for City, and that merely confirmed to me that they must be mine. Thinking back, I could have chosen a number of clubs: Blackburn, Bolton, and Preston were all closer than Manchester. I suppose it's possible that I was a glory-seeker. In the light of subsequent events, it is hardly worth commenting further on that!

I don't remember much about my first proper City match on 17 April 1971. I presume that I had nagged my dad until he somehow got us to a First Division game at Maine Road, probably hoping that I would lose interest after that. The opposition was Chelsea, I sat in the Platt Lane End, and the match itself was far from being a classic. City scraped a 1-1 draw. Keith Weller scored for Chelsea and, joy of joys, Francis Lee scored for City. I'm almost certain that Lee's goal was a thunderous penalty won by the great man himself. If my recollection is false, I don't wish to know, because nothing could have been more apt. Lee was especially famed for two things: a talent for winning penalties in artistic fashion, and a thunderbolt shot. I got to see both in my first match and I was hooked.

By reading the programme, which also cost five pence, suggesting that the *Magpie Review* was overpriced, I realise now that City had quite serious injury problems and were in the middle of a vital two-legged European Cup Winner's Cup match against, of all people, Chelsea. City had already lost the first leg 1-0 at Stamford Bridge. They went on to lose the second by the same scoreline, thus failing in their attempts to retain the trophy. The programme also informed the public of the opportunity to purchase, amongst other things, a Manchester City nylon watch strap from the Souvenir Shop for 27-and-a-half pence, a bargain I would say. The match I saw was not a terribly important one, but it was clear from the size of the crowd and their reactions, that even this match mattered to an awful lot of people. Clearly there was something here that could not be offered by Chorley FC. I would have been back there every week had it been feasible. However, getting to games at Maine Road was not easy for a little squirt with expanding hair, and so I had to make do with memories and imagination, for the time being.

For a while, I went to Burnden Park to watch Bolton Wanderers matches because a friend of my dad's used to follow them and he offered transport to all and sundry in the back of his van. We always left before the end of a match, to avoid the traffic, and consequently missed goals quite regularly. My first visit to Burnden Park, in September 1970, ended in a Second Division 2-0 defeat by Oxford United, who boasted none other than Big (as in Fat) Ron (Atkinson) on the team sheet. The programme notes described him as ' model of consistency'. The most notable name on the Wanderers team sheet was Roger Hunt, and the manager was the legendary Nat Lofthouse. My next visit to Burnden Park was the following September, for a Third Division match against Halifax Town. The programme for that game has an editorial which begins with the sentence, 'At last Bolton Wanderers have lost a match!' – which strikes me as a little disloyal. In 1973 and 1974, I had a period of regular visits to watch Bolton, by then back in Division Two. I saw a promising youngster called Peter Reid break into the Bolton side. My only ever visit to Deepdale, succumbing to the persuasion of a friend, was a 1973 Division Two game between Preston North End and Sunderland. This was another opportunity to see some fading stars, a common occurrence in the lower leagues. Come to think of it, it's a regular occurrence at Maine Road as well. Preston had Nobby Stiles in their side and were managed by Bobby Charlton. In contrast, Bob Stokoe's Sunderland team included Dennis Tueart, very much a rising star. Preston won 1-0, with a penalty from ex-City hero Neil Young, and there was trouble outside the ground afterwards. I was not tempted to return. My last visit to Burnden Park as a Bolton sympathiser was in October 1976, when Bobby Moore, Rodney Marsh and George Best played on the losing side for Fulham. I had already moved on to bigger and better things (or so I thought), but the match had a certain curiosity value.

My second visit to Maine Road, on 30 September 1972, was blessed with yet another Franny Lee penalty, in a 2-1 win over West Bromwich Albion, whose number 11 that day was Asa Hartford. These pilgrimages were all too infrequent, but by season 1974/75, persistent pestering of my dad was beginning to yield rewards, despite the fact that by now Francis Lee had become *persona non grata* because of his transfer away from City, something which I took as an enormous act of betrayal. The likes of Dennis Tueart, Rodney Marsh and Asa Hartford had replaced some of the old guard, and Tony Book, the captain of the all-conquering Joe Mercer team, was manager. However, Summerbee, Bell, Doyle and Oakes were still in the team when City played QPR on 28 September 1974. It was a spectacular winning goal by Rodney Marsh, an overhead kick in the closing stages of the match to seal a 1-0 win, that confirmed my view that City occupied a different level from anything I could see at Chorley or Bolton – not that I needed much convincing. You have to remember that things were very different in 1974. I probably wouldn't back City's first team against Chorley nowadays, never mind Bolton. I had the dubious privilege of sharing attendance at this game with England manager Don Revie, a well-known personality of the time.

After the Rodney Marsh overhead kick match, I went back to Burnden Park a few more times but it just wasn't the same. My next Maine Road game was a goalless City draw against Wolves, who had Steve Daley as a substitute. My first major trauma came when City played host to Brian Clough's Derby County team (28 December 1974), amongst whose number was Francis Lee, who had left City before the start of the season. The outcome was a famous winning goal by my erstwhile hero. Lee celebrated by indicating his pleasure at the goal and his displeasure with the City Chairman, Peter Swales. On 'Match of the Day' this was accompanied by Barry Davies's screeching entreaty to, 45Look at his face, just look at his face.' If Francis Lee's shot had continued on its trajectory, passing through the net and uninfluenced by the inconvenience of gravity, it would have struck me full in the face, two-thirds of the way back in the Platt Lane Stand. It certainly felt like a smack in the face. The match finished off City's Championship hopes for that season. They were still only two points off the lead, despite being eighth, but it was a blow from which they never recovered. Their challenge had been based on invincibility at home – *yes*, I am still talking about Manchester City. Prior to the Derby County match, City had won 10 and drawn two League games at Maine Road. This was the first home defeat of the season. I couldn't believe that Francis Lee would do something like that to me, after all that we had been through. I was glad that I had reversed all my Francis Lee pennants, so that they faced the bedroom wall and I didn't have to look at him. I hadn't taken them off the wall, mind you. I must have had some garbled notion that he might come back. And I was right. He did come back, eventually.

The visits to Burnden Park ceased and I went to three more City home games. A 1-0 home victory over Coventry was not memorable but the programme, a bargain at 10 pence, contained the final line-up for the Miss Manchester City competition, including a voting form to chose your City Soccer Queen. The lucky winner, chosen by a panel including Mr Peter Swales, Tony Book and Denis Law, was on for a free holiday in Gibraltar. Third place was a weekend in Blackpool with a hire car thrown in. Wow!

For fans able to match the judgement of Mr Swales and company by predicting the first three, there was the promise of a free season ticket. I didn't enter the competition. I must have decided that there was no chance of me being in agreement with Peter Swales. The winner, announced in the match programme of a 2-0 win over Burnley, was Susan Cuff (5ft 6ins, and 35-24-35).

My last match of the season was City's final home game, a 1-1 draw against Ipswich. I had suffered my first traumas: the Francis Lee goal and the City Soccer Queen competition; survived and returned for more. I would like to claim that I can recall these details because of my incredible photographic memory, but the credit goes mainly to the several volumes of notebooks containing entirely neutral reports on all games attended, and the scrapbooks of newspaper cuttings. Yes, I was an anorak! But I have made an almost complete recovery.

Looking back on the decision, if it was a conscious decision, to be a Manchester City fan, it seems reasonable to pose the question: if I had known then what I know now, would I still have opted for a lifetime supporting Manchester City? The honest answer is no, at least not to the same degree. I would probably have contented myself, like many others, with a lifetime sniping bitterly at *The Nation's Team*. I still go to matches expecting or, at least, hoping for victory. If I knew, *really knew*, that we were going to lose, then there would be no point in going. City fans may have masochistic tendencies, but we're not that daft.

One of the main driving forces behind still carrying on is the fear that, if I stopped now, City would become great again, and I would miss out after going through all of the nightmare times. I've invested so much in that team that if the payback comes, I want my share. Apparently this psychological quirk has a name: the sunk cost fallacy. It is usually applied to gamblers who continually sink money into their losses in the mistaken expectation that their luck must change; that their losses will be compensated in the fullness of time. In fact, each time they bet, the likelihood of losing is exactly the same. It is irrational behaviour. That's what football fandom is all about.

The return of Francis Lee as Chairman seemed such an obvious way of bringing back the good times. If the pennants had still been on my bedroom wall, I would have turned his chubby face round again. As for the good times, I'm still waiting.

The Nation's Team

It is a necessity for most football fans to have a team on which to focus their loathing. Manchester City fans are particularly blessed in this respect. In fact, we are the envy of genuine football fans throughout the country. There is a team based in the borough of Trafford that I cannot avoid mentioning. Well, to be honest, they are not so much a football team as a renowned financial concern and fashion house. However, they do claim some vague connection to football. As I am heartily sick of seeing their name in print, and not wishing to contribute in any way to this unfortunate trend, I have decided to refer to them euphemistically throughout. They are sometimes called the Swampmen, the Scum, or the RAGS (Red Arrogant Gits – normally aimed at their fans), and I was tempted to recognise their personification of evil and refer to them throughout as The Evil Ones. Instead, however, I have settled on calling them *The Nation's Team*, in reference to their general appeal (*The World's Team* might be more appropriate). They are the enemy.

Try as I may, and believe me I have tried, there is simply no ignoring or avoiding them. 'Take no notice,' people say. 'They are nothing to do with us.' Sadly this is not true. They haunt City like a monstrously deformed Siamese twin. Media pundits seem unable to cover any story concerning City without referring to *The Nation's Team*. In fact, there's hardly a television programme or newspaper page that can be guaranteed as free from a mention. Certainly, any sports programme is unlikely to proceed for more than a few minutes without a gratuitous reference. Ceefax often has a lead story concerning the non-injury of one of their players, or the fact that a transfer to or from *The Nation's Team* will not be taking place. A couple of years ago, during a commentary on Radio Five Live, Alan Green explained a sudden cheer in the Press Box by saying that it was because *!THEY* had just scored in a match elsewhere. The fact that *they* were not playing in the commentary match is a surprise in itself, since virtually their every kick can be monitored on television at home and abroad. For this and many other reasons, they have people who describe themselves as fans all over the world, and all over this country, following their every fashion parade on television. The media has always given their shirts massive amounts of free advertising and marketing, and promoted the whole operation shamelessly, even before their recent prominence on the field of play. They are the living proof that if you spend enough money over a long enough period, you can buy the League Championship. In fact, Blackburn Rovers bought it in a much shorter time, which certainly gave me some fleeting satisfaction.

It was apt that they waited until the formation of the Premier League to achieve this, because the Premier League was made for them. Even now the sight of somebody wearing a shirt of their famous colours – red, speckled blue, green and yellow, black, pink with yellow dots, puce and orange stripes, invisible grey – makes me wince. The only comfort comes when the accent of the wearer reveals origins somewhere between 150 and several thousand miles from Manchester.

I am in most respects quite a rational person. I have a number of dislikes such as McDonalds, Noel Edmonds, showjumping, advertisements and people who seek to overtake on the inside on roundabouts. Actually, I've just realised that this list could take up the whole book. Maybe 'rational' isn't the right word. But whatever my many dislikes, none has rivalled my loathing for this football club. This is explained by the fact that I have had to put up with the inexplicable love of the media for this team over the whole of my football life. Even when they were rubbish, they were still the main news. The origin of all this pre-dates my interest, but the sheer level of publicity ensures that little boys, even nowadays, will claim to support *The Nation's Team* because they are the only team they have heard of, and because it's easy. Success is guaranteed because of the self-propagating financial clout, and you don't ever have to leave your living room. You just sit there in front of the television, wearing one of your myriad choice of official replica shirts, and then you go and unleash your misguided superiority complex on your friends, who happen to support the local team and sometimes, maybe, even go to watch matches. Whilst I was in Zambia a couple of years ago for a period of 10 days, there were three games involving *The Nation's Team*. All three of them were covered live on television in Zambia, on a programme introduced by one of their ex-players, Gary Bailey. Wherever you go in the world, the shirts will catch up with you. It's an epidemic.

I believe that now may be a good time for my rant to degenerate further into paranoia. There are certain things that you learn to take for granted with *The Nation's Team*. Match officials seem to like them. The current count in derby matches, since I've been an active sufferer, is seven penalties to one in favour of *The Nation's Team*. The one penalty that City were awarded was so blatant that the offender concerned, Steve Bruce, didn't even argue. For a player representing *The Nation's Team* not to argue about a decision is a major thing in itself. I don't say that all seven penalties against were dubious, it's just that the slightest excuse to give a penalty always seems to be seized upon. In fact, the penalties are merely the most dramatic manifestation of a wider phenomenon. The major frustrations come from all those little decisions. I fight constantly against the tendency of all football fans to believe that match officials are

seeking to undermine their team, and for the most part I have been relatively successful. The exception is when my team is required to play against *The Nation's Team*.

When I was still attending primary school, I remember a last day of term when we
were all allowed to play games. At our school we had an identifiable school bully. It
wasn't an official or advertised post. He wasn't even very good at it; his nickname was
Ducky which, in retrospect, is hardly the most suitable of names for an aspiring school
bully – he was the best we could afford. I do hope that my old school has successfully
applied for Lottery funding to provide for a more convincing bully to terrorise Chorley's current pre-teens.

On this occasion, the school bully was lording it over a game of Subbuteo football
that was ostensibly winner-stays-on, but he always won. This was achieved by a bend-
ing of the rules, enabling him to employ all his troops up on the halfway line. Any opposition player touching the ball in his half of the pitch was deemed to be offside. It
was certainly a curious interpretation. When it was my turn, I decided that the best idea
would be to deploy exactly the same tactics. Thus all the players were up on the halfway line; a bit like an English League match when a goal kick is about to be taken. This
did not go down well. It was decided that, because he thought of it first, only he could
adopt the tactic.

To me a derby match is a little bit like playing Ducky at Subbuteo. In fact, anyone
playing against *The Nation's Team* should not be surprised if offside decisions are interpreted in a remarkably similar spirit. Indeed, if anyone should ask you to explain to
them the offside rule, and you are feeling a little lazy, all you need to do is await the arrival of *The Nation's Team* on your television screen – seldom a long wait – for the
simplified version: offside is when two or more players stick their hands in the air in
unison and glare meaningfully at a referee's assistant.

I can get even more paranoid. English teams were banned from Europe in the 1980s
until *The Nation's Team* qualified for a competition, then there was a sudden limited
unbarring. After *The Nation's Team* failed miserably to qualify for the group system
of the Champion's League, the rules were changed so that they were automatically
given a bye through to the group stage next time, guaranteeing obscene amounts of
money. Now the top **two** teams from certain selected countries are allocated a place in
the Champion's League, just in case *The Nation's Team* can manage only second
place.

Their omnipotence is now guaranteed and, most gallingly of all, they achieve dominance with a considerable contribution from a youth system vastly superior to City's. I
no longer put myself through the agony of watching their games on television; unless
they lose, in which case I can take some pleasure from viewing the highlights. It may
be that they have good players (although I must confess that my mind is unable to
grasp such an unpalatable concept), but that will not alter the fact that whoever, wher-
ever and whenever *The Nation's Team* play, I will support the opposition. This would
apply even if the opposition boasted Mussolini in goal, with a back four of Kissinger,
Saddam Hussein, Pol Pot and Hitler, a midfield with Thatcher on the right, Stalin on
the left, a couple of Radio One DJs (circa 1980s and not John Peel) in the middle, and
Rupert Murdoch up front with David Mellor. Well, maybe I'd settle for a draw with
Mellor in the team.

There are plenty of other examples supporting the concept of *The Nation's Team*. To name but two, Juventus and Real Madrid fulfil similar roles in Italy and Spain respectively. Their appeal is not restricted to the city in which they are based. Glory-seekers from far and wide claim allegiance. As a consequence, they inspire intense loathing from genuine supporters of other clubs. Maybe there is a common genetic predisposition to supporting *The Nation's Team*. I prefer to blame nurture rather than nature. Either way, it takes a positive act of will to avoid the clutches of *The Nation's Team* and thus steer clear of the soft option. *The Nation's Team* obviously satisfy some need as crutch or hate-target, depending on your perspective. Of course, rationality must be sacrificed in order to make full use of the possibilities offered by *The Nation's Team*. This is a sacrifice that I, for one, am more than willing to make.

I have never knowingly spoken to a professional footballer. The closest I've come to such an experience was in the early 1980s, when I found myself standing behind Denis Law in the ticket office of the Apollo Theatre. As I recall, Denis was there to collect what were probably freebie tickets for a Shirley Bassey performance. I was there to obtain tickets to see somebody like The Specials or The Clash. We were the only two people in the office. The person supposed to be serving had temporarily disappeared from sight. Denis complained to me about the service, in a polite, conversational and very British manner. He said something like, 'It's chaos in here,' or 'Typical, isn't it?' It was just one of those things that anyone might say in a queue.

I don't really like to think of footballers as people. This most certainly applies to those representing *The Nation's Team*. It is less easy to condemn someone as an embodiment of the Antichrist when you have had a brief chat and they seem like a nice bloke. It may have been a bit rich for Denis to be complaining about slow service if his tickets were complimentary, but it was hardly the behaviour of the Antichrist.

Denis Law, of course, played a dual role in history, having represented both teams, albeit more famously *The Nation's Team*. I can recall listening to the radio when *The Nation's Team* were relegated in disgrace as a crowd invasion caused the premature end of a derby match, which City were leading 1-0 thanks to Denis Law's cheeky back-heeled goal. There were fires on the Stretford End and attacks on City players. The victims of these assaults graciously declined to make a fuss about it.

Much earlier, City provided *The Nation's Team* with a place to play after the bombing of *The Swamp* in the war. It has since been alleged, on T-shirts and in chants at Maine Road, that Uwé Rösler's grandad carried out this bombing, but no compelling evidence is forthcoming. The fact that fans of Manchester City would see this as a positive act, to be applauded most vociferously, is indicative of a wider attitude to *The Nation's Team*, many aspects of which would make me seem like an enemy sympathiser. I feel much better after that rant. RAGS would explain these kinds of outbursts as jealousy. That is why they are known as RAGS.

Meanwhile, back to the comfortable world of the early 1970s, when I was enviously eyeing other people's platform shoes and parallels (trousers even more ridiculous than flares). *The Nation's Team* had just gained promotion, having wrecked a number of Second Division grounds and beaten City 1-0 in a League Cup match, with the winning goal coming from a penalty.

Part One: The Good Old Days

Dennis Tueart at Wembley in 1976: genuine photographic evidence that MCFC once won something. The subject is camouflaged to reduce the danger of shock-induced trauma amongst younger fans.

Season 75/76: The Zenith

This was my first proper season as a Manchester City fan, a regular devotee at the Academy of Football Farce. Prospects seemed pretty bright and, before a ball was kicked, expectations were high. My idea of a bad season would have been to win nothing and finish lower than third in the League. On the whole, this was what most people would have thought. City enjoyed an enviable status as a club, and manager Tony Book was under pressure to win trophies. The team had performed poorly away from home, and Book was already the fourth manager since the departure of Joe Mercer. Malcolm Allison had a spell in charge, followed by Johnny Hart, whom I don't recall at all. Ron Saunders also came and went, largely unnoticed by me, with just a League Cup Final defeat in 1974 to remember him by. Mr Saunders went on to take Aston Villa to the League title. He wasn't the last to move on to better things after leaving Maine Road.

By now my dad was resigned to driving me to home matches; not yet all home matches, but most. I was 14 years old and edging away from my T-Rex, Bowie, Gary Glitter devotions into a much more alarming Progressive Rock phase where I got into the pretentious output of bands such as Yes (featuring City fan, keyboard wizard Rick Wakeman), Pink Floyd, and Emerson, Lake and Palmer. You see, pop music was for girls and kids. Sophisticates like myself required something more challenging. Pseudo-intellectual gobbledegook from bands who only ever made albums, often double or triple albums, was just right. Throw in a few long drum solos and every self-respecting teenage boy was in feigned seventh heaven.

The Manchester City team beginning the 1975/76 season looked impressive. Colin Bell, still very much the athletic, goalscoring midfield player, was an England regular who performed consistently well for the national team. Rodney Marsh, a forward with skill in abundance, has one of those names always quoted by those who claim that football was full of 'characters' and 'entertainers' in the seventies, although he was blamed by many for costing City a possible second Championship title. Joe Corrigan, a massive goalkeeper who didn't look athletic and was consequently underrated by those outside Maine Road, was a man who came through considerable difficulties. By the time I was a regular feature on the Platt Lane benches, he was a figure of awesome authority and reassurance. When the ball was hovering ominously above the City penalty area, I knew that I could sit back and relax because Big Joe would catch it. Since the days of Joe Corrigan this feeling has not returned. Nowadays if the ball is in the air, I cringe, expecting any guardian of the City goal to stand on his line observing events in a disconcertingly detached fashion, as if it were none of his business, or alternatively to rush out and flap blindly at the football as if wafting away an irritating wasp. Either way, the outcome is at the discretion of the gods of football.

In the City defence were stalwarts Mike Doyle, famed for his hatred of *The Nation's Team*, and Willie Donachie, a magnificently consistent left-back. Donachie is unfortunate to be remembered by many for a rare cock-up when he was playing for Scotland and scored an amusing own goal in a televised Home International game. Despite Doyle's inimitable presence, Dave Watson, signed from Sunderland and destined for a regular England spot, was the central figure in defence. Alan Oakes was another long-serving player in midfield and Dennis Tueart, another signing from Sunderland, was the new darling of the fans, up front or on the wing. Tueart inspired banners claiming *Dennis bites yer legs*. I cannot confirm the validity of this statement. I certainly never witnessed any leg-biting.

The presence of old-fashioned centre forward Joe Royle meant that there was serious competition for attacking places. This led eventually to the departure of *the entertainer*, Rodney Marsh. My favourite player, and we all have them, was Asa Hartford, a combative but creative midfielder of the type that Scotland seemed to specialise in. The whole team played through Hartford, whose awesome consistency made him City's most reliable player. Hartford was known for a well-publicised transfer deal that fell through when Leeds United had a change of mind because of a hole discovered in the player's heart. It is unfortunate, therefore, that Barry Davies once described him as a 'whole-hearted player'. This may be technically inaccurate, but the sentiments are valid enough. As far as signing Asa is concerned, City got it right for once.

Television coverage was simple and civilised back in 1975. 'Match of the Day' occupied the prime Saturday night slot, and Granada TV broke up many a dull Sunday with their highlights programme. The BBC coverage was, and remains, better, but Manchester City appeared more often on ITV because of its regional nature. The matches were all played on Saturday afternoon, not Friday night, Monday night or Sunday morning. There were midweek matches, of course, and the BBC with 'Sportsnight', or ITV, would show highlights every now and again, particularly of Cup matches. Naturally, even then, *The Nation's Team* were televised more than anybody else, but 'Match of the Day' did endeavour to spread the coverage around far more than it does now. It was not unusual for lower division matches to be featured. Granada TV also covered games involving the many teams in the North-West. The BBC commentators included Barry Davies and John Motson, and the ITV commentators included Brian Moore and Gerald Sinstadt. What other profession can boast such little turnover of personnel in over 20 years? I have some advice for all aspiring commentators. If you get on the ladder now, there may be an opening for the 2030/31 Sky New Double Super Premier League season.

Back in the mid-seventies I watched all the football on television. Nowadays I don't even watch all the football still available on terrestrial television. There are some advantages to televised football, but not many. The idea of having an action replay is quite an attractive one. Sometimes I wish it were common at live matches. I know that it is possible with a modern, hi-tech, large electronic screen, but at Maine Road they still have puny electronic scoreboards. These are incapable of imparting anything but the most basic information and tacky advertising slogans, such as *Ooh Aah Daily Star*, which could hardly be more ill-judged.

Despite the superficial attractions of televised football, such as not being cold and wet, being able to see what happened in the crowded penalty area, knowing that you were right to slag off the linesman rather than merely assuming so, not having to pay (much), having access to toilet facilities unlikely to threaten your immediate health prospects, and being allowed to drink and eat as much as you like, every genuine fan will tell you that it is no substitute for the real thing. A football match is an event. At a live game, you can experience the mood, feel the climatic conditions, observe all of the participants, smell the bad breath of your neighbour, hurl abuse with some prospect of it being heard, and wince as the spittle from a deranged Neanderthal behind you takes refuge in your hair. A football match is all about the human condition at its most illuminating. It is frequently disgusting, often frustrating and infuriating, but occasionally uplifting. And most importantly, a victory witnessed first-hand is a victory earned.

The armchair supporter is an increasingly familiar feature of modern football. I think that such people should be banned from describing themselves as supporters. There should be a minimum qualification in terms of matches attended, indignities suffered and costs incurred. It should be against the law for such people to boast or gloat in the presence of genuine supporters. They do not possess the requisite moral authority. I believe that some sort of apprenticeship is in order. Learner fans should be forced to identify themselves with insignia. Not necessarily L-plates – I'm prepared to be flexible. Only when they have sacrificed and suffered enough should they be allowed into the fold and given the right to berate others of an alternative persuasion.

I have practised being an armchair supporter only in relation to Italian football. When watching English matches, I carry with me so much baggage: petty dislikes and grudges harboured for unreasonable periods of time, that I often wish both sides to lose. My long and expanding list of grievances also makes it virtually impossible for any England manager to select a side that I find acceptable, particularly when the manager himself occupies a lofty position in my grudge charts. This does not apply to foreign football; at least, not to anywhere near the same extent. I can view Italian football with an air of detachment, which is just as well considering the number of laughable penalty decisions. There is also the additional advantage of James Richardson, the best football presenter on television. Having said that, it is hard for those covering English football to ever satisfy me. I can detect nuances of bias that are not apparent to any sensible people.

Yet I still haven't quite got the hang of being an armchair fan. I decided to adopt Fiorentina when they sacked their manager, despite being in the top five in Serie A, and appointed a television pundit. The outcome was a dramatic slide to relegation, culminating in a last match 5-0 win that was not sufficient to save them. That's my team, I thought.

I suppose that I should have gone for Torino, the nearest equivalent to City, who are even worse. The experienced armchair supporter, in search of glory, would have chosen Juventus or one of the Milan clubs. Mind you, I have at least been to Florence, and even walked outside the stadium – not inside, mind you – which puts me ahead of large numbers of armchair supporters purporting to have a connection with *The Nation's Team*. When I watch Italian football on television, I know that I am not really involved. It is an entirely different experience from being a genuine fan. It is only a game.

People whose only experience of football is the sanitised version served up by television don't realise the limitations. You get no inkling of the movement, or lack of it, involved in a game of football. There's even no guarantee that you get to follow the whereabouts of the ball. Television directors seem obsessed with close-ups of dour looking managers or, at World Cups, crowds performing Mexican waves. They also have a curious habit of zooming in on a player who has just made a complete mess of a golden opportunity, just in time for the whole world to lip-read the expletive, and witness the angry and forceful ejection of mucous liquid from various facial orifices. As for representing the atmosphere of a football match, it never ceases to amaze me how inept commentators are at interpreting crowd chants and reactions. Chanting is often attributed to the wrong set of fans altogether. Television directors also seem over-keen to demonstrate all the toys available to them. When a close-up becomes so close-up that you have no idea where the action is on the pitch, or if indeed they are still on the pitch rather than on somebody's front lawn, then it ceases to have meaning. When a replay of a goal is shown for the fourth time from a different angle, whilst play is still ongoing and the other team is equalising, it makes you wonder why they bother to cover matches live at all.

Back in 1975 you didn't get a comprehensive television round-up of all the First Division goals scored. If your team was featured on a highlights programme, you got to see the goals; if not, then the goals disappeared forever into the ether. A lot of goals have gone that way. It's a sobering thought. Nowadays, I can record all of City's goals on video, or buy the highlights video at the end of the season. Unfortunately, nowadays they don't score many. I don't spend a great deal on video tapes.

The 1975/76 season began at Maine Road on 16 August 1975 with a 3-0 win over Norwich City, who had World Cup winner Martin Peters in their side. Colin Bell *slammed* in the first goal, according to my notes, and Dennis Tueart scored twice, including one of his speciality overhead kicks. My next match, against Newcastle United, ended in a 4-0 win for City, including two Dennis Tueart penalties. Joe Royle also ended a personal goal drought by scoring twice. City were unable to make any progress in away matches, but at Maine Road they were formidable. Four-nil was also the score against Middlesbrough, with two-goal-Rodney Marsh starring, according to myself (I, like reporters in some newspapers, used to give the players marks out of 10 and pick a star performer) and the Sunday People. Marsh got a staggering 10 from the newspaper (using the term 'newspaper' in the broadest possible sense), whereas I awarded only a picky nine.

The League Cup began for City on Wednesday, 10 September 1975, against Norwich City at Carrow Road. The match ended 1-1 after two late goals, including one scored by Watson, who equalised for City five minutes from the end. The replay at Maine Road was on the following Wednesday. I still wasn't always able to get to midweek matches. That meant staying at home with ears glued (not literally, that would be stupid) to Radio Manchester and Piccadilly Radio, switching from one to the other to catch all the reports. On Piccadilly Radio, two jingles, *It's a goal!* and *Oh, no!* always trumpeted an alteration in scorelines, depending on whether the goal was for or against a local team. This led to an anxious few seconds before the identity of the goalscorer was revealed. After all, *It's a goal!* could be unwelcome news from *The Swamp*. These gut-wrenching moments of anticipation were often ended by news of a goal at Spotland or Gigg Lane, but the anticipation never waned. Even when City were not playing, I would listen to any radio station with reports on any match. Radio City, covering, amongst others, Liverpool and Everton, was an obvious second choice, but as long as there was a match taking place somewhere, there was likely to be a reporter working for a station that I could tune in to. I didn't have to be all that interested in the matches taking place. The radio often provided mere background noise, giving me something to listen to whilst practising my Subbuteo moves.

The League Cup replay ended 2-2 after extra time. There were no penalty shoot-outs in the old days. The two teams were obliged to carry on playing until they got thoroughly bored with each other and one of them simply couldn't take it any more. The third match was played on a Monday night at Stamford Bridge, sensibly inaccessible to all interested parties. In front of a desultory 6,238 people, City won 6-1 with a Tueart hat-trick (including two more penalties). I distinctly remember listening to that one because City away wins were not common, and big away wins were very rare indeed. The Subbuteo practice went well that night.

Between the first and second Norwich replay there was a home game against *The Nation's Team*, the first since their return to the First Division. There had been a history of crowd trouble at derby matches; these were the days when football violence was still a popular pastime. In school, talk seemed to be just as often about which set of fans *took* the other team's end, not just who won the game. These accounts were invariably exaggerated, but there were problems at football matches because for some young men or old boys it was seen as an attractive way to fill time. The pleasures of drugs and joyriding had yet to catch the attention. Because of this general atmosphere, the derby match was thought to be too risky at the time. It finished in a 2-2 draw. The home games I did get to were not particularly inspiring. City achieved a 1-0 win against Stoke City, but the beginning of my report on a 0-0 home draw with Burnley was less than enthusiastic:

> *'A terrible performance by the City defence and a referee who allowed Burnley to run riot with fouling turned this match into monotonous rubbish.'*

The *Sunday People* described the City performance as 'one of their most frustrating, enigmatic displays,' which probably amounts to much the same thing. The only interesting angle was the return of Mike Summerbee, now playing for Burnley.

My report on a 1-1 draw with Ipswich Town begins with admirable impartiality:

> *'Manchester City were robbed of a point in the final minute of this match when referee David Wallace turned down a penalty appeal when Mick Mills controlled the ball in his own area with his hand.'*

Shame on you Mr Wallace. I have not forgotten! Mind you, just to show how objective I was, I gave him six out of 10, which for a referee was pretty good. This game was also notable as the first to be played following the transfer-listing of Rodney Marsh, whose days were very definitely numbered.

For the younger generation, I should explain that there used to be two points awarded for a win, no points for losing, and in the event of a drawn game, the two points were shared, one each. We seem to have acquired another point from somewhere. Maybe it's inflation. After all, a pint of beer cost less than 40 pence back in the seventies.

Meanwhile, City edged past Nottingham Forest (a very early Brian Clough version) in the League Cup and finally won an away game, 3-2 at Arsenal, covered for posterity by 'Match of the Day'. That Saturday night must have been a rare treat. In fact, City were climbing up the League. A 2-0 win over Birmingham City, notable for two Colin Bell goals and a star billing for 16-year-old winger Peter Barnes, helped to consolidate this upward momentum. I was at that game but still a little on the periphery when it came to the really big matches. On Wednesday, 12 November 1975, there was a massive League Cup game for City, against *The Nation's Team*. The combination of midweek and possible crowd trouble meant that I missed this one. By the following season I had succeeded in engineering a change to the rules, but it was too late to witness City inflict a heart-warmingly large thrashing on the team in red shirts. 'Doc's kids get spanking,' was the Daily Mirror headline. Two of City's goals in the 4-0 win came from Dennis Tueart, and there was one each from Asa Hartford and Joe Royle. City were 3-0 up and cruising after only 27 minutes. Happily, highlights were featured on 'Sportsnight' and I could revel in the occasion, preparing my joyous glow to take into school the following day. It was not an entirely blissful affair. A challenge by Martin Buchan on Colin Bell in the opening minutes left the City demigod seriously injured. He never fully recovered from that injury. He made comebacks, but was unable to regain his former stature.

Rodney Marsh was gone and virtually forgotten now that City were in the League Cup quarter-final and on a bit of a roll in the League. Paul Power, destined to play throughout long and difficult times for City, was edging into the side, and Peter Barnes was making quite a name for himself. Barnes ended up winning the Young Footballer of the Year award for 1976. He marked the occasion by making a memorable acceptance speech at the awards ceremony. I can remember it well. After beginning with, 'I would like to thank all professional footballers for this award,' he paused and gave a remarkable impersonation of a startled rabbit facing up to the headlights of a 10-ton truck. Amongst the audience there was embarrassed shuffling and coughing as the excruciating silence from the platform persisted. Eventually, young Peter managed to regain sufficient composure to finish off with, 'and I would like to thank all professional footballers for this award.' Who said that the age of oratory is over?

I was back at Maine Road as City beat Tottenham 2-1, and I banded about high marks as if they were worthless confetti rather than treasured garlands. A 4-0 win at Wolves took City to seventh in the League, still below *The Nation's Team*, but with the knowledge that the Cup win had blocked off any possibility of gloating from that direction. The League Cup quarter-final opponents were Third Division Mansfield Town, whose manager, Dave Smith, endeared himself to the City Faithful by saying that Mansfield would be a tougher nut for City to crack than their previous opponents. By now I had talked my dad into midweek matches. I watched the Mansfield Town game with all the confidence of a supporter following a big club playing no-hope inferiors. I was a bit of a BAG (Blue Arrogant Git). If you had told me then that there would come a time when City might play sides not unlike Mansfield on an equal basis, I would have laughed scornfully. In fact, Mansfield performed admirably. They allowed City fans full scope to be patronising as we applauded their plucky efforts in a 4-2 defeat that was never really in doubt, but provided enough worrying moments to be interesting. Nowadays, my attitude to a game against Mansfield Town would be dominated by trepidation. In fact, come to think of it, that now applies to all matches.

As the season cruised into December, Maine Road games included a goalless draw that put Queens Park Rangers top of the League, and a 4-2 win over Coventry City. Coventry's star performer was Tommy Hutchison, a man destined to play a prominent role at the Academy. Leeds United ruined Christmas by scraping a 1-0 win that left me less than complimentary. I blamed luck and awful refereeing, although I did acknowledge Frank Gray's effective marking job on Barnes, which was rather mature of me, I thought. To lose a home game, or indeed any game that I witnessed live (I still wasn't allowed to go to away matches) was a rare thing. The Leeds defeat was City's first of the season at Maine Road. It was quite difficult to handle at the time. It still isn't very easy, but it has certainly lost its novelty shock value. It's just like losing your virginity. Well, maybe not.

A defeat at Liverpool added to the Christmas gloom and sent City plunging towards mid-table, from where they never really escaped, at best hovering on the edge of the real action. A 6-0 win against Hartlepool United in the FA Cup was a hearty warm-up for the important business of the League Cup semi-final over two legs, against Jack Charlton's Middlesbrough, who boasted one of the meanest defences around. Up to and including the 10 January 1976, when they beat City by their favourite scoreline, 1-0, Boro' had conceded just two goals in 12 home matches. Three days after beating City 1-0, Middlesbrough beat City, you've guessed it, 1-0, in the first leg of the semi-final.

In the build-up to the second leg, City found themselves with an unwanted injury and suspension crisis. In addition to long-term casualty Colin Bell, Dave Watson and Dennis Tueart were unable to play. In retrospect this doesn't seem like much of a crisis. In recent years City have developed a permanent, if variable, injury list which never dips below four. Maybe they don't make footballer's groins like they used to. Having said that, the absence of three England internationals is not the kind of problem that a modern Manchester City manager would be likely to face. Back in 1976, the loss of Watson and Tueart meant that the leading defender and leading forward would be missing, necessitating some serious rearrangements in the team. Kenny Clements (resplendent in a Leo Sayer hairstyle) was switched from full-back to emergency central defender, and youngster Gerard 'Ged' Keegan, whose previous appearances had been rare, was drafted into midfield, with Peter Barnes given extra freedom to join Joe Royle in attack. As Power, Barnes, Clements and Barrett were all in the starting line-up, it was an inexperienced City team facing up to a miserly Middlesbrough side that included a young Graeme Souness, who was already attracting the attention of bigger clubs.

The moment I entered the ground on that night, I could sense the extra excitement and anticipation amongst the crowd. There is always a special exhilaration about night matches. The atmosphere seems more intensive and intimate. It helps when it's the biggest match you've ever been to and the prize is a Cup Final at Wembley. I was a bit anxious about this match, and the noise and elation in the crowd, right from the start of the game, served to increase the anxiety. I began to better comprehend the importance of the outcome. Previously, I hadn't seen many changes to the City team, and that aspect also made me more nervous than usual. Since that era, it has often been more of a surprise for City to send the same team out twice in succession. You're lucky if it's the same manager as the last match.

In 1976, stability was the norm so there was an element of fear of the unknown associated with this particular match. A lot of the pundits in the press, of whom as a naïve 14-year-old I still took some notice, reckoned that Middlesbrough's mean defence, and the threat of the odd breakaway from the likes of David Mills and David Armstrong, made them the favourites against City's inexperienced side. In fact, the threat never materialised, as City turned the whole tie around in the first 11 minutes. It took only six minutes for City to make the aggregate score level. Ged Keegan, whose City career peaked that night, headed a Peter Barnes cross into the net in front of the North Stand, to send the already excitable crowd into a frenzy. This had hardly abated when, five minutes later, Alan Oakes scored with a low shot after Keegan had set up the opportunity. At that moment, all of my fears disappeared and I knew that City would make the final.

A suicidal back-pass led to Peter Barnes scoring early in the second half, and there was no way back for Middlesbrough. The crowd and both teams were willing the end of the game, for different reasons, when another sloppy defensive pass was intercepted by Joe Royle, who made it 4-0 in the last minute. The scoreline of the earlier League match had been repeated.

For the next five weeks, the League form was predictable: wins at home and defeats away. In addition to being a trophy to play for, the League Cup also represented the best opportunity of qualifying for a European competition. City still hovered around the UEFA Cup places, but any realistic chance of the League Championship had been lost because of an inability to pick up points away from Maine Road. This probably gave me a distorted view of how good the team was, since I still couldn't go to away matches.

The next problem on the horizon was getting to Wembley. We didn't yet have season tickets, and demand would be high. As a member of the Junior Blues, a fine organisation devoted to the indoctrination of young children, I was able to enter a draw for the opportunity of getting one of a limited number of places on an official Junior Blues trip to the League Cup Final. I don't know what the odds were, but I entered and won and in the early hours of Saturday, 28 February 1976, my dad drove me to Maine Road to catch the coach, with mum coming along for the ride. After waving a fond farewell, I was on my way to Wembley. My dad was marginally too old to be a Junior Blue and had to miss out. Life's a bitch!

In fact, even I felt a bit old on that trip. Most of the Junior Blues were junior to me. I was at the age when everybody younger seems childish and stupid, so I didn't talk much to anybody on the journey down, preferring to daydream about the match. This probably accounts for the fact that after the game was over, during an anxious 20 minutes, the poor grown-ups in charge were driven to despair by my inability to give even the most rudimentary description of the person who had sat beside me for over 200 miles, and who hadn't arrived back at the coach when everybody else did. Eventually, the youngster reappeared, much to the relief of those carrying the burden of responsibility, and I did vaguely recognise him. The story was that a Newcastle United fan had stolen the youngster's hat, and the ensuing chase and attempts at retrieval accounted for the delay. I borrowed part of that story to explain the mysterious disappearance of the bobble from my bobble-hat. In reality, I took it off myself. Everybody knew that a bobble-hat with a bobble was simply not cool. For years my mother suffered under the illusion that Newcastle United fans went around stealing the bobbles off children's bobble-hats. I came clean about it eventually. Spookily enough, I lost a hat during another Cup Final five years later, but that's another story.

We arrived quite early and were trooped into the ground to take up position. The Wembley terraces at the tunnel end had very steep steps that didn't look particularly safe should there be a lot of movement in the crowd, but did allow for good views of the pitch, even for little squirts like us. Opposite was a simple and restrained scoreboard with *Manchester City 0 Newcastle United 0* in white letters on a black background. The pre-match entertainment consisted of a few physical jerks (blokes demonstrating an early form of aerobics) and brass bands and so on. I was glad that I was only 14 and therefore hadn't drunk several pints of beer because prospects for toilet-visiting were growing more and more bleak as kick-off approached. Eventually, the teams made their entrance to much noise and waving of flags and banners. When the waving of flags and banners died down a little, I could actually see the teams.

For City, Ged Keegan filled the problem right-back spot and Tommy Booth was playing in an unaccustomed midfield position. Apart from these minor variations, the team was back to a recognisable norm. Newcastle, of course, had plenty of support and boasted none other than Supermac, Malcolm MacDonald, in attack alongside Alan Gowling, who, I have since discovered, was described by one inspired scribe as the 'Galloping Chip'. This was, in effect, my first away game as a City fan, so the sight of so many opposition supporters was a novel one. Everyone seemed in friendly high spirits before the game and, in fairness, it was much the same afterwards, except that those in black and white colours were not in such high spirits. The match itself was really rather good. City, kicking towards their fans, started well. After 10 minutes, Asa Hartford floated a free-kick into the penalty area, Mike Doyle headed it back across goal, and Peter Barnes sneaked in unmarked to put City in front. To be honest, it all seemed a bit unreal. The surroundings were imposing, the sheer number of people quite alarming, and yet everything was proceeding so smoothly. This was Wembley, it was a Cup Final, City had scored!

There were opportunities for the Blues to add to their lead, but Newcastle were always in contention. Ten minutes before half-time, MacDonald crossed low and Gowling scored. Dennis Tueart squandered chances to restore City's lead before the break, but those minor indiscretions were forgiven in an instant, a minute into the second half. Willie Donachie's cross was headed back into the centre by Booth, and Tueart, positioned back to goal near the penalty spot, scored with the most precise of overhead kicks. It is a goal that is legendary at Maine Road and deserves to be so. If there was any justice (which there usually isn't), it had to be the winning goal, and it was, despite growing Newcastle pressure as the end of the game approached. Joe Corrigan, in the City goal, was one of many who made significant contributions that day but, after the Newcastle players had received their medals, it was my man of the match, City-captain Mike Doyle, who lifted the Cup towards the City fans. After the celebrations and the lap of honour, we hung around to allow most of the crowd to clear. Looking across at the scoreboard, I could see, quite clearly, *Manchester City 2 Newcastle United 1*. It was all true!

It seemed to be a bit of a doddle, this football-supporting lark. There may be one or two setbacks to be endured every now and then, but on the whole you get comfortable home wins and the occasional trip to Wembley to see a trophy collected. It would have been inconceivable to me then that this should be the high point of my life as a Manchester City fan. Looking back, I can't help but think that I didn't fully appreciate that day because it had all come so easily and so quickly. I've always wanted to repeat the experience, safe in the knowledge that I now know all about the other side of football and would appreciate a bit of success much more because of it. Unfortunately, the League Cup Final of 1976, when Dennis Tueart scored a winning goal to dream about, has not proven to be easily repeatable.

After the long and tedious trip back to Maine Road, I found my parents waiting patiently to collect me. The traffic around London was bad, and we arrived later than anticipated. The League Cup Final wasn't covered live on television in 1976, so my dad had to make do with my rambling description until the highlights on ITV the following day. I was able to relive the whole thing again, this time with close-ups and replays – not as enjoyable as the real thing, but a highly acceptable way to fill a Sunday afternoon.

After the Cup Final, the remainder of the League season was a mere formality. In the next home match, a 4-0 win against Sheffield United, Tueart repeated his overhead kick goal, just to show that it wasn't a fluke. To emphasise his fallibility, however, Tueart marked my first League match away from home, at Turf Moor, Burnley, by missing two penalties. To miss one penalty might be considered unfortunate, but to miss two suggests that he did it just to ruin my day out. To make matters worse, Burnley were down to 10 men for the whole second half. My second away match, at Stoke City, also ended 0-0. I was beginning to get the message that things were not so simple away from Maine Road.

Franny Lee returned to Maine Road with Derby County in an eventful match that severely dented his chances of another Championship Winner's medal. The game was noteworthy for a number of reasons. Colin Bell returned to the team, and Mike Doyle was sent off, in an opening 20-minute spell when City also scored three goals. Eventually, the Blues won 4-3, with Dennis Tueart and Bruce Rioch scoring two goals each. Also amongst the scorers was Paul Power: his first City goal.

My debut visit to Elland Road was the penultimate away game of the season. Although City dominated for the first hour, with Colin Bell scoring a goal that I described at the time as 'sizzling', two Leeds goals in as many minutes undid all the hard work and gave me my first experience of away defeat. Compared to Turf Moor and the Victoria Ground, Elland Road was an intimidating place for visiting fans, giving me a taste of less wholesome experiences to come. However, nothing was going to deter me from going to away matches. A bit of adversity is part of the attraction. You expect to be outnumbered, unless you go to places such as Coventry, and you expect to be up against it. If you're following City nowadays, you also expect to lose.

A dismal Easter was completed by my first of many Maine Road thrashings at the hands of Liverpool, the dominant team of that and many other seasons. All the goals came in the last 20 minutes. Two of them were scored by 'super-sub', David Fairclough, who had been on from the start and wasn't actually any kind of sub on this occasion. The presence of a surprising number of Liverpool fans in the Platt Lane Stand was revealed when the goals started going in by a raucous rendition of 'We Shall not be Moved'. That 3-0 win was essential to Liverpool's Championship win. It kept them a point clear of QPR with one game each remaining.

City's final home game of the season had an end-of-term feeling about it. Even my mum came along to see what all the fuss was about. It ended in a 3-1 win over Arsenal, with a young Gary Owen given a rare first team opportunity. Owen was to feature far more prominently the following season. Alan Ball was star man for Arsenal that day. The less said about that the better. I was obviously feeling in a relaxed and benign mood because I even awarded referee Derek Civil eight out of 10.

There was one remaining fixture, but it had to wait until after the FA Cup Final. Both matches involved *The Nation's Team*. The FA Cup was won by underdogs Southampton, thanks to a splendid winning goal by Bobby Stokes. Unfortunately, the Old Trafford derby game, which I did not attend, ended 2-0 to the home side. Any City fan would have settled for the results of those two games being that way around rather than the other.

Manchester City finished the 1976/77 season in eighth place, with a trophy in the cabinet and a 6-4 aggregate win over three games against *The Nation's Team*. Contentment and serenity reigned.

Season 1976/77: On the Brink

With Mike Doyle and Joe Corrigan, both capped by England over the summer, adding to an expanding collection of international players, City began season 1976/77 amongst the favourites, with the proviso that their poor away form should improve. I wasn't fortunate enough to witness the pre-season Tennant-Caledonian Cup semi-final against Southampton at Ibrox Park where, after a 1-1 draw, both sides scored all 11 penalties before City lost on the toss of a coin. I also missed the opening League game at Leicester, where the Blues came from behind twice to draw 2-2. I was, however, at Maine Road, in proud occupation of my new season-ticket seat in the Platt Lane Stand (Block Y2, Row 24, Seat 4), in a crowd of 41,007 to see City take on Aston Villa in their first home game of the season. To view every match from the same seat made quite a contrast from the nomadic wanderings of the previous season. Positioned halfway back, slightly to the left of the goal, it was a good view, marred only by an irritating post, presumably contributing to holding the stand up, behind which the players seemed to revel in hiding.

On Wednesday, 25 August 1976, at the grand age of 15, I handed in my season ticket slip at the turnstile and entered Maine Road with anticipation. I had endured a football-free summer that was far too long. There were a few additions to the squad, notably Brian Kidd, formerly of *The Nation's Team*, whose presence put considerable pressure on Joe Royle. Other significant additions were Michael Docherty, right-back and son of Thomas Docherty, *The Nation's Team* manager, and Jimmy Conway, a midfield player providing additional cover for the absence of Colin Bell, whose premature comeback was short-lived. The other change, noted by many, was the alteration in general attitude, with a less cavalier approach, particularly away from home. This resulted in fewer high scoring wins, but more wins overall. The press didn't approve of this development but I, like most honest football fans, already held winning in far higher regard than artistic impression.

Aston Villa, with Brian Little and Andy Gray in their team, were no easy opponents for the first home game, but City started well with headers from Dennis Tueart and Dave Watson giving them a two-goal lead after half-an-hour's play. It was a cushion they maintained. The following Saturday, Stoke City held firm for a goalless draw, and when this was followed by another goal-free game at Arsenal, Tony Book's more cautious approach prompted a *Sunday People* headline of, 'By The Book City A Bore'. Alan Ball was also quoted as saying, 'I remember when it was a pleasure to play against City.' Twenty years later, Ball, as Manchester City manager, in an act of commendable consistency, practised what he preached by making City a pleasure to play against for all and sundry.

In the meantime, the Blues fell at the first hurdle in their attempt to retain the League Cup, and were beaten 3-0 by Aston Villa. After this slightly subdued start to the season, City reverted to a two-wingers approach for the home match against Bristol City. Both of them, Barnes and Tueart, scored classic winger goals, dribbling and shimmying past a couple of defenders before firing shots past the goalkeeper. The two first-half goals were again sufficient, despite a late consolation goal from Bristol City. Bristol were experiencing a rare sojourn in Division One, and boasted muppet-like Gerry Gow, a tigerish and intimidating midfield player, amongst their number.

By now I was experiencing one of the potential downsides of a seat season ticket: you are surrounded by the same people every match. If they happen to get on your nerves with persistent inane comments, ridiculous observations or a running commentary of mind-numbing stupidity, there is nothing you can do about it. Directly behind me were seated a dad and two sons whose constant babbling often bordered on the excruciating. The dad appeared to be a RAG at heart, which was somewhat disconcerting, and spent a lot of his time teasing junior-one and junior-two about how inferior City were. I cringed in anticipation every time either junior asked a question and daddy prepared to impart his words of wisdom, which usually amounted to absolute nonsense and often contradicted his previous pronouncements. I had to tolerate this for six years.

One of the consequences of winning the 1976 League Cup was a place in the UEFA Cup. The first-round draw could not have been worse for City. On 15 September 1976, at Maine Road, in the first leg, I had my unforgettable first experience of a European tie and, in particular, of a Juventus team whose attitude to the game demonstrated a level of cynicism that I have seldom seen matched. After just a few minutes, Dennis Tueart was assaulted by the inaptly named Claudio Gentile, as he attempted to go past the defender. This tactic persisted for the whole match. On the other wing, Peter Barnes received similar attentions and didn't quite know what to do. Eventually, he was taken off with a limp and a lot of bruises. City won the game 1-0, with a goal by Brian Kidd from a corner just before half-time. Prior to that, Dino Zoff had made some impressive saves in the Juventus goal. Tueart had struck the crossbar with a fierce shot, after bravely side-stepping two defenders with considerable risk to life and limb. The sheer speed of the rare breaks by Juventus, and particularly Franco Causio, warned of more testing times to come in the second leg. The one goal lead didn't look enough. Juvé had players like Tardelli, Bettega and Benetti in their team, and they dominated the return match in Turin. Goals from Scirea and Boninsigna led to an aggregate 2-1 win for the Italians. Joe Royle nearly snatched it for City late in the game, but Dino Zoff made the save.

In the League, a 2-0 away win at Sunderland left City second only to Liverpool, but calamity struck in the next home game, my first-ever live derby match. This was a most painful experience. My hatred for *The Nation's Team* grew enormously as a result of this game. City dominated and took the lead with a Tueart header early on, only for goals to come from the first two enemy attacks. The second goal was a real trauma. Doyle deflected a cross against Corrigan, and the ball bounced straight to a grateful McCreery, who couldn't miss. Even so, City had many chances to score again. They thought they had when Martin Buchan appeared to clear the ball from behind the goal line after a Paul Power effort, but the referee and linesman hadn't noticed. The fact that television evidence indicated that the goal should have been given was of some consolation because it was ammunition to take to school. The final score was a flattering 1-3. On this occasion, I put it down to good fortune and even had the generosity to award one of their players, Lou Macari, nine out of 10. At that time, I had expectations that derby-match good fortune might even out over time.

Following on from two major defeats, the home match against West Ham was a low-key affair. City won 4-2, with a first goal for 18-year-old Gary Owen. A Tuesday night trip to Goodison Park raised the spirits a little. It was my first experience of the sheer hatred that a Merseyside crowd can exude. The atmosphere of general intimidation was quite tangible, despite the relatively modest 31,370 crowd. Even I feared a little for the match officials, and could forgive them occasional acts of generosity to the home side. I realise now that my experience was distorted by having spent most games in the Platt Lane Stand at Maine Road. Standing behind the goal at Goodison Park, so much closer to the pitch, everything was so much more intense. Incidentally, I also feared for myself and my dad. This was not a baseless fear. There were children lobbing bricks off bridges over the East Lancs Road on the journey back, and the City fans were not entirely joking when they chanted, 'We're gonna get our fuckin' heads kicked in.'

City needed a point to go to the top of the League table, albeit temporarily. They started well, but a header from Martin Dobson gave Everton the lead, lifting the mood of the home team and the crowd. City had to survive some intense pressure before recovering to score themselves before half-time, Asa Hartford contributing a rare headed goal from Brian Kidd's cross. City were much improved in the second half and looked the more likely scorers when, with just over a quarter of an hour left, Mr Ashley, the referee, awarded an indirect free-kick to Everton, seven yards from the City goal. Despite having all 11 players lined up on the goal line, the Blues failed to survive the ensuing pinball machine-like array of shots, which ended when Andy King's effort found its way through the crowd and into the net. With the Blues demonstrating commendable spirit, Paul Power equalised with a looping header within a minute, and it was City who looked most likely to score a winner. The game ended 2-2, we got home alive, and City were top of the table.

The summit was soon occupied by others as City played out two successive goalless draws at home, with a 1-0 away loss at Ipswich sandwiched in between. In the 0-0 draw with QPR, both teams contrived to miss a penalty. The game against Newcastle was simply dull. Both matches were played in front of around 40,000 people. Dennis Tueart, whose own form, notwithstanding the odd penalty miss, was exceptional, eventually broke the goal drought at Maine Road with a spectacular early winner against West Bromwich Albion. He followed that up with a last-minute winner against Derby County, in a positive goal-fest that finished 3-2. Meanwhile, dull goalless draws at Birmingham and Middlesbrough confirmed City's growing resilience away from home. If that meant boring the home fans a little, then so be it. That was how Liverpool were winning Championships.

After a draw at Tottenham, City faced a home game against Coventry, with the chance to stretch their unbeaten run to nine games. A first-half header from Brian Kidd and a late goal from Dennis Tueart, who also managed to miss another penalty, gave the Blues a comfortable win to set them up for two crucial Christmas matches.

I look back on Dennis Tueart as a tremendous, skilful player, who could take on defenders and score both spectacular and routine goals. I also look back on him as a good penalty-taker, but he did miss a few. He probably missed more penalties than City have had in the Premier League. With Tueart playing well as an attacking winger, and Brian Kidd contributing regular goals, City had a well-balanced side with flexibility. Either Tueart or Royle could play alongside Kidd as a second striker, with Paul Power filling the left side of midfield when required. Peter Barnes provided additional attacking options on the other wing, and the centre of midfield, under the stewardship of the ever-impressive Asa Hartford and his young and improving sidekick, Gary Owen, was as good as it's ever been. In Hartford and Owen, City had two creative midfield players who could also tackle and defend when necessary. This is something that Manchester City have lacked ever since. There was also stability in defence, with Doyle, Watson and Donachie well-established, Corrigan at his peak in goal, and only the right-back position, currently occupied by Clements, open to any dispute. All in all, it was the best City team of my time as a fan. I think that it's worth dwelling on that for a moment because, quite soon, it's all downhill from here.

That's enough dwelling. Back at Christmas 1976, City faced a match against Leeds United at Elland Road on 27 December. The match was not all-ticket, and we drove across the Pennines in cheerful mood, anticipating a good result. There was a good result, but unfortunately we didn't get to see it. The match should have been all-ticket, and we had to suffer the frustration of joining several different queues, some of which moved a little, and then being led to various other turnstiles with the promise of entry, whilst the teams came out and the match began. Two goals from Brian Kidd, after 10 and 28 minutes, were scored. We could hear the noise of the 49,000 crowd, but we were still outside. Eventually the police decided that, although there was some space inside, we would not be allowed entrance because there was fighting in there, and we might not like it. We gave up and drove back home. Despite a 2-0 win I was forlorn. A win over Leeds was to be treasured because of their stature, but I didn't see it, therefore it didn't count.

On a chilly evening two days later, there was the opportunity for making amends: a home game against Liverpool. A City win would put them level with Liverpool at the head of the table, with a game in hand. It really was bitterly cold. Bitterly, bitterly cold. There were tights on display and the players slid around on the frozen pitch like a Bambi-on-ice convention. Despite the inclement conditions, 52,020 paid to escape from the Christmas family trauma and witness some sporting theatre. Unfortunately for City, it was a tragedy with comic elements. The latter can only be appreciated with the passage of time.

I've already made the point that City had a strong team. It goes without saying that Liverpool also had a strong team. The names would be familiar to anyone with a basic knowledge of seventies English football. On this occasion, they did have a couple of notable absentees. Keegan was injured and Toshack rested, but they were still a formidable hurdle to overcome, representing a psychological barrier beyond which was the promise of riches untold. If City had won that night, world domination would have been a formality within five years. England would have become a land of prosperity and fairness for all and the New Romantics would never have been taken seriously. Poverty and starvation would have become things of the past, and Simon Bates would not have been allowed on national daytime radio. Eric Cantona would have stuck to philosophy etc. etc.. . . .

Back in Christmas 1976, Liverpool adapted quicker to the conditions, but it was always going to be a difficult night for the players. Yet, after a confusing goalmouth scramble, with bodies sliding and falling over in amusing fashion, Joe Royle shot City ahead 10 minutes before half-time. The Blues grew in confidence. Chances to score were rare. Time was running out. It all seemed possible. The Liverpool threat faded, City looked in control, and with just a few minutes left and all the players tiring, victory seemed inevitable. Then suddenly, and somewhat typically, City decided to press the big, red, metaphorical button labelled 'Do not press or this game will self-destruct'. There were three minutes remaining when Ian Callaghan wellied a hopeful long ball upfield. After one bounce, slightly higher than normal because of the hard pitch, but nothing to worry about, the ball travelled comfortably in the direction of the head of the lonesome defender, Dave Watson. Goalkeeper Joe Corrigan came off his line to collect, anticipating that Watson would let the ball go harmlessly through. On reflection, leaving the spherical object unhindered to complete its natural journey might well have been the preferable option. Corrigan would have picked up the ball, wasted as much time as he could get away with, and launched it back into the Liverpool half. The option chosen by Watson did not have quite such benign consequences. I can't say whether he heard a call from Corrigan and, in any case, blame is a little pointless now. Suffice to say that Watson headed the ball back and up, intending it as a back-pass to Corrigan, who was not anticipating such an eventuality. The ball passed comfortably by Joe Corrigan, to his right. An agonising little race ensued as both Big Joe and David Fairclough, who had appeared from nowhere, chased in vain. They finished second and third respectively to the ball, which trickled, quite unconcerned, over the goal line, just beyond the reach of Corrigan. Oh dear, I thought.

I wrote a juvenile 'we wuz robbed' at the end of my report on that game. We messed it up would have been more accurate. The result of this match may not have made a difference to the eventual outcome of the Championship, but it was a huge psychological blow for City players and fans alike. City ended 1976 in third place, behind Liverpool and Ipswich Town.

The first match of 1977 was a third-round FA Cup tie against West Bromwich Albion. Willie Johnston shocked the Maine Road crowd with a 30-yard screamer just before half-time. Brian Kidd's goal earned City a replay. This was in a second half which contained a good old-fashioned, free-for-all punch up. City scrambled a 1-0 win in the replay. Back in the League, Liverpool were stuttering a little, and both Ipswich and City were collecting games in hand due to postponements. It was 22 January before City played a 1977 League match. A 5-0 thrashing of mid-table Leicester at Maine Road, with Brian Kidd helping himself to four goals, suggested that City's title hopes were still intact. They were now just three points behind Liverpool, having played three fewer matches. Ipswich were even better placed: two points ahead of City, having played the same number of games.

The Blues advanced to the fifth round of the FA Cup with a 3-1 win over Newcastle at St James's Park, a result achieved without my presence. A radio phone-in suggested that the decision not to go was a wise one. This match had not proven to be a pleasant experience for many City fans. I was present at the next League away match at the Victoria Ground, Stoke, where City gave the best away performance I had seen. It was not particularly spectacular, apart from Dennis Tueart's first-half goal, the result of an intricate run past several bemused defenders, but it was comfortable. This was something that City had been striving for on their travels. They contained the home team without looking likely to concede a goal, and they threatened continually on the break. One such break, late in the game, led to Joe Royle adding a second goal, despite the best efforts of Peter Shilton in the Stoke goal. City looked like potential champions that day.

Back at Maine Road, the Blues scrapped, quite literally, for a 1-0 win in a bad-tempered home match against Arsenal, with lots of minor fisticuffs and macho posturing on display. Joe Royle's second-half header from a Dennis Tueart cross settled a match that was noteworthy for another dominant performance by Asa Hartford, and the relief that greeted the final whistle. Every point was precious. Away from home, City carelessly lost a two-goal lead to draw at Newcastle, and followed it up by losing 1-0 at lowly Bristol City, bringing an end to a 17-match unbeaten run. Despite these results, they were still well placed in the table.

In the FA Cup, my dad and myself paid our second visit of the season to Elland Road. This time we actually got inside the ground. It had crossed my mind on more than one occasion that a League and Cup double was still on. Oh, the folly of youth! The FA Cup was all that Leeds had left to play for and, particularly in the early stages, it showed. Joe Jordan, whose every contribution to a football game always seemed like a foul to me, led the home attack, in a very real sense. There were good opportunities for either team in an eventful game, but the two goalkeepers, David Harvey and Joe Corrigan, were both in excellent form. Joe Corrigan made the best save I have ever seen when he stopped an unintentional header from Alan Oakes from flying into his own net, midway through the second half. Corrigan was initially going the wrong way, but readjusted and flung himself Gordon Banks-like to make a one-handed save. Corrigan then got involved in a fracas with Jordan, who had repeated his habit of challenging late. I expect he was still making some of his tackles after the match was over and everyone had gone home.

I was fretting prematurely about getting tickets for the midweek replay when Leeds attacked with four minutes left. Jordan headed the ball into a dangerous region of the penalty area. Mike Doyle blocked Trevor Cherry, leaving both men on the ground, and the ball stuck in the mud. Cherry got up first, spotted the whereabouts of the ball, and slid it past Joe Corrigan and into the net. I sank to my haunches in despair. I was amongst a large number of City fans, appreciating for the first time the importance of the FA Cup. I rather fancied some more of it, but it wasn't to be. In the last minute, Jimmy Conway, who had not been a regular in the team since the early stages of the season, crossed and Dennis Tueart headed against the crossbar. Football is basically a cruel game. So much for the double.

Tueart and Hartford were at their dominant best as City resumed their quest for the single at home to Norwich City. The Blues were unable to score in the first half, and it took four Dennis Tueart penalties in the space of as many minutes to settle the match 2-0. Let me explain. Tueart was felled in the penalty area and, after a bit of a discussion, decided that, despite a couple of penalty misses earlier in the season, he would take the kick himself. Tueart scored, only for the referee to order a re-take due to encroachment by a City player into the penalty area. Tueart scored with a replica penalty, only for the referee to object once more on the same grounds. And I said that you didn't get action replays at live matches. Tueart again put the penalty into the same spot, and this time the City players finally had the sense to stay well away. Four minutes later, the Blues were awarded another penalty, which Tueart dispatched first time into the same corner but higher up. City moved to second place, one point behind Liverpool with just one game in hand. The pressure was beginning to show.

My first visit to *The Swamp* for a derby match resulted in *Return of the Derby Horror* or *Derby Nightmare II*. This has since developed into a very long series. Again Docherty's spindly-legged, offside-trap-obsessed waifs and strays scored with their first two efforts on goal, after a nervy opening twenty minutes. Again there was more than an element of fortune involved as Pearson, clearly offside, scored the opening goal. It came as a result of a McIllroy shot that deflected off Watson into Pearson's path. The referee's interpretation that Pearson had not been interfering with play was an obvious one. After all, since when has scoring a goal been interfering with play? These things do happen from time to time. They just seem to happen more frequently some times rather than others. Within minutes, a Macari shot deflected into the path of Hill, who scored a second goal. Again the referee consulted a linesman, because Pearson was offside when Hill scored. This time it would have been harsh to disallow the goal. But let's face it, there was never any realistic chance of that happening.

Coppell added a third goal early in the second half, as the City nightmare continued. I felt distinctly uncomfortable squeezed into my pen behind the goal at the Scoreboard End, dodging the spit being hurled from above, as the stewards looked on in mild amusement. City pulled one goal back through Joe Royle and began a bit of a fightback. Asa Hartford struck bar and post, but the finishing was not good enough to cause any real worry for the opposition. According to the records, 58,595 people were there. Although I knew virtually none of them, I took an instant dislike to most.

For some reason, I have an abiding memory of skinny legs when it comes to the Doc's version of *The Nation's Team*. Maybe they wore big shorts. Maybe I have a subconscious skinny-leg fixation of which I am unaware. My memory, somewhat influenced by an inbuilt blue filter, also hints at lots of penalty kicks, own goals and deflected free-kicks, as well as a rigorously employed offside-trap designed to kill the game. Curiously the latter was portrayed in a positive light, until later adoption by the likes of Arsenal. English football has never quite recovered from this abomination, despite the best efforts of clubs like City, who often deploy the tactic in the largely ineffective staggered formation.

Back at the Academy, a crowd in excess of 40,000 saw City scrape a 1-0 win against Sunderland. The anxiety and tension was beginning to stifle the players' ability. It wasn't doing much for me either. Incredibly, it was another Tueart penalty, just before half-time, that won the two points. Michael Docherty, whose City career was short-lived, could have equalised for Sunderland, but he muffed his opportunity in a big way. City were only one point behind Liverpool, with a game in hand. Ipswich were still squeezed between them. There were no other realistic contenders with a quarter of the season's matches remaining.

A 1-0 defeat at West Ham was a setback for the Blues. Some consolation came from Ipswich suffering a similar fate at the hands of Sunderland, whilst Liverpool were winning in the FA Cup quarter-finals, and Chorley were drawing 1-1 with Dagenham in the FA Trophy quarter-finals. The really big game of the day, the latter, was the match I attended, along with 4,759 others. Chorley lost the replay 5-1.

Another goalless affair at Loftus Road, against QPR, meant that City's title bid was at a critical point when Ipswich Town came to Maine Road on 2 April 1977. Ipswich had sneaked ahead of Liverpool on goal difference, leaving City three points adrift of both. The Blues still had a game in hand on the others, but a defeat by Ipswich would have virtually ended all hope. Brian Kidd gave City a deserved lead 10 minutes before half-time. There was no evidence of anxiety in the first-half performance. Indeed the lead could have been greater. This was, however, a game of two halves. A neat goal by Trevor Whymark, 10 minutes into the second half, brought Ipswich level, and all the fretfulness flooded back into City's play. It was only when Ipswich appeared to settle back, content with a draw, that City found the inspiration to keep their dreams of a League title alive. From a Barnes corner, Dave Watson launched a thunderous header into the top corner of the net, leaving City with three minutes to hold on. They were the kind of three minutes that go on for hours; the kind that you never quite learn to deal with, when your team is hanging on desperately and everyone is just wishing the time away. Brain Talbot should have equalised for Ipswich. He didn't, and City won 2-1.

Titles are often decided at Easter time, and although City still had seven games to play after Easter, there was no doubting the significance of the three matches against Leeds, Liverpool and Middlesbrough on Easter Friday, Saturday and Monday. This gruelling schedule would have today's managers reaching for the Valium. City games, even at Maine Road, had degenerated into desperate struggles, and an early Leeds goal by Joe Jordan did little to lift the mood of the majority of a 47,727 crowd. The equaliser from Kidd came just before half-time. He had been standing around, minding his own business, when the ball dropped fortuitously at his feet. All presents were gratefully accepted. City attacked with some conviction in the second half, and they took the lead after a Barnes corner led to a mad scramble in the penalty area. Asa Hartford's shot was flicked in by Kidd for the winning goal.

I wasn't able to get a ticket for the clash with the mighty Liverpool. In the event, Liverpool dominated, with Keegan scoring just before the break. To their credit, City refused to give way, and when Brian Kidd scored with only 13 minutes left, a miracle looked possible. A draw would have been an excellent result for City, but it turned out to be a typical City ploy of raising hopes only to dash them again. Within a minute, Liverpool re-established their lead and their position as title favourites.

Two days later, City's beleaguered troops faced up to a resolute Middlesbrough defence at Maine Road. For most of the match the Blues attacked without being able to make a breakthrough. With 15 minutes to go, the visitors broke. Souness played a clever through-ball, and David Mills had the opportunity to just about finish City off for the season. Generously, he blasted his shot over the crossbar. With only a few minutes left to play, an incredible looping header by Asa Hartford sent the remaining crowd into raptures of delight. Many had left, believing that City were destined not to score. The crowd became increasingly desperate as the referee played four minutes of injury time, due mainly to the earlier time-wasting that had led to two bookings for Middlesbrough players. City were still hanging on, just.

A much needed 2-0 win at West Bromwich Albion, who had a midfield player called Bryan Robson carried off with a broken leg, was followed by a midweek home game against Birmingham City. Again, it was an ordeal. After just seven minutes, Corrigan parried a shot from Trevor Francis and Kenny Burns, playing as a striker, followed up to score. It took a bit of individual flair by Peter Barnes to bring City level. Barnes skipped past a couple of defenders to set up a goal for Brian Kidd, his one-hundredth in league football, although many of them would not be considered by me as a matter for celebration.

In the second half, City increased the pressure, and Kidd headed a second goal. More goals should have come to ease the apprehension, but the finishing was wasteful. Luckily, Birmingham didn't appear to have much enthusiasm for an equaliser. That result left City level on points with top-of-the-table Liverpool, having now played one game more. There was still all to play for with five matches left and Liverpool having the additional distractions of the FA Cup and European Cup.

The City title bid effectively ended in high farce on Saturday, 30 April 1977, at the Baseball Ground. When my dad and I eventually arrived, after a tortuous journey, and handed our ticket stubs in at the turnstiles, we were directed to our designated perches, high in an alarmingly steep stand. We sat down expecting to see a football pitch, and instead saw a vision not unlike a slab of Southport beach with goalposts at either end. The pitch contributed heartily to the comic qualities of the occasion. The central character was Mr J. Yates of Redditch, who was refereeing his last match and no doubt wished to make it one to remember. Well, Mr Yates, you succeeded.

The first half was relatively uneventful. The ball bumped and bounced unpredictably. There was the odd shot at either end, when the ball arrived by chance at the feet of a well-placed player. At half-time the referee made an announcement chastising members of the crowd for whistling. He endeavoured to overcome this in the second half by whistling constantly himself. Whilst the announcement was being made, Joe Corrigan amused himself by making a little sand sculpture, on a pie theme, in the goalmouth. As the second half progressed, Derby seemed to be adjusting better to the requirements of beach football. Corrigan saved well from Kevin Hector, and Gerry Daly (ex-*The Nation's Team*) shot wide after Donachie had fallen over in the sand. In response, City had their best spell. Brian Kidd missed a good chance, Dave Watson headed against the crossbar, and Ged Keegan had a shot saved. And then the whole world caved in on Manchester City in a memorable five-minute period. A weird bounce allowed Powell to elude Donachie and prompt an attack that ended with Gemmill sneaking in at the far post to score from Hector's cross. Within a few minutes, Derby added a second goal, following a corner. As tempers were lost, the match deteriorated into a series of scuffles and arguments. Most involved Archie Gemmill, even when an incident appeared to have nothing to do with him – a Roy Keane of his day. Four players were booked within a minute as Mr Yates suffered an on-field mid-life crisis. Things degenerated even further for City when the ball bobbled comically in front of Joe Corrigan, causing him to parry it straight to Kevin Hector, who made the score 3-0. Brian Kidd got involved in more scuffling and was sent off; a one-sided punishment, I thought.

The best was yet to come. Gemmill toppled rather unconvincingly in the penalty area: an attempted triple-twisting, backward somersault with pike, I believe. Gemmill was refreshingly candid about his theatrical display when interviewed on 'Match of the Day'. Mr Yates was certainly impressed. He awarded a penalty. I cannot in all honesty say that Mr Yates pointed to the penalty spot, because there was no penalty spot. The referee paced out about 10 yards and put the ball down in what he considered a suitable position to take a penalty. Everyone else could see that the ball was too close to the goal. Joe Corrigan pointed this out, started pacing the correct 12 yards and was booked for his trouble. The referee eventually succumbed to reason and called for a groundsman with a tape measure and some whitewash. It looked to most people as though Corrigan had been right, but he wasn't *un*-booked. Daly scored from the penalty. City had been without Hartford and Tueart, but there is no doubt that this was a poor performance. It was a very long trip home.

After the disaster in Derby, a 1-1 draw at Villa Park was not good enough. In the next game at Maine Road, against Tottenham, City played with a freedom suggesting that they had given up any real hopes of winning the title. Tommy Booth's header gave them a half-time lead, and Dennis Tueart added a second goal early in the second half. Barnes chipped a third and Hartford volleyed a fourth, with nearly half an hour still remaining. Brian Kidd scored again near the end, to leave Spurs well and truly relegated.

Three days later, another home game, against Everton, ended 1-1, with City fading after a bright start. Kidd's first-half goal was cancelled out by Lyons, and 38,440 had witnessed the final Maine Road action of a season that had promised much but not, in the end, delivered. When City won their final game, 1-0 at Coventry, with a rare goal from Conway, Liverpool were already Champions, a point ahead of City with still one match remaining. In fact, they lost that match against Bristol City. Liverpool had also drawn 0-0 against perennial strugglers Coventry, on the same night as City's drawn match with Everton. These points contributed greatly to the survival of both Coventry and Bristol City, at the expense of Sunderland. When all the points were added up, Liverpool had won the League by only one point from City, with Ipswich a further four adrift. With FA Cup and European Cup Finals to think about, Liverpool may have been winding down in their last couple of matches, but I can't help thinking back to that cold Christmas evening, when Watson's own goal let Liverpool off the hook at Maine Road.

To make matters worse, Liverpool lost the FA Cup Final by the jammiest goal ever seen at Wembley: the ball deflected in off somewhere in the vicinity of Jimmy Greenoff's nipple, following a chronic shot by Lou Macari. They did win the European Cup, but that was scant consolation to me.

Season 1977/78: Getting In Behind People

With the worst excesses of the seventies fading into deserved oblivion, shoe heels were almost back to normal in 1977, although there was a dubious clog fad in the Chorley area. Meanwhile, the music revolution prompted by the Sex Pistols and others was well underway. Completely hooked by these short, angry and highly subversive noises, I bought 145Anarchy In The UK' on EMI Records prior to it being withdrawn in response to a public outcry. I played it over and over again, alternating with 'New Rose' by The Damned. It was possible to play each one four times in the time it took to complete one Yes track. Wow!

I hadn't completely dumped my pretentious adolescent leanings, but I was well on the way to swapping them for new ones. With Sixth Form College already beckoning and *New Musical Express* competing with the sports pages for my attention, I welcomed back the football season with open arms.

One of the enduring images of this period in City's history is the sight of Mike Channon on his backside, having failed in an attempt to keep his cross in play. This is grossly unfair on a player who was an England regular, and whose overall record at City does not look all that bad, in retrospect. But since when was football fair? The problem stems from the fact that Channon was supposed to be the big signing to transform City from runners-up to Champions, the elusive missing link. Channon was always a likeable chap. He was game enough to appear on local radio football phone-ins, answering such incisive questions from fans as, 'Why do you spend so much time on your backside?' Channon was enthusiastic about football. You could tell that from his performances as an expert pundit on television, where his answer to all problems was to encourage players to do a lot more 'getting in behind people'. He was a West Country boy who seemed destined to play his whole career at Southampton, where he had so much success and where he returned for another spell later, teaming up with Alan Ball amongst others. Famed for his arm-twirling goal celebrations, the embodiment of a runaway windmill on speed, Channon scored plenty of goals for club and country. His acquisition by City demonstrated the size and pulling power of the club. It should have been that final piece in the jigsaw.

With Barnes and Owen receiving rave reviews for their England Under-21 performances, and a positive cornucopia of full internationals on show, City began the season amongst the really hot, hot favourites; the vindaloo favourites. The addition of a record £300,000 signing, Mike Channon, persuaded a number of the expert pundits to predict City as Champions, and Maine Road was buzzing with anticipation of great things when City took to the pitch for the opening match against Leicester City. The event was undeserving of the anticipation as a defensive Leicester stifled City to earn a 0-0 draw. The surprise result of the day was a 3-1 win by freshly promoted Nottingham Forest away to Everton. We all knew that was a flash in the pan.

This unsatisfactory start was quickly forgotten after City's first two away games of the new season: a 4-1 win at Villa Park, inspired by a Tueart hat-trick, and a 1-0 win against West Ham, with the winner coming from Joe Royle. Royle was in the side because of Brian Kidd's absence, but was widely assumed to be under threat because of the arrival of Channon. With optimism fully restored, City returned to Maine Road to take on Norwich City. There was already media talk of a Channon goal drought! Such nonsense was dispelled as Channon treated the home crowd to a virtuoso performance, impressing even sceptics like myself. Channon merited full marks for his two-goal performance, as he linked up splendidly with Brian Kidd for the first time. Even though City were without the injured Tueart, Barnes and Power provided the attacking width to supplement the midfield domination of Hartford and Owen. City cruised to an emphatic 4-0 win, with lots of frills thrown in to keep the fans ecstatic. Channon's two goals, a header and a free run at goal after interception of a poor defensive pass, were unremarkable, but he also played a major part in the other two goals, scored by Power and Hartford. It was arguably his peak as a City player, and it sent City to the top of the League, ahead of Liverpool and *The Nation's Team* on goal difference.

The subsequent match, on a rainy Saturday, 11 September 1977, was also at Maine Road, with the opposition provided by *The Nation's Team* themselves; a top-of-the-table clash with the added edge of unbridled hatred. Over 50,000 were packed into Maine Road to see City reverse a run of three consecutive derby defeats. Despite being my very first derby victory, it was actually something of an anticlimax. The win was achieved with such great ease that the Blues did not need to be at their best. The scoring commenced after 14 minutes, when a Brian Kidd free-kick seemed to go right through the defensive wall before flying into the corner of the net. The Blues, dominating in the slippery conditions, increased their lead early in the second half, when Kidd's shot was half-stopped by Stepney, but still trickled over the line. Kidd came close to completing a hat-trick, missing one chance and having a goal disallowed, ostensibly for a foul on Stepney, but it was Channon who sent City into the comfort zone 12 minutes from time, shooting home after some poor defending. The opposition had chances, but a City win never looked under serious threat. In the end, a long-range effort from Nicholl provided some inadequate consolation for our esteemed visitors, and the match ended 3-1. City remained top of the League.

In the 1977/78 season, the UEFA Cup draw was kinder to City. When the Polish side Widzew Lodz came to Maine Road for a first leg match, City were in prime form and the crowd expected goals. The Blues put their opponents under extreme pressure early in the game, and goalkeeper Stanislaw Burzyonski looked decidedly unsure of himself as Lodz survived a couple of early goalmouth scrambles. Burzyonski did save Brian Kidd's shot after 11 minutes, but couldn't prevent Peter Barnes from following up to score from the rebound. The Lodz team had one worthy effort in the opening half. It was a dipping shot by a chap with an unpronounceable-looking first name, Zbigniew Boniek. This was the same ginger-haired Boniek who went on to fame and fortune at Juventus.

City were not on top form, but a second goal, scored by Channon early in the second half, seemed to have settled the matter. The Blues were heading for the comfortable first-leg lead that they required. At least, that's what was supposed to happen. What actually happened was that Zbigniew Boniek scored twice in the space of five minutes, the first from a deflected long-range shot, the second from a penalty. Frantic attacking by City in the remaining 15 minutes amounted to nothing, and Donachie was sent off in the last minute, for allegedly kicking a Pole (ouch!), just to add to the misery. In the return leg, despite having the chances, City failed to score, and another sojourn into Europe ended prematurely, by virtue of the away goals rule.

Welcoming this opportunity to concentrate on the League, City followed a draw at QPR with a 2-0 win over Bristol City at Maine Road, despite mounting injury troubles. A goal in each half by young starlets Barnes and Owen kept City in first place, level on points with Liverpool and Nottingham Forest. Of course, everyone knew that Forest would fade.

For our second visit to Goodison Park, in the interests of personal safety, my dad and I opted for seats. Being a standing away fan meant that the police would hold you back *en masse* after the game had ended and then, just when it was absolutely clear, to anyone who might wish to know, that all the people about to leave the ground were enemy supporters, the police would release you *en masse* to face up to any locals who were waiting in ambush. If you didn't require frogmarching to coaches or trains, you had to peel away from the *masse* without anybody noticing. Why the police didn't just brand *legitimate target* on our foreheads, I don't know. Actually, I do know. It would be time-consuming, expensive and rather silly.

Two brilliant saves by Joe Corrigan kept City level as Everton provided the main threat. The Blues did have their moments, particularly when Tommy Booth's header was pushed on to the crossbar and post by the Everton goalkeeper, George Wood. Tony Book was forced to reshuffle the defence when injury prevented Tommy Booth from taking part in the second half. City were indebted to Asa Hartford for a deflected shot that gave them an early second-half lead because Everton attacked with menace. Thankfully, a header by Bob Latchford was all that they could manage in the way of goals, so the game finished 1-1. My dad and I spent the next hour trying to track down the whereabouts of the car. We remembered the street name, but when confronted with street after street of identical terraced housing, we were unable to re-trace our steps. We asked a number of locals for assistance in our search and eventually somebody came up with a piece of useful information, but at least two people, living in adjacent streets, hadn't got a clue where our street was. By the time we were starting our journey back, all the traffic had cleared. City were still unbeaten and still top of the table.

Three days later, the first cracks began to appear and City relinquished their position at the head of the First Division. After dominating Coventry City at Highfield Road, and leading 2-1 at half-time, City collapsed to a 4-2 defeat despite Dennis Tueart marking his return to the team with a goal. In a bad-tempered affair back at Maine Road, City renewed acquaintance with Malcolm MacDonald, now of Arsenal. Peter Barnes chipped Pat Jennings to give City an early lead, but MacDonald equalised for Arsenal before the break. The City lead was restored after an hour's play, thanks to a penalty by Dennis Tueart. Arsenal could have drawn level immediately when Frank Stapleton was put through by Liam Brady, but he obligingly failed in his attempt to beat Joe Corrigan. One scything tackle too many on Peter Barnes resulted in Peter

Simpson being sent off, and the referee also collected several other names as the game degenerated into fits of petulance and misplaced aggression. The outcome was a 2-1 win that left the Blues just a point behind the leaders, Forest. Since it was clear to all that Forest wouldn't last the pace, City were effectively still top. When City and Forest clashed at the City ground the following week, the Blues took an early lead but eventually lost to a late Peter Withe goal. Brian Clough's team was becoming an irritation.

It was during City's next game, at home to Wolves, that the cracks began to resemble baby chasms, revealing ominous fundamental flaws in City's aspirations. Asa Hartford had talked himself into a booking against Arsenal, and consequently a ban for three matches, and City were also without Tueart, but there could be no excuses for the first home defeat in 13 months. Tony Henry was given his debut, ahead of the transfer-listed Joe Royle, but defensive frailties were to the fore as John Richards scored two unanswered first-half goals. City had done most of the attacking before half-time, but after the break, as confidence drained, Wolves threatened to make the scoreline worse. John Richards should have completed a hat-trick, but it ended 0-2.

After what amounted to an alarming slump in form, City's next fixture was not one to be relished. For the first hour Liverpool strolled around Maine Road as if they owned the place, a familiar sight. City had their chances, but Liverpool actually looked like Champions. Fairclough had already squandered one opportunity when he linked well with Dalglish and shot past Joe Corrigan to give Liverpool the lead. Liverpool did everything except add to their lead, thanks to stout defending and incompetent finishing. In an astonishing final 30 minutes, Liverpool paid the full price for their wastefulness as the Blues roused themselves in dramatic fashion. Brian Kidd fired City level, Channon scored with an angled drive, and in a late breakaway reminiscent of Liverpool themselves, Peter Barnes, despite being felled by Alan Hansen, set up Joe Royle for the third City goal. It is, without question, a funny old game.

As October drifted by, the clocks went forward and November made its appearance. City lost their third away match in a row, thanks to a goal for Ipswich by ex-Chorley boy Paul Mariner, and found themselves embroiled in a League Cup mini-series against Second Division Luton Town. Episode One finished 1-1, with the teams separated for only four minutes. Back at Maine Road, Episode Two failed to produce any goals. The Luton team included the blond Futcher brothers: Ron, the striker who scored the first goal of the tie, and Paul, a composed central defender widely thought to have a great future. Luton's Maine Road performance was essentially one of stout rearguard action, with goalkeeper Milija Aleksic in elastic form. Having said that, a chap called Gary Heale blew his opportunity of getting his surname into some amusing tabloid headlines by missing the best chance of the match in the last of the 90 minutes. City should have scored in extra time, but they were unable to get the football past Aleksic.

The second replay took place at *The Swamp* in front of a meagre crowd of 13,042. The match had been declared all-ticket and had already been postponed from the previous day, leading to general confusion and consequent lack of interest. I sat in a half empty Scoreboard End, with no worries about dodging spittle, as Gary Heale made a second bid for stardom by scoring two goals in the opening half an hour. The curse of Old Trafford appeared to be taking effect. The general gloom had been compounded by Dennis Tueart's transfer request, following his relegation to the substitutes' bench for the first replay. Tueart was recalled for Episode Three and started brightly, but the whole team was taken aback by events. It took a fortunate penalty, scored before half-time by Tueart, to bring some spluttering life into the flagging City machine. The match developed into a classic cup-tie, with Heale squandering a hat-trick chance before Channon drew City level. It was all jolly, end-to-end stuff. A Peter Barnes shot disturbed the framework of the goal in the last minute, but couldn't prevent another dose of extra time.

The Luton manager, Harry Haslam, had some justification in feeling aggrieved at the referee, who charitably awarded City another penalty in the final minute of the opening period of extra time. Even more generously, Tueart missed it, although credit must once more go to elastic Aleksic. After 115 minutes of play, and with everyone contemplating the horrors of yet another match, Brian Kidd headed the winning goal to round off a game that deserved a bigger crowd. It was my only ever experience of victory at *The Swamp*. Luton played well, but the clear message was that City were not the force that they had been relatively recently.

The visit of Leeds on 12 November 1977 did not prove to be the beginning of a revival in the League. The first half was promising enough, and City should have had more than Channon's deflected goal to show for it. After half-time, however, City's defensive fragility was flaunted with gusto. Carl Harris should have scored and Joe Jordan did score, with a header. A couple of minutes later, Arthur Graham gave Leeds the lead as Joe Corrigan was left unaided to face two opponents. City defenders Doyle, Watson and Clements behaved as if they were not acquainted, and although City rallied temporarily, Hankin added a third Leeds goal. Peter Barnes, called into the England squad by Ron Greenwood, scored to give City some hope, but Leeds held firm.

Barnes played on the opposite wing to Steve Coppell as England's World Cup hopes officially expired during a 2-0 defeat in Italy. The Press were uncharacteristically constructive about the performance, hardly uttering a bad word, and Greenwood persevered with this positive approach, making Barnes yet another England international of note in the City ranks. It was all the more maddening, therefore, that the team had fallen to eighth place.

A goalless draw away to third-placed West Bromwich Albion marked a welcome pause in City's slump. The next home match, against Chelsea, signalled the possibility of upward mobility once more. It was a game that contained just about everything. We had a comical own goal from Graham Wilkins after nine minutes, when he took the rolled ball from Peter Bonetti, spotted Peter Barnes bearing down on him, and hurriedly returned it whence it came – only to discover that Bonetti had moved. We had truly inspired wing play by Barnes, who tormented the opposition cruelly. When one of his shots was saved, Tueart followed up to make it 2-0. The home fans were anticipating a landslide but Ray Wilkins pulled a goal back after 24 minutes, and three minutes later Chelsea equalised from a penalty. The anxiety didn't have long to register. A deflected Tueart shot restored City's lead within minutes, and Peter Barnes was the inspiration behind a Channon goal that made the half-time score 4-2.

The second half was subdued by comparison. Barnes sprinted clear of the defence to score a deserved goal, and the hapless Graham Wilkins, already booked, upended Barnes twice in a minute to merit his marching orders. Six minutes from the end, Dennis Tueart, still seemingly intent on leaving, completed his hat-trick. A hat-trick, a penalty, a sending off, eight goals including a comedy own goal; this match had everything except an eleven-a-side love-in in the centre circle. Actually, that may have happened when I visited the toilets at half-time.

A win at Ipswich kept City in the League Cup, but tempers flared once more at Derby, this time without me, as referee Derek Civil blew his final whistle a split second before a Dennis Tueart header crossed the goal line. The outcome was a 2-1 win for Derby, who, to make matters worse, were now managed by Tommy Docherty. A 3-0 home win against Birmingham City looked impressive enough on paper. On grass, it was a tribute to the excellence of Joe Corrigan, who made a number of high-class saves. Dennis Tueart once more starred amongst the outfield players, breaking the deadlock with a volley after 55 minutes. It wasn't until the closing 10 minutes that City added to their lead with goals from Owen and Channon. Trevor Francis was the main man to suffer from Corrigan's gymnastics in goal.

As Christmas approached, we drove over the Pennines for yet another deeply disappointing visit to Elland Road. On this occasion, City looked back to their best, dominating for virtually the whole match. Of course, none of that matters in football. City may have been fluent and impressive, but Leeds scored the only goals. Gordon McQueen, looking suspiciously offside, gave Leeds an early lead. After City had wasted a series of chances, Paul Power broke through. His clash with David Harvey should, by common consent, have resulted in a penalty. It didn't. I admit to bias, but the newspapers also questioned both decisions. Honestly! As frustration mounted, too many City players lost their tempers and got their names into the referee's notebook. This lack of discipline was becoming a regular feature and an unwelcome distraction. Eventually, Leeds broke from their defensive barrage and Tony Currie set up Trevor Cherry for a decisive second goal 20 minutes from the end. In the trade it's referred to as one of those days.

I was beginning to believe in a personal Elland Road jinx. Unfortunately, the FA Cup third-round draw ensured that another visit was imminent. The FA Cup was now the main object of my covetous attention. I had seen a League Cup triumph, and in an act of commendable realism, I was starting to accept that a League Championship was an over-optimistic aspiration. The FA Cup was desirable and, I thought, attainable. Yes, the FA Cup would do very nicely.

Beginning on Boxing Day 1978, there was a period of five weeks that shaped not only that season, but those following it. City had an outstanding Christmas period, something that looked unlikely at half-time of a dull Boxing Day home game against Newcastle. It was the return of Colin Bell that seemed to inspire the Blues. After only a handful of First Division matches since his injury suffered in November 1975, Bell emerged as substitute for the second half and was straight into the action, heading just over the bar and then forcing a save from goalkeeper Carr. Bell was not destined to score, but his appearance eclipsed yet another Dennis Tueart hat-trick. Tueart opened the scoring with a gliding header and, following a Brian Kidd goal, he added a tap-in and a 20-yard drive to complete a 4-0 win. The emotional high carried over to the following day at Ayrsome Park, where City beat Middlesbrough 2-0. On New Year's Eve, at home to Aston Villa, City completed their exceptional Yuletide run with an impressive win in front of 46,074 elated fans. Well, obviously they weren't all elated. Some wanted Villa to win. The match was dominated by City, but they had to work for their two goals, scored in the second half by Peter Barnes, and Brian Kidd, the latter a thunderous header from a Barnes cross.

The build-up to the FA Cup match at Leeds could hardly have been better. When the match started, amidst eager anticipation, City carried on from the earlier League meeting by dominating the opening half, only to again fail in their attempts to actually score a goal. Leeds threatened an improvement at the beginning of the second half and I began to sense the Elland Road jinx hovering. In the event, I had nothing to fear on the football side. Sitting behind the relevant goal, I had the perfect view when, after 63 minutes of play, Watson crossed, Bell headed back across goal and Tueart headed into the roof of the net, sending the fans behind the goal, including me, into fits of frenzy. City streamed forward looking for more goals and 10 minutes later they had one. Peter Barnes lashed the ball in after Colin Bell's header had been pushed on to the crossbar by the beleaguered David Harvey.

With 15 minutes remaining, a Leeds threat eventually emerged, but not from a conventional source. The source of this threat was not the Leeds United players, but the disgruntled fans massed behind the opposite goal. It began with a lone fan running on to the pitch and appearing to attack Joe Corrigan, a very large man wearing football boots. I'll leave you to judge the wisdom of such an action and the mental capacity of the individual involved. Big Joe then drew the attention of the referee to the fact that the crowd behind the goal were hurling objects at him. Within a few minutes, hundreds of Leeds fans had invaded the pitch with the obvious cunning plan of getting the match abandoned. As police and stewards tried in vain to force the fans back, the referee, Colin Seel, had no alternative but to take the players off the field. That having been achieved, Mr Seel re-emerged with a microphone to announce that the match would not be abandoned, and that they would play until midnight if necessary. I didn't like the sound of that, but this was one of those rare occasions when I actually admired a referee. Unfortunately, his commendable defiance had no effect whatsoever.

Picture the scene: little me, complete with scarf and bobble-less bob-hat, seated only a few rows from the front and facing up to massed ranks of irate Yorkshiremen who had already marched, in what could easily pass for organised formation, approximately a third of the length of the pitch towards me. It was a great relief when, after a nervous interlude, a gaggle of crash-helmeted riot police on horseback emerged from nowhere to herd the angry mob back into the stands. It's the only occasion when I have been able to see the point of mounted police, other than as a means to trample people standing in orderly queues. When the players eventually returned, neither team looked particularly focused on playing football. In the final minute of the match, Joe Corrigan, understandably reluctant to stay too close to his line, brought down Tony Currie, and Frank Gray converted the penalty. The crowd trouble overshadowed one of the best City performances I've ever seen, and I was even denied the treat of a repeat, in the safety of my own home, by an industrial dispute that led to the cancellation of 'Match of the Day'. Is it any wonder that I'm paranoid?

Another big crowd turned out for the next home match, a 3-2 victory over West Ham. Peter Barnes scored the pick of the goals in a match where City never quite got away from the opposition. Trevor Brooking, one of the West Ham scorers that day, was always able to create enough to keep them interested. The all-important result maintained City's interest in higher matters, the League title. Fifth place, six points behind leaders Forest, but only two behind Liverpool, re-established them as serious contenders. We were all still waiting for the widely anticipated decline of Forest.

For Manchester City, the Cup competitions returned to centre stage in late January and early February. In the quarter-finals of the League Cup, City faced a home tie with Arsenal. An outstanding performance by Pat Jennings in the Arsenal goal, with spectacular saves to deny Tueart and Barnes, left the match goalless. Before embracing the challenge of the replay, City won 3-1 at Norwich to jump into second place in the League. The season was approaching a make or break period, with vital matches in quick succession: the replay against Arsenal in the League Cup, and the FA Cup fourth round, where City had been drawn away to Nottingham Forest.

City failed to clear the first of those hurdles, losing 1-0 at Arsenal to a late penalty. That made the trip to Forest so much more vital. By now Channon, dropped by England, had been relegated to the City substitutes' bench, with Kidd and Tueart undisputedly forming the best striking partnership. Tueart was, however, still in dispute with the club. On 28 January 1978, a cold and frosty Saturday, we set off on the long trip to Nottingham, driving all the way to the last M1 service station before the turn-off, only to discover from other bemused supporters that the game had been belatedly postponed. Reaching Nottingham for a Tuesday match on a normal working day for my dad, and a normal college day for me, was not an easy matter, but somehow we managed it.

The match itself was an exceptionally good one and was a notable turning point for many reasons, most of them detrimental to City. As soon as the game began I could tell that Brian Clough had worked a minor miracle with his mixture of rejects, almost has-beens and never-heard-ofs. The man was obviously as near as it is possible to get to a football genius. John Robertson, one of Cloughie's most notable reformed characters, cut in off the wing to score with a dream of a shot after only four minutes, and for 20 minutes or so Forest were rampant. Gradually, City resurrected their own passing game, although they never fully stemmed the lightning Forest counter-attacks. As the City midfield began to dominate, it took a reflex save from Shilton to prevent Kidd from equalising, and to maintain Forest's lead at half-time.

Tony Book's half-time decision to replace Gary Owen with Mike Channon seemed an odd one. Owen and Hartford had been increasing their grip on midfield, and the introduction of a third forward player did not seem logical. I have learned since then that managers seem to revel in being illogical. Tony Book was a relatively minor offender compared to most of his successors. Forest continued to look dangerous, and when Peter Withe scored following a corner, everything seemed lost. It wasn't quite. Within two minutes, Brian Kidd flicked a Kenny Clements cross past Shilton and City hopes revived. The Blues rarely threatened an equaliser, however, and Forest could easily have added to their score as they consistently broke at speed through City's lightweight midfield. Joe Corrigan was able to foil Martin O'Neill, but had to rely on the kindness of a post to prevent a second Withe goal.

I left the match convinced that Forest were good enough to win the League, and aware that City's season was in tatters. I also cast anxious glances at the Trent, which seemed a little too close for comfort should any local pre-Stuart Pearce psychos decide to start some trouble. In the cold light of day, I was able to manage relatively mature reflection on this particular match. Previously, I had put most defeats down to bad luck or bad refereeing. Some defeats could be attributed to over-generous City defending, but I rarely credited the opposition with having much of a role. Mind you, at least I never blamed the colour of the team shirts. I viewed the Forest game as a match where City played well, but their opponents played better. In keeping with recent precedents, if I couldn't blame the shirts, I should have complained that Forest were trying too hard.

The repercussions of the Forest game were considerable. Dennis Tueart, at the peak of his career, left City to join the New York Cosmos in the doomed American League. This said much about the reality of City's Championship hopes, or at least Tueart's opinion of them. After having seen Forest, I had to admit that a six-point lead did look ominously large.

Nearly 40,000 people still turned up to the next home match, a comedy on ice co-starring QPR. For much of the time, the snow-covered pitch made staying upright the limit of ambition for the players. QPR seemed to be better at it, and Joe Corrigan was again in outstanding form as he dived about in the snow like an oversized husky. With Stan Bowles having one of his better days, it looked as if QPR would take advantage of City's Cup hangovers, but a more direct second-half approach by the Blues led to a Channon goal. This was soon followed by a rapturously received goal from Colin Bell, his first since returning to the side. City eventually hung on for a 2-1 win.

A run of seven successive League wins came to an end at Bristol City, where two revenge goals by Joe Royle gave City a mountain to climb. They got halfway up the mountain, probably to one of the intermediate base camps, to force a 2-2 draw. That result meant that the Blues dipped below Everton in the pack still chasing Forest at the top of the table. On 25 February 1978, two days after Blondie's first British gig, attended by yours truly at Blackburn King George's Hall, Everton were the visitors to Maine Road. For some reason, the overwhelming urge of most males to rush to the front when Blondie took the stage was not evident when Everton trudged on to the pitch. I don't suppose that anyone was too keen to catch a glimpse up Mick Lyons's shorts. City restored genuine hope with an impressive performance lacking only in the most important aspect, the end product. George Wood made a series of excellent saves in the Everton goal, and it looked as though the visitors would repay City for the fortunate draw at Goodison Park earlier in the season. Instead, the Blues made the breakthrough with 10 minutes left, when Brian Kidd followed up to head in after Colin Bell's shot was blocked by Wood. It was tough on the goalkeeper, but I make a habit of never having genuine sympathy for the opposition.

The 3-0 defeat at Arsenal in the next match was a result that City could not afford. It meant that the derby match at *The Swamp* on Wednesday, March 15 was unlikely to have a significant bearing on the title. But who cares about the title? It still meant a lot to me. We had a car crisis leading up to the match and it looked as if I wouldn't get to see it. A considerable amount of sulking and the generosity of one of my dad's pals, who lent us an old van, resolved the crisis. After resolving a subsequent van-parking crisis, we were in position behind the Scoreboard End goal just in time for kick-off. Having learned from previous experience, we stood quite near to the front, out of range of potential gobbers or urinators. The match was memorable for a number of reasons, not least the reaction of the media afterwards. It was certainly a controversial match, but the moments of controversy depended very much on your point of view. The referee, the infamous Clive Thomas, booked seven players and made a number of more telling contributions. After eight minutes, he awarded a penalty. The referee had no hesitation, as the media always puts it. That doesn't mean that he was right. The relevant incident took place in front of the Stretford End, therefore my own view was not a particularly good one. Gordon Hill scored. Wind and heavy rainfall heightened the frenetic activity, with Stepney in the home goal having particular difficulty, but City were strangely disinclined to take advantage.

To be honest, which is difficult, there could have been goals at either end. Maybe Mr Thomas decided that the teams needed a little assistance. Twelve minutes into the second half, at a distance of no more than 15 yards from where I was standing, and only inches inside the penalty area, Asa Hartford aimed a kick at the ball and missed everything. At least, it looked to me as though he missed everything. However, at precisely the same moment as Hartford's foot swung, an unknown force seemed to remove all structural support from Jimmy Greenoff, who was somehow propelled forward as if coshed from behind with a massive blunt instrument. Hill scored penalty number two.

The *Curse of the Swamp* looked set to decide matters once more, until Stepney parried Kidd's shot and Peter Barnes followed up to score with 12 minutes remaining. Two minutes later, Asa Hartford chipped the ball brilliantly over the defenders, foiling the irritating and overused offside-trap by chasing after it himself. As he approached Stepney, Hartford squared the ball to Brian Kidd, who came from a position behind Hartford and therefore could not be offside. Kidd scored the simplest of tap-ins and the linesman stuck his flag up in the air for offside. Mr Thomas went over to consult the linesman, but to my great surprise still awarded the goal. Maybe he went over to explain the rules. In any case, amidst much whinging and name-taking it was 2-2. The

Press chose to ignore the penalty decisions and moan about the City equaliser. Video evidence proved the referee right, a rare occurrence indeed.

Despite all the excitement and debate, a draw had not improved City's title hopes. After another draw at Wolves, things were getting a little desperate by the time Middlesbrough visited Maine Road in the next home match. The Blues did not play like title contenders, but a close-range header by Channon in the eighty-ninth minute, his second goal of the match, looked like earning them a 2-1 win. It didn't. Middlesbrough equalised with the last kick of the match. Another 2-2 draw at Newcastle was notable for two debut goals by 19-year-old striker Roger Palmer. Palmer was the first of City's local black players to make it into the first team, and his goalscoring ability was on view again in the next home match. He controlled the ball, turned and shot passed Ipswich goalkeeper Paul Cooper to give City the lead just before half-time. Channon added the second in a distinctly low-key 2-1 win, with Paul Mariner again scoring against the Blues. Ipswich had their minds on the FA Cup, with a semi-final against West Bromwich Albion looming.

When Forest came to Maine Road for a midweek fixture that should have been a clash of the titans, their Championship lead was already looking unassailable. This was a more cautious and professional Forest. They came for a point, and with City, Asa Hartford excepted, suffering apparent fatigue, achieved their goal in a match of few chances. It was the only goal achieved that night.

In the next home match, West Bromwich Albion, who had lost their semi-final match against Ipswich the previous Saturday, extracted their revenge on an increasingly forlorn City team. Cyrille Regis sprinted clear to give the Baggies the lead, and goals from Cunningham and Ally Brown made matters worse. City were unable to take advantage of the chances they did make, and were even more unable to cope with the speed of the counter-attacks. A Brian Kidd consolation goal was all that they managed.

With a place in Europe seriously under threat, City found some timely form to win 4-1 at Birmingham and 3-1 at home to Coventry. They ended the Maine Road season, however, with another dour performance against Derby County. Mike Channon gave the Blues the lead but it was short-lived, Gerry Daly scoring before half-time. The City fans chanted for substitute Peter Barnes to be brought on. When they were finally granted their wish, the cheers turned to boos as Gary Owen was taken off. There seemed to be so many more suitable candidates. The fans were beginning to vent their frustration on Tony Book.

Many of them were fortunate enough not to make the trip to Anfield for City's penultimate match of the season. I was one of the unlucky ones who witnessed City's worst performance of the season, a comprehensive 4-0 demolition by Liverpool. It didn't look too ominous in the first half, despite City's defensive outlook and a goal by Dalglish. After half-time, however, City had no answer to Dalglish and Fairclough. A Phil Neal penalty and two further goals from Dalglish, the first one a gem, completed City's misery.

The trip to Anfield was not without external incident. Despite the comprehensive win, there were nervous moments outside the ground as local youngsters came to ascertain allegiances, with big brothers hovering further down the road. We assumed looks of contentment, pretending to be Liverpool fans. It wasn't necessary to appear too smug. After all, it had been a disappointing season for Liverpool. They won only the European Cup.

The final match of the season, a goalless draw at a muddy Chelsea, was almost an afterthought. City actually finished fourth, which doesn't seem so bad in retrospect, but didn't seem too good at the time. Forest, of course, won the League by seven points from Liverpool. City were a further five points adrift, three behind third-placed Everton. Asa Hartford was my clear choice for player of the season, with the departed Dennis Tueart in second place. Mike Channon was never in contention. Storm clouds were gathering over Maine Road.

Season 1978/79: From San Siro to Gay Meadow – the return of a false Messiah?

I spent the June of 1978 overdosing on late-night televised World Cup matches and revelling in the sheer magnificence of it all, right up until the unsavoury concluding stage. I embrace every World Cup with relish, but the competition usually seems to pass from the exciting early matches, full of the promise of future delights, to the unsatisfactory climax, without a discernible intervening period. Maybe the real thrill is in the anticipation, and the enthusiasm declines as matters proceed. The 1978 World Cup had the added drawback of ending on a dubious and unpalatable note as Argentina, needing a heavy victory over Peru to make the final, achieved their objective rather too easily. In the final against Holland, fortune seemed to favour the home side once more.

The end of a World Cup always leaves me wondering what on earth to do with all that spare time. Having spent the best part of a month watching football games every day, sometimes several in the same day and occasionally two at once, it takes a while to remember what it was that used to fill the pre-World Cup waking hours. I would have been quite happy to see the tournament start all over again. Unfortunately, there was only Test Match cricket to keep me going through the summer until, at last, the new football season arrived.

Tony Book had understandably attempted to improve City's faltering defence. The major transfer activity involved a deal with Luton Town, a club with which City were particularly familiar after the League Cup epic of the previous season. There may have been some confusion in the City management when they contacted Luton Town expressing an interest in Futcher. Perhaps they recalled being impressed by *a* Futcher, but they couldn't remember *which* Futcher. The outcome was that they bought both Futcher twins.

Paul Futcher, an England Under-21 international, was elegant, confident in possession of the ball, and never hurried. He gave every impression of being a superior kind of British central defender. Unfortunately, he also had a seemingly inbuilt self-destruct mechanism that triggered just often enough to suggest that the general impression he gave was largely superficial. Brother Ron was a centre forward from whom little was expected apart from some cover for injuries. The only other signing of note, Colin Viljoen, was at the stage of his career where he was unlikely to have a big impact in midfield, which was, in any case, causing City the fewest concerns.

With Dennis Tueart a fond but fading memory, Mike Channon was expected to fill the resulting goalscoring and general mega-hero void. Perhaps 'expected' is the wrong word to use. We all hoped that Channon would fill the gap. There was nobody else.

City did not get off to a particularly impressive start to the new season. An opening day draw at Derby was followed by another at Maine Road against Arsenal. In their first home game, City started badly, and Stapleton had already wasted chances to score for Arsenal before Malcolm MacDonald obliged. After half-time, an improved City managed to equalise through Kidd, who was also City's goalscorer at Derby. With Dave Watson absent from the City defence, the next home match, against Liverpool, was always likely to be tricky. It turned out to be embarrassing. A Souness goal, taken with considerable aplomb following McDermott's through pass, was cancelled out by Brian Kidd's third goal of the season, but the City defence was assuming sieve-like qualities and it wasn't long before Ray Kennedy re-established Liverpool's lead. Early in the second half, Souness scored from close-range, and with only 55 tortuous minutes having expired, Kenny Dalglish took advantage of his isolation in front of goal, to add the fourth. The whole occasion is best summed up as City, and particularly Channon, lumbering about in attack, firing shots hither and thither, whilst Liverpool eased their way through a dazed defence, picking off goals as and when they chose to. One Channon shot ballooned into the crowd near the end of the match provoked jeers of derision. Prospects were not looking too encouraging.

In the League Cup, City only just edged past Fourth Division Grimsby, thanks largely to a Kevin Moore header flying into his own net. Roger Palmer scored the second on a night to forget. With Kidd injured, Channon scored his first goal of the season in a 1-1 draw at Norwich, before City secured their first League win, at home to Leeds. The Blues were again shaky in the opening exchanges, and a linesman's flag was the only thing preventing Leeds from taking the lead. Actually, the flag alone would have been insufficient. Credit must also be given to the fine, upstanding citizen in charge of the flag. I'm sure that the offside decision was impeccable. After all, the match officials are dedicated professionals who know precisely what they are doing.

Immediately following the disallowed Leeds goal, City advanced to the other end of the Maine Road pitch and Dave Watson volleyed the Blues ahead. In the City attack, it was Roger Palmer who made the significant impact, swooping on to a back-pass to make it 2-0 after 16 minutes, and lurking in the ideal position to add another goal 10 minutes from time. Palmer's opportunities in the team were limited, possibly because he looked as though a strong breeze might blow him over. There were also long periods in matches when his presence would go unnoticed, but there is little doubt that Palmer's finishing was formidable. Since football matches are decided by the team scoring the most goals, I would have thought that Palmer's main asset was a pretty good one to have, and that he merited more games for City.

A remarkable and unexpected hat-trick by Ron Futcher inspired a 4-1 win at Chelsea, and 'the other Futcher' scored again in a 2-0 home win over Spurs, in a match where Joe Corrigan was City's busiest and best player, as the Blues again struggled for long periods. Those results catapulted the Blues into fourth place in the League as they prepared for a second leg UEFA Cup tie against Twente Enschede of Holland. In the first leg match, City actually took the lead through Watson. Even though Twente did equalise to force a 1-1 draw, the Blues faced up to the home match knowing that any kind of a win was all that was required, and that they had one of those much coveted away goals that so excite the likes of John Motson.

In fact, as is almost always the case, the away goal was an irrelevance to a tremendous cup-tie. After only eight minutes, a Gary Owen cross was diverted into his own net by the aptly named Wildschut. Brian Kidd was through on goal but missed, and Gary Owen, finding himself in a similar position, shot against the post as City looked to capitalise on the good start. After a tentative beginning, Twente played their way back into contention and equalised just after half-time. Bearing in mind recent European adventures, it was not surprising that the Twente goal gave both crowd and team the jitters. The sight of Colin Bell entering the fray as substitute, for his first outing of the season, seemed to boost morale. With 20 minutes left, Brian Kidd stormed forward and unleashed a swerving long-range shot that ended its brief but exhilarating journey in the top corner of the net. With eight minutes remaining, Colin Bell scored and we were able to relax for fully three minutes, until Gritter also scored from close-range. There were still agonising moments to endure before the referee finally ended the match. It was City's tie, 4-3 on aggregate. At last I had seen a win in European competition.

I was still recovering from an incredible Free Trade Hall performance by The Ramones the night before (about 30 songs in 45 minutes – surely the most action-packed 45 minutes of the season), as the teams marched on to *The Swamp* to take part in a nasty, violent and frankly poor League derby match. For the record, there was the obligatory dubious decision, Channon's goal ruled out because Kidd was standing in an offside position. In addition, the referee failed pitifully in his attempts to control some violent confrontations. One particularly rash challenge by Albiston on Barnes had the desired effect. The City winger seemed to lose all interest in the ball. In truth, none of this would have bothered me much had the day not been spoiled by Joe Jordan's last-minute winner, a shot that somehow found a route to goal through a crowded penalty area.

This fixture provided an opportunity for City fans to make double use of the tune from the popular ditty 'Jilted John', a hit single performed by Jilted John. Not only could 'Gordon is a moron' be directed at Gordon McQueen but 'Jordan is a moron' could be thrown in as a bonus. Full use was made of the opportunity. One City fan had an additional touching memento to remember the day by, consisting of a newspaper photograph of himself with a dart in his head. Most others preferred to forget the day as quickly as possible.

A few days later, I went on a seaside excursion to see City given a considerable fright in the League Cup by Third Division Blackpool. Despite starting well and taking the lead through Channon, City were made to struggle by a hard-working side clearly intent on embarrassing big-city neighbours. Within two minutes of going behind, Blackpool were level, and the remaining 55 minutes belonged to them. Only poor finishing prevented City's ignominious departure from the competition.

Goals from Kidd and Ron Futcher enabled the Blues to register a much needed 2-1 win at Birmingham in the next League match. By now, brother Paul had been dropped from the City defence. When Blackpool visited Maine Road for the League Cup replay, it took a penalty by Owen to break Blackpool's dogged resistance. Owen and Booth added further goals. Two more Owen penalties were required to see off Coventry at Maine Road, and propel City to a respectable fifth in the League in the approach to another European night at Maine Road.

The UEFA Cup second-round opponents on 18 October 1978 were Standard Liege of Belgium. Liege were not exactly brimming with well-known players. Michel Preud'homme, the goalkeeper preferred to a chap called Jean Paul Cricifix, went on to play for the Belgian national side for a number of years. I hesitate to suggest that Cricifix may well have been better on crosses. There were also a few current Belgian internationals, such as Gerets, Renquin and Wellens, and the odd foreign international. Defence looked like their strong point, and most of their approach to the first leg match was dictated by that philosophy. After only 13 minutes, City made a crucial breakthrough, Barnes supplying the cross for Hartford to head low into the net. There should have been more goals as City piled forward, although there was a warning against complacency just prior to half-time, when Willens, clear through on goal, was thwarted by Joe Corrigan. Preud'homme continued to be the busier goalkeeper, making a number of saves, including one where he kicked a ball from Brian Kidd off the line, against the underside of the crossbar and away to safety. As City became frustrated by their inability to make the tie safe, breaks from Liege increased in frequency. It looked as though the Belgian tactics were working well. In the previous round, against Dundee United, there had been only a single goal over the two legs, as Liege edged through 1-0. Although they had conceded one goal at Maine Road, the Liege players and coach must have been happy with a night of containment. The City fans, however, were far from happy, and were jeering well before the finish. My, we were certainly spoilt in those days!

Football being the unpredictable game that it is, everything changed completely in the final five minutes of the match. The dramatic finale was triggered by the Romanian referee, who spotted a Belgian handball. It certainly wasn't easy to spot, but the television pictures suggested he was right. In the absence of the banned Owen, Brian Kidd stepped up to score from the penalty. A minute later, Kidd scored again, with a glancing header, after a spectacular piece of wing play by Peter Barnes. Amidst a barrage of noise from a rather more supportive crowd, the party climaxed with a fourth goal, again set up by the irrepressible Barnes, and this time finished by Palmer. The Belgian tactics had collapsed in dramatic fashion, proving that old and entirely obvious maxim, 'it ain't over 'til it's over.'

Even City couldn't squander a 4-0 lead, although they did have their moments in the second leg, when Liege scored twice, once from a penalty. Gary Owen celebrated his return from a Euro-ban by getting himself sent off near the end to earn another one. City progressed 4-2 on aggregate.

Meanwhile, back in the League, I had the opportunity to return to Burnden Park, this time very much in the away end. Bolton Wanderers, after a number of agonising near misses, had finally succeeded in being promoted. They celebrated by nailing some plastic seats to the terracing behind the goal, and renting their use to visiting support- ers. These included some that were situated directly behind the metal girders holding up the ancient stand. These were not so much restricted view as no view. Luckily, my seat was more fortunately located, and I had a good view of an excellent match. Fol- lowing an even opening period, Roger Palmer gave City the lead after winning a chase to reach a Kenny Clements defensive hoof. That merely inspired Bolton to exert some pressure of their own, and they equalised before the break when Alan Gowling headed in, following some trickery from Frank Worthington. Worthington, one of the Stan Bowles and Rodney Marsh school of entertainers, was clearly Bolton's inspiration, and he flicked the home side into the lead just after half-time. With Peter Reid looking dominant in midfield, City were looking vulnerable. Gowling twice came close, and Tommy Booth cleared off the line from Worthington. Having survived the onslaught, City began to force Bolton back. Brian Kidd headed against the bar, and Gary Owen hit a fine equaliser with 20 minutes left. City finished the stronger of the two sides and Brian Kidd shot against the post as Bolton took their turn at desperate defending. A draw was probably a fair result, but who cares about fair?

The next League match, at home to West Bromwich Albion, also ended in a 2-2 draw. Whilst it was a highly entertaining match, played in front of a 40,000 crowd, it was not a win, and City needed to win. Having said that, Albion came into the match fresh from putting seven goals past Coventry, and in proud occupation of fourth place in the League, one higher than City. Channon returned from injury to give City the lead after 16 minutes. Injury to Watson meant another chance for Paul Futcher, al- though he might have preferred lesser opponents for such an opportunity. Cyrille Re- gis, the scourge of all Division One defences, equalised for Albion. Asa Hartford restored City's lead with a left-foot volley struck with considerable force, only for Bryan Robson to cancel that out from close-range, and all before half-time. Albion's manager was, of course, none other than ex-Oxford United star, Big Ron Atkinson.

A Gary Owen penalty was required to earn City a draw at Aston Villa, but yet an- other Owen penalty was insufficient to save City from defeat at home to Tommy Do- cherty's Derby County. Goalkeeper John Middleton was in maddeningly good form as City contrived to waste somewhere between a string and a gaggle of scoring chances. Derby's goals, scored by John Duncan and Gerry Daly, the latter a penalty, proved too much to recover.

City were, therefore, not in the best of form for a trip to Anfield the following week. Yet they actually gave an encouraging performance. Although Liverpool started brightly, City matched them and might even have taken the lead if Roger Palmer hadn't shown rare mercy in front of goal. In the second half, City played as well as they had all season, but it was all to no avail and referee Walmsley took centre stage in a bad-tempered finale. Alan Kennedy went down in the penalty area but, much to everyone's surprise, the referee resisted the pressure and did not award a penalty. Amidst the sort of intimidating atmosphere that makes match officials and fans alike fear for their personal future, tempers flared and there were several bookings. In one incident Tommy Booth attacked Jimmy Case with a mud pie, which is not something you see every day of the week. I cannot say whether penalty number one should have been given. The fact that I don't dwell on it much in my post-match report suggests that Liverpool might have had cause for complaint. However, there was universal agreement that the referee's decision to award Liverpool a penalty a few minutes later was a poor one. By 'universal' I mean myself, two newspaper reporters and the players involved in the incident. OK, so it's a small universe.

Phil Neal scored from the penalty, and with only four minutes remaining there was no way back for City. I can remember a very long and frustrating wait in the car park after the match as the traffic took an eternity to depart. There seems to have been an epidemic of penalties in City matches during this period. This one sent City plummeting into mid-table, 10 points adrift of the League leaders, Liverpool.

On the afternoon of Thursday, 23 November 1978, City played a UEFA Cup third-round first leg match in the San Siro Stadium against AC Milan. The match was postponed from the previous night because of fog, and an under-strength City side, without Channon, Barnes and Owen, was expected to struggle against the Italian giants. Instead, a first-half Kidd header and a Paul Power shot, the culmination of a run that had taken him almost the entire length of the pitch, gave City a truly astonishing two-goal lead with half an hour to play. Milan had never lost a European match at home, and although they pulled one goal back almost immediately, the prospect of defeat had the crowd jeering and throwing cushions. I've never been to the San Siro Stadium, but I imagine that you'd need a pretty good shot to hit a player with a cushion, and even if you did, it wouldn't hurt. In the end, City had to settle for being the first team to score twice in a European tie against Milan in the San Siro, because with eight minutes to go, Bigon scored his second goal of the night. Even so, a 2-2 draw in Milan was a tremendous result for City.

Two days later, 38,527 people turned out to welcome the returning heroes and to see the home debut of Kazimierz Deyna, the finest Polish international of his generation. Deyna, at 31, had reached an age where he was permitted to head west and earn some hard currency. He was instrumental to the success of the Polish team that finished third in the 1974 World Cup, knocking out England in the qualifiers. Lato got the goals, but Deyna was the brains behind the operation in midfield. Kaziu Deyna was an athletic, skilful, creative midfield player, with a commendable knack of scoring goals and an ability to make the difficult look simple. He was one of the best players who ever played for City, a Polish Colin Bell. Unfortunately for him, his arrival at Maine Road could hardly have been more ill-timed. If Deyna had an agent, he would have been justified in suing him. Deyna was about to find himself in the middle of a revolution.

Deyna's home debut against Ipswich was not a success. Kenny Clements suffered a broken leg and it was another overseas player, Arnold Muhren, who starred as the visitors won deservedly, 2-1. Dismissing the Ipswich game as a mere blip brought on by tiredness, we settled down for the return leg of the AC Milan tie and one of the most remarkable nights seen at Maine Road. Sadly, Franco Baresi, whose name appeared on the original teamsheet, did not play, but the Milan team included their captain, the legendary Gianni Rivera. Milan were battling it out at the top of Serie A, having finished fourth the previous season, yet they were brushed aside in the most emphatic fashion in a first half that was almost too good to be true. After 15 minutes, the veteran goalkeeper Albertosi was beaten by a Tommy Booth header. On 31 minutes, Asa Hartford drove a sweet shot into the top corner of the Milan net to make it 2-0, and just before half-time, Hartford's quick free-kick caught the Milan defenders in slumberland as Kidd was left unchallenged to head the third goal. Both sides missed second-half chances and Joe Corrigan had to earn his pay, but there were no further goals. The final score: Manchester City 3, AC Milan 0 (aggregate score 5-2). I just had to see that in writing!

Having belittled one of the giants of European football, and given a passable impersonation of a quality football team, City returned to planet earth by allowing Southampton their first away win of the season. The deadlock was broken by Viljoen's stunning volley. Unfortunately, it was into his own net. Phil Boyer added a second goal for Southampton just after half-time. Paul Power halved that lead but the visitors, captained by Alan Ball, hung on for a 2-1 win. Three days later, on a mudbath of a pitch at The Dell, the scoreline was repeated as City exited from the League Cup. Another 2-1 defeat followed at QPR to send City drifting further down the League table. Clearly, European success was not proving to be an inspiration.

There were improved performances over the Christmas period, but no wins. A hard-fought goalless draw at home to champions Nottingham Forest was followed by a Boxing Day trip to Goodison Park. Having risen from my sickbed and, much to the chagrin of my mother, declared myself fit for the match, I was there to witness City lose to a Billy Wright strike, despite offering much to admire. A 1-1 draw at Bristol City made it 11 League matches without a win.

Although City had been unfortunate in many of those matches, the defence was looking fragile and the goals were not flowing to compensate. Deyna had already been sidelined, unable, as yet, to cope with the pace of the games or the inadequacies of his colleagues. It was at this point that Mr Swales pressed the panic button. Malcolm Allison, amidst a frenzied media circus, returned to Maine Road to take on joint team responsibilities with Tony Book. Bill Taylor, the coach credited with masterminding the downfall of Milan, was unceremoniously dumped. Allison was greeted by all as the Messiah whose return would prompt the re-emergence of City. On 13 January 1979, a cigar-puffing Allison was in place at Elland Road to see the Blues scramble another draw, 1-1, with a late Kidd goal. If anyone wanted evidence that an instant miracle was not imminent, the goalless FA Cup home draw against Third Division Rotherham

United provided it. However, it was not all gloom. City did manage to win 4-2 in the replay to set up a fourth-round tie against Shrewsbury Town.

Back at Maine Road on 20 January, City's home foibles seemed to be getting worse. Chelsea, the visitors, were languishing second from the bottom of the League. Kaziu Deyna, now considered fit enough to make a contribution, was given a place in the side, and as an attacking force City prospered because of it. Paul Power gave them the lead, only for a rare Corrigan misjudgement of a cruel bounce to allow a Duncan McKenzie equaliser. It took a deflected Ron Futcher goal to restore City's lead before half-time, and that slender lead should have been increased. Yet 15 minutes from the end, Peter Osgood equalised for Chelsea and, three minutes later, Clive Walker scored off a City corner. Yes, I do mean a City corner. As the corner was cleared, Walker found himself with a free run on goal and somehow managed to squeeze the ball through Corrigan's legs.

The following Saturday, I travelled to Shrewsbury with much on my mind, not least whether we would get there through the fog still alive, and whether there would be a match to see even if we did. Because of the treacherous driving conditions, my dad was all for turning back on a number of occasions, but I was insistent. Just before we reached Shrewsbury, the fog retreated miraculously, revealing nearly clear skies and bright sunshine. City did not want the match to go ahead on the sandy but icy pitch. By all accounts, they spent most of the morning and early afternoon complaining about it. Certainly, it was less than ideal, but with the 'Match of the Day' cameras gathered, like vultures, in hope of a big-name demise, and a place in the FA Cup fifth round at stake, the City team should have had incentive enough to ignore the imperfections of the pitch and fight for a win.

The thought of Gay Meadow conjures images of frisky lambs frolicking, children skipping and buxom damsels doing whatever buxom damsels do in gay meadows. At Anfield, opposing teams are intimidated by the sight of a sign proclaiming *This is Anfield*, situated in a position where players cannot avoid viewing it, just prior to running on to the pitch. I don't know if Third Division Shrewsbury Town chose to mimic this by having a sign stating *This is Gay Meadow* to unnerve the opposition by reducing them to fits of laughter. They certainly must have had something up their sleeves to account for the outcome of this match, which kicked-off in pleasant but cold conditions at three o'clock, as intended. Channon, despite having made a transfer request, was selected in a full-strength City team that started in competent fashion, exchanging some neat, short passes and flicks in midfield. But after only nine minutes, defender Keay punted the ball forward and Paul Futcher made a typical and costly misjudgement, performing an admirable impersonation of an elephant on roller skates in the process. Paul Maguire found himself through on goal. Corrigan saved the first effort, but Maguire was able to follow it up to give the home side the lead. A similar approach brought further opportunities for Steve Biggins, who had one shot blocked by Corrigan, and a reasonable request for a penalty denied when Donachie bundled him over. City passed it around nicely and made a couple of chances, but with Futcher having a recurring nightmare, particularly against the lively Maguire, who cost all of £3,000, Joe Corrigan was a busy man.

At half-time, we all expected some improvement. A bewildered Deyna was taken off and Colin Bell, treading gingerly on the slippery surface, was brought on as City made a number of tactical switches. Yet Shrewsbury continued to break through, outpacing City defenders and, in particular, the hapless Futcher. Chapman headed a deserved second goal from a Maguire corner, and it became clear that City were in serious trouble. Channon wasted good opportunities to give the Blues some hope of salvation, but Joe Corrigan was City's best player by some distance, which just about says it all. Shrewsbury had no need to waste time as the finish approached. They wanted more goals. 'Match of the Day' collected their scalp. With most of the other matches falling victim to the weather, City were big news.

City's topsy-turvy form was getting more bizarre by the match. They followed the ignominy of a home defeat by Chelsea and the Gay Meadow *outing*, with a 3-0 win at Tottenham. That should have augured well for the Maine Road clash with the Spawn of Beelzebub. It should have, but it didn't. The pitch was hard and balance difficult, and the City players seemed either unable or disinclined to cope with it. *The Nation's Team*, obviously aided by the devil's trickery, and being, on the whole, smaller and more nimble, coped very nicely. I've tried hard to come up with a reason to attach blame to the referee for the 0-3 fiasco, but apart from a minor suspicion of handball in the build-up to one of the goals, I've struck a blank. City were appalling. Steve Coppell scored twice, including one fortunate volley that might have appeared, to the untrained eye, to have been a good goal. I know better. All goals scored by *The Nation's Team* are either lucky or illegal.

With two goals from Channon and one from Kidd, City emphasised their unpredictability by winning 3-0 at Coventry in the very next match. That was followed by another inconclusive home match against Norwich, in front of the lowest crowd of the season, 30,012. City fell behind early in the match, but a Gary Owen header brought them level. After Peter Barnes had been tripped on the edge of the penalty area, a second Owen goal, from a dubious penalty, put City in the lead. But the Norwich captain and World Cup hero, Martin Peters, earned his team a point with a goal 10 minutes from time. City had not won a Maine Road League match for five months.

This unwelcome run was finally ended when Bolton Wanderers visited Maine Road on 4 March 1979. After spurning a number of opportunities, City eventually took a sixteenth minute lead when Mike Channon scored. Despite creating plenty of other chances, it required another fortunate penalty, when Neil McNab made fleeting contact with Gary Owen, for City to extend their lead. At 2-0, it was surely the signal for the crowd to relax and enjoy as City exhibited their skills. Of course it wasn't. It was the signal for Frank Worthington to score with a magnificent volley and for Bolton to put the City fans through 16 minutes (plus injury time) of agony as they threatened the equaliser. This is a sensation to which City fans have become accustomed, yet it gets no easier with practice. City hung on to win 2-1, end an appalling run of home matches, and offer some encouragement for the visit of Borussia Mönchengladbach in the UEFA Cup quarter-final first leg, four days later.

Borussia, with Danish mega-star Allan Simonsen in their side, had qualified for the

UEFA Cup by finishing second in the Bundesliga, with only goal difference costing them the title. They would have been formidable opposition at the best of times. These, for City, were not the best of times. There had been a long and eventful gap since City's improbable win against AC Milan and nobody was anticipating a repeat. Malcolm Allison, who was already assuming prominence over Tony Book, tried his best to confuse the Germans, known for their meticulous analysis of opponents, by replacing the suspended Owen with 18-year-old Nicky Reid, who had not previously played for the first team. To the credit of both the player and Allison, Reid performed well in midfield alongside Hartford, particularly in the first half, when City put Borussia under considerable pressure. After 25 minutes, Channon gave City the lead when the Borussia defence failed to clear a Hartford cross and, with a bit more composure near goal, a shock might have been possible. However, an impressive demonstration of the art of finishing was provided 20 minutes into the second half by Ewald Lienen, following a rapid breakaway inspired by Simonsen. Hartford and Barnes had clear chances to regain the lead for City, but it was Bruns for Borussia who came closest to scoring with a rasping shot against the post. Borussia's attacks may have lacked quantity, but they had quality. Despite a late Deyna goal for City, Borussia won the second leg 3-1 with considerable comfort, and went on to win the competition, beating Red Star Belgrade in the final.

That match signalled the end of any hope that City might rescue something from a highly disappointing and inconsistent season. The transfer-listed Channon scored in two 1-1 away draws, against Arsenal and Wolves, as City began to cast anxious glances at the diminishing number of teams below them in the League table. A 2-1 defeat at Ipswich, followed by a 4-0 thrashing at West Bromwich Albion, did nothing to improve matters. It was during this spell that a new City signing was introduced amidst much fanfare and numerous media appearances, with the player involved pronouncing to all and sundry his intention of being a star. The man in question, Barry Silkman, was a chirpy, cockney midfield player with a hairstyle ordered from the Kevin Keegan catalogue. He had signed from Plymouth Argyle, costing City a cut-price £65,000, after protracted negotiations and doubts about fitness. By all accounts, the goal he scored on his debut at Ipswich in the 1-2 defeat, a neat chip over Paul Cooper, was rather a good one. Silkman declared it one of his best, so we can only assume that it must have been quite good. In his home debut against Wolves, Silkman was the star turn in a much needed 3-1 win, and provided some relief in an otherwise dull encounter. After Channon had given City the lead midway through the first half, Silkman took to centre stage, dribbling past defenders and firing in shots. Early in the second half, it was Silkman's through-ball that led to Roger Palmer's goal, and although Hibbitt pulled one back immediately for Wolves, Silkman had the last word, heading City's third goal. The fans must have been cheered up because when Mike Channon limped off with an injury before the end, he received healthy applause. This was City's first home game since the transfer of Brian Kidd to Everton for £150,000. Kidd had comfortably been the top scorer in the previous season, with 16 League goals, and had contributed 14 in all competitions since, despite absences through injury. His departure was received with some incredulity around Maine Road. Little did we all know that this was merely the appetiser.

City fans took advantage of an opportunity to chant 'Kiddo' in City's next home game, against Everton. Kidd received very little service from his new colleagues, as a defensive Everton clung on for a goalless draw, with goalkeeper George Wood outstanding, and Roger Palmer unusually wasteful in front of goal. Once more it was Asa Hartford who controlled what was one of City's better displays of recent weeks. Worrying rumours concerning the future of a number of players, including Hartford, were beginning to circulate. It was reassuring to see Hartford performing in such emphatic style. The main rumours suggested Allison's wish to alter the style of play, and his inability to convince some senior players.

City lost 2-0 at Middlesbrough, and were the targets of slow handclapping in a depressing affair at home to Queens Park Rangers. A spectacular effort from Silkman was cancelled out by Busby before half-time and the crowd were not impressed by City's efforts to rectify the situation. Two goals in a six-minute spell near the end of the match rescued the Blues. Gary Owen scored both, the first following up his own disputed penalty, the second a much more emphatic shot. The points made City's First Division survival a certainty, but the natives were getting restless. Malcolm Allison's magical powers were being questioned.

Three days later, Asa Hartford and Peter Barnes were both omitted from the team for an evening match against Middlesbrough following disagreements with the management and questions about attitude. The 28,264 crowd, the first to dip below 30,000 all season, reacted to City's first-half display with a number of inflammatory chants including, 'Book out', 'Asa Hartford', and, rather optimistically, 'We want Tueart'. It was Kaziu Deyna, press-ganged into a forward role, who won the match with a cool finish. Deyna was clearly operating on a different plane from his fellow midfield players. The move forward actually proved quite fruitful. The man was the calmest finisher I have ever seen.

The following day, the club made the astonishing announcement that both Hartford and Barnes had been transfer listed. Ironically, Channon had been taken off the transfer list. I added a special section to my little reports' book to mark the occasion. I was not a happy bunny, making comments such as,

> *'Manchester City are finished as a force in football; Tueart, Doyle, Kidd, Barnes, Hartford, Bill Taylor…who is next? Corrigan, Watson or Owen perhaps; relegation for next year is already in the thoughts and if Hartford and Barnes leave this means that Tony Book has completed his demolision job.'*

In retrospect, there were three errors in this bitter outburst. I probably credited Tony Book falsely, the demolition job had most emphatically not yet been completed, and I spelt the word *demolition* incorrectly.

I didn't really expect that club captain and England regular, Dave Watson, the rock of City's defence, or England Under-21 captain and City boy through and through, Gary Owen, would be under threat. I wasn't totally convinced that Hartford and Barnes would really leave. After all, Asa Hartford had been City's most consistent and influential outfield player for a number of seasons, including the current one. Surely the management would do all in their powers to persuade him to remain at the club. In ad-

56

Bleak & Blue

dition, Peter Barnes, an England regular and only 22 years old, may have been suffering from a loss of confidence, but you don't get rid of talented players with so much of their career ahead of them, do you?

Meanwhile, back at the Academy, City were facing up to four remaining matches, three of them at home. The first, against already relegated Birmingham City, attracted City's lowest home gate of the season, and rarely progressed beyond end-of-term going through the motions. Channon, enjoying being in the good books, was the provider for all three City goals. Paul Power scored the first one, but even a demoralised Birmingham were able to level before the break. City spurned a plethora of scoring opportunities, Channon himself striking bar and post with the same shot, but it wasn't until 13 minutes from the end that Kaziu Deyna restored their lead with a diving header. Four minutes from time, Deyna added a trademark goal, nonchalantly sliding the ball beyond the goalkeeper with effortless precision, having apparently occupied a personal time warp in the penalty area, allowing him longer than seemed reasonable.

For the following home match against Bristol City, Asa Hartford returned to the side, replacing Gary Owen, the victim of influenza. It was easy to see why Hartford had fallen out with the management, and with Malcolm Allison in particular, as City appeared to adopt a direct, long-ball game, missing out the midfield altogether. The method did not lead to the creation of many opportunities, and City were indebted, once more, to the Kaziu Deyna school of clinical and outrageously cool finishing. Latching on to Channon's header, Deyna ambled around goalkeeper Shaw without a care in the world, taking time out for a little rest before passing the ball quite casually between two defenders who happened to be guarding the goal line. Bristol City, with Gerry Gow outdoing Silkman for the worse midfield haircut, and Joe Royle itching to embarrass his former club, could easily have got something from this match, but a neat Deyna dummy set up Asa Hartford for City's second goal late on.

In the penultimate match of the season, City were brushed aside 3-1 by European Cup finalists, Nottingham Forest. Larry Lloyd took pity on the Blues and scored a goal for them. The final act of the season was played out at Maine Road against Aston Villa on Tuesday, 15 May 1979, one of a number of leftover matches caused by the long, cold winter. Asa Hartford was preferred to Gary Owen, now also rumoured to be in dispute with Allison. But once more it was the ex-Polish captain, Kazimierz Deyna, who caught the eye, as he gave City a third-minute lead, effortlessly rounding goalkeeper Jimmy Rimmer, before sliding the ball home. Deyna came close to adding to his goal tally with a volley, but City's approach left Villa with most of the possession. Just after half-time, the visitors exploited this advantage to equalise through Cropley. However, Deyna restored the City lead with a spectacular free-kick, just to prove that there was variety to his goal scoring. Mortimer and Deehan spoilt the Deyna show by both scoring in a four-minute spell. The crowd didn't react too badly to this 2-3 defeat. The exploits of Kazimierz Deyna were providing an entertaining sideshow to end an otherwise uninspiring season, with City finishing in fifteenth place.

The players dispersed, many joining up with national teams. Peter Barnes and Dave Watson featured prominently in England matches, with Joe Corrigan also getting an outing. Barnes was particularly impressive in a 3-0 European Championship win in Bulgaria, scoring the third goal. Watson, the first-choice central defender, scored one of the other goals. Asa Hartford, as always, was a fixture in the Scotland team, and Gary Owen was a senior player in the England Under-21 side. Clearly, City had not performed well in season 1978/79 but there was still strength in the team. Most people, myself included, would have said that the essential players were Corrigan, Watson and Hartford. Gary Owen had almost played himself into that category and Peter Barnes, despite a disappointing season, had the ability to destroy teams, and still had many years left to prove it. With Kaziu Deyna, albeit as an emergency striker, beginning to show his quality, and with a number of promising young players such as Ray Ranson, impressive at right-back, Nicky Reid, Tony Henry and Roger Palmer, in addition to those who might emerge from City's FA Youth Cup finalists team, the future did not look too bad. A bit of tinkering should do the trick. At least, that's what most people thought.

On 16 July 1979, Malcolm Allison officially took sole charge of team affairs at Manchester City, leaving Tony Book with essentially administrative duties. That was the date of the official announcement. Big Mal had already been wielding his axe in a savage and seemingly indiscriminate fashion long before the official date. It was an eventful summer. The back pages revelled in the constant transfer activity in and out of Maine Road. The wisdom of Big Mal's revolution was about to be tested, and I was off to Manchester to experience it all at first hand. These were exciting times.

Season 1979/80: Revolution

Dramatic things were afoot in the summer and autumn of 1979. First and foremost, I was off to university, the first of our family to do so, and therefore relatively clueless as to what it would entail. I had carefully analysed many a university prospectus, studied all the courses on offer, weighed up all the pros and cons, and made my sound academic choices. Three of those choices just happened to be University of Manchester Institute of Science and Technology (UMIST), University of Manchester, and University of Salford, all of which were, by some happy coincidence, located in pretty close proximity to the home of Manchester City Football Club. Wasn't that fortunate?

I managed to scrape together enough grades of sufficient quality to get me into my first choice, UMIST, and I was eagerly anticipating my move to the seething metropolis and city of dreams as the summer progressed.

The other dramatic events were unfolding in and around Maine Road. If you hung around outside the ground for more than five minutes, you were likely to see some player or other leave or arrive. There were more arrivals and departures than at Victoria Station on a wet Sunday morning; I could have said at rush hour, but that would have been an exaggeration. One thing that can be said about Malcolm Allison is that he is not a man to compromise. It was the most action-packed summer in Manchester City history. It was Malcolm Allison's revolution, his massive gamble.

I do him an injustice when I suggest that the Allison axe fell indiscriminately. In fact, there was definite method in his madness. Allison seemed determined to produce a team of players that was emphatically his. Of those players around when Allison arrived, only the inexperienced survived and prospered for any length of time, with the exceptions of Joe Corrigan and Paul Power. Corrigan's career spanned the two Allison periods, and therefore he was a man on whom Allison could rely. The reason for Power's survival is not so clear, although Allison's eventual promotion of the player to captain made even Paul Power very much an Allison man. Power was always a reliable and hard-working player, but he lacked the skill of many of those who left. There were some other experienced players, such as Tommy Booth and Willie Donachie, who also managed to survive the clear-out, but there was a distinct trend to the transfer activity. During Tony Book's spell as manager, changes in personnel had been minor and gradual. From the moment Allison arrived, there was friction and discontent amongst the players. The impression given to an outside observer was that Big Mal's answer to dressing room discontent was to bring together a whole new set of players, untainted by the temptation to contradict the master's teaching. Yet, unlike some fans, I do not condemn Allison and attribute to him sole blame for the entire subsequent decline of the club. There were two sides to Malcolm Allison's City management style. The first, the identifier, promoter and organiser of young talent was much to be admired. However, the second, the transfer market wheeler-dealer, would have trouble in convincing even the most sympathetic admirer. If only somebody had controlled Allison's use of the cheque book. City were on the verge of crippling themselves financially for years to come.

The City match magazine for the opening game of the 1979/80 season catalogues the summer events. It begins on 27 May 1979, when the club expressed an interest in signing midfielder Steve Daley from Wolves for £600,000. By then, a tearful Gary Owen had already been transferred, against his wishes, to West Bromwich Albion for £450,000. On 4 June, the Wrexham winger/striker – I never was very sure – Bobby Shinton signed. His transfer fee was eventually set at £300,000. On 21 June, Dave Watson, the City captain and top of my ratings chart for the previous season, beating even Asa Hartford, signed for Werder Bremen for a laughable £100,000. On 26 June, 20-year-old striker Michael Robinson signed from Preston North End for a staggering £756,000, making him the second most expensive player in the country. A day later, the 1979 City Player of the Year, Asa Hartford, was transferred to Nottingham Forest for £500,000. Unable to get on with Brian Clough, Hartford was soon on his way to Everton. On 10 July, a bid of £880,000 for Steve Daley was turned down. Surely that was the end of that!

On 13 July, Peter Barnes was transferred to West Bromwich Albion for £750,000. On 26 July, the services of Yugoslavian defender Dragoslav Stepanovic were purchased for £140,000 from German Second Division side Wormacia. It was rumoured that Stepanovic had earlier been on offer for only £25,000 but nobody had wanted him. City also revealed their plans to buy Crystal Palace midfield player Steve Mackenzie for £250,000, despite the fact that he had never played a first team game, and had made only a few appearances in the reserves.

The media ran most of these stories as headline news, particularly revelling in the signings of Robinson and Mackenzie. Although Joe Corrigan was named as club captain, Allison added to the general mirth by announcing that Stepanovic, who spoke no English, would be team captain on the field. It was also announced that the 16-year-old Tommy Caton would be the partner for Stepanovic at the centre of the City defence. Meanwhile, Allison was still chasing after Steve Daley, with increasing desperation as the season drew near. An interest in Norwich City striker Kevin Reeves was also being added to the rumour mill.

To say that I was not impressed with all this at the time would be an understatement of considerable proportions. The sale of Barnes and Owen begged the question, what is the point of having a youth system if you sell players off just as they are becoming established and valuable contributors? I was also unconvinced about the intended replacements for Watson and Hartford. I could not deny that Allison had created anticipation and excitement for the approaching season. Nobody knew what would happen. They might not win a single match. On the other hand, maybe Big Mal was a saviour after all. Maybe a miracle was about to happen.

On Saturday, 18 August 1979, 40,681 apprehensive but curious fans made the pilgrimage to Maine Road for the opening match of the season. Allison's revolution had some unexpected effects on us all. With so many fresh faces on show simultaneously, it was hard to make much of an assessment of the new players. Many of those in the City team were around my age, some even younger. This had the curious effect of making the crowd much less inclined to show their discontent. After all, they didn't know what the players were capable of, so they could hardly berate them for not living up to it. Perhaps the biggest alteration of all was in the expectation of the Faithful. Suddenly, any sort of a win would be considered an achievement, whereas in the past only comfortable and entertaining wins would do.

The team for the opening game against Crystal Palace merits close attention. Pre-season injuries to Donachie and Shinton upset Allison's plans a little, and initially Tommy Booth, not Stepanovic, was made captain. Reassuringly, Joe Corrigan was still the goalkeeper, a fact that almost certainly saved City from relegation. The 19-year-old Ray Ranson, a veteran of eight previous first team appearances, was chosen as right-back, with Stepanovic playing at left-back. Alongside Booth at the centre of the City defence was, as promised, Kirby boy Tommy Caton, complete with blond, curly locks and a tall but slight frame which made you worry for his safety when the likes of Cyrille Regis were in the vicinity. Power and Henry, the workers in midfield, were joined by City 'star' Barry Silkman and Steve MacKenzie, aged 17 and playing his debut first team match of any kind, against the club that had sold him to City. Mike Robinson, looking on the old side at 21 years of age, was joined in attack by the Polish maestro Kazimierz Deyna.

The opposition, Terry Venables' newly promoted Crystal Palace, included Gerry Francis. This was the basis of a team dubbed 'the team of the eighties' by some, prematurely as it turned out. In the match itself, the new boys all performed well, especially Tommy Caton, who received much acclaim for a commanding display. The match produced no goals, but the crowd seemed reasonably pleased, serving to emphasise the change in expectations. If anything, Palace had the better chances, but it was not a disaster. For most of us, that was enough. Even the sceptics amongst us, and that was the majority, had a sneaking admiration for the sheer audacity of Allison. We were willing the youngsters to prove us, and more importantly the rest of the world, wrong.

A dose of reality was at hand within days as City crashed 3-0 at Middlesbrough. Channon and Viljoen were recalled ahead of Deyna and Henry for the next game. This was another home match against a newly promoted side – Brighton, captained by Brian Horton. It was a game that City dominated, with first-half goals from Power and Channon giving them the lead at half-time, 2-1. When Ranson was fouled near the edge of the penalty area, City were grateful for the penalty, dispatched by Robinson, to give them a 3-1 lead. The Blues should have put the match beyond doubt, but Brighton emerged as a threat late on. Horton generously missed a penalty, but Peter Ward did score two minutes from the end. The final whistle came as a matter of some relief.

City continued to struggle away from Maine Road. Joe Corrigan was the saviour in a 1-1 League Cup draw at Third Division Sheffield Wednesday, and the only consolation from a 2-1 defeat at Spurs was a first goal for Mackenzie. Back at Maine Road for the League Cup second leg, very little happened until a hyperactive closing 10 minutes. Wednesday took the lead from a retaken penalty. Referee Colin Seel booked Donachie and Corrigan for protesting about the decision to allow a retake. Penalty-taker Brian Hornsby dummied in his approach to taking the penalty, inducing Corrigan to move. Maybe the referee was just anxious to avoid extra time. Mark Smith scored from the second attempt. Remarkably, Tony Henry scored twice in the last two minutes to rescue City, but the honeymoon period was already coming to an end.

On Wednesday, 5 September, Malcolm Allison revealed his pièce de resistance. The 26-year-old England B international Steve Daley was to sign from Wolves for the staggering and record-breaking sum of £1,450,227. There were collective gulps of amazement. The rumours had been that Wolves were insistent on Paul Power being part of the transaction. Nobody expected a price tag so high for a player who was not even a full international. Wolves spent the money on striker Andy Gray. I will leave posterity to judge who got the best deal. I doubt that a vote will be required to settle the issue.

City also signed striker Stuart Lee from Stockport County, for a more modest £80,000, and both players made their debuts against Southampton at Maine Road, in front of a crowd now expecting some return on the investments made. For that kind of money, Daley had to be a more than adequate replacement for Asa Hartford at the heart of the City midfield. Of course, nobody could expect instant success. And instant success was not what happened. With most of the City team still relative strangers to one another, a twenty-fourth-minute goal from Holmes gave Southampton a lead to which they clung grimly. With Tommy Booth injured, Allison had preferred to play Willie Donachie at centre half rather than recall Paul Futcher, and Dragoslav Stepanovic was captain for the first time. Southampton's new £250,000 signing, Mike Channon, had not rejoined his old club in time to play. Channon's departure surprised nobody.

Meanwhile, Colin Bell had finally given up his fight to continue playing. Bell soldiered on, and featured in a number of matches in season 1978/79, but was unable to recover anything like his previous mobility. It was a sad end to a fine City career. A crowd of 24,000 turned up to see a combined Manchester team beat a combined Merseyside team 2-1 in Bell's testimonial match. Manchester also won the old-favourite's penalty competition. I am pleased to report that Francis Lee scored from both of his penalties, but Bobby Charlton missed one of his. Stuart Lee and Tommy Caton scored the real goals. Trying to enthuse for a team including enemy representatives was not easy. They should stick to Manchester derby testimonials.

Back in the real world, Gary Owen was amongst the scorers as City received a severe 4-0 hammering at the Hawthorns against West Bromich Albion. Peter Barnes had a less happy time, pulling a hamstring and limping out of the match, but plenty of points were proven. After that result, the Blues found themselves propping up the First Division League table. The novelty of all the new faces was beginning to wear thin.

The prospect of my imminent arrival as a resident of Manchester seemed to kick-start City into action, just in the nick of time. It all began with a home match against Coventry City on 22 September. Paul Futcher partnered Caton at the centre of the City defence, allowing Donachie to return to his proper left-back position. Stepanovic joined MacKenzie and Power in midfield as support for the new maestro, Steve Daley, whose arrival prompted the relegation of Barry Silkman to substitute. With Kaziu Deyna injured, Dave Bennett was the latest local youngster to make the starting line-up, preferred in attack to Stuart Lee, whose first team career was already on the wane. Coventry City, who included Tommy Hutchison and Bobby McDonald in their team, had won all their home matches and lost all their away matches. It was easy to see why the latter was the case as the City youngsters swept into a 3-0 half-time lead, with two goals from Robinson and a third emphatically driven into the net by Mackenzie. There were no further goals, but this convincing win was enough to lift City clear of the relegation zone. A few days later, Robinson was on target again as City came from behind to draw 1-1 with Sunderland in the League Cup at Maine Road. City lost the replay 1-0 at Roker Park, but between the two encounters, the Blues registered their first win away from home, with Kaziu Deyna scoring the winner in a 2-1 victory at Leeds. Admittedly, the sending off of Leeds defender Paul Hart was a considerable help, but who cares?

It was around this time that I made the move to Chandos Hall, just minutes away from the centre of Manchester. Life changed immediately. The revolution on the pitch at Maine Road was matched by a lifestyle revolution for yours truly. There were clubs and discos that played the best music, rather than the monolithic seventies disco typical of small-town establishments. There was a constant stream of bands, the best, most obscure bands, the bands ignored by Radio One. This was the era of New Wave, when British modern popular music was undergoing an explosion of post-punk invention and Manchester was the best place to experience it. Joy Division, Magazine, A Certain Ratio and The Fall were amongst the local talent, and the best of the rest came to play at the myriad of venues. I was in cultural heaven and the euphoria spilt over into the football, at least for a while.

City followed a 0-0 draw at Arsenal with a midweek1-0 home win against Middlesbrough, an occasion momentous as my first trip to Maine Road since my move to the city of Manchester. I could have walked to the match, or caught a number thirty-something bus down Oxford Road. Instead, I exploited my dad's attendance to cadge a lift and exchange parcels of dirty washing (outgoing) and food parcels (incoming). The latter included my mother's popular steak and apple pies (that's two different types of pie), a definite hit with the denizens of G Floor. Bobby Shinton made little impression on his home debut, and it was Kaziu Deyna who, once more, rescued City with a late, headed goal.

Three days later, City were back at Maine Road to face the European Champions, Nottingham Forest. It was a match of high quality, with Forest looking threatening from their famous lightning counter-attacks. City looked sharp and creative themselves, particularly Kaziu Deyna, who gave a virtuoso performance prompting marks of 10 out of 10 from two national newspapers and even from me. With the second half a couple of minutes old, Robinson crossed and Deyna controlled the ball, dummied, turned and blasted his shot past Shilton for the winning goal. From then onwards, Deyna looked a class apart from the rest, exploiting the space left by Forest's requirement to be more positive. A combination of Shilton's excellence in goal, and wasteful finishing by Deyna's colleagues, meant that Forest were always in the match, and Joe Corrigan was called into the action, with one particularly good save to thwart Birtles. The result not only lifted City into eighth position, but provided proof that they could compete with the best teams. The victory was achieved without the injured Daley, and the latest victims of the Allison axe, Shinton and Stepanovic.

Following a 2-2 draw at Norwich, courtesy of two Dave Bennett goals, City crashed down to earth with an emphatic home defeat by Liverpool, an event in danger of becoming something of an annual ritual. A combination of cock-ups by Mackenzie and Futcher led to an early Johnson goal. The muscular Robinson did thunder a shot against the Liverpool post, but Dalglish was left unmarked to add to the Liverpool lead after 31 minutes. Dalglish and Kennedy added further second-half goals to make a severe dent in City's goal difference. A similar scoreline would be a suitable metaphor for my experience of the following night, when unfancied Joy Division blew main band The Buzzcocks off the stage at the Apollo Theatre. At least, I thought they did, and that's all that matters.

A 2-0 defeat at Crystal Palace followed, but that was a mere trifle compared to the big match on 10 November 1979. City were at home to *The Nation's Team*, who were at the top of the League table. All City fans knew that the full range of possibilities was on offer, from absolute humiliation to untold ecstasy. In the event, it was much, much closer to the latter as City, prospering as underdogs, out-chased, out-harried and out-played their rivals in front of over 50,000 spectators. Malcolm Allison had increased pre-match anxiety amongst the Faithful by again making a number of changes. Futcher and Mackenzie were omitted in favour of Tommy Booth and Tony Henry.

The pitch was heavy and the action was hectic as both sides embraced the derby ethic of 'no surrender' to an admirable degree. Opportunities were limited. A Coppell shot struck the post at one end and a Power shot unerringly found the obstacle of Gary Bailey's legs at the other, when scoring looked the easier option. Ten minutes after half-time, the game changed dramatically. Tony Henry (at 22, one of the older youngsters) rewarded Allison's team selection by putting an untidy scramble out of its misery with a sweet shot. Nicholl might have equalised, when Henry sought to undo his good work by under-hitting a back-pass, but the tide was turning in City's favour. *The Nation's Team* survived a couple of goalmouth scrambles, but after neat work by Bennett, a precise finish from Robinson sealed the victory with 17 minutes remaining. This really was a derby victory to savour.

The following week, I was stood on the exposed terracing at Burnden Park on a cold, wet day to witness a rare occurrence, a Steve Daley goal. For some reason the seating behind the opposite goal was no longer available for away fans, and we had switched ends. The match never came close to matching the excitement of the previous week, but Daley's right-foot shot, from the edge of the penalty area after half an hour, was all that was required for maximum points. Corrigan had to make good saves from Gowling, Greaves and, near the end, Whatmore, who should have scored. Jim McDonough in the Bolton goal also had his moments. Happily, there was no Frank Worthington in the Bolton line-up on this occasion. The Daley goal was perceived as a milestone. His influence to date had not been out of proportion to his massive price tag. A popular theory was that his first goal would inspire improvement. Yes, well, we can all dream.

With City sitting comfortably in mid-table, I could slurp coffee from my Manchester City mug with pride. But the course of City fandom seldom runs smoothly for long, and a 1-0 defeat at Bristol City followed, with Paul Power receiving marching orders, rather surprisingly for 'foul and abusive language'. And he's such an educated boy. Power was suspended for the visit of Wolves. Lucky him.

Andy Gray brushed off Caton as if he were a minor irritant to open the scoring, and prospects would have deteriorated further had it not been for feckless finishing. When Roger Palmer, deputising for the injured Robinson, slotted City level five minutes before the break, it looked as though the Blues might be enjoying a fortunate day. Within a minute, Hibbitt dispelled such unmerited optimism by restoring the Wolves lead and they went on to win 3-2. A late goal from Deyna made the final score closer than City deserved. The City captain, Steve Daley, did not have a happy reunion with his Wolves ex-team-mates. Britain's most expensive player, Andy Gray, bought with the Daley money, had a much more enjoyable day out. City performed even worse in their next away match, losing 4-0 at Ipswich.

Away from the football, I had already taken in some splendid performances from the likes of Stiff Little Fingers, Gang of Four, The Jam, XTC and Talking Heads. Manchester was thoroughly to my liking. Many of the city centre drinking establishments had been honoured with my presence, and it was unusual to be doing nothing in the evening. Quite how the student grant stretched so far, I don't know. It was an enjoyable time. And let's face it, City were doing better than might have been anticipated.

The end of my first term was already approaching as the Blues disposed of a reassuringly awful Derby County side at Maine Road. Allison, constantly tampering with the line-up, had brought Shinton back into the reckoning at the expense of Deyna. Palmer also found himself once more out of favour, and Steve Mackenzie was still being rested. A crisp shot by Mike Robinson gave City an early lead. The Blues then wasted several chances, with Power, Henry and the struggling Shinton amongst the chief culprits. Eventually, Tony Henry increased the City lead, and David Webb kindly shot into his own net, to leave City celebrating a welcome 3-0 win.

Three days before Christmas, I found myself at Goodison Park, watching Asa Hartford and Brian Kidd in an Everton team playing City on a rock-hard pitch. I was about to see City win on Merseyside for the first time. That's the first time for me, not the first time ever for City.

Steve Daley's measured shot gave the Blues the lead after 12 minutes. Fifteen minutes later, Tony Henry volleyed the second, following a demonstration of Dave Bennett's tricky dribbling skills. As was so often the case, however, Joe Corrigan was City's star performer. Everton did manage to beat him once, Brian Kidd scoring after 64 minutes. Strangely, the Everton threat subsided after they had scored, and City might even have added to their own goal tally. A 2-1 win was good enough for me.

The Maine Road Boxing Day clash with Stoke City took a long time to show signs of life. Mike Doyle was back on familiar ground, in a Stoke City side that also included the exciting, young prospect, Adrian Heath. However, it was Doyle's fellow defender, Dodd, who gave Stoke an early lead, which was cancelled out by Paul Power. With the Christmas puddings sitting heavily on the stomach, it was only in the last 20 minutes that City began to threaten with conviction. There was a scramble, with Henry coming close, a bad Robinson miss, a breathtaking save by Peter Fox to deny Bennett, and another to stop a close-range Daley volley. To cap it all, there was a long-range Caton shot against the inside of the post, but it finished 1-1.

City ended 1979 with a 4-1 defeat at Brighton. It was Stuart Lee's turn to be brought in from the cold, and he scored City's goal. With half of the season gone, the jury was still out on the Allison revolution. The anniversary of his arrival was upon us, and it would have been difficult to say, with any conviction, what Allison's best team was. His constant chopping and changing suggested that he didn't know himself. Still, the FA Cup was about to begin, presenting the opportunity for some glamour, and relief from the increasing tribulations of an unpredictable League season. With a third-round tie against Fourth Division opposition, City could already look forward to the possibility of a morale-building Cup run.

On Saturday, 5 January 1980, I stood on a muddy hill, amongst a crowd of 12,599 packed into the Shay, to welcome the new decade with a match between Halifax Town, a mid-table Fourth Division side, and big-spending Manchester City. The two o'clock kick-off time meant that the winners would be the first team through to the FA Cup fourth round. The pitch was a muddy quagmire. The match-ball sponsors were

Briggs Priestly Ltd of Halifax, '*Your local trophy suppliers and engravers*'. They were obviously touting for business from Manchester City.

The City team should be recorded for posterity. With Donachie and Booth injured, Corrigan's reshuffled defence consisted of Ranson, Power, Reid and Caton. Allison might not have been tempted to turn to Futcher, with memories of Gay Meadow still vivid. In fact, Futcher, along with Stepanovic, was also unavailable because of injury. Viljoen, Daley and Henry were in the City midfield, with additional back-up from Bennett. Mike Robinson was the main striker, with Bobby Shinton in support.

City had an early fright when Paul Hendrie shot narrowly wide from close-range, but recovered to take control, or so it seemed. Robinson and Shinton both squandered opportunities, but surely a goal was imminent. Just before half-time, the Blues had another fright: Corrigan saving from David Evans. Early in the second half, Hendrie again came close. One or two of us on the muddy hill were beginning to get a little twitchy. One or two of us were transmitting this anxiety to the players in no uncertain terms. Bobby Shinton, still to make any kind of mark in a City shirt, shot straight at goalkeeper John Kilner from a few yards out, to waste the best chance of the match. Hands covered faces on the muddy hill. Then, with 15 minutes remaining, Halifax advanced towards the muddy hill with their best attack of the match. A chap called John Smith put Hendrie in the clear, and it was one fright too many for City. This time Hendrie scored. City's desperate efforts to rescue the situation failed, and they were the first First Division side to exit the competition. Oh dear.

Halifax Town ended the season seventh from bottom of the Fourth Division. They subsequently slipped out of the League altogether. The day they beat Manchester City will no doubt remain one of their proudest memories. However, since they have managed to get back into the Nationwide League, I cannot rule out the possibility of a repeat meeting, quite possibly in a League match.

Almost 12 months on from defeat at Shrewsbury, City had once again delighted their detractors with a leading role in the major giant-killing. Allison, with all his experimentation, seemed no nearer to finding a team capable of competing consistently with the better teams. Barry Silkman had disappeared, on loan to Israeli club Macabbi, and his replacement as star midfield dynamo, Steve Daley, had yet to convince anyone, including, I suspect, himself. Daley did have some things in common with Asa Hartford: one head, two legs and the letter 'a' in his surname, for example, but few considered him an exact or even remotely adequate replacement. I returned to university somewhat more sheepish about my allegiances and casting anxious glances at the League table.

Mike Robinson had some relief from the personal, mounting criticism, including some from Allison, when he struck the penalty to give City the lead in their next match, at home to Spurs. But the Blues were outplayed by a visiting midfield including Ardiles, Villa and Hoddle. Joe Corrigan performed heroics, but couldn't prevent Hoddle's equaliser 20 minutes from the end. Soon after the goal, the teams left the pitch for several minutes whilst frantic attempts were made to find a replacement for an injured linesman. When they returned, both sides seemed to settle for the draw.

A 4-1 thrashing at Southampton followed, with Mike Channon and Dave Watson, whose move to Bremen had been a brief one, amongst the scorers. Further revenge was on the menu for the following match at Maine Road, as Peter Barnes and Gary Owen returned for the first time since their transfers to West Bromwich Albion. Albion had been unable to match the success of their previous season and were actually below City in the table. At least, that was the situation before the match. Regis gave Albion a first-half lead, which was extended by Barnes, who scored the easiest of goals to silence the minority of fans who taunted him with chants of 'City reject'. Although Stuart Lee pulled a goal back to raise City hopes, the reject had the last word, scoring his second goal near the end. Albion, still managed by Ron Atkinson, had a midfield player, Bryan Robson, who was celebrating his first international call-up. I didn't reckon much of him.

The management attempted to control mounting criticism by announcing the likely return of Dennis Tueart, two years after his departure had sparked off City's decline. Meanwhile, I was busily engaged in the alternative distractions Manchester had to offer, cramming The Mekons, The Ramones, The Clash, Iggy Pop and Joy Division into the space of a couple of weeks. The last two were actually on the same night. After Iggy had finished performing, three of us legged it from the Apollo Theatre back to Piccadilly and then, for what seemed like miles, down Oldham Road to reach an obscure venue called the New Osborne Club. I dread to think what the Old Osborne Club was like. Within minutes of arriving, sweaty and knackered, we had squirmed our way to the front, just in time for Joy Division to take the stage. It was the most mesmeric performance I have ever seen. Mind you, I do have a taste for bleak music. This was proof of how uplifting despondency can be. If only it worked in football.

Back at the Academy, City were facing up to Leeds United, having earned a 0-0 draw at Coventry, once again thanks mainly to the acrobatics of Joe Corrigan. Dennis Tueart, now aged 30, had returned to City but was unavailable due to injury. With Robinson also injured, Palmer and Bennett formed an all-black attack for the first time. However, despite the return of Mackenzie, the forwards received poor service from midfield. In a stupefying first half, Arthur Graham scored following a corner, and the gloom descended. Brighter moments, particularly from Bennett, led to a second-half improvement. On the hour, Allison lost patience with Steve Daley, who still seemed incapable of exerting any real influence. Nicky Reid was brought on to replace him, and within minutes City equalised, Bennett setting up Paul Power. Bennett might have capped a good display with the winning goal, but City had to settle for another draw.

Away from Maine Road, Joe Corrigan was consistently City's man of the match as the Blues were overwhelmed by their opponents. Even in heavy defeats, such as the 4-0 crushing at Nottingham Forest in City's next game, Corrigan performed heroics and saved his colleagues from further embarrassment. There was some improvement at Villa Park, where Robinson, Power and Donachie were all on the scoresheet. Unfortunately, Donachie's effort was an own goal that supplied Villa with a late equaliser in a 2-2 draw. When John Bond brought his Norwich team to Maine Road on 1 March

1980, City had only a five-point cushion saving them from the clutches of the relegation zone. Dennis Tueart made his comeback and, 10 minutes into the second half, the inexplicably long-forgotten Deyna made an appearance as substitute. Tueart was full of ideas, but most of his colleagues were unable to interpret them. There were a few occasions when City might have scored, which is more than could be said of Norwich, but the match finished goalless. Norwich City striker, Kevin Reeves, was largely a spectator. Another Joe Corrigan rearguard action was able to frustrate Liverpool at Anfield, until Tommy Caton put one past him. The Blues lost 2-0.

With City's position looking increasingly precarious, Allison forked out £1 million to sign Kevin Reeves in time for a home debut in City's next match, against Arsenal. Things could hardly have turned out worse. Tueart limped off early in the match to be replaced by Robinson. Dave Bennett struck a shot against the post, but with injuries to Power and Deyna unsettling City, Joe Corrigan was again a busy man in the City goal. In the second half, the Reeves debut degenerated further as his clumsy challenge led to the penalty dispatched by Liam Brady. Further goals from Stapleton and Brady finished off a dispirited City. On the same day, Andy Gray scored the winner as Wolves won the League Cup at Wembley.

Miraculously, the five-point cushion separating City from the dreaded relegation zone was still intact, thanks to the inability of Derby, Bristol City and Bolton to take advantage of City's demise. The one-hundredth league derby at Old Trafford was a dismal affair. In the build-up, neither side had managed a goal in their previous three matches. I was seated in the luxury of K Stand to witness Maine Road's derby hero, Tony Henry, break that run a minute into the second half. A shot from Mickey Thomas looped up off Henry's boot and over Joe Corrigan's head. Joe Jordan came close to adding to the lead but City rallied to show some late defiance. Reeves was suspiciously flattened by Ashley Grimes, but little short of murder will get you a penalty at Old Trafford. Roger Palmer squandered City's best chance to level the scores. The run of matches without a win was extended to 13 games.

City's first win of 1980 looked a distinct possibility in the next home match, when bottom-of-the-table Bolton Wanderers were the visitors. The goal drought was ended by City's prodigal son, Dennis Tueart, who volleyed the Blues ahead after nine minutes, and added a second goal two minutes into the second half. Neil Whatmore's diving header, five minutes later, scotched any hopes of a relaxing afternoon. As City wasted their opportunities, Bolton took advantage of the increasing defensive jitters. In injury time, Peter Reid, Bolton's captain, attempted to flick the ball past Ray Ranson, but the defender's arm got in the way. To the utter despair of the City fans and players, a Mr Alan Seville, dressed in matching black shirt, shorts and socks, pointed to the penalty spot. Reid, who took the penalty himself, was not in merciful mood.

Everton, level on points with City, were the visitors in a crucial midweek match. Asa Hartford and Brian Kidd both featured in the Everton starting line-up, as did a youthful Gary Megson. With Kaziu Deyna recovered from injury and currently back in favour, City made a reasonable start. Kevin Reeves almost broke his scoring duck, but it was left to Deyna to provide the finish after 30 minutes, demonstrating typical serenity in the penalty area. Just before half-time, a more spectacular Deyna effort was ruled out because Dennis Tueart was loitering in an offside position. A second-half revival by Everton left the Blues ruing that decision. With the City offside-trap in pitifully poor mode, Hartford shot against the post, and Joe Corrigan made excellent saves to prevent Eastoe and King from scoring. There were 18 minutes remaining when midfield maestro Steve Daley played a crucial through-ball to set up the second goal of the match. The under-hit back-pass left Joe Corrigan stranded, and Andy King nipped in to score. We were already in April and City had yet to win a game in 1980.

Being in masochistic mood, I made the Easter trip to City's next match against another of the Division's strugglers. Stoke City, only two points better off than the Boys in Blue, looked even more jittery than City. With Kaziu Deyna in inspirational form, Peter Fox was the more active goalkeeper, denying Reeves, Daley and Tueart early on. City old boy Mike Doyle headed off the line to prevent a first Reeves goal for the Blues, but there could be no excuse just before the break, when a defensive error left Reeves clear. Again Fox saved, but he shouldn't have been allowed to. Just after half-time, Garth Crooks forced Corrigan into some acrobatics, but this was one of Joe's quieter days. However, City were unable to capitalise on their better chances and had to settle for another 0-0 draw. There was a particularly pertinent comment from the Stoke manager, Alan Durban, after the match. He was quoted as saying, 'Deyna was superb. The problem is that he's playing football at Radio Four level while the rest of the team are on Luxembourg.' Depending on your opinion of the relative merits of Radio Four and Radio Luxembourg (circa 1980) that just about sums up Deyna's time at City. There is more than a passing resemblance to the City career of Gio Kinkladze.

On Easter Monday, fifth-placed Aston Villa were the visitors as City tried once more to break their 1980 duck, in front of a disappointing crowd of 32,584. Just before half-time, David Geddis gave Villa the lead. An improved City fought hard in the second half, and Paul Power brought them level. Geddis threatened further damage on the counter-attack for Villa, but Kaziu Deyna created enough opportunities for the Blues to finally win a match. They seemed incapable of doing so.

Meanwhile, Willie Donachie and Stuart Lee became the latest departures, both heading for Portland Timbers in the USA. With Nicky Reid impressing in the first team at left-back, Donachie's departure, after a long and valuable career at City, was no great surprise. Stuart Lee, a victim of one of Malcolm Allison's whims, only ever enjoyed limited opportunities.

On 12 April, several important milestones were achieved at Molineux. As City got worse, my compulsion to attend every match seemed to increase. I take this as a sign of true City fandom. At considerable expense, my father and I sat in the impressive Molin Stand at Molineux somewhat perplexed by three things: the oversized match magazine, the price of coffee, and the fact that the football pitch was so far away that another stand could fit comfortably in the intervening space. I never was able to fathom at what stage Wolves were in their new ground plans. I do know that these undoubtedly ambitious plans were soon to be accompanied by relegation, as often seems to be the case. At the time of this vital encounter, Wolves were comfortably placed in the top half of the table, with the League Cup sitting proudly in their trophy cabinet. They did not appear to be missing Steve Daley much.

With old stager Emlyn Hughes in defence and Wayne 'Sniffer' Clarke partnering Andy Gray in attack, these were relatively exciting times at Molineux. The players were such small figures that it was like watching a game of Subbuteo. I kept expecting an oversized knee to accidentally crush one of the defenders or dislodge the goalposts. The early action was in the City penalty area as Wolves forced a number of corners, but Daley missed the first real chance, to the delight of the home fans. Luckily, the Wolves defence was in generous mood. After 15 minutes, Geoff Palmer struck a firm back-pass beyond goalkeeper Bradshaw, and Kevin Reeves was left with an open goal to score for City, at last.

Steve Daley must have been desperate to get a goal in a match against his old club. After 21 minutes he achieved his ambition. Clearly feeling that the Wolves generosity should be returned, Daley stuck out his head to glance a Parkin free-kick beyond Corrigan's reach, and the home team were level. Early in the second half, the Blues were living dangerously. A deflection off Nicky Reid sent a shot looping over Corrigan, and a repeat of the derby match own goal was only just averted when the ball cleared the crossbar by inches. In addition, Joe Corrigan made two fine saves, and Andy Gray had a goal disallowed, as Wolves threatened to take control. However, after 52 minutes City broke and Willie Carr handled the ball whilst still on the floor, after slipping during his attempts to stop Tueart. Tueart scored from the penalty, and the City players began to play with hitherto rarely displayed levels of confidence. As Wolves pushed players forward, City counter-attacked with real menace, and should have increased the winning margin. But let's face it, any win was most welcome after a wait of four and a half months.

City completed their escape from relegation trouble with victory over Bristol City, the side in twenty-first place whose games in hand represented the only serious threat to survival. With Kevin Reeves injured, Mike Robinson was recalled to the side, and he looked determined to prove a point. Robinson was still a very young player, and his pace and strength were enough to give him a reasonably successful career in the top division. The problem at Maine Road was that, with so many young players around, much was expected of those who cost plenty of money. Robinson went on to play for Brighton and Liverpool, before heading for a spell in Spain that resulted in him becoming a presenter for Spanish television, where he does a most convincing imitation of a native. He looks as if he could be reading the news on Channel 9 in the 45Fast Show'. The match against Bristol City turned out to be his last for the Blues.

Robinson had already threatened with a typically strong run before striking a right-foot volley into the net after 12 minutes. Bristol City had plenty of possession, and with the City defence still looking nervous, Joe Royle was close to scoring another goal against his old club. The Blues were reduced to counter-attacking, but the consolation was that they seemed to be rather good at it. Nicky Reid made a break from the halfway line, and although his shot was saved, Kaziu Deyna was on hand to score from the rebound. The visitors continued to enjoy the best of the possession, but a Tueart header sent City into half-time with a 3-0 lead. Strangely, City played better in the second half, but the only goal was a consolation effort for the doomed Bristol City team.

City's final away game was at the Baseball Ground. The Faithful turned out in force and were in good voice. My second trip to Derby County was no more successful than my first, the infamous 4-0 defeat featuring the mystery of the missing penalty spot. The first half was not dissimilar to the Bristol City game, except that City were on the receiving end. David Swindlehurst, who had signed for Derby on the pitch amidst chants of 'What a waste of money' from City fans, took only six minutes to score his first goal for the club. After 14 minutes, a Gerry Daly cross was deflected into his own net by Nicky Reid. Just before half-time, Futcher clashed with Alan Biley, prompting the referee to award a penalty kick, which was taken and scored by the hideously coiffured Biley himself. In between all this, City were actually playing quite well. Despite totally dominating the second half, a late Dennis Tueart goal was their only reward. Just to complete a slightly surreal afternoon, the results filtering through from other matches confirmed that City were safe and Derby were relegated. Both sets of fans seemed to take the news as a cause for joyous celebration. In truth, Derby were all but relegated before the match began. Admirably enough, their fans were determined to make the most of it.

I turned down the chance of a ticket for the Rugby League Challenge Cup Final, between Hull and Hull KR, in favour of City's last match of the season and a Magazine gig at the PSV Club. Ipswich Town came to Maine Road occupying third place in the League table and with an unbeaten run of 25 games behind them. With Tueart injured, Allison decided to give a debut to the diminutive 19-year-old, Paul Sugrue, a recent signing from non-league Nuneaton. All the goals came in the opening 12 minutes. Kevin Reeves scored from close-range, but a Hunter header made the lead a short-lived one. Tony Henry restored the City lead with another header and, for once, Chorley boy Paul Mariner, who was in the team along with the Dutchmen Mühren and Thijssen, failed to score. City won 2-1 and Hull KR beat Hull.

In the evening, I stupidly went to the Magazine gig on an empty stomach and very nearly blacked out in the stifling and oxygen-rare atmosphere. I'm pretty sure that the band was on top form, but I spent most of the time outside in the fresh Hulme air.

The season had to be considered a relative success. Survival was the main thing, and that had been achieved with City finishing seventeenth, three places above the relegation zone. Joe Corrigan was my clear choice as player of the season, with Kaziu Deyna the closest of the outfield players. Youngsters Reid, Bennett, Ranson and Caton had all impressed, as had Mackenzie, although he struggled to last the pace in his first full season. Far more worrying was the form of Allison's most expensive signings. Reeves had shown promising signs, but Steve Daley had not come close to justifying his fee. The average home attendance of 34,842 was down a couple of thousand on the previous season, but most fans were willing to give Allison the benefit of the doubt now that City had survived the first phase of revolution. Having made so many changes simultaneously, and having provided so many young players with a year's experience, we could only hope that Allison's judgement would be proved correct in the second season. Mackenzie, Caton, Reid and Ranson were soon to be lining up together in the

England Under-21 team, and with the City Youth team, including rising stars like Steve Kinsey and Clive Wilson, again making the Youth Cup Final, the future could be faced with optimism.

There was one minor proviso, one note of caution: City had to get off to a reasonable start to season 1980/81. Allison knew that. We all knew that.

Season 1980/81: Dreaming of a Blue Wembley

The summer of 1980 marked my return to Chorley. Manchester had surpassed all expectations and it was strange to discover that my own changes were not mirrored in Chorley, which had stubbornly remained the same. Yet I soon settled back into a routine, following all major sporting events on the television. A Phil Neal blunder against Italy received most of the credit for England's exit from the European Championship, which was won by West Germany in the summer of 1980. The only City player in the squad, Joe Corrigan, didn't get a game, but Dave Watson was still first choice as a central defender. Tommy Caton and Steve Mackenzie did feature strongly in England's European Youth Cup win, which was obviously far more important.

There were conflicting signs from City's pre-season build-up. In Portugal, victory against Sporting Lisbon and a draw against Porto suggested great things, but back at Maine Road, a 5-1 defeat to Legia Warsaw was somewhat less impressive. Pre-season friendlies are, of course, notoriously unreliable. Malcolm Allison had been actively offloading players over the summer. Mike Robinson was sold to Brighton for £400,000, a devaluation of £356,000 in one season. Paul Futcher followed Kenny Clements to Oldham for £150,000, and Barry Silkman, after returning from his loan period at Macabbi Tel Aviv, was sold to Brentford. Allison was candid about his reasons for these deals, citing temperament in the case of Futcher and an inability to get on with other players in the case of Silkman. (I wonder why that was. He seemed like such a shy, unassuming boy.) Allison claimed that Robinson needed to improve, and the time needed for such improvement simply wasn't available. The latter part proved rather too accurate for the manager's liking.

With a respectable start to the season so important, it was unfortunate that the first game was away, against Southampton. The Dell was not a happy hunting ground for City. Mike Channon must have taken considerable pleasure from scoring both goals in a 2-0 win for the home side. Still, there was no reason to panic. A nice home encounter with recently promoted Sunderland offered the opportunity to acquire some points four days later.

The Sunderland match could hardly have been more catastrophic for City and, in particular, Allison. Only an alien landing and mass abduction of the entire first team could have had a more detrimental effect on morale. Even then, at least the fans would have been better entertained. More defensive tampering by the City boss proved to be a mistake. Ranson was omitted, causing a switch to right-back for Reid, and Stepanovic was surprisingly recalled to partner Booth, leaving Caton to move to an unaccustomed left-back position. Paul Sugrue was preferred to Deyna as a striking partner for Kevin Reeves, with Tueart providing additional attacking options. Daley, Henry and

Power constituted the remainder of a fragile-looking midfield. After 12 minutes, with City's offside-trap in its customary shambles, Stan Cummins scored the simplest of goals. Although Dennis Tueart should have equalised for City, John Hawley was equally wasteful, heading over for Sunderland. The visitors were cheered on by their delighted fans, whilst the Faithful became increasingly disgruntled.

In the second half, the Blues degenerated alarmingly. Hawley scored from a penalty in the opening minute, and seven minutes later the unthinkable happened: Joe Corrigan made a mistake. We had all become so accustomed to the man's infallibility, that a dropped cross seemed an impossibility. It happened, and Hawley scored again. I'm pleased to say that this was merely an isolated aberration. Normal Corrigan service was quickly resumed. City wasted several chances to at least get on the scoresheet, but in the last minute, Hawley completed his hat-trick and City's misery.

The final score of 0-4 was an enormous psychological blow. We were all relying on some points from this game. The forthcoming fixtures were already taking on a much more daunting appearance. Ranson and Mackenzie were drafted in for the visit of Aston Villa, but it didn't take long for bleakness to descend once more as Peter Withe cracked a volley in off the City post fewer than 10 minutes into the game. City responded well, but their first goal of the season was elusive, and Villa remained a threat on the counter-attack. With 15 minutes left, Gordan Cowans executed a destructive pass and Withe scored Villa's second. Roger Palmer blasted over the bar for City, and it was beginning to look as though they were incapable of scoring. Remarkably, the Blues were rescued by two goals in the final 10 minutes. The referee spotted a handball, and who am I to argue? Dennis Tueart proved that City were capable of scoring, albeit from a penalty kick. This lifted the spirits of a flagging City team and, with only two minutes remaining, a deflected Ranson shot brought the scores level. The Blues got a rapturous reception at the end of the match, but they were still left propping up the First Division table.

The League Cup second-round first leg match at Stoke offered some relief from an already troubled League campaign. At least, it should have done. I was still trying to work out which Stoke player was Loek Ursem when Lee Chapman's first-minute header put City behind. Joe Corrigan then suffered an injury diving at the feet of Jeff Cook, who was also hurt and hobbled off soon afterwards. In the meantime, City were playing their way into the match, but when Kevin Reeves did manage to get a shot past Peter Fox, the post returned it. When Chapman was left clear but missed, it became apparent that Corrigan's injury was causing him to struggle, and he didn't emerge for the second half. Tommy Booth ended up in goal, with Nicky Reid moving to central defence and Paul Power to left-back. These were positions that both players were destined to occupy with considerable success for longer periods. Everything pointed to an early Cup exit, but the crisis provoked a marked improvement from City, and Booth spent most of his adventure as a spectator. With Steve Daley looking uncharacteristically dominant in midfield, and the travelling support in good voice, Tueart and Caton both headed against the crossbar before a Tony Henry shot was deflected in for a deserved equaliser. It was quite a week for Joe Corrigan. He had been rewarded with a two-week suspension by the club after criticising Allison in the media. This was later rescinded, but because of the injury, it was about to happen anyway.

The Stoke match programme, the same price as City's at 30 pence, contained very little about Stoke City. It was filled with the kind of articles normally found as page fillers for magazines adorned with pictures of young ladies in states of undress – so I'm told. I wouldn't know, obviously. There were articles on bikes and cars (entitled Hatchback Haters) and, my favourite, a short history of snooker. There was even a page devoted to music gossip, containing the tenuous connection that Meatloaf was a soccer fan. The proof of this was that he had just bought into a New York Softball team. Curious. There were some references to football. There were articles on Clive Allen, Kevin Keegan, Alan Mullery and Diego Maradona, none of whom featured in the Stoke City line-up. Maybe they were all injured.

City's 2-2 draw at Middlesbrough, where they were the victims of a last-minute equaliser, lifted the Blues one place off the bottom, above Stoke City. There was still no Maradona in the Stoke line-up for the League Cup second leg match, but Maradona's spitting image, Lee Chapman, could have given the visitors an early lead had long-forgotten reserve goalkeeper Keith Macrae not made the save. Dave Bennett, making the most of his recall, created the opportunity from which Henry scored with a delicate chip, and then added the second goal himself, to give City a 2-0 half-time lead. A Bennett headed goal, from a Reeves cross early in the second half, offered City fans the almost forgotten opportunity to relax, as the Boys in Blue sought to add more goals. With Tueart, who would normally take penalties, sitting on the substitutes' bench, a late handball could have given Bennett a hat-trick opportunity. For some reason Tommy Booth took it upon himself to blast the penalty kick over the bar.

There is no doubt that City were beginning to play like a team capable of competing in the First Division, but they lacked points and, as Bruce Forsyth would be at pains to emphasise, points mean prizes. With Dave Bennett catching the eye in attack, and Steve Mackenzie looking increasingly the part in midfield, the City performance against Arsenal at Maine Road on 6 September 1980 had everything except the all-important result. Pat Jennings was in formidable form, but Reeves, in particular, seemed keen to give the Arsenal goalkeeper ample opportunities to show off, rather than shoot beyond him. With City unable to make the breakthrough, there was always the danger that Arsenal would. Macrae came to the rescue on a couple of occasions in the first half. The bubble-headed Alan Sunderland, who had wasted those opportunities, made amends by setting up the chance for the extra-large, ginger-haired Scotsman, Willie Young, to score early in the second half. The Blues demonstrated admirable spirit, but the Arsenal goal seemed to be charmed. It took a Tueart penalty, awarded for handball, to rescue a point, but City really needed both.

In the next match the Blues won much admiration as they gave Forest a scare at the City Ground. Unfortunately, admiration was all they won. Despite leading 2-1 at half-time, with Bennett and Henry replying to an early Forest lead, City lost 3-2. Many nice things were said and written about them, but City were still languishing in the bottom three. Six Kaziu Deyna goals in two matches had propelled the reserve team to the top of the Central League table, but somehow that wasn't much consolation. Deyna was recalled for the injured Reeves in the next match, at home to Stoke, again. Surely this was the signal for an emphatic first League win.

Of course it wasn't. Chapman struck a warning shot against the bar early on, as City gave a strangely lethargic display, undoing much of the recent good work. As the break approached, goals in quick succession, from the Dutchman Ursem and Lee Chapman, stunned the crowd. Tueart replied for City just before half-time, but that failed to spark off a second-half revival. The recently recovered Corrigan was kept busy, and although City had chances to salvage a draw, they failed to take them.

The Blues edged through a League Cup tie at Luton with goals from Bennett and Henry. A Yugoslav chap called Raddy Antic scored for Luton. Thus City went into the Old Trafford derby match giving off conflicting signals. With Mackenzie and Tueart missing through injury, Paul Power was drafted back into midfield. Things began badly for City. Bennett was cynically scythed down by Albiston when clear through on goal. Back in 1980 the punishment was only a booking. City received the bigger punishment because the injured Bennett had to be replaced by Sugrue. A handball by Jimmy Nicholl could have given the Blues a penalty chance. That will have to suffice for the obligatory dubious refereeing decision.

Soon afterwards, Steve Coppell scored, following up his first shot, which had been blocked by Corrigan. City were not playing badly, and just before half-time, right in front of the assembled Faithful, Kevin Reeves headed in from a Daley corner, and I spent a difficult few minutes trying to stay on my feet. The Blues played less convincingly after half-time, continually giving the ball away and largely reduced to hanging on. As usual, Corrigan came to the rescue until, as City attempted their consistently poor offside-trap, Albiston shot into the net through a crowd of players. The referee immediately disallowed the goal, and I thought for one joyous moment that City were going to benefit from a referee's generosity in a derby match. The moment passed. The referee consulted his linesman and the goal was awarded. No doubt the linesman pointed out that Ray Ranson had been behind the referee, playing everyone onside. He should also have pointed out that this was the reason why linesmen usually give the offside decisions. Maybe the referee was just toying with our fragile emotions, building up hope only to dash it once more. I suppose that City did not merit an equaliser, but who cares? Roger Palmer had already wasted one chance to bring the Blues level when, with two minutes to go, he made the most of his second opportunity, and I went home happy.

The next home match was the one most to be dreaded. A crowd of 41,022 turned up to see Liverpool complete their annual demolition of City, who looked pitifully out of their depth. The only surprise was that the match was already 38 minutes old before a classic Dalglish finish put Liverpool ahead. For once, Fairclough missed his chances and supersub was himself substituted. Souness added a second goal, and a cracking Sammy Lee shot completed the scoring. Actually, 0-3 at home to Liverpool was not bad for City in that era.

The Blues sank to second from bottom, but at least the Liverpool game was out of the way. Although term had restarted, I was still struggling to find somewhere to live in Manchester. Temporarily, I was commuting in every day and flat-searching whenever possible. It was a strange time. I was not disheartened by City's results. I truly believed that they were close to getting it right. What worried me more was that Peter Swales would press the panic button again, and ruin what might be achieved. I may have got the wrong impression but the fans, particularly at away matches, seemed to be giving the Allison and Book regime their full support.

On 8 October 1980, I traversed the Pennines for a midweek match against Leeds United, who were only one point better off than City. We were all unaware that this was to be the last battle of the Allison revolution. It was a fairly uneventful match. Tommy Booth nearly gave City an early lead, but that dismal offside-trap failed again, allowing good opportunities for Sabella and Curtis. Corrigan was once more called upon to compensate for defensive inadequacies. City had their chances. Reeves wasted the best, after a terrible Leeds back-pass had put him in the clear. Early in the second half Leeds, under their new manager Allan 'the real Sniffer' Clarke, stepped up the pressure. The Blues succumbed, and Harris gave Leeds the lead. Kaziu Deyna came on and might have equalised, but he didn't. The fans were in good spirits throughout, amusing themselves when necessary, but supporting the team to the full, and demonstrating strong backing for Allison to the end. City might easily have drawn the match and possibly even won, but they didn't.

The following day Peter Swales reached once more for the panic button. I, for one, regretted the decision. Allison was certainly a risk-taker. He could have played safe and made the changes more gradually, but he seemed to revel in being outrageous. The transfer activity caused his downfall and cost City financially. Having said that, players like Ranson, Reid, Caton, Henry, Mackenzie and Bennett had all benefited from substantial experience at a tender age, and were already valuable assets, particularly Mackenzie and Caton. The team had demonstrated considerable ability, but the consistency was lacking. I wrote a touching little epitaph at the time expressing the opinion that, given more time, Allison would have succeeded in producing a good team. In the light of subsequent events, I'm willing to stand by that. Considering that nobody is in a position to prove me right or wrong, this is not an opinion requiring much bravery.

The most important immediate consequence of the Allison dismissal was a further deterioration in form. Defensive frailties were cruelly exposed in a 3-1 defeat at West Bromwich Albion, under the temporary charge of the great survivor, Tony Book. Gary Owen and Peter Barnes, in the absence of the incentive of proving Allison wrong, were not amongst the goalscorers. John Bond, the Norwich City manager of seven years, was named as Allison's successor in time for him to view a dismal and spiritless performance at home to Birmingham City. For various reasons too dull to recount, this was my first match experienced from the Main Stand. I must admit that the view from amongst the posh folk was an excellent one. Unfortunately, the match, despite a respectable but subdued 30,040 crowd, was one of the worse that I have ever seen. City had a couple of efforts on goal, Steve Daley taking the prize for the worst miss. Birmingham City didn't make a single chance in the match until the last minute, when a clumsy challenge by Power gave Archie Gemmill the opportunity to complete a perfect Maine Road day by scoring the penalty kick winner. City slumped to the bottom of the League.

Allison had been unable or unwilling to supplement his young talent with a few choice experienced players. Bond's first major contribution to City, apart from scrapping the appalling offside-trap, was to make three indisputably excellent signings for modest sums of money. As a veteran of survival on low budgets, Bond made a habit of snapping up players in their twilight years. Now was the right time to do this for City. It was a pragmatic short-term measure in the interests of survival. Bond's problem was that he didn't know when to stop.

The three new player were all Scots. Tommy Hutchison (£47,000), complete with straggly hair and Mexican-bandit moustache, was bought to provide some consistent, quality service from the flanks. Gerry Gow (£175,000) may have looked like an overweight Bobby Ball, but he provided much needed muscle in midfield, where City were far too lightweight. Bobby McDonald (£270,000), quite a contrast from the other two with his cropped hair, was a particularly astute signing. He contributed solidity as a genuine left-back, with the additional bonus of a propensity for goalscoring, particularly from set pieces.

The immediate effect was staggering. Even before the three were eligible to play, City registered their first League win of the season, at the thirteenth attempt. With youngster Gary Buckley filling in for the injured Bennett, City set about Spurs right from the start. Kevin Reeves, whose inability to finish had cost Allison dearly, found his goalscoring touch after renewing his career under Bond. A fourth-minute header by Reeves put City ahead. The speculation was already mounting about the future of Steve Daley. Perhaps aware that there may not be many more chances, Daley took the opportunity to score his first Maine Road goal just before half-time. After the break, Spurs found some form, but a third City goal by Mackenzie finished them off. Hoddle's late goal was a mere consolation.

Hutchison and McDonald made their debut appearances at Brighton in a 2-1 win, but it was Dennis Tueart who scored both goals. Mike Robinson scored for Brighton near the finish, but City held on to lift themselves off bottom place. Despite the new signings being cup-tied and Daley suspended, the newly confident City dismissed Notts County in the League Cup fourth-round with ease. Dave Bennett latched on to a poor back-pass to score the first goal, but it was Dennis Tueart who gave a vintage performance, scoring the other four goals in a 5-1 win.

McDonald, Hutchison and Gow were all given home debuts against Bond's old club, Norwich, in the next League match, with Daley dropped to substitute. However, an early injury to Hutchison allowed Daley to get back into the action quicker than anticipated. The first half was less than inspiring, but a tremendous shot by City captain Paul Power gave the Blues a sixtieth-minute lead and triggered the team into action. The lack of additional goals left us all with a nervous closing 10 minutes, but City held on for the all-important points. For the first time, the Blues edged out of the relegation zone.

Tueart scored again in a 1-1 draw at Leicester, but City suffered a setback at Sunderland, losing 2-0 despite a promising display. Of course, we all knew about promising displays, and we all preferred points.

Meanwhile Bond was ringing the changes to the back-room staff. Steve Fleet, an extremely successful youth team coach, and Dave Ewing, in charge of the League-topping reserve side, were both dismissed. On the playing side, Bond had made it clear that Deyna and Stepanovic would not be featuring in his plans, and Steve Daley had indicated his own desire to leave. Roger Palmer was on the verge of a move to Oldham Athletic, where he was to provoke the excellent chant of 'Oooh! Roger Palmer' for many years. On the incoming side, Bond had already indicated his interest in Phil Boyer, a player whose Gloria Hunniford-style bouffant hair bore a remarkable resemblance to Bond's own.

Southampton, featuring Keegan, Channon and Phil Boyer, were the next visitors to Maine Road, in the first of two successive home matches. In a disappointing first half, Channon won a fortunate penalty for Southampton, which Holmes obligingly missed. It was the slice of luck City needed. After the break, the increasingly influential Hutchison delivered a precise free-kick, Reeves laid the ball back, and Gow struck his first City goal. Southampton's morale began to crumble, and a perfect Hutchison cross enabled Bennett to head the second goal. A Reeves glancing header completed a satisfying win.

The 3-0 scoreline was repeated when Coventry City visited Maine Road the following week. With a sweet volley, Reeves scored the kind of goal we had all been waiting for, and City could have scored twice more before a Power diving header increased their lead, all within the first seven minutes. With Mackenzie revelling in the back-up from Gow, and Bennett free to display his skills with confidence, City could have scored an embarrassing quantity of goals. As the Blues penetrated the Coventry defence with awesome regularity, a third goal was inevitable. Dave Bennett was the deserving scorer in the second half. City were completely transformed from the often pretty, seldom dominant and never ruthless side of earlier days. Survival was beginning to look like a formality. Support for John Bond was, naturally, total and unconditional, although the first hints of what was to come were detectable. In addition to Boyer, Bond was already expressing his intention to purchase his own son, Kevin.

City continued their meteoric rise with a 3-2 win at Crystal Palace, who were soon to give new employment to Malcolm Allison. A first-minute Reeves goal established control on the match. Gow scored both the other City goals.

By now I had moved into a shared flat in a large, old house in Whalley Range, only 20 minutes walk from Maine Road itself. The location was not particularly salubrious. Had I been female, I would have received the regular attention of kerb-crawlers. Had I been black, my bag would have been inspected frequently by the local constabulary. The drinking establishments offered the full range of attractions from the Whalley Hotel and Caught on the Hop, if you desired a walk on the wild side, to the Great Western for Irish nationalist sing-songs at the weekend. If you could bear the longer walk, The Seymour or The Throstle's Nest were for the slightly more up-market clientele. We visited them all, as well as quaffing huge quantities of Newcastle Brown Ale in the flat. At that time, it was only acceptable to drink Newcy Brown in the safety of your own home. To do so publicly risked association with heavy-metal biker types or hippies.

After emptying sufficient bottles, we embarked on the compulsory student experimentation with home-brew. The flat was too cold for it to be successful in terms of taste, but what it lacked in aesthetic value was more than compensated by potency. And so the long, cold winter nights were passed getting paralytic on home-brew, and listening to the likes of Young Marble Giants, Joy Division, The Fall, Public Image Ltd, Talking Heads and Magazine, and ultimately, dreaming of a Blue Wembley.

Almost unnoticed, City had progressed to the quarter-final of the League Cup. The match took place on Wednesday, 3 December 1980, against West Bromwich Albion, complete with Owen, Barnes and Bryan Robson. Gow, Hutchison and McDonald were cup-tied, which meant that the team competing for City was essentially Allison's. The exception was Bond's new signing, the 31-one-year-old Gloria Hunniford, sorry Phil Boyer (£225,000). I can say, with some honesty, that up until this point in my role as supporter, I had not actively disliked any City players. For some reason, Boyer was my first exception to this. I'm afraid to admit that there have been many since, as managerial decisions have become increasingly bizarre and inexplicable.

Albion were lying third in the League table, and when Tommy Booth sliced the ball into his own net for a third-minute own goal, the portents did not look favourable. However, the spirit in the City ranks was much improved. Within eight minutes of going behind, a delicate flick by Reeves gave Bennett the opportunity to demonstrate neat finishing skills, and City were level. Henry struck a post as the Blues piled forward. On the hour, Tony Henry headed Bennett's cross into the net for the winning goal. Albion put the City defence under plenty of pressure towards the end, but sheer determination saw the Blues through to the semi-final.

Three days later, City faced their biggest test to date under John Bond, as high-flying and much admired Ipswich Town visited Maine Road. Bobby Robson's side was at its peak, with a midfield, including Dutchmen Thijssen and Mühren, oozing class and dominating matches. Arnold Mühren gave Ipswich an early lead and their passing ability made if difficult for City to get into the game. Again City's new fighting spirit came to the fore in an impressive second-half recovery, completed by a Gow equaliser, 15 minutes from the end.

The remarkable events at Maine Road received national attention. Bond was announced as winner of Manager of the Month for November, with Steve Mackenzie receiving the award for Young Player of the Month. There was a minor setback when City suffered a 2-1 defeat at Tottenham despite, by all accounts, dominating the match. Boyer scored his first goal for the Blues.

Back at Maine Road, City gained revenge over a disappointing and negative Leeds United side. Tommy Booth suffered a significant injury after 30 minutes of the match. His partnership alongside Nicky Reid had been one of the features of City's improvement. Indeed, Reid had been something of a revelation as a central defender. Booth's injury was the opportunity for Tommy Caton to return to the first team. The Reid-Caton combination subsequently became the first choice. For most of the match, the Leeds tactic of holding on for a goalless draw looked likely to succeed, but in the last minute, the revitalised Reeves, with his back to goal, exhibited good chest control and a neat turn before firing a stunning shot beyond John Lukic.

City's improved fortunes were there for all to see at Goodison Park on Boxing Day, as Everton's unbeaten home record succumbed to the increasing momentum of the City bandwagon. Reid and Caton stood firm at the centre of City's defence as Everton, prompted by Hartford and Steve McMahon in midfield, dominated the first half without making a breakthrough. This was largely thanks to the exploits of Joe Corrigan, yet again. With the second half only a couple of minutes old, Gerry Gow took advantage of a defensive mix-up to give City a surprise lead. I watched with increasing anxiety from the Bullen's Stand as Everton applied the pressure, but Corrigan made all the saves required of him, and two minutes from the end, Paul Power finished a neat counter-attack to leave City with a flattering 2-0 victory. The match programme featured a magnificent photograph of Gary Megson looking as if he has a particularly hairy ginger cat sitting on his head. Young Gary revealed that his favourite newspaper was the *Daily Star* and that his post-match routine often involved a night on the town with Steve McMahon.

The following day, City were back at Maine Road to complete a perfect Christmas with victory over Wolves. The ambitions of most visiting teams seemed restricted to survival against the new, improved City, and for an hour these tactics were successful for Wolves. Eventually, however, Bobby McDonald scored his first City goal, from a corner. This opened the way for three goals in the last 10 minutes to complete an emphatic win. Two Tommy Hutchison goals either side of a Kevin Reeves header emphasised the reinstatement of Maine Road as a ground to be feared by opposing teams, in a way not seen since the heady days of 1976.

On 3 January 1981, Malcolm Allison returned to Maine Road, as manager of bottom-of-the-League Crystal Palace, for an FA Cup third-round tie. In foul weather, City failed to make a first-half breakthrough, despite winning a succession of corners. After 53 minutes, a push on Boyer was penalised, and Kevin Reeves opened the scoring with a penalty kick. Paul Power added a second goal, although it's doubtful that the deflection off his thigh was actually intended. After wasting a couple of excellent chances, Boyer finally scored from close-range to make it 3-0, and Reeves added another near the end to complete a 4-0 win. Allison received a good reception from the City fans, but it must have been galling for him to see a City team, inspired by his players, in such confident form.

City had to rely on a dubious Mackenzie goal for a draw at Coventry, as the Blues reached the dizzy heights of twelfth in the League. That stroke of luck was more than wiped out in the next Maine Road game, the League Cup semi-final first leg against the Champions, Liverpool. There was a long-overdue return to the side for Bennett. Tueart and Henry were also drafted in to replace the cup-tied players as City took the field in front of 48,045, facing their biggest match for some considerable time. After three minutes of passion and aggression, City pierced the Liverpool defences with Kevin Reeves leaping to head a goal for City. It was a joyous moment, encapsulating the tenacity and spirit of a resurrected City. Regrettably, it was also a fleeting moment. Reeves was harshly penalised. The goal was disallowed.

In a frantic first half, all of City's other chances fell to Boyer, who was unable to convert any. Fairclough threatened on the break for Liverpool, but City could be pleased with their performance. The second half was a tight affair. With nine minutes remaining, as City players stupidly argued over the award of a free-kick, McDermott's pass to Ray Kennedy proved to be the decisive act. Kennedy scored to give Liverpool an unmerited, first-leg lead. The one big consolation for everyone connected with City was that the contrast between this display and the one earlier in the season at home to Liverpool could hardly have been more stark.

With City occupying a comfortable mid-table position, the League matches were taking on a more mundane appearance. When Middlesbrough visited Maine Road, the atmosphere of anticlimax was heightened by an early Hodgson goal, reversing recent trends. This prompted City into action, and headed goals from McDonald and Reeves secured a half-time lead. The referee decided to draw attention to himself by sending both David Hodgson and Nicky Reid off for no more than a touch of push-and-shove. Two goals from Middlesbrough captain Tony McAndrew in the last 20 minutes could have spelt trouble for City had McAndrew's final effort not been directed past his own goalkeeper. City won 3-2.

With the sideshow of the League out of the way temporarily, City could concentrate on the important business of the FA Cup fourth round, and an unprecedented second home draw in succession. One of those strange quirks of fate had matched City with John Bond's old club, Norwich, complete with skipper Kevin Bond and a forward line of Joe Royle and Justin Fashanu. Dave Bennett was also in the starting line-up. Unfortunately, that was the white Dave Bennett who played for Norwich. Bond still preferred Boyer to City's Dave Bennett, who was substitute. Ranson and Reid were also missing for City, but this didn't prevent one of the most impressive displays of goalscoring I have ever seen from a Manchester City team. The Blues actually had a fairly shaky start, and Corrigan was called upon to make an early save from Fashanu. After 17 minutes, Kevin Bond clattered Boyer, who had to be replaced by our own Dave Bennett.

I cannot deny feeling a measure of cruel satisfaction at the turn of events, and it seemed to lift the whole City team. In fact, the injury was quite a serious one and Boyer was ruled out for the rest of the season. Within a minute of the Boyer incident, City scored their first goal. Gow played the ball in to Reeves, on the edge of the penalty area. Reeves controlled the ball adeptly, swivelled and volleyed an unstoppable shot into the roof of the net. That £1 million price tag was looking more justifiable by the match. After 25 minutes, McDonald rolled a free-kick into the path of Gow, who curled a delightful shot around the Norwich defensive wall for City's second. Just before half-time, a long-range effort from Mackenzie struck the crossbar and Power followed up to demonstrate similar precision by whacking a shot against the post.

After 74 minutes, Mackenzie's luck improved when a similar effort flew in with the help of a deflection. Two splendid counter-attacks in the space of three minutes led to additional goals. Dave Bennett latched on to a Reeves flick after 79 minutes to run clear from the halfway line, finishing with aplomb. Three minutes later, Hutchison, Bennett and Gow combined to set Power a chase, which he won to lob the Norwich goalkeeper and score City's fifth, and probably best, goal. The final action of the game, a McDonald headed goal from a Hutchison corner, was routine in comparison. John Bond's reaction to City completing their 6-0 demolition job was to attempt to rush on to the pitch from his position in the Main Stand, with the intention of consoling his son. Bond Senior made himself a figure of ridicule by tripping over the advertising boards in his attempt to reach the hallowed turf. It wasn't the last time that Mr Bond's actions would invite ridicule.

A narrow defeat away to Aston Villa, then second in the table, was followed by a disappointing home encounter with Nottingham Forest. Paul Power gave City an early lead, but it was all a bit of a struggle after that. A Trevor Francis goal in the second half completed the scoring in a 1-1 stalemate. It was not an auspicious build-up for the League Cup semi-final second leg at Anfield, but there, from my seat in the Kemlyn Road Stand, I was able to witness the finest performance by Malcolm Allison's Manchester City team. With the exception of Gary Buckley, this was Allison's team, but it was a team with new belief in their own abilities.

City did not win the match, but they gave Liverpool a real scare, attacking right from the start in an attempt to recover the one-goal deficit. After 22 minutes, the task looked impossible, when Dalglish scored from a corner to give Liverpool a 2-0 aggregate lead. Yet City responded with more attacks. Five minutes into the second half, the Blues at last received some reward and Reeves scored after Clemence could only parry a Mackenzie shot. In a hectic, open cup-tie, the home defence had many anxious moments. Of course, Liverpool might have added to their own score, but they were reduced to making occasional breaks. With 20 minutes remaining, Buckley crossed and Dave Bennett directed a header against the underside of the crossbar. Bennett had another chance later, but dragged his shot agonisingly wide. Liverpool went through to the final, but seldom have I taken so much pride in a City display. Ranson, Caton, Reid, Buckley, Bennett and Henry, products of the City youth system, played their parts to the full. I thought that it was the nearest City were ever likely to come to winning at Anfield. I was actually wrong about that.

Living in Whalley Range was a great advantage when it came to queuing for tickets, a pastime I indulged in with increasing regularity. The FA Cup draw had given the Blues a tricky-looking away tie against Peterborough United of the Fourth Division. With memories of Halifax and Shrewsbury still painfully raw, this was not a match to be taken lightly. I managed to get myself a ticket for the game and a place on a Finglands coach to London Road, where I was not surprised to see the 'Match of the Day' cameras waiting in eager anticipation of another City fiasco. The afternoon was not an entirely comfortable one. Packed into the old stand behind the goal, with a difficult view and a lot of swaying amongst those attempting to see, the attractions of seating to the vertically challenged were becoming clear. Peterborough, or 'the Posh', gave City some anxious moments in the first half. The match was not a classic, but we were all grateful when Tommy Booth, preferred to Caton, cracked home his first City goal for two years just before half-time, after Peterborough had failed to clear a Tommy Huchison cross. The second half was uneventful. Before the start and throughout the match, the City fans were having a kind-of chant workshop, creating a new song. To the tune of 'Ant Music' by the popular combo Adam and the Ants, the song went:

> *Come down to Maine Road*
> *And do yourselves a favour*
> *Your football has lost its taste*
> *So try another flavour*
> *Man City, oy, oy, oy, oy!*

It didn't catch on. I never heard it again. Presumably it failed to meet the high standards of the Kippax Song Validation Committee. I can't imagine why.

On the following Saturday, the one-hundred-and-second Manchester derby match took place, with most people's minds on other things. Despite a crowd in excess of 50,000, the match was a low-key, understated affair. Yes, that does mean that it was crap. However, the overall entertainment value was rendered irrelevant by the result, a second consecutive derby home win by City. The goal came after 59 minutes. With a neat pass, Bennett found Power on the left wing, and the City captain's low cross was swept in by Steve Mackenzie. Smugness abounded amongst the Maine Road Faithful.

Hardly anyone noticed when, towards the end of February, Steve Daley followed Kaziu Deyna to the USA. Daley was transferred to Seattle Sounders for £300,000 with little fanfare. City lost over £1 million on the deal. That's pretty impressive when you consider that Daley was an active first team player for barely more than one season.

After the Blues had lost 2-0 at Arsenal in a midweek fixture, the postponement of an away match at Stoke City left us all with time to ponder and dream. At 12.30 on the Monday following the FA Cup fifth-round win at Peterborough, I was nervously clutching a little transistor radio to my ear in the UMIST Students' Union building, praying for a home draw in the quarter-final. Not being religious, I had nobody to blame for the numbered balls dictating instead that the Blues would have to travel to Everton. The FA Cup quarter-final represented the greatest progress made by City in that competition during my time as a genuine follower. I now had very fixed ideas about my ambitions as a Manchester City supporter. They were relatively modest ones. Firstly, I wished to see a Blue victory at *The Swamp* against the *Spawn of Satan*. Surely, that would not be too much to ask.

My bigger ambition was to see City win the FA Cup, having personally attended every match on the way. It had to be the FA Cup. Even though I was too young to fully appreciate it at the time, I had already seen a League Cup win and, in any case, the League Cup has always been the poor relation of the cup competitions. Having had my taste of bad times, I was certainly ready to appreciate the significance of an FA Cup victory in 1981, and the thought was seldom far from my mind. I recall preparing myself mentally for the discomfort of frog's leg-twitching experiments in the Stopford Building of the Medical School, all in the name of Physiology, by daydreaming on the outcome of City's Cup matches. I could vividly imagine the commentary on famous City victories, and I was willing them to happen. I was also beginning to get nervous because *I had* been to every match, and an away draw against Everton meant that I would also be able to attend the quarter-final without difficulty. By now, we were regular seat season ticket holders, and that meant priority for tickets, as long as you were prepared to queue. I was able to walk to the ground, hangover permitting, therefore queuing for tickets was not a problem.

On Saturday, 7 March 1981, sitting in Row P, Seat 49 of the Park End Stand at Goodison Park, I was about to find out whether the dream could continue. The two sides were safely tucked away in mid-table, which meant that the FA Cup was crucial to both, if real interest for the remainder of the season was to be maintained. The importance was not lost on either the players or the crowd of 52,791. In the Everton midfield were Asa Hartford and Steve McMahon, and in attack was promising youngster, Imre Varadi. Sadly, there was no place for either Gary Megson or the ginger cat.

Jim McDonough made a fine reflex save to stop a close-range Reeves header early on, as City settled well. Steve Mackenzie went one better, beating McDonough with a long-range shot, only for the ball to come back off the crossbar. It was a real blow to morale therefore when, two minutes before half-time, Everton took the lead. Varadi crossed, Hartford flicked the ball on, and Trevor Ross was left clear at the far post to side-foot a comfortable goal. Within a minute, Gerry Gow had equalised, lifting the ball over the advancing McDonough. The game was well and truly on.

Everton started well in the second half and they had a vital stroke of fortune. The referee's decision to award a penalty for Caton holding Varadi seemed a trifle severe. With four minutes of the second half gone, Everton restored their lead, courtesy of a Trevor Ross penalty kick. I was beginning to fear the worst as City searched in vain for an equaliser, leaving themselves vulnerable in defence. Imre Varadi, latching on to an atrocious McDonald back-pass, somehow contrived to miss, despite seemingly taking the ball around the despairing Corrigan. Following an Everton corner, the ball struck a City post and Reid cleared off the line during the ensuing scramble. These were trying moments. Another Everton goal would have certainly finished the dream off. With only six minutes left, Kevin Reeves hit a delicate chip over the Everton defence for Paul Power to chase. As McDonough came off his line, Power chipped the ball over the goalkeeper and towards the net in front of us. In the ball went, and I began to believe that the dream was, indeed, going to come true.

A hard-fought match, with tempers never fully contained, and tackles only just the right side of GBH, degenerated further in the later stages. A young Kevin Ratcliffe, playing at left-back, was sent off, and the mood of the home fans turned ugly. Tueart nearly scored a winner in the dying seconds. If he had, I may not have lived to tell the story. I escaped the cauldron of Goodison Park in a state of euphoria. City had survived a stern test and, this being 1981, when the FA Cup was the FA Cup, the replay was all but upon us. Four days after the first encounter, 52,532 people were somehow crammed into Maine Road for the most pulsating night I can ever recall in that stadium. The crowd were seldom much below a state of hysteria throughout the evening. The traffic nearly caused my dad to be late, and there were all kinds of problems parking. I only just got into the stadium as the teams emerged into an atmosphere of tangible delirium. City had to win. There was no doubt about it. And I fully expected that they would.

There had been three days of continuous rain, which did little to help the quality of the football. McDonough and Corrigan both made important saves in a tense and inconclusive first half. In the opening 20 minutes of the second half, the conditions seemed to be gaining the upper hand and both sides struggled to play any constructive football. Then, in the space of two minutes, City won the match. Bobby McDonald scored with a low, skidding shot through a crowded penalty area, and followed it up by placing a firm header from Tommy Hutchison's cross beyond McDonough. It was 2-0 and everyone was stunned by the suddenness of it all. In fact, the City left-back could have scored a hat-trick. McDonald's header against the crossbar, after 80 minutes, looked the easiest of his opportunities. With five minutes remaining, Paul Power scored City's third, following a smart break from defence. In the final minute, a shot from Hartford was saved by Corrigan and Eastoe followed up to score. Nobody cared. City had won 3-1 and advanced to the semi-final.

I had already been through the trauma of listening anxiously to the semi-final draw on my transistor radio, praying that City should avoid Ipswich Town, clearly the best team left in the competition. They didn't.

The League matches were now no more than a distraction from the real action. Back at Maine Road, just three days after the quarter-final euphoria, City had a relatively comfortable time against fourth-placed West Bromwich Albion. An early Bobby McDonald header, from a corner flicked on by Caton, was followed by a Tueart goal just before half-time. Alex Williams, deputising for the injured Corrigan, had the odd save to make but, despite plenty of possession, the visitors were largely ineffective. Bryan Robson headed a late consolation goal, but this wasn't a happy return for the ex-City boys Barnes and, in particular, Owen, who had to be replaced because of injury.

The victory over West Bromwich Albion proved to be the only one achieved in a disappointing build-up to the FA Cup semi-final. There were some mitigating circumstances, such as a few injuries and some players rested, to partly account for two poor away performances in the space of three days. In the rearranged fixture against Stoke City, the Blues led when Bobby McDonald scored, again from a near-post corner flicked on by Reeves, but just before half-time Mike Doyle headed the equaliser. After the break, Stoke seemed keener to win. O'Callaghan scored a deserved winner for the home side, leaving me with my first taste of defeat at the Victoria Ground.

A similar experience was in store at St Andrew's. It was the first time that I had been to Birmingham City's ground. I can remember my father driving past the ground on an overpass, with no visible means of exiting to get at the stadium. When we did eventually find a way through the maze, it was to witness an embarrassing opening half an hour, with Birmingham scoring through Frank Worthington and Tony Evans, and only Joe Corrigan's heroics preventing more damage. City improved, but never seriously threatened a recovery.

Gerry Gow had been absent for both of those matches, and although the overall standard of hairstyle was improved as a consequence, the steel in City's midfield was conspicuous by its absence. There was another passionless display in the next home match, against lowly Brighton. After a goalless first half, Brighton took the lead, and it required a Mackenzie volley to rescue a point. Three days later, another struggling side, Leicester City, were the visitors to Maine Road, in front of a disappointing 26,141 crowd. A much-improved City established a 2-0 lead, with both goals scored by Kevin Reeves. But three goals in the space of eight minutes, midway through the second half, turned the match on its head – if football matches can have heads. The third Leicester goal, by Jim Melrose, prompted City into some face-saving activity, and Tony Henry rescued a point with a late equaliser. A 2-0 defeat at Norwich followed. This was a truly cataclysmic event. Until 1997, in all my time as an active Blue, this was the only occasion on which Norwich were able to win a match against City.

Thus, the preparation for City's biggest match for many years was not impressive. My own preparation had included the tortuous experience of purchasing tickets for the match whilst suffering a top-notch, grade-one hangover. With head still swimming and stomach raising serious objections, I somehow crawled out of bed at the intended hour and made it out of the house. Slightly revived by the fresh Mancunian air, I walked to Maine Road feeling increasingly confident that the task could be achieved without vomiting or passing out. The fact that my walk took me past Hydes-Anvil Brewery, with its attendant smell, caused a temporary dip in confidence. But having survived that obstacle and the slightly less pungent aroma from the Harp Brewery further down the road, I arrived to join the ever-growing queue. The cold air allowed me to reach my initial objective of the ticket office windows without untoward incident, but when I strolled into a local newsagent's shop to book tickets for the Finglands coach to Villa Park, it all became too much. I had to crouch down on the floor whilst the tickets were being filled out in order to avoid falling into a state of unconsciousness. I would have much preferred to remain standing, but given the compromised state of my nervous system, my legs felt unable to cope. Eventually, I made it back with all the necessary tickets and stumbled into bed.

On the day of the match, having controlled my alcohol intake the previous evening, the most sobering thought was the quality of the opposition. Bobby Robson's team was the best in England that season. They were brimming with talent and were in serious contention for three trophies: The League Championship, FA Cup and UEFA Cup. Paul Cooper was in goal; the defence of Mills, Butcher, Osman and Beattie could hardly have been stronger; Mühren, Thijssen and Wark were a dominating midfield trio; and Gates supplemented Brazil and Mariner in attack. There was no apparent weakness. In fact, Ipswich went on to lose the League title to Aston Villa, and ended up winning only the UEFA Cup. And it all began to go wrong for them on Saturday, 11 April 1981, at Villa Park.

The City fans were packed into the Witton End to greet their red and black-striped heroes. Actually, only the shirts were striped; not the heroes themselves. The chanting was all relatively predictable. There was the 'We're on the march with John Bond's army, we're all going to Wem-ber-ley' chant and the 'I'm dreaming of a blue Wembley, just like the one's I used to know' chant. There were also a limited number of variations on chants for each of the City players, but I don't know how many fans really believed that City would win the match. Crucially, Gow had been restored to supplement the City midfield of Mackenzie, Hutchison and Power, and Dave Bennett was preferred to Tueart as a partner for Reeves in attack. Booth was Reid's central-defensive partner, with Ranson and McDonald the full-backs.

For the first 30 minutes of the match, City were transfixed as Ipswich passed the ball with confidence, hoarding possession and creating opportunities with alarming ease. Eric Gates volleyed wide and Alan Brazil wasted a glorious chance, barely making contact with the ball as he swung his leg. The ball itself flew across goal and to safety. Hutchison cleared off the line following a Beattie header, as Ipswich continued to dominate. Yet gradually, City began to show the sort of fight that had deserted them in recent matches. In the second half, Mühren and Thijssen were given no time to dwell on the ball and City edged themselves into the match as an attacking force. Paul Power had been close on a couple of occasions, but this was a typical semi-final and clear-cut opportunities were rare. The 90 minutes produced no goals. As the match moved into extra time, Ipswich began to look tired. Hutchison's cross produced a good chance for Bennett, but his header was tipped over the bar by Cooper. City, attacking towards their own fans, won a number of free-kicks near the Ipswich penalty area. With the match 100 minutes old, Mackenzie rolled a free-kick into the path of Paul Power, who bent a left-foot shot around the Ipswich wall and low into the corner of the net, revealing hitherto hidden talents as a free-kick specialist. Paul Power had been nothing short of a goalscoring machine during City's Cup run. The goal was greeted with unbridled pandemonium from behind the goal and elsewhere. It was one of my most extraordinary moments as a follower of the club.

The rest of the match was accompanied by deafening noise. Ipswich were unable to threaten a recovery and the final whistle went. Incredibly, City had made it to the FA Cup Final. When I got back to the coach, the radio was playing the commentary of the other semi-final. It was still in extra time, having kicked off later than our match. I didn't care who won between Wolves and Spurs because we had just beaten Ipswich. If we could beat Ipswich, then we could win the final, whoever it was against. I do believe that I was suffering from a fit of unrestrained optimism. This did not prove to be a regular occurrence subsequently.

With Gerry Gow on the cusp of a suspension, as it were, Bond decided to rest City's muppet to avoid the calamity of a suspension for the FA Cup Final. Despite this, City won 3-1 at Wolves, with Bennett scoring twice. Back at Maine Road, in the absence of several first-choice players, City repeated their FA Cup result against Everton in a League match. After a dull first half, goals from Bennett and Reeves established City's supremacy. Imre Varadi pulled a goal back for Everton, but Steve Mackenzie snuffed out any thoughts of a revival by scoring City's third.

City's penultimate away match of the season allowed Ipswich to keep their faltering title hopes alive with a 1-0 win. The final home match, against relegated Crystal Palace, resolved the one remaining Cup Final selection problem: the competition between Tueart and Bennett. Dave Bennett's first-half headed goal was the highlight of an impressive personal performance in an otherwise ordinary City display. A late equaliser left Palace with an extra point to take down with them to Division Two. City's final position of twelfth in the table was assured.

On Saturday, 9 May 1981, my dad drove us down to Wembley for the centenary FA Cup Final against Tottenham Hotspur. Four of us made the trip: me, my girlfriend, and both parents. We were always entitled to two tickets, but managed to acquire two more through Chorley FC. I suppose that this kind of thing explains why there are never enough tickets around come Cup Final day. My girlfriend had also been at the semi-final, and was obviously getting a warped view of life as a City supporter. Before that season, she had never been to a match. This didn't prevent her from claiming to suffer more when the Blues lost. My mum and dad had the stand tickets, and found themselves in an area full of Spurs fans. In the end, they managed to swap, which was probably just as well.

It had been clear in the build-up to the final where the allegiance of the media would lie. Glenn Hoddle was the darling of the media, and the appeal of the City youngsters angle paled in comparison with that of the cute and loveable foreigner. It was ironic that, within a year, Argentineans would be considered the lowest form of life by that same media.

I stood at the Tunnel End, in much the same spot as my previous Wembley visit, but in a different frame of mind. This was my Cup Final. I had seen every game on the way, and it only required one more win for my dream to come true. Surely, City would not let me down now. Spurs had Ardiles and Hoddle, but City had the determination and the fighting qualities required to be winners. As the teams emerged, I waved my flag and joined in the chants. It was an emotional day and my team did not let me down. There were many heroic performances from City in this match. In particular, Joe Corrigan was awesome in goal whenever called upon, and Nicky Reid was outstanding at the centre of the City defence. This should have been City's day, and the dream should have come true.

There were close calls at both ends in the opening exchanges. On 30 minutes, City, attacking the Tunnel End, took the lead with an unlikely goal. Ray Ranson's floated cross from the right wing was headed by Tommy Hutchison, of all people, beyond the reach of Aleksic and into the top corner of the net. All hell broke loose behind the goal. I lost a hat in the ensuing frenzy and I didn't even realise it until half-time. Spurs were visibly shaken, and Reeves wasted a good chance to add to the City lead. Half-time was reached with everything going nicely. I never did find my hat.

Spurs began quite well after the break, but on 55 minutes a combination of two delicate one-twos between Mackenzie and Reeves, left Steve Mackenzie clear on goal. He seemed to get around Aleksic, but could only run the ball against the post. The importance of that moment can hardly be exaggerated. Soon afterwards, the disappointing Ricardo Villa was substituted. I can still recall him trudging off in a long, dejected walk towards the tunnel and the derision of the City fans; an image of disconsolate hairiness. Spurs increased the pressure, but Corrigan looked unbeatable. As the final 10 minutes approached, it looked as though City would hold on for a win. I didn't care that it had been an unspectacular final. I was only interested in seeing the final stage of the dream. Ardiles was fouled, and Spurs had a free-kick in a dangerous position. Hoddle attempted to curl a shot into the left corner of the City goal, but Corrigan had it covered. Unfortunately, Tommy Hutchison's shoulder diverted the ball into the opposite corner of the net. I can still remember it clearly. I saw it all the way. My heart sank. The goal, a clear fluke, was attributed to the genius of Saint Glenn.

As the match went into extra time, City looked the fitter and stronger team. At various stages during extra time, four Spurs players were incapacitated, presumably by cramp, but the Blues could not force home their advantage. Gerry Gow had the best opportunity but he blasted his shot wide. The match ended in a huge anticlimax. Amidst some confusion as to the correct protocol, the players trooped up to be greeted by the Queen. It was only the second drawn FA Cup Final at Wembley. My optimism was on the wane. Surely this was an opportunity missed.

When I joined it the following Monday, the queue for replay tickets stretched most of the way around Maine Road. The replay had been scheduled for Thursday, back at Wembley, with a large proportion of the neutral tickets being sold at Wembley Stadium itself. I went to the replay on my own, on a coach whose passengers included the legendary Helen, a large lady who for many years sat behind the goal in the North Stand, occasionally ringing a large bell. The crowd capacity for the replay was reduced from 100,000 to 92,000 and, more importantly, the match programme price was reduced from 80 to 60 pence. I left my flag at home, deciding to be mature about it, but as soon as I saw Wembley again, I bought another one.

The replay has often been cited as one of the great FA Cup Finals. That isn't how I view it at all. For me, it was a cruel calamity. City were the team who looked jaded and tired, and they failed to reproduce the form of the first match. Spurs, on the other hand, presumably lifted by their late escape from defeat, were much improved. City's best spell of sustained pressure came in the opening minutes. Despite that, after only eight minutes, it was Spurs who took the lead. Ardiles set up a chance for Archibald, and although Corrigan saved, a somewhat more cheerful Villa scored from the rebound. Two minutes later, with most people around me looking to their left where a crowd rumpus was suspected, my hope was revived by the sight of Steve Mackenzie thundering a long-range volley into the roof of the Spurs net. It was a tremendous goal, but sadly out of step with City's general play. Corrigan produced several excellent saves and Hoddle struck a free-kick against the post as City hung on for half-time.

There was an improvement in City's second-half performance. Within four minutes, Reeves headed into the path of Bennett, who was brought down by a combination of two Spurs defenders. City had a golden opportunity to retake the lead. Who cared that it was against the balance of play? Who cared that it was from a penalty kick? I didn't.

I merely prayed, again, that Kevin Reeves, facing the City Faithful, would not miss the kick, and spend the rest of his days having to suffer reminders of it. For once, my prayers were answered. The penalty was emphatically converted, despite a good guess from the goalkeeper as to the intended direction of the shot, and the dream was still on. For the first time in the game, City began to match Spurs. The determination seemed to be flowing back. Maybe it was our year, after all.

Of course, it wasn't. With 20 minutes left, Garth Crooks equalised. With 13 minutes left, four City defenders failed in their attempts to tackle Ricardo Villa and *that* goal was scored. Nicky Reid, City's star of the night as far as I am concerned, was not one of the four challenging defenders. I wish he had been. The dream was shattered. There was still time for Tueart to come on as substitute and miss a couple of good chances, but my optimism had already dissipated. When the final whistle went, I just wanted to leave and get home as quickly as possible.

The journey back seemed endless. Helen kept wandering up and down the coach try-ing to lift spirits, but I was inconsolable. City having taken part in a great FA Cup Final meant nothing to me. The whole thing had turned out disastrously. Some Spurs fans lobbed bricks at our coach. I've hated Spurs ever since. Why should they lob bricks at our coach when they have just won? They even went back to Wembley and won again the following season, which made me hate them even more. They didn't even need to win our Cup Final. And in any case, there can be absolutely no excuse whatsoever for Chas and Dave, snooker-loopy or not.

In the early hours of the morning, there was a lone figure wandering disconsolately through the streets of Moss Side and Whalley Range, trailing a limp flag over his shoulder. I sulked for days.

The Blues lost an irrelevant leftover League match 1-0 at Anfield, without my pres-ence, to complete an astonishing but ultimately disappointing season. One semi-final and one final seemed unlikely in those bleak, early days, but to come so close and end up with nothing is not a pleasant feeling. My player of the season was Nicky Reid, he-roic in the Cup Finals, and number one central defender as far as I was concerned. Joe Corrigan and Tommy Hutchison, the unfortunate Cup Final villain, came close, with Reeves and Mackenzie not far behind. In fact, I was quite happy with my team, proud of them even. If I hadn't been inconsolable, I might have dwelt on a promising future with young players like Reid, Mackenzie, Bennett, Ranson and Caton to the fore. In-stead, I was too busy masochistically replaying a tape of the Piccaddilly Radio match commentary that I had asked somebody to make (featuring James H. Reeve as a sum-mariser, I recall), and dreaming of next year. Surely City would get back to Wembley and put it all right next time round, or at least soon. It certainly didn't occur to me that John Bond would dismantle the team.

Season 1981/82: Tricky Trevor

My stay in Whalley Range had been an interesting and enlightening experience. There were riots in the summer of 1981, a reaction to Margaret Thatcher doing to the country what John Bond was about to do to City. Being in the full flush of youthful folly, late in the night following the Moss Side disturbances, I walked back from the town centre with a friend. We wandered in a relatively oblivious state right past the police station that had been the site of the biggest battle of the evening. All was quiet. The calm after the storm.

For me, the music scene had also calmed down a little. This was partly because of the increased expense and effort required to make it into town, and partly because when all of the bands came around for a second time, the novelty factor was missing. There had, however, been notable high spots. Being a happening guy, I knew a friend of a friend who had inside information about the first performance by New Order, resurrected from the ashes of my beloved Joy Division. The event was taking place at the Manchester College of Higher Education (acronym Comanche) Student's Union. Being a slightly misinformed happening guy, I turned up by mistake a week early to see Rolf and the Pony-Tails. Mind you, they were very good. Their version of the 'Hawaii-5-0' theme tune was particularly splendid and, as I recall, they also did a little number warning of the perils of the National Trust, which was more than a little bizarre. The following week, I saw the first New Order performance, with Gillian revealed on keyboards, and Barney *singing* for the first time – it was excellent.

Other highlights I can remember include The Fall's tour of Manchester and an Icelandic band called Purkirr Pilnik, who supported Mark E. Smith and the boys at the Band on the Wall. They were the precursor band for The Sugar Cubes, minus Björk. The singer, who was probably head-Sugar Cube, Einar Örn, revelled in jumping off the stage, running up to members of the audience and yelling, 'Excuse me, I have nothing to say.' He would then leap back on to the stage. I could tell that boy would go far.

I moved back into Chandos Hall for my final year, a time given over to indulgence in all that Manchester had to offer. It seemed like every evening was spent at one of the nearby hostelries, such as the Old Garrett, which served fine and cheap Boddington's bitter, or the Bull's Head. After closing time, my clique and I often strolled over to the Cyprus Tavern to continue our excessive drinking into the small hours. There we would boogie away to the latest alternative sounds – alternative to Radio One, that is. Or we would complain as the music degenerated into a session of dirges by the likes of Bauhaus, whereupon students dressed like members of the Addams Family would emerge from the gloom, sending us scuttling back to our pints. Happy days.

Changes were afoot in the world of football at the start of the 1981/82 season. The three points for a win system, now staggeringly adopted by the whole world, was introduced. This ensured that visiting teams who adopt stifling defensive tactics, but surprise their frustrated opponents by scoring from their one breakaway attack of the match, should have maximum reward, whilst teams battling out an enthralling 3-3 draw should both be penalised.

Back at the Academy, Paul Power and Steve Kinsey were announced as the winners of the 1981 supporters' Player of the Year and Young Player of the Year awards respectively. John Bond set a few alarm bells ringing with the inexplicable sale of Steve Mackenzie to West Bromwich Albion for an insulting £450,000. The 19-year-old England 'B' international gave every sign that he was just about to mature into a fine player. He was the best passer at the club and lacked only in fitness and stamina, defects likely to be rectified with age and experience. Bond blamed the financial situation for making the deal unavoidable. It seemed strange, therefore, that Martin O'Neill, a player entering the twilight of his career, had been signed from Nottingham Forest for £275,000.

The biggest news in the first match magazine of the new season concerned the

£6 million plan for City's 54,000 capacity Maine Road development. Peter Swales is quoted as saying, 'We are committing ourselves to a lot of money, but I'm sure it is the right way to spend it. There is no question of putting the ground before the team.' The first stage, to be completed before the start of the next season, was a new roof for the Main Stand at a cost of £1.5 million. That was Phase One. Everything was abandoned before we ever got to Phase Two.

Despite the baffling sale of Steve Mackenzie, the new season was greeted with some optimism. By a strange quirk of fate, Mackenzie was involved in the first City match of the season, a Maine Road encounter with West Bromwich Albion, under new management since the departure of Ron Atkinson to do the devil's work. Bryan Robson was still alongside Gary Owen in the Albion midfield, but not for much longer. The City team differed from the Cup Final heroes in the replacement of Mackenzie and the suspended Gow with O'Neill and Tueart, and the preference for Phil 'Gloria' Boyer over Dave Bennett. A first-time right-foot shot by Hutchison, and a close-range Tueart header gave City a 2-0 lead after 30 minutes. It was a lead that they maintained until the seventy-third minute. Then, just to make the City fans uncomfortable, a bubble-haired David Mills pulled one goal back from a penalty kick, following a clumsy O'Neill challenge. In a low-key opening to the season, a Bobby McDonald goal earned City a 1-1 draw at Notts County in City's first away match, but the real excitement was just about to begin.

My first away trip of the season was yet another visit to the Victoria Ground, Stoke, but this match had a greater significance than usual. The morale of everyone at Maine Road had been lifted by the £1.2 million signing of Trevor Francis from Nottingham Forest. There was high excitement amongst the travelling Faithful at the prospect of his first match, and I was amongst them, behind the goal in the Stoke End Stand, to see one of the most impressive debuts ever made by a City player. I had not been a particularly big fan of Tricky Trevor, and I feared another Channon fiasco, but it took only one match to win me over. The Stoke match programme had its finger right on the pulse, with an article entitled, 'It's make or break season for Trevor Francis *and Forest*.' It was obviously break rather than make.

The match itself was an excellent and exciting one. Stoke had some promising young talent, with Bracewell and Heath buzzing around in midfield, and Lee Chapman, a tall, blond, exceptionally awkward centre forward, causing all manner of problems for the City defenders. Stoke, still with Mike Doyle at the heart of their defence, had won both of their opening matches, and began confidently. Joe Corrigan was forced to save from Chapman, but City replied with a Hutchison shot that collided with the inside of a post and scuttled across the face of goal, before escaping past the other post. In the Stoke goal, Peter Fox denied Kevin Reeves with a fine save as City sought to counter the home side's enthusiasm.

With the action passing to and fro, it was the moment for Tricky Trevor to make his mark. His pace had already been apparent, and an obvious worry to the Stoke defenders. It was the combination of pace and skill that allowed Francis to latch on to a long ball from McDonald, slip deftly past the final defender and slide the ball beyond the advancing Fox to open the scoring after 36 minutes. Delight was plenteous amongst the Faithful behind the goal. After 62 minutes, Chapman took advantage of a Caton error to bring Stoke level and threaten to dampen the City celebrations. The reply was immediate. Well, it was within two minutes, which is nearly immediate. Francis demonstrated his goal-making skills by skipping down the wing, again outpacing hapless defenders, before hitting a threatening cross. A massive scramble in the Stoke goalmouth ensued, the result of which was a goal for substitute Boyer. Fox bravely fought a one-man rearguard action to keep the score down, but with three minutes left he was beaten again when Francis made the most of a Gerry Gow through-ball to apply a steadfast finish. The final score was 3-1, and the impact on expectations was considerable.

A crowd of 42,003 turned up in eager anticipation of the home debut of Trevor Francis. A happy, smiley Francis was pictured alongside an even more happy, smiley John Bond on the cover of the match magazine. Inevitably, the match was an anticlimax. Kevin Keegan's penalty gave Southampton the lead, and Reeves equalised for City just before half-time. There were no more goals in a poor second half.

Whilst everyone's attention was taken up by the headline-grabbing arrival of Trevor Francis, the more alarming purchase of John Bond's son, Kevin, from Norwich (via Seattle Sounders) for £350,000 was quietly confirmed. With Caton and Reid performing well as a young but rapidly maturing central-defensive partnership, the acquisition of Bond Junior was hard to justify, particularly when bearing in mind the suggestion that Steve Mackenzie had been sold because of a cash crisis. Caton had just received his first England Under-21 cap, and Reid had established himself as a nimble defender with pace and good tackling ability. John Bond was inviting accusations of nepotism. The RSVP message did not go unanswered.

Such accusations were hard to refute when, after being quoted as saying that young Kevin would have to fight hard to get into the team, Bond Senior dropped Ray Ranson to play his son at right-back in the very next match, at Birmingham. Bobby McDonald was also omitted, with Caton switching to left-back and Tommy Booth being restored to central defence. The result was an unhappy return to St Andrew's for Trevor Francis, and me. With some disconcertingly cheerful and sarcastic local policemen making comments throughout, just behind my standing position, I watched Birmingham go into the lead in the second minute. Tony Evans went on to complete a hat-trick, with two further goals in the second half. But for a Frank Worthington free-kick being resolutely blocked by the post, the scoreline could have been even worse than the already shabby 3-0. Bond's defensive reshuffle was not a success.

Sanity was resumed the following week, with the return of Ranson and McDonald, and the restoration of the Reid-Caton partnership. Without Boyer, O'Neill and Kevin Bond, City registered their biggest win of the season against a Leeds side that included Peter Barnes, signed from West Bromwich Albion. Bond had unsuccessfully tried to re-sign Barnes for City as part of the Mackenzie transfer deal, but Leeds won that particular battle. In the programme notes, Bond was already making excuses for his son. He said, 'I've put Kevin in an unfortunate position and I'll have to do something about it quickly. The crux of the matter is that he's in his best position at centre half, and it's not getting the best out of his defensive capabilities to play him at full-back as I did last Saturday.' Bond also made a point of criticising Nicky Reid. Subtlety was not his middle name. Actually, I haven't checked that, but I'm probably right.

First-half goals from Tueart and Reeves gave City a nice half-time cushion against Leeds. However, the most crucial incident of the match came after 60 minutes, when Trevor Francis suffered an injury during a challenge with John Lukic, the Leeds goalkeeper. When the ball fell loose, Tueart pounced to make the score 3-0, but the injury to Francis was not a trivial one. From that moment, the on-off injury saga was an all too familiar feature of the Tricky Trevor spell at Maine Road. The effect on the rest of the team of being without Francis was striking.

After Francis had limped off, Kevin Reeves made the final score against Leeds 4-0, and City were in proud occupation of fourth place in the League table. Three days later, with Boyer replacing the injured Francis, the Blues were back at Maine Road to face Tottenham. With Ray Clemence looking shaky in the Spurs goal, City had their chances, particularly when Caton miskicked against the crossbar after Clemence had fumbled the ball. However, the only goal of the match was scored for Spurs early in the second half by Mark Falco, cementing their place as my second most-hated team.

Meanwhile, largely unnoticed, Bond had continued his apparent mission to sell most of City's youngsters, with the transfers of Dave Bennett to Cardiff (£125,000) and Tony Henry (£125,000) to Bolton. Bennett re-emerged years later to take personal revenge on Spurs in Coventry City's FA Cup win. For the next game, a visit to Brighton, Kevin Bond was selected to play at the centre of the City defence, with Reid being moved into midfield. City lost 4-1.

Undaunted, Bond Senior retained Bond Junior in a 2-0 League Cup first leg win over, yet again, Stoke City at Maine Road. With Gow about to have an operation on his knee, Bond had decided to strengthen the midfield with the re-signing of Asa Hartford from Everton for £350,000. Hartford, now aged thirty, was thus reunited with Tueart, now aged thirty-one. In their first spell together at City this pair had been pretty much the dream ticket, but isn't there a saying along the lines that you should never go back? If there is, it doesn't hold when you wish to reverse your car out of a parking space, or when you've discovered a flaw in your otherwise incredibly chic Marks and Spencer outfit, but in the case of Tueart and Hartford, there may be an element of truth in it.

A first-half own goal by Dennis Smith, and an Asa Hartford goal on his return, scored from an acute angle near the end of the match, looked like a sufficient first leg lead against Stoke. With Bobby McDonald dropped, the 19-year-old Clive Wilson made his debut first team appearance, at left-back, as Bond continued to experiment.

The omens were not promising for the derby match at Maine Road on 10 October 1981. Under the influence of alcohol, on the night before the match, I had clumsily dropped my Manchester City mug on to the floor of G Floor kitchen, causing it to break – the mug, that is, not the floor. Although I am not superstitious, honestly, such portents can only fill a fan with foreboding. The Blues held Big Ron's lackeys of Lucifer even if they did have Moses playing for them – to a goalless draw and, under the circumstances, I was quite happy to settle for that. Bryan Robson was making his debut and Steve Coppell was dropped, although he later came on to replace the legendary Garry Birtles (as in 'You're worse than . . .'). It was a scrappy affair. Bond's latest formation in the defensive game of musical chairs, apparently designed to get Kevin into the team, was to play Reid and Bond as central defenders with Caton at left-back. Most of the crowd of 52,037 went home content in the knowledge that it could have been worse.

Booth and Buckley were next to leave Maine Road, both going to Preston North End. There were also rumours about a possible move to Arsenal for Tommy Caton. As the Bond changes continued, a 1-0 defeat at Highbury sent Tricky Trevor-less City slumping to fifteenth place in the League table. I suspect that Francis would have particularly liked to play against his old club, Nottingham Forest, in City's next home match. The match certainly needed something to rescue it. A typically efficient Forest display led to a stifling encounter of few opportunities. John Robertson might even have taken all the points for Forest, had it not been for alert work by Joe Corrigan. Another scoreless match left City in sixteenth place.

I regret to say that I missed the League Cup second leg tie against Stoke, where City surrendered their two-goal lead but edged through 9-8 in a marathon penalty shoot-out. I did, however, make the journey to Goodison Park for the next League game against Howard Kendall's Everton, but without a great deal of optimism. The match was memorable for a number of peculiar happenings rather than the football itself. Before the game started, the PA announcer struggled with the pronunciation of City's new Norwegian signing, Aage Hareide (£10,000 from Molde). As he reached the relevant point on the team sheet, there was an embarrassing delay as the announcer assessed the possible alternatives. Eventually, he elected for 'age areeed' – City fans, being well versed in Nordic linguistics, were well aware that the correct pronunciation was 'awger hareider'. I can only presume that the PA man no longer holds the same job. If he were still in the post, there would be regular delayed kick-offs at Goodison Park because of the time taken to announce the Premier League multinational team line-ups.

The tall, blond and athletic Hareide, a positive cliché of Norwegian-ness, had quite an eventful afternoon on his full debut. In the opening exchanges Kevin Reeves spurned two good opportunities, neither of which was as appetising as the one missed by Boyer, following a poor back-pass. City's run of four matches without a goal was no fluke. The finishing simply wasn't there. As sixth-placed Everton recovered from their poor start, Joe Corrigan was called upon to perform his usual rescue act. Fortunately, the home side proved equally incapable in front of goal. A single second-half goal was enough to give City a surprise win. Aage Hareide galloped down the right wing like an Arctic reindeer on heat – although, to be honest, I haven't seen many Arctic reindeer, on heat or otherwise. But this was exactly how I would imagine them to gallop across the frozen tundra, if I did imagine them at all that is. He then crossed perfectly for Tueart to score with a far-post header.

The match had been a bad-tempered affair and the crowd were not, on the whole, terribly enamoured with the outcome. My dad and I sneaked out of the ground unmolested, and even managed to locate the road on which our car was parked. What we hadn't bargained for was something akin to a scene from a Derek Jarman film on the theme of alienation and desolation. As we walked down the road, hunched and trying to look unhappy, two youths sprinted down the opposite pavement. On the way, one of them had cried out, 'The sledgehammer will considerably reinforce our position with regard to the ongoing dispute with those vagabonds and villains.' Or words to that effect. They reached a car, stopped, opened the boot, picked up a heavy item looking remarkably like a sledgehammer, and disappeared back whence they came, somewhat in a hurry. I was concentrating earnestly on my feet as much as possible. When their footsteps could no longer be heard, and fearing that I might walk into a lamp-post, I looked up and saw a house on fire with flames billowing out of the upper windows. There were people watching it all happen without any signs of concern. The house may have been derelict, but it was still an unnerving little scene. We reached the car and made our retreat. My dad was strangely reluctant to go to Goodison Park again, and so, for several years, was I.

City had arrested their slide, but with little conviction. On 7 November 1981, Tricky Trevor was welcomed back from the land of the injured for the home match against Middlesbrough. After an inauspicious start, Francis obliged his adoring public with a header to give City the lead, and followed it up by playing a major role in a Kevin Reeves goal for City's second. Bottom-of-the-table Middlesbrough were given heart by a deflected goal just before half-time, and began quite promisingly after the break. When Thomson curled in a free-kick to bring them level, there were many glum faces to be seen around the Platt Lane Stand, including mine. It took a harsh penalty award, converted by Tueart, to steal all the points for City in a 3-2 win.

Northampton, struggling in the Fourth Division, also made City toil at Maine Road, in a League Cup third-round tie. Trevor Francis darted and threatened but was unable to inspire his colleagues. Francis had a couple of shots cleared off the line, and from the second, Bobby McDonald followed up to give City a half-time lead. When a chap called Tony Mahoney, on loan from Fulham, scored a spectacular equaliser, early in the second half, City gave every impression of being shell-shocked. It took a good Joe Corrigan save to prevent Mahoney heading Northampton into the lead. The Blues were clearly toying with the idea of another famous Cup defeat. A defensive lapse allowed Dennis Tueart to restore sanity following a corner, and Tueart completed his face-saving act with an overhead kick, to leave City flattering 3-1 winners.

The Blues continued their climb up the League table with an impressive 4-0 home win against third-placed Swansea City, who were enjoying an unusual and ultimately brief experience of the rarefied atmosphere of football's upper echelons, under the guidance of manager John Toshack. Toshack had moved on from his days as co-presenter of 'Mac-N-Tosh', an excruciating Merseyside radio show, also featuring Duncan Mackenzie. A decision to move into management, rather than a career in the media, was soundly based.

It took a Tueart penalty to break the deadlock of an evenly balanced first half. After the break, Tommy Hutchison followed a close-range shot against the crossbar with an inviting cross, which was directed into the net by Kevin Reeves, despite the best efforts of Dai Davies in the Swansea goal. Tricky Trevor was the inspiration behind a second Reeves goal and another Tueart goal as City rounded off a most satisfactory afternoon's work. Even referee George Courtney escaped any criticism in my match report. Kevin Reeves seemed inspired when playing alongside Francis. In particular, his often tentative finishing became far more positive. It was becoming clear that City were increasingly reliant on Tricky Trevor to get results. The true extent of this reliance would only emerge when the man packed his bags for sunnier climes.

Meanwhile, even the presence of Tricky Trevor could not prevent a 2-0 defeat away to high-flying Ipswich. I made the coach trip to Oakwell, home of Barnsley Football Club, on a damp and murky December night, in a reasonably confident mood, as the prospect of a League Cup fourth-round tie beckoned. Barnsley were going well in Division Two, and their fans seemed to be quite pleased with the work being carried out by manager Norman Hunter, the ex-Leeds United, archetypal hard man. I can recall the coach climbing a hill in the gloom as we neared the ground, eventually coming to rest on what looked very much like a drenched slag heap. I picked my way gingerly, and in complete darkness, through the black, indeterminate substance, which was interspersed with mucky puddles of variable depth. I was heading as best as I could in the vague direction of the floodlights. By the time I got inside the ground, the rain had relented somewhat, and I was treated to a seemingly endless rendition of 'Norman Hunter's Red and White Army'. This was repeated over and over again, without respite, for the best part of an hour, by a band of fanatical, bordering on psychotic, Barnsley fans positioned in a corner of the ground close to the City Faithful. The match magazine, *Oakwell Review*, contained a curious little story under the heading 'Tommy Tyke Sez'. Written in broad Yorkshire, it was all about someone trying to get tickets for the City match, and the punchline involved pork pies. I gather that it was a regular feature.

Norman Hunter's team did not contain many well-known personalities. One of the central defenders was the typically gritty Yorkshireman, Mick McCarthy, and in attack was their top scorer, Trevor Aylott. City were without Francis, an ill omen, especially when the replacement was Phil Boyer. After an uneventful first half, which caused few distractions to upset the Barnsley bid for the longest running repetitive chant ever on a wet Wednesday, Aylott headed the home side in front. This was just a few minutes after a curling shot by Hutchison had struck the inside of a Barnsley post. The goal spurred City into action, but they failed to convert pressure into goals, and might even have gone further behind had Corrigan not saved a fierce Aylott shot. I collected yet another giant-killing.

After the match, I negotiated the lagoon-ridden slag heap with the consolation that the FA Cup was my priority, and with the cries of 'Norman Hunter's Red and White Army' fading into the background. I didn't expect to be going back to Oakwell.

City were in ninth place in the League when they took on Aston Villa at Maine Road on 5 December 1981. Tricky Trevor had made a surprisingly quick recovery from a thigh strain, an injury less serious than his earlier knee trouble, and he was quickly into the action, hammering a shot against the post from an unlikely angle. Although they had been unable to recapture the previous season's form, Villa were still formidable opposition, and only a series of fine saves from Joe Corrigan kept City in the contest. It was during City's brightest period, midway through the second half, that Tueart's glancing header gave them a slender lead. Missed opportunities by Tony Morley and Peter Withe late in the game were the main reason for City maintaining the lead. Tueart also scored the only goal at Coventry, to lift the Blues into seventh place.

Back at Maine Road, bottom-of-the-League Sunderland, including 19-year-old Ally McCoist, were the pre-Christmas visitors. On a freezing day, City's under-soil heating made them the only highly placed team with a match. The prospect of a comfortable win propelling them into fourth place seemed like too good an opportunity to spurn. Naturally, they lost. In fact, not only did they lose but top-scorer Dennis Tueart suffered an Achilles tendon injury, leaving him unable to play for the remainder of the season. The fans were left wishing that the under-soil heating had been faulty, and that they had been Christmas shopping in central Manchester. That's how bad it was.

Although Stan Cummins scored a spectacular opening goal a minute before half-time, 11 minutes into the second half City actually led after Trevor Francis scored twice. The Blues then threatened further goals and were thwarted only by ex-Trotters goalkeeper, Barry Siddall. With eight minutes remaining, City still led 2-1. The crucial moment seemed to be the appearance of substitute Barry Venison, a man whose haircut made Phil Boyer's look respectable. *Super-bouffant-sub* Venison set up an equaliser for Gary Rowell and then, following a glaring miss by McCoist, scored the winner himself. Happy Christmas!

It was with some trepidation, therefore, that I made the Boxing Day trip with my dad to a snow-bound Anfield, for a match against a Liverpool side languishing in mid-table. It turned out to be the high point of the whole season. We parked the car on a snowy street full of other parked cars. This earned my dad a parking ticket because beneath the snow there were double yellow lines. Needless to say, it was cold inside, although the necessity to avoid the darts being hurled by Liverpool fans in other sections of the Anfield Road End tended to encourage huddling as far away from the danger area as possible. There was netting to prevent any bottles being thrown at visiting fans. This did not, however, provide much of a barrier to coins or darts.

The match was one of only two surviving First Division fixtures. In fact, Mother Nature was about to propel City to the top of the table. I was glad to see the waif-like but speedy Steve Kinsey being given an opportunity to deputise for Tueart, ahead of Boyer, but I could not in all honesty claim optimism before the match began. The Liverpool team had the usual awesome look about it. Yet City started splendidly. After only six minutes, Kinsey skipped down the right wing and crossed for Asa Hartford to head beyond Grobbelaar and into the net. The goal was disallowed, but even though the match was featured later on television, I don't know why. It didn't matter, because within a few minutes, Hartford had latched on to a Kevin Reeves cross to give City a lead that counted.

This prompted a response from Liverpool, and in particular Kenny Dalglish, who shot against the crossbar and forced Joe Corrigan to make a fine, smothering save. But Bruce Grobbelaar was in reassuringly clownish form, flapping at every cross and offering hope whenever the ball was in the Liverpool penalty area. In addition, the Liverpool finishing was strangely ineffective, and Joe Corrigan was able to block the way when called upon to do so. After opportunities at both ends of the field, the crucial moment came in the second half, when Phil Thomson made a fine fingertips save to prevent a Steve Kinsey goal. Kinsey's chance came about because the real Liverpool goalkeeper had dropped another cross. This time he was punished for his error. Kevin Bond scored from the penalty kick.

With only 10 minutes remaining, Whelan found the quality of finishing required to beat even Joe Corrigan. I expected panic and surrender, but instead City regained the initiative. When Kinsey sped once more down the right wing and his cross was flicked goalwards by Kevin Reeves, Grobbelaar should probably have prevented the ball from crossing the line. He didn't. Astonishingly City led 3-1. This was all too much for one Liverpool fan in the Kop. A bottle was thrown, with the sort of accuracy uncharacteristically lacking from the Liverpool forwards. It struck Joe Corrigan on the back of the head and sent him plummeting to the floor. There was a delay as the man-mountain was restored to the land of the living, and the match was played out without further incident.

It was City's first League win at Anfield in 28 years, and they haven't won there since. Liverpool were so stunned by this result, which left them in the bottom half of the table, that they embarked on an awesome run of form that eventually drove them to the League title. They owe it all to City.

Two days later, with the weather again thwarting all their rivals, City had the opportunity to go to the top of the League. A win at Maine Road against struggling Wolves was all that was required. The under-soil heating had proven effective once more, but City did not look like repeating their Anfield heroics in an uneventful first half. Asa Hartford opened the scoring after half-time, but Peter Daniel equalised direct from a free-kick awarded because Joe Corrigan was adjudged to have handled outside the penalty area. Only a desperate goal line clearance from League-debutant Clive Wilson, deputising for the injured McDonald, prevented Wolves from taking the lead. City struggled to give anything like a passable impersonation of League leaders. With five minutes remaining, Kevin Reeves flicked on a long clearance from Joe Corrigan, and Tricky Trevor chased after the ball at an angle taking him further away from goal. Without breaking stride, he unleashed an astonishing right-foot shot. The ball flew inside the post, past a bemused Paul Bradshaw. At that moment, life seemed so much more worth living. It was the kind of goal to which words cannot do justice. City were top of the table. Of course, all the other teams had games in hand, but City *were* top of the table.

The Blues began the New Year, and their mission to return to Wembley in the FA Cup, with a 3-1 home win against Second Division Cardiff City, who included Dave Bennett in their side. Trevor Francis gave City the lead, and although Paul Maddy equalised for the visitors, a fine Bobby McDonald header restored City's advantage before half-time. Another ex-City player, Paul Sugrue, made an appearance as a second-half substitute, but both old boys went back to Wales disappointed. Francis scored the only second-half goal. The match was notable for the return from injury of Gerry Gow, without his Afro-perm. However, it was a return from injury that didn't last long.

Martin O'Neill made a return from beyond the grave as a replacement for Gow in the next match at Maine Road, against Stoke City. O'Callaghan gave the visitors the lead in a ghostly first half. Trevor Francis provided some much needed relief from the boredom with a splendid second-half equaliser, but it was insufficient to prevent City losing top spot, and they never seriously threatened to recover it.

The season's lowest point came on 23 January 1982, when Coventry City came to Maine Road for an FA Cup fourth-round tie. The mere thought of the Cup should have been enough to inspire the City team. The Faithful had been building themselves up for the start of the FA Cup, and the chance to relive the heady days of the previous season's run. The home draw against lowly Coventry was ideal, and the media pre-match hype had progressed at full throttle. Everything was in place. The referee blew his whistle to start the match, and then, nothing . . .

After just two minutes, with the City defenders behaving like disinterested spectators, Steve Hunt gave Coventry the lead. That was sure to spark a passionate response from City we all thought, or at least some of us thought, possibly. Instead, with the City defenders behaving like shy and awkward teenagers at a gathering for halitosis sufferers, Mark Hateley, yes *that* Mark Hateley, was left with plenty of time to add a second goal. This was thanks in part to a weird deflection off some loose turf. The visitors, who to add insult included ex-member of *The Nation's Teaml*, Gerry Daly, as captain, also had a goal disallowed.

Clearly things were not going to plan. At half-time, Bond abandoned his idea of using Gow to fill in at right-back for the suspended Ranson, and Nicky Reid was allowed, at last, to return to defensive duties. City improved, but demonstrated that their finishing could be as woeful as their first-half defending. To add to the general mood of the day, referee George Courtney decided to dismiss Asa Hartford for a second bookable offence. This temporarily inspired City, and Trevor Francis earned a penalty, which was converted by Kevin Bond. There followed a period of relentless City pressure, with numerous scrambles and close calls, a disallowed goal, and the kitchen sink (probably). The final gilt-edged and glorious opportunity fell to youngster Steve Kinsey. With the weight of expectation exerting intolerable pressure on his flimsy frame, Kinsey shot straight at goalkeeper Jim Blyth. Soon afterwards, Coventry took advantage of City's numerical defensive disadvantage to break away and add a third, a neat chip by Peter Bodak. This was not a happy day at the Academy. More than a few cats had reason to fear that Saturday night.

With the season rapidly becoming devoid of meaning, City played their fifth consecutive home match against Birmingham City in front of a disappointing crowd of fewer than 30,000. Bond took the opportunity to rant and rave in the match magazine, threatening mass clear-outs and generally foaming at the mouth. Only four players were deemed exempt from his wrath following the Coventry disaster: Tricky Trevor, Tommy Hutch, Nicky Reid ('to a certain extent') and, naturally, Bond Junior. The Coventry game had proven to be Gow's last for City. He was sold to Rotherham. Tommy Hutchison and Phil Boyer were on the verge of temporary transfers to the Hong Kong club, Bulova, and Martin O'Neill was poised to return to Norwich. Bond's other widespread changes amounted to very little. Paul Power returned from injury and John Ryan, a free transfer and the kind of 'experienced' player Bond specialised in signing, replaced the injured Reid. The crowd had little opportunity to be disgruntled in a first half containing six goals. After 38 minutes, City were 4-0 ahead, Francis and Reeves both scoring twice. Steve Kinsey darted around to good effect but slips by Bond and Caton let Frank Worthington in for two goals before half-time. Worthington, Francis and Reeves each had at least one opportunity to complete a hat-trick, but there were no second-half goals.

One point from their next two away matches confirmed what everybody knew: City were not genuine contenders for the Championship. The next visitors to Maine Road were Brighton who, with players like Andy Ritchie, Neil McNab, Jimmy Case and Gordon Smith in their side, were comfortably placed in the top half of the League table. Francis scored from a free-kick and manufactured an opportunity for Reeves to inspire City to a 2-0 half-time lead. Bobby McDonald and an own goal from Gary Stevens completed an emphatic 4-0 win. The best goal, a classy 30-yard shot curled into the top corner by Tricky Trevor, was disallowed because there was somebody in a blue shirt watching admiringly from an offside position.

A 2-0 defeat at Spurs followed, leaving City in seventh position, with a place in Europe looking an increasingly forlorn hope. The tide of opinion was beginning to turn against John Bond. Most fans were painfully aware that should Trevor Francis be removed from the City line-up, the future did not look bright. Maybe this accounts for the cautious approach adopted in the derby game on 26 February 1982 at *The Swamp*. With Francis again missing because of injury, Bond's policy of selling without replacing was exposed. Aage Hareide made a rare appearance, and 17-year-old Gary Jackson was drafted in for a debut, leaving Kevin Reeves a lone figure in attack. Bond chose to keep Kinsey on the substitutes' bench. The result was an uncomfortable afternoon for those of us behind the goal at the Scoreboard End. We cheered ourselves with chants concerning the rotundity of Mr Atkinson, but it was chiefly an exercise in watch-watching. After withstanding an early onslaught, City took a surprise lead. Ray Ranson made a decisive run down the right wing and hit the perfect near-post cross for Kevin Reeves to score with a glancing header, right in front of the Faithful.

The Nation's Team were temporarily shaken, but they restored parity before half-time, when Moran's header flew beyond the reach of Joe Corrigan. For most of the second half the ball seemed to be heading our way. The big Bond idea appeared to involve Hareide following Bryan Robson around wherever he went. I suppose it worked, although the best second-half chance fell to Robson, following one of many corners. Robson hit his shot into the ground and the bounce took it into the crowd, skimming the crossbar on its way. It was a second half to make a true-Blue cringe, but City held on for a draw. *The Nation's Team*, who rather fancied that they might win the Championship, went home disappointed and that, after all, was the most important thing.

Bond was so reliant on Tricky Trevor that he gambled by playing Francis in the next match, against Arsenal at Maine Road. Francis limped off after half an hour, leaving Aage Hareide to play as a makeshift forward. The match was dreary. City right-back Ray Ranson was their most effective attacking player, which adequately sums it up.

A midweek 1-0 away victory against strugglers Leeds United was achieved without my presence. Kevin Reeves scored the goal to give the Blues a rare win away from Maine Road. They followed it with a respectable 1-1 draw away to Nottingham Forest, with Tommy Caton scoring his first City goal. There was more good news in an overlong and premature wind-down to the season, as Ranson, Reid and Caton all played in the same England Under-21 side against Poland.

Tricky Trevor turned villain in City's next home match, against Everton. In a lively first half, Adrian Heath gave Everton the lead after only five minutes. Within a minute, a long-range shot from Kevin Bond brought City level. The match degenerated when Neville Southall failed to hold a shot and Francis challenged for the loose ball. In time-honoured fashion, as Southall lay injured, the Everton defenders surrounded Francis and engaged in the normal display of masculine posturing with shoving, grunting of oaths and general stern looks. For some reason, Tricky Trevor decided to head-butt one of the Everton defenders, Billy Wright, leaving the referee with little option but to direct the City star to the dressing room. Joe Corrigan came to the rescue with an inspired second-half display as City held on for a point. The closest Everton came to a winner was a Steve MacMahon shot that came perilously close to breaking the crossbar.

Whilst City maintained their push for mid-table obscurity, a goalless draw at Middlesbrough was followed by a home defeat against West Ham. With Francis and Bond Junior suspended, the cupboard was very nearly bare for the West Ham match. John Ryan was joined in an overcrowded, yet strangely anonymous, midfield by Jackson, Hareide, Hartford and Power. Bond once more snubbed Steve Kinsey, preferring instead to leave Kevin Reeves alone in attack. The result was largely a tedious stalemate. Paul Goddard had two second-half opportunities for the Hammers. Joe Corrigan thwarted the first one, but Goddard scored from the second. McDonald shot against the bar in the dying minutes, and Jackson blasted the rebound wide as City sought a point to keep their dwindling European hopes alive. It was all in vain.

Worse was to follow as two matches in as many days left City with Easter egg all over their faces. It was a very different Liverpool side that visited Maine Road on 10 April 1982 from the Christmas puddings on that cold Anfield day back in December. The result was a humiliation for an increasingly dishevelled and spiritless City team. With Kevin Bond the latest to be given a run out in midfield, and Hartford's powers on the wane, Liverpool swept through the middle of the City team with disdain. The only hope for inspiration, Trevor Francis, was still suspended, and with Liverpool on an awesome run, City were like lambs to the slaughter, only with less aggression. Sammy

Lee hammered in the first goal from distance, giving Joe Corrigan no chance. The City goalkeeper fought bravely to deny Johnston and Kennedy, but when Caton's tackle on Rush was penalised, Phil Neal increased Liverpool's lead with a penalty.

Just after half-time, there was evidence of some spirit in the City ranks, prompted by Steve Kinsey, and Reeves should have scored from a Kinsey cross. They didn't get another chance. Rush set up Craig Johnston for Liverpool's third and a mis-hit Kennedy cross drifted fortuitously in for the fourth. Dalglish laid on the simplest of chances for Ian Rush to make it 0-5, with the City defence and midfield – let's face it, *the whole team* – AWOL. City completed their impressive Easter with a 4-1 defeat at Wolves, despite the return of Trevor Francis.

A 2-0 defeat at Swansea was followed by a brief respite, with Francis scoring the only goal at West Bromwich Albion. Second-placed Ipswich were the next visitors at Maine Road. Alan Brazil gave them a first-half lead, but City demonstrated some character, and Asa Hartford's goal earned a point. The major credit, once more, went to Joe Corrigan, who made a number of excellent saves as Ipswich broke through the City back-line with alarming regularity.

On 28 April 1982, I took a break from the increasing monotony of the City season to watch an Under-21 international match. England played Scotland at Maine Road in the UEFA Under-21 Championship semi-final second leg. Tommy Caton, Nicky Reid and Steve Mackenzie all played, but Ray Ranson, who had been captain in all three previous internationals, missed out because of injury. It was a rather disappointing game, although the 1-1 draw was enough to send England through 2-1 on aggregate. Clearly, the dullness of England internationals was being nurtured from an early age.

Only 24,443 people turned up to see City's penultimate home game, against Notts County. This uninspiring, end-of-term, mid-table contest, followed on from a goalless draw at Aston Villa. Sixteen minutes from the end, Paul Power scored his only goal of a season badly disrupted by injury, and City held on for a 1-0 win.

The supporters voted for Tommy Caton as the Player of the Year, with Steve Kinsey once more winning the Young Player of the Year vote. The season seemed to be drifting serenely to a sleepy close when John Bond made a decision that lost him any remaining scrap of my support. Nicky Reid was sold off to Seattle Sounders, albeit with a buy-back clause, leaving Bond Junior as the unsurprising winner of that particular battle. Having split up the promising Caton-Reid central-defensive partnership, and played Nicky Reid as a midfield filler, Bond may have hoped that nobody would notice when Reid was sold off. On the contrary, in the last home match of the season, against Coventry, Kevin Bond was barracked by the crowd, and the first shouts of 'Bond Out' gathered momentum. It didn't help that the City display was dismal. Steve Whitton had completed a hat-trick for the visitors before Trevor Francis, fighting a one-man battle, managed a late consolation goal.

My clear choice as Player of the Season was Tricky Trevor, despite his many absences. Tueart, Ranson and Corrigan were also in contention, with Nicky Reid and Tommy Caton just behind. Kevin Bond was well down the field. This is partly because, like many City fans, I found it difficult to accept the manager's son. The fact that Bond Senior was oblivious to the problems that might be caused by buying his own son says much about the man's sensitivity. In fact, Reid did return to City at the end of his spell in the USA, but the damage to Bond's credibility with the fans was already done, and Nicky Reid, his confidence dented by Bond's machinations, never quite fulfilled that exceptional early promise.

City ended the season with a 2-0 defeat at Sunderland and finished in tenth place which, looking back with the benefit of hindsight, doesn't seem all that bad. In the FA Cup Final, much to my chagrin, Spurs (without Ardiles or Villa) beat QPR after a replay. Two successive FA Cups – that's just greedy.

Season 1982/83: Into the Abyss

I finished my final examinations at UMIST and sat back to enjoy the 1982 World Cup. I had an active interest in the England team because of the presence of Trevor Francis, who played well and scored goals in probably England's best World Cup since 1966. They remained undefeated, did not rely on scabby victories, as they did in Italia '90, and only an over-cautious approach to the second-stage match against West Germany prevented a possible appearance in the final. West Germany's 2-0 win over Spain left England with too much to do in their own match against the hosts. The media, as ever, expected nothing short of overall victory. I can't imagine on what they base their expectations.

Italy were always going to be the winners after their incredible 3-2 win over Brazil, the match of the tournament, and one of the best ever, with Paulo Rossi scoring a hat-trick. Being an awkward git, I reacted against the excessive media hype of Brazil, a feature of most World Cups regardless of merit, and was, therefore, delighted with the Italian victory. I doubt whether anyone could have stopped their inevitable progress after that performance. It was an excellent World Cup, with worthy winners.

And then I returned to Chorley and reality. A degree did not mean a job. I was one of Maggie's millions. At first, admittedly, I had not tried terribly hard to escape her clutches. As time progressed, it became clear that I couldn't. Letter after letter of application was dispatched, and rejection after rejection was received, although many prospective employers gave no reply at all. A few interviews were endured, including two in the great city itself. None were successful. I was in for the long haul. At first, I was desperate to stay in, or at least close to, Manchester itself, but as time progressed I became merely desperate, and gradually adjusted my target geographical area accordingly.

Matters also degenerated rapidly on the football front. Trevor Francis was sold to Sampdoria, but not to worry: we didn't so much lose a star striker as gain a roof. Tricky Trevor's replacement was the undulating and incongruous construction atop the Main Stand. It stands to this day as a monument to folly. Francis and the roof were both valued at £1 million. You can see Mr Swales's point. After all, we might only have watched Trevor Francis for a few more seasons. We can still sit and admire the roof. It isn't as if the Main Stand didn't already have a roof. Still, I'm sure that this roof is a much better expression of architectural artistry than the old roof – and it undulates!

John Bond's transfer dealings smacked of a hard day's work at a car boot sale, or an evening furtively sniffing around skips. David Cross (aged 31), a bearded centre forward who scored regularly for West Ham United, but cannot by any stretch of the imagination be described as a replacement for Tricky Trevor, signed for £135,000. The long-haired Chris Jones, having made a mere six first team appearances for Spurs the previous season, was signed on a free transfer, as was Ian Davies from Newcastle. The only slightly encouraging signing was Graham Baker, a 23-year-old midfield player signed from Southampton for £225,000. He had once scored a televised debut goal that prompted an excited Barry Davies to screech, 'Oh! **yes** for the youngster!' The only other change of note was that John Ryan had been moved to the coaching staff.

The season began, therefore, in an atmosphere of general apathy. The fixture list had been kind, giving the Blues an opening day fixture away to Norwich City, followed by consecutive home matches against Stoke City and recently promoted Watford. City won all three and sat proudly at the top of the table. Let that be a cautionary lesson to you all.

At Norwich, the 'Match of the Day' cameras were there to record a 2-1 win, with David Cross scoring on his debut, after only two minutes. Paul Power scored City's second. My first sight of the Blues in the 1982/83 season was amongst a pitiful crowd of 27,847 for the Stoke match. The low turnout clearly reflected the general mood around Maine Road in the aftermath of the departure of Trevor Francis. The match itself was quite entertaining. John Bond's latest fad was to use son Kevin as a sweeper. This allowed Ray Ranson to venture forward more often. One drive from the City full-back came back off the Stoke post. The only goal of the match was scored early in the second half, when a defensive blunder by the six-foot Scot David McAughtrie was punished by David Cross, allowing us all to imagine temporarily that maybe he could replace Tricky Trevor. The woodwork was clattered at both ends of the pitch, but there were no more goals.

There was even more drama in the match against Watford, who had also won both of their opening matches. After only three minutes, Joe Corrigan dislocated his shoulder in a clash with Nigel Callaghan. That brought the game's two heroes to centre-stage. Dennis Tueart came on as substitute, for his first appearance after a long injury absence, and Bobby McDonald took over in goal, intent on thwarting the likes of John Barnes and Luther Blissett. It was a typically British, stiff upper lip response to adversity. Watford had most of the possession, but McDonald was equal to all they could muster. With 14 minutes left, an Asa Hartford corner flicked off the head of Luther Blissett, and Dennis Tueart dived in to head the winning goal. McDonald made dramatic and impressive saves to foil Gerry Armstrong and to prevent a Caton header from flying into his own net. The post did its bit by denying a John Barnes header, and the match ended amongst much euphoria. It was classic blood-and-guts entertainment, after which City found themselves two points clear at the top of the League. I recall having a night out in celebration, including a trip to the Cyprus Tavern. After a few pints, it wasn't too difficult to convince myself that maybe I was wrong, and that City were not so bad after all.

A 1-0 defeat at Notts County was a setback, but a 2-1 victory at Spurs, with both goals scored by Graham Baker, helped to maintain City's bright start. One of Baker's goals was either a fluke or a stroke of genius. It was similar to the Poborsky goal for the Czech Republic against Portugal in Euro '96, a scoop-shot over the advancing goal-keeper. I put both of them down to flukes. City's 20-year-old goalkeeper, local boy Alex Williams, responded well to his first significant run in the team, playing a star-ring role at Spurs and in City's next game, at home to Aston Villa. However, it was clear that many City fans remained unconvinced by the unexpectedly bright start to the season. Once more fewer than 30,000 spectators were there to witness the proceedings. In the absence of the injured Cross, Chris Jones made his home debut for City, but it was only when substitute Dennis Tueart entered the fray that City's attack carried any threat. Gary Shaw's first-half goal for Villa was well deserved, and only hero-ics from Alex Williams prevented a more emphatic margin of victory. A 4-1 defeat at West Ham followed to put City's early season results into perspective. Hartford and Bond were both sent off, and Alex Williams saved a penalty. By all accounts, City could have conceded eight.

Nicky Reid's return from Seattle offered some hope of defensive improvement. Hareide and Caton had been acting as markers, with Bond Junior the sweeper. Reid was not in the team that took on Coventry at Maine Road, in front of 25,105. A 16-year-old Paul Simpson was given a surprise debut on the left wing, as Paul Power re-verted to left-back. With the Blues defence in disarray early on, Scotsman Jim Mel-rose gave Coventry the lead. Baker brought City level before half-time, and an improved City scored two further goals in the second half. Tommy Caton blasted a shot into the roof of the net after Les Sealey had been penalised for taking too many steps whilst holding on to the ball, and David Cross added the third goal. Garry Thompson scored to subject the City fans to the usual uneasy last 10 minutes, but the Blues held on for all three points.

A wet Tuesday in Wigan was my first experience of City away from home in season 1982/83. The occasion was a Milk Cup second-round first leg tie at Springfield Park. Larry Lloyd was player-manager of the Third Division side, who also included Archie Gemmill in their line-up. The constant rain reduced the match to farce. Alex Williams had a busy first half as Wigan, prompted by Eamon O'Keefe, a £60,000 signing from Everton, created the best chances. City kept their feet better in the second half, and Dennis Tueart headed them into the lead. Ten minutes from the end, Tommy Caton also found the net with a header. Unfortunately this goal was scored at the wrong end. It finished in a 1-1 draw.

Back at the Academy, Corrigan, Reid and Kinsey were all in the City line-up for the visit of Sunderland. A 2-1 defeat at Goodison Park the previous week had left the Blues in seventh place. City's recent record against Sunderland was not an impressive one, and when Ally McCoist scored after 30 minutes the run looked set to continue. There was much relief early in the second half when Kevin Reeves diverted a Kinsey cross into the Sunderland goal, ending a personal goal famine. Without Francis along-side him, Reeves was a shadow of his former self. An uncharacteristic blunder by Nicky Reid led to Mick Buckley restoring Sunderland's lead. It was a cross by substitute Paul Simpson that inspired the City equaliser, another goal for David Cross. City had chances to win the match, but they failed to convert any of them.

On the 23 October 1982, I was back at *The Swamp*, behind the goal at the Scoreboard End. *The Nation's Team* led the First Division, and with eight full internationals, three Under-21 internationals and some very expensive signings in their team, there was no doubting who went into the game as favourites. In the event, this turned out to be the closest City have come to a win at *The Swamp* during my time as a card-carrying member of the Academy.

After 12 minutes, and a promising start, City scored from a Paul Power corner flicked on at the near post by Kevin Reeves. Dennis Tueart was the man who headed the Blues in front, at the Scoreboard End. City then had to withstand a number of attacks. Gordon McQueen fluffed a chance, doing, in the process, a very good impression of a clumsy oaf. In addition, Coppell fired a shot against the underside of the crossbar, and Joe Corrigan performed familiar heroics.

City began the second half brightly, but few of us expected the impressively devastating counter-attack that led to a second City goal after 47 minutes. Ranson fed the ball up to Kevin Reeves, who released Baker on a right-wing overlap, and Baker's cross was swept past Gary Bailey by David Cross. Suddenly, a win was an actual possibility, and *The Nation's Team* were visibly shaken. However, from the bowels of the earth, they conjured up a goal six minutes later, Stapleton curling a shot into the top corner of the City net: a real stomach-churner. And so, we were faced with the agony of 37 minutes attempting to hang on to a precious but slender lead. Failing to win from 2-0 was not a pleasant prospect.

The pressure mounted, the goalmouth scrambles became desperate. Robson blasted over the bar, Corrigan saved from Whiteside and Macari, and then City broke. Cross headed back across goal and Tueart had the chance to restore City's two-goal cushion. He was thwarted by a reflex save by Bailey, and the action switched back to the other end. With 10 minutes remaining, the mere thought crossed my mind that everything was becoming calmer, and that City might hold on. This unforgivable mental lapse had inevitable consequences. Stapleton prodded an equaliser over the line, despite Ranson's valiant attempts to clear, and defeat became an unbearable possibility. Joe Corrigan was called upon to make one more breathtaking save, to prevent a corner entering the net via an inadvertent deflection off the head of David Cross, but City at least held on for a bitter-sweet draw, leaving both sides the losers under the three points for a win rule.

The atmosphere was somewhat less frenetic as City cruised past Wigan in the second leg of the Milk Cup tie, with two first-half goals by Paul Power. In the match magazine for the next home game against Swansea City, Bond announced that he had given up on plans to sign Archie Gemmill, who was on a match-by-match contract at Wigan. Quite how such an acquisition would have fitted the requirements of a long-term strategy, only Mr Bond knows.

Lifted by their performance in the derby match, City gave an encouraging display against Swansea. The opening goal, after 16 minutes, was something of a classic. An indirect free-kick inside the penalty area, but at an oblique angle to goal, was cheekily flicked up by Hartford, and blasted over the wall and into the net by Dennis Tueart.

City attacked with purpose, and could have added further goals. Eventually, Asa Hartford scored City's second, but that old goal-poacher Bob Latchford replied two minutes later, to leave the Blues with another difficult final 20 minutes.

Another home match, against Southampton, brought three more points for City, propelling them into second place in the First Division table, behind only Liverpool. A mix-up between Mark Wright and Peter Shilton presented Kevin Reeves with the opportunity to put City in the lead after only 10 minutes. Although Shilton later saved a Kevin Bond penalty to keep the Saints in the game, the City near-post corner routine led to a second goal midway through the second half. Hartford's corner, flicked on by Bond, was headed in by Bobby McDonald. It all looked so simple. The match finished 2-0.

Four days later, only 17,463 turned up at Maine Road to see if City could repeat their performance against Southampton in a Milk Cup third-round tie. They couldn't. Kevin Reeves earned City a penalty, care of a clumsy Mark Wright tackle, and Dennis Tueart gave the Blues the lead. Within two minutes, Wright made amends by heading the equaliser. City had the better of the second half, but failed to add to their score. They lost the replay 4-0.

After another defeat, 0-1 away to Ipswich Town, the only cheers on a bleak November afternoon at Maine Road, in a goalless draw against Birmingham City, were provoked by a stray dog, whose pace and anticipation caused 22 grown men to abandon a game of football for 10 minutes. Referee Don Shaw took the players off the pitch as hapless officials engaged in a hearty exhibition of slapstick. When the players felt able to continue, a young Tony Coton in the Birmingham goal caught the eye as City dominated without being able to score. After his initial burst of success, David Cross was proving to be one of the main culprits in City's apparent 'shoot to miss' policy.

Despite continuous speculation concerning players on the Bond shopping list, events drifted on much the same as Christmas approached. Chris Jones departed on another free transfer, and City lost another away game, 3-0 at Forest. The visit of a meek-looking Arsenal team provided some cheer for the denizens of Maine Road. In the first half, the Blues came up against a serious wood problem. George Wood, in the Arsenal goal, appeared to attract the ball, and the wood of the crossbar prevented a Dennis Tueart overhead kick from taking us all on a pleasant trip down memory lane. Two second-half headers by Tommy Caton temporarily solved City's goalscoring problem. The second goal, a minute from the end, proved to be the winner.

David Cross ended his goal drought by scoring at Luton. Unfortunately, the home side managed the same feat on three occasions. As the Christmas fixtures arrived, City had drifted into unobtrusive mid-table. The FA Cup offered the only hope of excitement. Apart from a public falling-out between Bond and Ray Ranson, and the signing, on loan from *The Nation's Team*, of Peter Bodak, all was subdued at the Academy. With Baker injured, Bodak, a scorer in Coventry's 3-1 FA Cup win at Maine Road the previous season, and therefore not on most people's Christmas card list, made his first appearance against Brighton in another dismal match at Maine Road. The Brighton goalkeeper was called Perry Digweed, which amused me, and he generously presented Kevin Bond with a gift of a goal just before half-time. Andy Ritchie equalised and might even have won the game for Brighton who, as soon as they realised how bad City were, made a concerted effort to take all the points.

My reports were beginning to warn of dire consequences should City fail to improve, yet I doubt that I really anticipated what actually did occur. City were occupying ninth place in the League table, 11 points clear of Sunderland, Norwich and Birmingham City, the three teams occupying the dreaded relegation places. None of them ultimately suffered the indignity of relegation.

With games on consecutive days, City followed a 5-2 thrashing at Anfield with a reasonably encouraging 2-1 home win against West Bromwich Albion. Steve Kinsey, at last given an opportunity to play, celebrated by scoring City's first goal. It was a complete surprise when Ally Brown thundered a long-range equaliser. It took an own goal by captain Alistair Robertson to give the Blues a much needed win, once the agonising last few minutes had been endured.

City faced up to three consecutive away matches at the start of 1983. A 2-2 draw at Birmingham was followed by a 0-2 defeat at Watford. A 0-0 draw at Sunderland earned the Blues an FA Cup third-round replay, and at least kept hopes alive for a miracle. In the replay, City began with real determination. Kinsey and Tueart might have given the Blues the lead before Hartford scored a thirteenth-minute goal, following up after David Cross had headed against the bar. Cross himself added the second goal, five minutes before half-time, and everything seemed to be going our way. Kevin Reeves, dropped to midfield after scoring only twice all season, emphasised his determination not to score by hammering a shot against the crossbar early in the second half. Dennis Tueart also struck the frame of the goal as City endeavoured to make the tie safe. However, a stunning goal by Gordon Chisholm was the signal for normal service to be resumed. The nomadic Frank Worthington, collecting yet another club, came close to an equaliser, and referee Joe Worrall contributed to the torture by adding four minutes of injury time for no apparent reason. But City held on.

On 15 January 1983, Norwich City, captained by Martin O'Neill, and including the on-loan Aage Hareide, were on the receiving end of a rare comfortable City win in a match of reunions. Even Mike Channon, a second-half substitute, made an appearance. He did not get a friendly reception. David Cross and Kevin Bond both scored with headers in the opening 15 minutes. Cross added another, before O'Neill's deflected free-kick gave Norwich some encouragement. In the second half, Kinsey struck the bar, but Hartford was more accurate, scoring City's fourth and final goal. With Reid back at the centre of the defence, Cross back amongst the goals, Kinsey looking lively, and Bodak providing some good service from the wing, things were looking up, right? Wrong.

City were in eighth place after the Norwich match, and although they dropped to tenth following a 1-1 draw away to Aston Villa, the Blues seemed to be safe in mid-table. Due partly to lack of funds, I was unable to get to many away matches in season 1982/83. There may have been other reasons. There was an atmosphere of general disillusionment around Maine Road. The crowds had fallen to around 22,000. The club seemed to be drifting and there was little enthusiasm for the matches. Of course, the FA Cup competition could have changed all of that.

On 29 January 1983, I was driving my dad's car back from a night out in Alsager at the same time as City were playing their FA Cup fourth-round tie at Brighton. I somehow managed to keep my concentration on the M6 as goal after goal went in. The match had hardly begun before it was all over for City. They lost 4-0 to a struggling team. It was a woeful performance. In the next match programme, Bond called the display 'disastrous' and proceeded to slag the whole team off, exempting only Corrigan and Reid. The programme notes were obviously written well before the game, against Spurs at Maine Road on Saturday, 5 February 1983. Two days earlier, to everyone's amazement, Bond had decided to resign as City manager. He was in charge for just under two years and four months. In his statement Bond said, 'I feel I have done as much as I can at this club. It would be wrong to stay and risk the chance of everything going sour.' He obviously had a highly effective sourness detector kit.

John Benson, Bond's assistant, was promoted to acting manager, with Tony Book, forever hovering in the background, his assistant. With only 17 matches remaining, finding a new manager was not going to be an easy matter. City still looked comfortable in mid-table, 10 points clear of the relegation zone. There didn't seem to be a need to rush through a permanent appointment. Most people were glad to see the back of Bond, although his timing could have been better.

I've been struggling to find the metaphor that adequately describes City's decline following the FA Cup exit. For those of you who watch 'Ski Sunday' because you can't be bothered to reach for the remote control, I want you to imagine that the Scandinavian in the horrifically lurid, snug-fitting lycra outfit, with the sticks in his hands, is poised at the top of the slope, rocking back and forth in readiness to set off. That represents the position that City occupied prior to the fateful Brighton game. Now, imagine if you will the couple of minutes after the signal to go, with the enthusiastic, yodelling noises of the crowd ringing in your ears. That just about sums up City's progress for the remainder of season 1982/83, only without the yodelling.

The decline was gentle to begin with. The first post-Bond match, against Spurs, was dominated by City. Cross smacked a shot against a post, and McDonald headed against the crossbar, but Spurs, who had themselves threatened occasionally on the break, rather selfishly took the lead with a penalty, after the lively Gibson had been felled. Two astonishing misses by David Cross followed, before Gibson added a second Spurs goal with only 14 minutes remaining. Cross finally found his heading range, only for Steve Perryman to intervene with a hand. Tueart's penalty gave City hope, and although Cross once more missed the target with a header, he followed up the rebound from the crossbar to rescue a point in a 2-2 draw.

This apparent display of fighting spirit from City was short-lived. After an emphatic 4-0 defeat at Coventry, the Blues gave a lethargic and feeble performance against Notts County at Maine Road. One of the rare scoring opportunities in a truly dismal match fell to Justin Fashanu, a transfer target for Bond earlier in the season. Fashanu's free-header, from an eighty-first minute corner, almost awoke the crowd and sank City further into the mire.

Caton and Reeves, the latter ending a run of 20 matches without a goal, both scored at Sunderland. Unfortunately, the home side scored three. Despite the slump, the Blues still maintained a 10-point lead over those occupying the relegation zone when Everton visited Maine Road on 2 March 1983. However, with three points for a win, and most of those below having games in hand, some reassurance from two consecutive home matches would have been welcome. City could hardly be faulted for effort against Everton, but they rarely looked like scoring. The best chance fell to Everton's David Johnson, who somehow managed to pick out the one defender on the line after Corrigan had made an initial save from a youthful Graeme Sharp.

Three days later City were faced with a vital derby match at Maine Road. *The Nation's Team* were third in the League, but not offering a serious threat to Liverpool. The match was of far greater importance to City. Heroics were required. 45,400 people were expectant.

The City players tried their hardest to deny the opposition time and space, and in the first half it worked well. Kevin Reeves headed the Blues into the lead in a match of limited opportunities, and an inspired performance looked possible. In the second half it all went horribly wrong. Rare indecision by Joe Corrigan allowed Stapleton to head the equaliser. Suddenly Corrigan was a busy man, making two excellent saves. And then another Stapleton header somehow squeezed between Corrigan and Hartford on the City goal line, and the Blues were left facing calamity. To add to the pain of an unhappy afternoon, Tommy Caton thundered a shot against the frame of the goal in the final minute.

There was little evidence of spirited resistance in the two away games that followed. Matches against Swansea and Southampton both ended 4-1. City were in free fall. In search of financial security at the end of an illustrious career, Joe Corrigan departed to Seattle Sounders, leaving the goalkeeping position in the safe hands of Alex Williams. The problem was the rest of the team. Ivan Golac was taken on loan. Geoff Lomax was handed a debut at left-back. Andy May was in and out of the side. Nothing, however, seemed to prevent the general atmosphere of gloom and self-pity pervading the playing staff. There had been some injury problems, notably Kinsey, and frequent suspensions, but little to account for such a dramatic collapse.

The home defeat by mid-table Ipswich Town had more than a hint of inevitability about it. After Joe Corrigan had said his fond farewell, his successor got a taste of life as a City goalkeeper, making a number of athletic saves, particularly from the Ipswich captain, Paul Mariner. There was nothing Williams could do about John Wark's second-half goal. Disconcertingly, one goal always looked sufficient, and so it proved.

At Easter, City finally ended their dismal run of 11 matches without a win, registering a surprising 2-0 victory away to West Bromwich Albion. Unfortunately, the fixture list ensured that the revival would be short-lived. Back at Maine Road two days later, Liverpool were due for their annual humiliation of City. Right from the beginning, despite the best efforts of Bruce Grobbelaar, both sets of players seemed to assume that Liverpool would win comfortably. After kicking-off, the visitors kept the ball for a good two minutes without allowing a City player a touch. Whelan's header, narrowly clearing the bar, at least allowed the Blues to join in. Surprisingly, it took 31 minutes for a Souness thunderbolt to open the scoring. Grobbelaar almost equalised for City, but it was Fairclough, deputising for Ian Rush, who scored the second goal, just before half-time.

Alex Williams was virtually the only City player offered the chance to shine, and he did. He was helped out by the post when Fairclough broke through yet again. With the completely out of sorts Baker replaced by May, City began to indicate some interest in making a contribution to the match. At the very least, they threatened to keep the score respectable for once. It was all to no avail. Two goals in the final seven minutes, from Kennedy and Fairclough, ended any such unfounded optimism. It was business as usual.

I made the trip to the Victoria Ground hopeful of some improvement. The need for points was becoming desperate. The teams below were getting closer, and the games in hand were still available. City matched Stoke in the opening half but, on the hour, ex-*Nation's Team* player, Sammy McIlroy, scored right in front of the City fans, after Mark Chamberlain's cross had been cleverly dummied by Paul Bracewell. The Blues enjoyed their brightest moments late in the match. A David Cross header flicked off two Stoke players, including goalkeeper Fox, before smacking the crossbar and flying clear. Tommy Caton volleyed over the goal from close-range. Paul Power had a goal disallowed for offside. It had been a reasonable effort. Unfortunately, only the result mattered.

Time was running out. The winner of the Miss Manchester City contest, Hadfield-housewife Margaret Bray, had already been announced. Anything short of victory over West Ham at Maine Road was unthinkable. John Benson dropped David Cross and Graham Baker, returned Dennis Tueart to the midfield, and pushed Reeves back into attack alongside Kinsey. For once, a City manager got something right. Bobby McDonald headed the first goal after 13 minutes and, eight minutes later, a handball by Billy Bonds offered Tueart the opportunity to extend City's lead from the penalty spot. This he did emphatically, and the Blues were in the unaccustomed position of leading 2-0. Kinsey and Reeves both came close to securing the points in the second half, but there were worrying moments. Alex Williams was forced to make a spectacular save from a Ray Stewart free-kick but, mercifully, West Ham failed to score. The cavalry, it seemed, were in sight.

A 3-0 defeat at Arsenal caused a few cavalry to fall off their horses, leaving City with another anxiety-ridden afternoon at Maine Road, against Nottingham Forest. An early goal, scored with a crisp, low shot by Ian Wallace, did nothing to ease the apprehension. Hartford, McDonald and Kinsey all squandered chances to bring the Blues level before half-time, but their best opportunity followed a dropped-ball in the Forest penalty area, early in the second half. When the ball fell fortunately for Asa Hartford, he blasted it against the Forest goalkeeper, van Breukelen, and it squirted agonisingly wide of the post. Soon afterwards, Forest broke quickly and John Robertson found Davenport, who scored the second goal. Kevin Bond, playing as a makeshift centre forward, struck a shot against the Forest crossbar, and created the opportunity for Baker to score. Despite a passionate final 20 minutes, City couldn't force an equaliser, and things looked bleak indeed. Many of the cavalry had stopped off for a few pints or were now heading in completely the wrong direction.

In the penultimate match of the season, a miracle appeared to occur. The cavalry were put on standby as Kevin Reeves headed a late winner to relegate Brighton and capture three vital points for City at the Goldstone Ground. I listened to the match on the radio with an air of detachment, but was suffering intense, internal turmoil. With City's win at Brighton, the mist cleared. Swansea and Brighton were doomed, and the final place was between City and Luton Town. As long as Luton failed to get any points from their game in hand, at Old Trafford of all places, City would require only a draw in their last match of the season. This would be at Maine Road and against Luton Town.

I don't know what possessed me to do it, but I actually stood in the Scoreboard Paddock, amongst the RAGS, to watch *The Nation's Team* defeat Luton 3-0 on the Wednesday before City's crucial relegation decider. I went along with a fan of the enemy. I've known him since childhood, but it was still a strange and uncomfortable experience. To them, it was just another win, a formality, lacking in importance. There was never any real doubt about the outcome, although *The Nation's Team* were a bit slow to take the lead, and Paul Walsh scurried about threateningly at times for Luton. It was a good result for City.

Saturday, 14 May 1983 was a sunny day. A crowd of 40,000 turned up to watch City take on Luton Town, requiring only a draw for First Division survival. The match attracted much media attention since most other issues had already been decided. There was an air of unreality as City kicked towards the North Stand in the first half. Neither side felt able to play much football. The stakes were too high and the tackles were often even higher.

Half-time was reached without much incident. Alex Williams had dealt well with Luton's brighter moments, and although the match was, to say the least, delicately poised, City looked capable of surviving. This was the first time for many years that the Blues had entered their final match of the season in danger of relegation. It was uncharted territory for players and fans alike. Yet as the game progressed, City seemed to improve. They were striving for a goal that would surely prove decisive. Attacking the Platt Lane End, there were a number of close calls, most involving Dennis Tueart, but the ball wouldn't quite run for us. As the final phase of the match approached, there was an ever-diminishing threat from Luton. They were more or less resigned to their fate. Paul Walsh had darted around, and Brian Horton had battled in midfield, but their time was just about up. Into the last 10 minutes we went. It was agonising, but it would soon be over.

And then, with only four minutes remaining, disaster struck. A hopeful cross from the right was partly cleared by Alex Williams to the feet of the Luton substitute, Raddy

Antic, outside the penalty area. Williams was back on his feet when Antic struck an unconvincing shot. The ball was deflected past the City goalkeeper and into the net. I had never experienced such overwhelming shock in a large crowd. The magnitude of the silence argued against the reality of what had happened. Yet Luton players and officials were jumping around in celebration, and the ball was back on the centre spot for City to kick-off. There was a small band of Luton fans crammed into the top corner of the Kippax, at the junction with the Platt Lane End, and I'm sure that they were cheering, but I could hear nothing. What remained of the cavalry had just gambled away their horses after an ill-advised session with a bunch of ruthless dominoes sharks.

After the goal had been scored, I decided not to watch the remainder of the match, preferring instead to hide my face in my hands. I suppose that I was offering up a sacrifice to the gods of football. I would forego the pleasure of seeing a goal. My reward was supposed to be that City would score one. I didn't actually know what to do.

There was crowd noise suggesting one or two near things. Then there was another, less striking version of the ominous silence. The match was over. I threw my programme to the floor and walked out of the ground immediately. I didn't see David Pleat's jig of delight, still replayed frequently on television – almost as often as Ricardo Villa's goal. I'll never know how he escaped a lynching. I've disliked the man intensely ever since. He was dancing on the grave of my club.

Raddy Antic turned up as manager of Atletico Madrid, steering them to a League and Cup double in 1996. His period in English football was unremarkable, apart from this one fateful contribution. I wonder if he realises the significance of his deflected goal. It had a profound effect on me. The unthinkable had happened. I could never again trust my team.

I didn't really require this additional opportunity to be miserable. I was without a job, the great British public had inexplicably reinstated the same despicable government, and now my team were relegated. On top of that, my love life had taken a turn for the worse. 1983 was not turning out to be a year to remember with any fondness.

Actually, thinking about it, I reckon it was around this time that our cat died as well. I should have written a country and western song about it. After all, there are plenty of rhymes for relegation. **Relegation** – I simply couldn't believe it. I didn't think that City could be relegated. I didn't think that it was actually possible for that to happen to a club like City. All my previous faith and beliefs were shattered. It really was the worse thing that had happened to me, and believe me, I took it very personally. It called for one almighty and sustained sulk, and I wallowed in self-pity for some considerable time, milking it for as long as possible, before I got bored.

How dare they get relegated? How dare they? My reports ceased from that moment. That was my retaliation! It was the best I could do.

Part Two: The Dark Ages

Jim Tolmie: hands up, if you like the hair.

Season 1983/84: Jim Tolmie's Hair

Looking on the bright side, not a habit in which I often indulge, 1983 was not a bad year for music. There were good albums from New Order, David Bowie (his last), The The and Cabaret Voltaire. 'The Tube' was a breath of fresh air on television, and The Smiths phenomenon was about to take hold of an unsuspecting world. This was also the year when I gave up my attempts to find a proper job and went back to student life, resigned to three more years in the hope of a PhD. If that didn't get me a job, I would have to resort to accountancy. I am *trying* to stay on the bright side.

The timing of my decision had a strong influence on my eventual destination. Initially, of course, I had hoped to stay in Manchester. Failing that, I had hoped to stay within 50 miles of Manchester. Eventually, I had to settle for 100 miles. I had been working on the assumption that the 100 miles could easily be bridged by rail or road. Unfortunately, I ended up in Bangor, North Wales, at the very limit of my exclusion zone, and with the slowest imaginable rail link to Manchester. Making the journey by motorised vehicle wasn't much of an alternative. The North Wales roads seemed specially designed for maximising traffic jams.

This new life was to begin in October 1983. My only previous experience of Bangor involved a lazy afternoon spent lounging around on an immobile raft in the Menai Straits, listening to a Cricket World Cup match on the radio whilst my girlfriend did something scientific with algae. I don't recall much about it, except that Graeme Fowler was out cheaply.

I left my accommodation-hunting a little late. I remember driving around the city in my dad's green Mini, listening to the excellent 'Chimera' by Bill Nelson (a short LP or a long EP), but failing to find anywhere suitable. There was a vacancy for a lodger with a devout family of chapelgoers, but for some reason this did not appeal to me. Reluctantly, I settled, at least temporarily, for Neuadd Emrys Evans, a hall of residence founded by old Emrys himself. He was clearly a cheerful soul. No women were allowed on the premises and no bar was permitted. Once the arrangements were made, I spent the remainder of my time in Chorley trying to forget that I would soon be departing for pastures new.

Throughout the summer of 1983, I did my utmost to pretend that relegation had been a bad dream. Then they published the fixture lists, and I was confronted with the unpalatable truth. The only consolation was the thought that City would spend a season brushing aside the inferior opposition of the Second Division and storm back into the top division. Does that sound familiar?

The Blues were instantly installed as promotion favourites. In fact, whenever Manchester City are about to begin a season outside the top division, they are *always* favourites for promotion. I didn't know that back in 1983. I could therefore give the sage predictions some credence. There were, however, nagging doubts about the reliability of such optimistic prognostications.

Malcolm Allison's transfer dealings had left the club in dire financial straits at the very moment when they were embarking on ambitious stadium plans. With their usual excellent timing, City had indulged in their spending spree at the peak of an expanding transfer market. It brings a whole new meaning to the phrase 'shop 'til you drop'. By 1983, football had entered a stage where a certain amount of reality was restored to the transfer market, too late to be of any benefit to City. John Bond's legacy to the Blues consisted of far too many players approaching the end of their career, and a squad lacking any depth. Soon after the season's end, Kevin Reeves was mysteriously dispatched to Burnley for a nominal fee. The decision had been driven by the necessity to reduce the wage bill. Although Reeves was not a prolific goalscorer, he was a player with more ability than most others at the club. The deal did little to cheer me up. Dennis Tueart also departed, for the second time.

On the face of it, the new season was not to be greeted with much relish. The one slightly positive occurrence of an otherwise depressing summer was the appointment of Billy McNeill, a big name at Celtic as both player and manager. McNeill was well known and respected. I can only imagine that Peter Swales didn't reveal to him the full extent of the Manchester City piggy bank crisis. The man obviously appreciated a challenge. The restoration of Manchester City's fortunes was certainly a challenging task, on a par with, say, world peace and the eradication of poverty.

The arrival of Billy McNeill prompted an invasion of Scottish hordes. Jimmy Frizzell left Oldham Athletic to become McNeill's assistant. The new management regime then used their insider knowledge of all things Caledonian to make a few canny acquisitions. Neil McNab, a combative midfield player purchased for £30,000 from Brighton, proved to be a long-term bargain. The immediate priority, however, was to buy a forward-line, and the unlikely pairing chosen was Derek Parlane, on a free transfer, and Jim Tolmie, who cost £30,000 and sported a hairstyle so unfashionable that it was almost trendsetting. Parlane, a Rangers stalwart for many years, and a former Scottish international, was in the twilight of his career. He signed from Leeds United, where his contribution had not lived up to expectations. On the face of it, this was a John Bond kind of signing, but at least Parlane was free.

Jim Tolmie, short, with ginger hair and a wispy moustache, looked like he had been dragged backwards through some gorse bushes. The mop-headed Columbian international, Carlos Valderrama, probably used a photograph of Jim Tolmie as his inspiration. There was never any difficulty in picking Tolmie out on a football field. Signed from the Belgian club Lokeren, having played previously for Morton, the 22-year-old was an obscure figure for the Maine Road Faithful. This can be advantageous for new players. Nobody had any preconceived ideas about Tolmie. Nobody had any idea who Tolmie was.

Newcomers always create interest and, despite the calamity of the previous season, as the day approached it was hard not to look forward to the season with some anticipation, if not enthusiasm. The fixture list had a strange look about it. There were, of course, a number of clubs in Division Two against which City were unaccustomed to competing. The Blues were, however, by no means the only big club fallen on hard times. City would be up against Newcastle United, complete with Kevin Keegan, Chelsea, Sheffield Wednesday and Leeds United.

The season began for City with consecutive away matches on 27 and 29 August 1983. Parlane scored on his debut as the Blues won 2-0 at Crystal Palace. Tolmie registered his first goal at Cardiff City in the second match, but it wasn't sufficient to prevent a 2-1 defeat. My first view of the new City was a home match against Barnsley on 3 September 1983, in front of a crowd of 25,105. The slimmer but more expensive match magazine (now priced 40 pence) had the management team on the front cover and the three new Scottish players on the back cover. The reality of the Second Division was brought home by looking at the team line-ups. Mick McCarthy was still the Barnsley captain, and there were one or two players whom I had vaguely heard of, but this definitely wasn't what I was accustomed to. City won the match 3-2. It wasn't terribly convincing, but Jim Tolmie was an instant hit with the fans, scoring twice and looking very much the part of the maverick eccentric. Tolmie's curling free-kick, the opening Maine Road goal of the season, was the lift that the Faithful were looking for. Parlane scored the other goal.

McNeill was quick to reduce the Scottish contingent after falling out with Bobby McDonald, who departed without experiencing a single Division Two match in City colours. Andy May, sporting a blond hairstyle which suggested an imminent audition for Wham!, took the left-back position.

The second home match, a 0-0 draw against Fulham, was less inspiring, but a 2-1 win at Portsmouth ensured that City were featuring amongst the leading sides. Jim Tolmie proved that he could take penalties, and Parlane scored again, to further justify McNeill's faith in his bargain-basement striking partnership.

The next match, at home to Blackburn Rovers, was of particular importance to me. There were friends from school days who had been waiting a very long time for this opportunity. Blackburn, before Jack Walker's money, had been no higher than Division Two for many years. City had always been in the First Division. In my time the two teams had not met. If Blackburn Rovers beat Manchester City now, nobody, least of all me, is surprised. In 1983, it was a frightful prospect, an indignity not to be contemplated. The day could hardly have gone better for me. It seemed that everything City tried worked. Blackburn didn't actually play that badly, but the Blues won 6-0, with Parlane scoring a hat-trick and Tolmie amongst the other goalscorers. An evening of unbridled smugness was guaranteed.

A 2-1 win at Leeds cemented City's second place in the League table as the day of my trip to Bangor finally arrived. City's good start to the season made the whole prospect far more palatable. It also offered me considerable sustenance when, having ascertained what Bangor had to offer, I plunged into post-traumatic culture shock. Where were the clubs? What did everyone do after 11 o'clock? Where were the people who had even heard of The Fall? Even the students at Bangor knew nothing of the culture to which I had become so accustomed. Pretty much the only bands to play Bangor were Lindisfarne and, a few weeks later, well, Lindisfarne again. Yes, there were hills, but I was only 22 years old. I didn't want hills!

Plenty of students chose Bangor for the rock-climbing, a pastime which, like Rugby Union, attracted more than its fair share of boisterous buffoons. They were full of japes and merriment, which largely took the form of drinking games, a propensity for trouser-dropping, and an unhealthy over-keenness to assemble naked human pyramids at the slightest provocation. All in all, I reckoned they were best avoided. It is little wonder that the locals were not too enamoured with the invading student population.

Trips to the football quickly became my link with civilisation as I saw it. Despite the interminable train journeys and my lack of motorised transport, in the interests of maintaining my sanity I paid regular visits to Manchester for home matches and cultural enlightenment. Luckily, I still knew plenty of people to stay with in the great city, and my overgenerous parents often lent me their car, especially if there were matches on consecutive weekends. The result was that I was able to see just about all of the City home matches. When it's over 100 miles to a home game, and you're not exactly swimming in cash, away matches become less of a priority.

To save money, and because it was a rip-off, I stopped buying the match magazine regularly. I had also finally abandoned my anorak-esque habit of writing reports on matches. These reports had been getting shorter. The relegation was the excuse I needed to give them up altogether. I rely heavily, therefore, on memory for this period of City's history. In more ways than one, the next five years represented, for me, the Manchester City dark ages.

The City team still had many familiar faces. Alex Williams was ever-present in goal. Ray Ranson was the first choice right-back, with youngster Geoff Lomax making occasional appearances. Left-back was more of a problem for the City management. Andy May was relied upon to fill the position for much of the season, with Ian Davies and Clive Wilson also making occasional appearances. Tommy Caton was partnered by Kevin Bond who, freed from his father's baggage, was less a target of fan disgruntlement, and had a pretty good season. That's the warmest praise that I can manage for the fruit of John Bond's loins. As far as I was concerned, Bond Senior carried most of the blame for our predicament.

Asa Hartford suffered early season injury, leaving the main midfield duties to McNab and Power, still the captain. The other positions were less fixed. Graham Baker and Nicky Reid were the main occupants in the first half of the season. To begin with there was no dispute about the striking positions, which were occupied with some distinction by Parlane and Tolmie.

On 1 October 1983, Jim Tolmie was a goalscorer once more as City beat Grimsby 2-1 at Maine Road, and maintained their strong early challenge. Parlane had already scored seven goals in his first seven League matches, and he was on hand once more to sweep Paul Power's cross into the net against Swansea, in City's next home game. The lead was lost when Bob Latchford took advantage of an unescorted moment in the City penalty area to bring Swansea level before half-time. It took a late goal from substitute, and latest Scottish recruit, Duncan Davidson to secure three more points for City.

Another narrow home victory, 2-1 against Middlesbrough, helped to make amends for a 1-0 defeat away to Charlton. By now, one or two changes were being forced due to injury and suspensions. The tall, blond and frighteningly awful Mike Walsh stepped in for a few matches at centre half, in the absence of Reid and Bond. On 29 October

1983, City fans and players received their first major jolt of the season. The Blues were hammered 5-0 at St James's Park by the Newcastle of the Keegan and Beardsley era.

With Nicky Reid stepping back into the defence, and Kinsey making a goalscoring return to the team, City won 3-1 at Shrewsbury to return to second place, but unwelcome doubts were beginning to obscure the earlier optimism. Parlane and Tolmie were still scoring goals. There was a goal each in a more reassuring 4-0 home win over Brighton. This followed a 3-0 exit at Villa Park in the Milk Cup, but to be quite honest, I didn't really care at all about the Milk Cup. Season 1983/4 was only about promotion. Nothing else mattered.

The contenders were already emerging. Sheffield Wednesday, Chelsea and Newcastle had all chosen this season to do their impersonation of awakening giants. City had already been thrashed by Newcastle. A home draw against Derby County and a 2-0 defeat at Carlisle did not appear to be an auspicious build-up to consecutive matches against the other two leading sides. When the Blues took on Chelsea at Stamford Bridge on 3 December 1983, I was still lying in bed with a Pernod-induced hangover of monumental proportions. I haven't touched the horrible stuff since.

There was some consolation to be had from the regular reports on BBC Radio Two. One of the major disadvantages of leaving the North-West was the impossibility of picking up the relevant local radio stations. Now that City were in Division Two, it was not always easy to get information about matches as they were in progress, but on this occasion even the 'Match of the Day' cameras were at Stamford Bridge to record City's 1-0 win. This was due entirely to a stunning free-kick by Jim Tolmie, and totally unmerited, by all accounts. I was well beyond the stage where I cared about merit. The recuperative qualities of the win were such that I even felt able to progress to solids. City were back in second place.

On 10 December, there were 41,862 people at Maine Road to see the Blues take on top-of-the-table Sheffield Wednesday. It was played in the aftermath of Tommy Caton's transfer to Arsenal for £460,000. The only new signing to compensate, another bargain-basement Scot, Gordon Dalziel, was a midfield player. Andy May was moved to centre half in a reshuffled defence. This was not a good time for experimentation. Wednesday, under manager Howard Wilkinson, were well organised and brimming with experience. It says much of Wilkinson's managerial ability that players like Gary Megson and Imre Varadi, scorer of a spectacular goal, were able to look so impressive. City were always struggling, and eventually lost 2-1. There was an ugly mood amongst the crowd. On the way out of the ground, one of my friends, who was wearing a non-committal scarf to counteract the cold, was attacked by a City thug for making the mistake of becoming temporarily detached from the rest of us. It was an unhappy day. City dropped to fourth place. There were only three automatic promotion places.

It was becoming apparent that promotion at the first attempt was crucial for the Blues. I could not tolerate another season of the two City promotion songs. Song Number One (to the tune of 'Give It Up' by K.C. and the Sunshine Band) went:

'Na, na, na, na, na, na, na, na, na, na, na,
City's goin' up, goin' up, City's goin' uh-up!'

Song Number Two (to the tune of 'Karma Chameleon' by Culture Club) was:

'Karma, karma, karma, karma, karma, come on City,
We're goin' up, we're goin', uh-uh-uh-up!'

Billy McNeill's pre-Christmas present to the fans, and the replacement for Tommy Caton, was Mick McCarthy (signed for £200,000). He was Barnsley-born and mostly bred – presumably there was some hint of Irish ancestry – and quite possibly chiselled out of granite, nutty slack, or some such suitable northern substance indicative of hard but unsophisticated Second Division central defenders. McCarthy made his debut in a goalless draw at Cambridge, in front of a crowd of 5,204. Nearly 36,000 saw his first Maine Road appearance for City, against Oldham Athletic on Boxing Day. It was actually McCarthy's second Maine Road match of the season. He had featured in the opening home fixture as Barnsley captain.

There were a number of reunions associated with the Oldham game. Kenny Clements was the Latics captain, Roger Palmer their leading goalscorer, and both Tony Henry and David Cross were in the Oldham side, as was Mark Ward, signed by Latics from Northwich Victoria for £10,000. Jimmy Frizzell's replacement as manager was another ex-City player, Joe Royle. There were, no doubt, a few scores to settle. The most telling contribution came from Steve Kinsey, who scored one goal and made the other as City won 2-0. Kinsey's appearance was a boost to City's attack. The striking partnership of Tolmie and Parlane was no longer functioning as well as it had in the early weeks of the season.

The holiday break gave me my first real opportunity of seeing City away from home. There was a bumper crowd at Leeds Road on 27 December 1983 as City sought a second win on consecutive days, against Huddersfield Town. The grim, old stadium, now defunct, looked like it belonged to another era altogether, but at least there was some shelter at the back of the Main Stand. Steve Kinsey, whose pace was too much for the unsuspecting Huddersfield defence, was again the inspiration behind City taking an early two-goal lead, Kinsey scoring the first himself. The other seasonal success, Geoff Lomax, scored a fluke goal, direct from a second-half cross as City went on to win 3-1 and force their way back into the promotion places. On New Year's Eve, I made a return trip to Oakwell on a cold and crisp day. City took a first-half lead through Derek Parlane, and with Barnsley old boy McCarthy looking reassuringly solid at the centre of the City defence, a third consecutive win looked likely. A late equaliser for the home side prevented it.

Although Jim Tolmie found the net for the first time in six matches, against Leeds on 2 January 1984, albeit from a penalty kick, City could only draw 1-1. Newcastle were able, once more, to displace City in the top three.

The FA Cup visit to Blackpool, on 7 January 1984, was memorable for all the wrong reasons. It seemed to me that the home side had sold far too many tickets for the enclosed stand, in which I was to spend a most uncomfortable couple of hours. Even before the game began, it was apparent that the space available was not sufficient for the numbers of standing spectators, who were crushed up against barriers and fences at the front, and a solid but rather decrepit-looking wall at the back. The roof above us didn't look particularly secure. General feelings of security were not helped by the fact that bits of it were encouraged to detach themselves by some alleged City fans with imbecilic tendencies. In addition, the exits were few and inaccessible once you were caught in the crush. Some fans sought escape by climbing over the fences and on to the pitch area. The police tried to stop them, and the incidents were reported as minor pitch invasions in the media. This was a taste of genuine disasters to come.

I saw little of the game itself, except how badly Mike Walsh played as a stand-in defender. There were own goals at either end, neither of which I saw clearly, and Blackpool emerged as 2-1 winners. My major concern had been to stay on my feet. When the game ended and the crowd began to disperse, the uppermost feeling was one of relief. An early exit from the FA Cup was nothing to be concerned about. We really did want to concentrate on the League. Honestly.

A 3-1 home win against Crystal Palace restored City to the top three and set everything up nicely for my first visit to Ewood Park. I was staying in Manchester at the time, and made the trip with a fellow-sufferer. I hadn't anticipated the sheer volume of traffic making the same journey, or the complete absence of anywhere to park once you got to Blackburn itself. By the time we had reached the turnstiles, there was a considerable queue and the game was already under way. I knew that City's 6-0 win earlier in the season would give me considerable protection from any baiting Blackburn fans, but I was keen that City should not lose this match, not least because of the urgent requirement for points. It was a blow, therefore, to receive the clear message that Blackburn had taken the lead.

We got into the ground in time to see Jim Tolmie win and convert a slightly fortunate penalty to equalise for City before half-time. In a scrappy second half, the referee compensated Blackburn with an even more dubious penalty award that proved to be decisive. Blackburn won the match 2-1 and I trudged back to the car to join the traffic jam.

I was once more reduced to listening out for scores on the radio when the Blues drew 1-1 at Grimsby in their next match. There was talk of a possible Paul Power goal that crossed the line but wasn't given. All that matters is that it wasn't given. Back at Maine Road, City were able to beat Portsmouth 2-1, but the tension was mounting. Tolmie again scored from a penalty. It had been two months since his last goal from open play.

On 18 February 1984, City lost a crucial Maine Road match against Newcastle, the team to which they could least afford to lose. A crowd of 41,767 turned up to will a victory, but City were unable to cope with the quicker and more confident visitors. Despite a Kinsey goal, City lost 2-1, with too many players looking jaded and lacking in confidence. The reality was becoming all too apparent. City were not good enough to finish in the top three.

A nervous 1-0 win over Shrewsbury at Maine Road kept the Blues in contact, with Nicky Reid scoring the only goal, but two consecutive away draws were not what was required. On 17 March 1984, City lost 5-1 to Fulham. I didn't see the match, but it must rank as one of City's worst performances. A home win against Cardiff was followed by a home defeat against Charlton as City's erratic and increasingly unconvincing form continued. A 2-0 win at Swansea City, featured on 'Match of the Day,' provided some last vestiges of hope. Parlane scored his first goal for two months, his left foot redirecting a Steve Kinsey cross into the Swansea net. Kinsey himself volleyed the spectacular second goal, to give City a half-time lead that they maintained. The Blues were now trailing third-placed Newcastle by seven points, and were only ahead of fifth-placed Grimsby Town on goal difference.

Parlane scored again in a 3-1 home victory over Carlisle United, a match that also featured a first City goal by another Scot, Gordon Smith. Smith, a £35,000 buy from Brighton, was the man famous for missing the chance to score a last-minute winner in the 1983 FA Cup Final against *The Nation's Team*, not a contribution to the history of football likely to endear him to the Faithful at Maine Road.

At least the win over Carlisle kept City's hopes alive, and the gap down to four points, as they entered the Easter period requiring maximum points from matches at Boundary Park, against Oldham, and at Maine Road against Huddersfield. In fact, Easter finished City off. My first visit to Boundary Park was to witness a lively match with plenty of excitement and four goals. Unfortunately, a 2-2 draw was simply not good enough

Back at Maine Road on Easter Monday, Huddersfield Town, featuring Mark Lillis in attack, played the kind of fearless football that only a side in comfortable mid-table can still afford as the end of the season approaches. The Blues, on the other hand, were nervous wrecks, wrapped in their own apprehension and carrying the burden of a large, desperate and imploring crowd. The visitors swept into a two-goal lead. In an act of unprecedented generosity, referee Derek Owen took pity on the suffering City players and awarded two penalties, both dubious, late in the first half. Tolmie, who had missed from the spot against Carlisle, and was suffering a severe confidence crisis, had been replaced as penalty-taker by Kevin Bond, who dispatched both to send City into the dressing room level at half-time. The kindness shown in allowing City back into the game was ultimately wasted. City were still unable to produce any kind of form, and the Huddersfield players, with the extra spur of the injustice suffered, restored their lead and deservedly won 3-2.

City's promotion challenge petered out with a whimper. The final nail was hammered emphatically into the coffin by second-placed Chelsea, who played at Maine Road on Friday, 4 May 1984. This was the first City League game to be featured live on terrestrial television. This was the day when Manchester City's long and appalling record of live terrestrial television humiliation commenced. Chelsea, with chief tormentor Pat Nevin amongst the scorers, were in celebratory mood as they won 2-0 against a dispirited City.

On my part, it had required some ingenious skiving to make a 7.15 kick-off time, but I succeeded and received my usual reward. There was, at least, the solace of a night out in Manchester. I went off with some friends to the Cyprus Tavern to indulge in a touch of consolatory, late night drinking. It became apparent that a large party of Chelsea fans had also happened upon the place. According to not terribly reliable sources, they had actually booked in advance. I was booked to sleep on the floor of a friend in Chandos Hall, and luckily for me, when he felt a bit ill and wanted to leave at midnight, I had to go with him. The following day I learned that within minutes of our leaving, the place had been stormed by irate City fans, many of whom often frequented the establishment, and some of whom resented their displacement by Chelsea fans. I dare say that the 2-0 defeat did not help. Suffice to say, there was an OK Corral-type fracas, which I was quite happy not to have witnessed.

Chelsea, along with Sheffield Wednesday and Newcastle, had broken clear at the top of the table. City managed to hold Wednesday to a goalless draw in their last away match of the season, and completed their fixtures with an emphatic 5-0 win over relegated Cambridge United at Maine Road. With the battle over, the confidence had returned. Even Jim Tolmie got himself on the scoresheet. This last match of the season was the only home League match that I missed. I simply couldn't whip up the enthusiasm for spending more money on the train to Manchester for what was a futile fixture.

The season had ended in great anticlimax. City finished in fourth place, but they may as well have been fourteenth. The outcome was the same. It would be another season of Second Division football to come, and another season of those football chants. Looking back with the considerable benefit of hindsight, Billy McNeill had done a remarkable job to keep City in contention at all with the players and funds available, and some progress had been made. McCarthy was the ideal, solid centre half for a promotion fight, and younger players such as Kinsey, May and Wilson gave some grounds for optimism. City, of course, would be promotion favourites once more when the new season started. But we all knew what that meant.

Season 1984/85:
Na, na, na, na, na, na, na, na, na, na, na, City's goin' up!

Having been looking for a job and then finding a job – sort of – but nonetheless ending up fairly miserable, I could relate quite nicely to the words of the great Morrissey. The lyrics of this fellow cheerful soul offered me solace during those days of indulgent self-pity. Wallowing in the incompetence of our beloved team is a natural and most enjoyable pastime for Manchester City fans, and I made the most of it. In fact, things didn't look nearly so bad during the summer. My alternative to experiencing the final match of season 1983/84 was a sunny day spent on the beach at Newborough, Anglesey, with Manchester-dwellers visiting me for a change. Things rarely look as bad when City are not playing.

There were other distractions as well in 1984. Being basically from mining stock, and unreconstructed old Labour, I was keen to man the barricades for the forthcoming revolution, or at least stand around the town centre on a Saturday, collecting for the striking miners. Mind you, when the football season recommenced, I wasn't quite so keen – the revolution had to play second fiddle to football. Such half-hearted commitment may well help to explain the absence of a decent, working-class revolution in British history. It certainly emphasised my priorities.

By the time that the summer of 1984 was reaching its close and the football season was rearing its ugly head, I had moved to somewhere unpronounceable on the edge of

Menai Bridge (the town, not the bridge), on Anglesey. The Smiths were almost permanently on the turntable, with the occasional interruption from The Wonderful and Frightening World of The Fall, and I was even looking forward to the opportunity to see New Order. The execution of this latter endeavour required a complex round trip of several hundred miles, the exact reasons for which are too uninteresting to merit further attention. This escapade is not entirely irrelevant, since it did tie in with the start of the new season.

City drew their first match 2-2, at Wimbledon on the Saturday of the bank holiday weekend. I was back in Chorley to listen to the drama unfold on the radio as the Blues rescued a point when a depressing opening to the campaign looked likely. On the Sunday, I drove my dad's car to a car park near Crewe railway station. The second leg of the journey involved an alarmingly fast van ride to Southampton, in a hired van driven by somebody else, and with a window seat offering a frighteningly good view of the proximity to the kerb. After a brief respite, the van trip was continued to the ultimate destination, Portsmouth, where a sterling performance by Barney and the team was witnessed. At this point, the plan went slightly awry. The difficulty of getting sufficiently drunk in Portsmouth, late on a Sunday had not been anticipated. The result was an uncomfortable and sleepless night in the van. This was almost entirely my own fault since I stupidly volunteered to sleep in the front, reckoning without the gearstick, which proved unavoidable whatever contortion I attempted.

Having just made the train to Manchester the following morning (Monday, 27 August), the rest of the convoluted route to Maine Road became a formality. The train to Crewe was followed by a car journey to the ground to see the opening home match against Grimsby Town. I arrived at two o' clock, when the ground was still rather becalmed. With the Blues having finished so close to the promotion places in the previous campaign, expectations amongst the Faithful were extremely high. Billy McNeill had managed to make a couple of purchases over the summer. Welshman David Phillips was a snip at £65,000 from Plymouth Argyle. There were extra appearance-related payments written into the deal, but considering that Phillips went on to enjoy a long career in the top English League, mostly not at City, the signing was undoubtedly a good one. Phillips played primarily in midfield, and earned himself a reputation for scoring spectacular goals, thanks mainly to an uncanny ability to produce his best moments in front of the 'Match of the Day' cameras. The other new player was ex-Barnsley striker Tony Cunningham, a £90,000 buy from Sheffield Wednesday. Cunningham was big and strong, but never looked quite so dangerous playing for City as he had done against City. The list of players falling into that category is long and ever-increasing. Even these modest purchases must have tested the Maine Road coffers. Presumably as some sort of compensation, the price of the match magazine was raised once more, to 50 pence.

The Blues began the season with a familiar line-up, relying heavily on home-grown talent. Alex Williams was to play in goal in every City game of the season. Ray Ranson's loss of favour with the City management meant that Phillips was chosen as right-back, with Paul Power, still captain, on the other flank. Mick McCarthy, who had rightly won the Player of the Year award for the previous season, despite not arriving at the club until Christmas time, was initially partnered by Kevin Bond, a combination that did not last long. McCarthy eventually formed a very effective partnership with Nicky Reid. Neil McNab, Graham Baker, Clive Wilson and Gordon Smith comprised the midfield for the opening matches. Wilson, an intelligent and skilful youngster who always looked comfortable in possession of the ball, played a prominent role as one of the few creative City players. With Tolmie reduced to substitute, Parlane was chosen to partner Cunningham in attack.

In the event, many more players were destined to play their part in a dramatic season at Maine Road, due largely to an injury crisis of almost epidemic proportions as the season approached its climax. Parlane and Smith, an elegant player who was able to add some calmness to the often frenetic midfield skirmishes typical of the Second Division, were goalscorers at Wimbledon, and both repeated the feat against Grimsby, to guarantee a happy first home game. A Bond penalty was the other goal scored in a comfortable 3-0 victory that would have raised expectations further had it not been for the fact that the Championship was already expected. There was, therefore, no further for expectations to go. Since only goal difference had separated the two teams at the close of the previous season, the result was encouraging for all of us. I was even able to stay awake sufficiently long to drive back to Bangor that evening.

Since this is Manchester City we are talking about, it should come as no surprise that in the next match, at home to Fulham, City gave a display as inept as their performance against Grimsby was impressive. Although Parlane scored twice, Fulham won 3-2, carving holes in the City defence with alarming regularity. The first League table was published with City occupying only ninth place. McNeill responded by making significant alterations to the team. Bond was dropped, to make way for Nicky Reid, and within a few weeks he was sold to Southampton for £75,000. This ended a not altogether happy association, until his surprise return to the staff a decade later. Andy May was also brought into defence, this time at right-back, enabling Phillips to move to midfield, where he continued to play for the remainder of the season.

A 2-0 defeat at Wolves, followed by a goalless draw at Carlisle, suggested little improvement, and City plunged to fourteenth in the table. It was a deflated City team that scraped a 1-0 home win against Huddersfield in the next match, in front of an ominously low crowd of 20,201. Graham Baker scored the only goal of a game in which Parlane was injured. It was a significant moment for his replacement, Steve Kinsey, who was widely reported as the star performer in a 3-0 win at Cardiff City that finally got the City season moving. Kinsey was still a slight figure, who looked strangely incongruous competing against the usual rugged and brawny central defenders. Despite giving the impression of flimsiness, Kinsey was able to make the average Second Division centre half look like a hippopotamus trying to keep track of a Yorkshire Terrier. Since most defences seemed designed primarily to counteract aerial bombardment, Kinsey's pace was enough to make them look foolish. If only his finishing had been more profitable.

The Cardiff victory was also notable for the first goals of the season by Cunningham and Wilson. For Cunningham, it ended a worrying run of six games without scoring, and he followed it up with two more in a League Cup tie against Blackpool, which City won 4-2.

With two consecutive home League matches to follow, the opportunity was there for City to make some real progress up the table. Against Crystal Palace, Gordon Smith gave the Blues a lead which they were careless enough to surrender before half-time. The sheer pace of Steve Kinsey resulted in the all-important winning goal. It was the match against high-flying Oxford United, on 6 October 1984, that gave the Faithful reason for genuine hope. The margin was only 1-0, with Steve Kinsey scoring the winner, but City played well enough to suggest that they could compete with the best the League had to offer.

Having established this fact, the Blues then proceeded to lose their next two matches. The first of these was against Shrewsbury Town. I decided to make the journey to Gay Meadow for the first time since the infamous FA Cup match. I had my parents' Mini in Bangor, and a look at the map confirmed that Shrewsbury was about as close a Division Two football ground to Bangor as there was. Having come to grips with the nature of road travel in North Wales, I allowed several hours for the journey and arrived far too early.

A football ground is an eerie place two hours before kick-off. For once, I was on my own, and having exhausted the option of wandering around Shrewsbury, I decided to enter the famous Gay Meadow. I had the enclosure behind the goal to myself for quite some time. It gave me a chance to read the match programme most thoroughly. The black-and-white photograph on the cover suggested that glossy colour had yet to reach Shrewsbury. The crossword was taxing. The clue for 11 across read, 'Follow the Maine one to Manchester? (Four letters).' Any ideas? The Secretary's notes were written under the headline 'The Big Boys Are Here'. He had obviously never seen Steve Kinsey, but it demonstrates the attitude of most of City's opponents in Division Two. In fact, Kinsey was injured and didn't play in this first League meeting between the two clubs. City made chances. City missed chances. Shrewsbury scored the only goal, at my end of the pitch, midway through the second half. I drove home disillusioned.

Kinsey returned and scored a goal at Middlesbrough, but City still lost 2-1, to remain in mid-table obscurity. The Blues needed an own goal to help them to a 2-1 win over Blackburn, a much more nail-biting affair than the previous season's encounter at Maine Road, but a 0-0 draw at Brighton suggested little grounds for increased optimism. Tony Cunningham had scored only one League goal in 13 starts. In fact, he never scored another League goal for City. His finest moment came in the Milk Cup third-round replay at Upton Park, where City won 2-1 with goals from Kinsey and Cunningham, following a scoreless first match at Maine Road. Cunningham's goal, scored after bursting through with a reasonable impersonation of pace, was his best for the club. Having said that, the competition was not fierce. It was strange to hear a City win described as a giant-killing. Giant-killing was what happened to City, rather frequently. Yet West Ham were the First Division team, so I suppose it was a giant-killing, of sorts. It was certainly a surprise.

David Phillips scored his first goal of the season in the twenty-fourth minute of an important 1-0 Maine Road win over Birmingham City, a team occupying one of those much sought after promotion places. Having beaten both Oxford and Birmingham, two of the division's pace-setters, City had no reason to fear any of the sides in the Second Division. Yet they were still hopelessly inconsistent. Having lost patience with Cunningham, and with Parlane and Tolmie both suffering injury problems, Billy McNeill brought another Scot, Jim Melrose, into the club to provide a much needed boost to the attack. The deal proved to be inspirational, at least in the short-term.

Draws against Sheffield United and Portsmouth, interspersed with an emphatic Milk Cup exit at Chelsea, did not appear to be the forerunner of great things, but on 1 December 1984, Melrose scored his first City goal in a 2-0 win at Oldham, launching City's rise up the table. The Blues remained in seventh place after a 2-0 home win over struggling Notts County the following week. This was a generally dull match, but the goal from Jim Melrose, blasted in from virtually the halfway line towards the bemused occupants of the North Stand, was simply breathtaking. I'm still not sure whether I dreamt it or not. City players are not in the habit of scoring such goals.

Melrose, understandably brimming with confidence, scored again in a 3-1 win at Charlton. On 22 December 1984, the Blues lost 3-2 at Fulham, a repeat of the score from the earlier Maine Road meeting, but a considerable improvement on the previous visit to Craven Cottage. Melrose scored a goal in that match and in the next game, a 1-1 home draw with Barnsley on Boxing Day that City really ought to have won. Three days later, despite an emphatic 4-0 win over Wolves at Maine Road, in which Melrose played a starring role without scoring himself, City were still placed only fifth in the League, a position not improved by a New Year's Day 1-1 draw at Leeds. That game marked Jim Melrose's final goal in a run of six goals in seven matches. He didn't score again for four months.

On 5 January 1985, I made the trip to Coventry to see the FA Cup third-round tie, anticipating the possibility of an incongruous giant-killing. City played exceptionally well and scored through Paul Power but, typically, Coventry somehow managed to score twice, without ever looking likely to. Their only player of note, Terry Gibson, was the man whose groin would have been far better strained on this occasion.

City obviously fared far better away from home when I was not in attendance. There were glowing reports for a 2-0 win at Huddersfield which marked Cunningham's last City appearance, albeit for only five minutes as a substitute. He was subsequently sold to Newcastle for £75,000. Parlane was also released, on a free transfer to Swansea.

Back at the Academy, the Blues recorded a comfortable win against Wimbledon. Gordon Smith's chip established a first-half lead. A first-time David Phillips left-foot shot that flew into the roof of the net confirmed the presence of the 'Match of the Day' cameras, and Graham Baker scrambled a third City goal, despite seemingly making every effort not to. The Wimbledon match began a run of four consecutive games featuring goals from David Phillips. With Smith, Baker and Wilson all contributing to the arduous task of scoring goals, City were not so reliant on the finishing of their forwards, which is just as well. The victory at Wimbledon also propelled City into third place, the last of the coveted promotion positions. The Blues came from behind to win 2-1 at Crystal Palace and consolidate their position. Then, just when everything looked to be running smoothly, and despite a spectacular David Phillips goal of the month for Jimmy Hill to drool over, City slumped to a 3-1 home defeat at the hands of Carlisle United.

Thankfully, it turned out to be only a minor setback, as goals from Phillips and Smith gave City a 2-0 home win against Brighton and second place in the table. On 2 March 1984, City faced the trip to Ewood Park. Being isolated many miles from anywhere of note, I was not able to attend many away games, but I considered the trip to Blackburn my duty. Rovers were themselves amongst the leading contenders for promotion, along with Oxford, Birmingham and Portsmouth. They were just as desperate for the points as City were.

The weather intervened to dangle an additional metaphorical carrot (or with footballers, maybe it should be steak and chips and a Luther Vandross LP) in front of the Manchester City team. The consequence of frost elsewhere was that cancellations had offered City the possibility of number one spot in the footballing charts, should they win. Hence, the Faithful maintained warmth and morale before the match with chants of 'We'll be top by five o'clock'.

Such chants would usually be just the inspiration City needed to lose heavily and in the most embarrassing fashion imaginable, but for once it didn't happen that way. The Ewood Park pitch did not look entirely frost-free itself, which made for a scrappy and largely unskilful match, as players battled to keep their balance. Steve Kinsey had an unfair advantage when it came to balance, and it was he who scrambled home the only goal of the match, after some comical defending. Staggeringly, after the match had finished the City fans were still chanting, 'We'll be top by five o'clock.' In fact, it was only 4.45pm when City were top of Division Two.

Back at Maine Road, Phillips scored the only goal against Middlesbrough to maintain City's position. A week later, the Blues registered their most emphatic win of the season, at home to Shrewsbury Town. Andy May was a revelation in midfield as the Blues won 4-0. May himself scored, along with Power, Smith and Kinsey. On that day, City really did appear to be Championship material, and they were looking comfortable in that top position. All was well with the world. At least, so it seemed.

A few injury problems had begun to emerge, including the loss of Clive Wilson for the remainder of the season. This was one of the reasons for Andy May switching to midfield. Kenny Clements returned to Maine Road on loan, as cover for the right-back position. Ken McNaught had already performed a similar cover for Nicky Reid at the centre of the City defence, prior to Reid's return. Frankly, resources at Maine Road were scarce. It didn't take many injuries and suspensions to cause severe disruption. An injury to Gordon Smith left City with very little room for manoeuvre. On a more positive note, Neil McNab did reappear, albeit looking a little rusty.

Whatever the excuses, City were unable to maintain the high point of 16 March

1985. A midweek goalless draw away to Birmingham City was a good result, but a 3-0 loss at Oxford United started those overused alarm bells ringing once more. The Blues could only manage a 2-2 draw at home to Cardiff City. The one bright spot of this match was the reappearance of City's young winger, Paul Simpson, who scored one of the goals, and impressed everyone with his energy and skill.

The Blues were still on top of the pile as the Easter programme began, but their position was looking more precarious. Because of the holiday break, I was able to make my third visit to Oakwell, Barnsley, in search of reassurance. It was nice to see that the Tommy Tyke column was still going strong in the *Oakwell Review*. Tommy, it seems, was a big fan of Barnsley old boy Mick McCarthy. He was also very complimentary about Asa Hartford, who had starred recently in Norwich City's League Cup win over Sunderland, in his first season after leaving City for the second time. The game itself was not an inspiring occasion. Confidence appeared to be lacking, and the players looked in need of Lucozade or something even stronger. The City fans amused themselves by directing a series of chants at an overactive Barnsley fan in a pink raincoat, who had the misfortune to be sitting close to our end. The chants varied from 'Fuck off, Pinkie' to 'Pinkie, give us a wave' and even 'We love you Pinkie, we do' – exhibiting a greater range of violent emotional mood swings than the average episode of 'Coronation Street'.

Whilst Pinkie continued his habit of leaping from his seat at regular intervals, City struggled in vain to make a breakthrough, despite the presence of Paul Futcher in the home defence. The match finished goalless, the Blues dropped to second place in the League, and Melrose picked up an injury that was to cause him difficulty for the rest of the season.

Worse was to follow back at Maine Road on Easter Monday. The young striker, Darren Beckford, made his first start for the Blues, but Baker was injured again, rather soon after making a comeback from an earlier problem. City's only goal came from a penalty, scored by Jim Tolmie, the substitute. It wasn't sufficient to prevent a damaging 2-1 defeat by Leeds United. City dropped to third place.

Even worse was to follow as City crashed 4-1 at Grimsby Town. Simpson scored a goal that was no consolation and the Blues slipped to fifth. An imminent increase in the suicide rate in the Manchester area was becoming a serious possibility. The fall from the position of prominence occupied so recently had been a shock to all connected with the club. It simply couldn't be allowed to continue any longer.

The Maine Road match against Sheffield United on 20 April 1985 was one of the most tense I have ever endured. Anybody misguided enough to consider football an entertainment needs to experience a gut-wrenching occasion like this one. City's promotion hopes were palpably leaking away as they strove, in vain, to recapture some form, and threaten an obtuse visiting defence. It was a match in which Jim Melrose made a premature attempt at a comeback as Billy McNeill gambled with some desperation. It was understandable desperation.

Three-quarters of the game had been completed and still there were no goals. A quick glance at the watch, about every 10 seconds, confirmed that time was indeed travelling at a faster than conventional rate. The whole season's work was in serious jeopardy unless City could make a breakthrough to revive their chances. A draw would simply not do. And then Jim Tolmie had probably his finest moment in a City shirt. When Paul Simpson played the through-ball to put Tolmie clear, the mop-haired Scot had the time to stop and consider before shooting. It wasn't a lot of time, but it would have been sufficient for a lesser man to realise the massive importance of the moment and shoot limply, overwhelmed by the responsibility. Instead, Tolmie slotted the ball beyond the goalkeeper and into the net with consummate ease. The relief around Maine Road was like the ending of the most massive constipation imaginable – not literally, I'm glad to say. The Blues even swept forward to score a second, finished by Kenny Clements of all people.

The win over Sheffield United still didn't put the Blues into a promotion spot, but defeat would have left them virtually finished off. Four matches remained, two at home and two away. The next match, against Alan Ball's Portsmouth, had the potential to be decisive. Portsmouth were just two points and one place behind City. Both sides needed a win to close the gap on Blackburn, who now occupied the third promotion place. Oxford, with John Aldridge scoring close to 30 goals, were virtually assured of the Championship, with Birmingham City, including Wayne 'Sniffer' Clarke, comfortably holding second place. There was only one place to play for, and the consequences of defeat for City at Fratton Park did not bear thinking about.

Regardless of cost and inaccessibility, I could not stay away from City matches now. I went to Southampton to stay with friends for the weekend, the main event of which was the match on 27 April 1985. The sun was shining as City took to the field in their red-and-black striped away shirts. With the stakes being so high, it was understandable that the opening half suggested fear of losing was outweighing hopes of winning. Whether by design or out of necessity, City played for quick breakaway attacks. Tolmie and Kinsey both had opportunities to put City ahead, but there were no goals in the first half. When the teams re-emerged for the second half, City were kicking towards the Faithful, massed behind the goal on a roofless terrace. The Blues took the lead soon after half-time, when a deep cross drifted beyond the final defender, and David Phillips headed the ball back across goal and into the net. All our hopes were raised in that moment, but the home side recovered from the blow to equalise with a scrambled effort by Nicky Morgan. Inspired by this, Portsmouth stormed forward and suddenly defeat loomed ominously. The City defence was forced to withstand a number of attacks, and Alex Williams made vital saves, including one particularly commendable effort to foil a Neil Webb shot. By now, I was willing to settle for the less disastrous outcome of a draw, even though that would inevitably leave Blackburn in a superior position. In the event, it wasn't necessary. With fewer than 10 minutes remaining, Paul Simpson chased after a long ball, and surprised everyone with an exquisite lob over the stranded Alan Knight in the Portsmouth goal. It was the most important City goal of the season. The deflated Pompey team tried to recover the damage, but it was City who threatened again, with Kinsey on the break. It is not in City's nature to make life more bearable for their fans and so we had to settle for 2-1. There was an inordinate and excruciating period of injury time, during which the referee's watch was obviously transported into a time warp of some description. The final whistle was eventually blown to rapturous relief from the Faithful. We didn't even mind being held behind for about 20 minutes whilst the disgruntled locals were ushered away to chants of, 'Bye, bye, Pompey, Pompey, bye, bye.' When the easily recognisable figure of Alan Ball edged on to the pitch for a post-match interview, the imitation of the Pompey chimes was repeated with 45Bally' instead of 'Pompey'. The mood of jollity was considerably enhanced by the news that Blackburn had lost.

This was Portsmouth's third consecutive defeat, a run for which everyone at Manchester City was grateful. Ultimately, City robbed Alan Ball of the chance to win promotion, but he certainly extracted his revenge. And when we were eventually released from Fratton Park, it emerged that the disgruntled locals had not been escorted very far away from the ground. Several cars were attacked on the presumption that their owners were City fans. We managed to escape without damage, much to the relief of the owner of the car in which we drove to the match.

After victory at Portsmouth, City were once more in control of their own destiny. That should have been good news. But all the doubts and frustrations returned with City to Maine Road, for the mass reunion with Oldham Athletic on 4 May 1985. A crowd of 28,933 turned up in the hope that City would virtually ensure promotion with a comfortable win. Instead, they had to endure a goalless draw, with the only consolation being provided by the news that Blackburn had fared even worse, leaving City's cushion intact. One win was required from our two remaining matches. Matters could have been far worse. With Andy May having been sent off for dissent just before half-time, City were understandably cautious about their approach to the second half. This was the first, and last, sending off suffered by a City player all season.

Ten thousand City fans joined me on Bank Holiday Monday, 6 May 1984, in the Kop End at Meadow Lane, the home of Notts County, whose relegation was imminent. Prior to the match, there was a party mood amongst the Faithful in the pubs near to the ground as City fans practised their singing and drinking, anticipating the successful conclusion to a season's work. The combination of results on the Saturday, despite City's failure to beat Oldham, had left City in a favourable position. Although Portsmouth and Blackburn were likely to win their bank holiday games, neither would be able to catch City in the event of a victory for the Blues. The two promotion songs were given plenty of airplay; not for much longer, I hoped.

Since their demise had become virtually inevitable, Notts County had actually improved, with Justin Fashanu locating the whereabouts of the net. They even had a couple of recent victories to look back on, but surely the greater importance of the match for City would make them the favourites? The party atmosphere was still in full swing when the teams kicked-off, with County heading in our direction, and City facing towards an end of the ground bereft of any kind of stand whatsoever. There had been such a long and good-natured build-up to the match, that it came as something of a shock when County scored an early goal, then another, and then a third before half-time. With players suffering from stage fright and fans from shock, the ghastly reality took time to sink in. When the players trudged off for half-time, the party turned sour as some of the fans, who had been practising their drinking too conscientiously, made minor incursions on to the pitch. The decision of the match officials to delay the start of the second half, whilst understandable, probably made matters worse. With nothing else to distract them, more idiots joined in, and it was several minutes before the teams re-emerged. A belatedly much-improved City battled hard to rescue an impossible situation in the second half. Paul Simpson scored two excellent individual goals and seriously threatened a third as City discovered all the form and urgency so lacking from their first-half display. Scores elsewhere, however, were not going our way, and as the other important games finished, it became clear that even a draw would be of no use to City. In any case, the Blues were unable to score a third goal and went down 3-2.

The whole day was a massive anticlimax but it did serve to clarify matters considerably. City were level on points with Portsmouth, but with a far superior goal difference. Blackburn were a further point adrift. Should City win their final match, they would be promoted. Any other result would open the door to either Portsmouth or Blackburn. If City lost, or even drew, then theoretically at least, even Leeds or Brighton, a further point behind Blackburn, might still sneak into third place. There was little doubt that the Blues were cutting it fine, but they were the only team who had complete control over their own destiny. With so many others ready to pounce, however, anything except a win in the final game at Maine Road, against Charlton Athletic, was very unlikely to be sufficient.

It was as simple and as frightening as that. Everyone reached for a good stiff drink, except me. I had to drive back to Bangor to stew on the situation for the rest of the week. Further analysis of the fixture list and the League table confirmed the necessity for a win in the final match. It was all or nothing. Despite my best efforts it was hard not to see the parallels with the nightmare match against Luton, the last occasion on which a large crowd had assembled at Maine Road to witness the culmination of a season's toil, all dependent on one game of football. On that dreadful day, the media spotlight was firmly directed at Maine Road, and with most other domestic League matters already settled, the same treatment could be anticipated. On my way into the ground, I could see the BBC vans parked in their usual spot behind the Main Stand, confirming the presence of the 'Match of the Day' cameras.

The Charlton Athletic team emerging from the Maine Road tunnel on that day was a depleted one. They had a 17-year-old goalkeeper, Lee Harmsworth, but they still had one or two notable players, including a young Robert Lee. City had problems of their own. With Reid and McCarthy both suspended, and Wilson, Smith and Baker still injured, Billy McNeill had to gamble on the fitness of Melrose once more. Kenny Clements and Andy May were acting as stand-in central defenders. The match magazine featured a headline of 'Come On, You Blues!' It may have been my imagination, but I detected a hint of desperation in that plea.

My main problem was that I had lost my trust in Manchester City. They had let me down on the big occasion too often, and the Luton game was still all too fresh in the memory. Whatever the outcome, it had been a strange end to the season. In March,

City had looked certainties for promotion. Their sudden slide in form had allowed Oxford and Birmingham to move clear, leaving Portsmouth in the best position to secure third place. At that point, Portsmouth suffered a costly run of defeats, including the one against City, to allow Blackburn through. When matters were in their own hands, Rovers also faltered to allow City back. It seemed that nobody wished to be promoted.

Consistent goalscoring had presented the Blues with a huge problem throughout the season. Steve Kinsey goals were sporadic. Melrose had begun with a spectacular run, only for that particular source to dry up completely, just as quickly as it emerged. Phillips also enjoyed a spell of goalscoring, but was not able to contribute regularly. In the latter stages of the promotion challenge, it was Paul Simpson who had become the chief supplier of goals. There had been little to suggest that a sheer adrenaline rush would inspire City to their biggest win of the season, but that's exactly what happened.

The crowd, nearing 50,000, roared City on from the start, and there seemed an extra energy about the whole team. Yet an early error by Andy May invited a calamitous opening. His back-pass failed to reach Alex Williams, and Steve Gritt should have scored. Eventually, Geoff Lomax scrambled the ball clear, to much relief, and the main action switched to the other end of the pitch. With the match still only a few minutes old, a quick break down the left wing sent City bursting forward in numbers, towards the inhabitants of an expectant North Stand. Simpson emerged with the ball on the wing, and crossed low for a completely unmarked Phillips to sweep City into the lead. After 15 minutes, Simpson floated a corner to the edge of the penalty area, and Andy May headed the ball with incredible precision into the smallest of gaps between a Charlton defender's head and the crossbar. City were 2-0 up before they had time to think. Not surprisingly, the match settled into a more normal pace for the remainder of the first half, with every forward movement by Charlton provoking mass anxiety.

At half-time, the news that Blackburn led relegated Wolves 1-0 met with a subdued response. If Charlton had pulled a goal back, it would have been the cue for unprecedented scenes of nail-biting, teeth-gnashing and psychotic rocking in the stands. Instead, City began the second half even better than the first, with a burst of three goals at the Platt Lane End. Paul Power's cross seemed to be too high for Melrose, but he somehow stretched backwards to direct a header beyond Harmsworth. The Charlton goalkeeper then suffered a mini-crisis of indecision as a long ball came towards him. Paul Simpson took advantage of Harmsworth's reluctance to leave the safety of his penalty area, to slip the ball around the young goalkeeper and slide it into the empty net, for his sixth goal in nine matches. Finally, David Phillips produced his usual fare for 'Match of the Day,' rifling a low, right-foot shot into the corner of the net.

At 5-0, even I was convinced that victory was assured. The match still had 30 minutes to go, but City seemed exhausted by their exertions and Charlton, I'm sure, just wanted to go home. There seemed little point in continuing, but rules are rules and the match was allowed to meander to its conclusion. When Robert Lee scored for Charlton, he received polite applause from the home fans. That was the final score, a 5-1 win, rendering victories for both Blackburn and Portsmouth irrelevant. City were back in Division One after two years in exile. It was one of the happier days at the Academy.

Season 1985/86: Few Members and Fewer Memories

The highlight of the summer of 1985 occurred when Manchester City played in Bangor. It was the beginning of a revolution in local entertainment. Soon to follow were The Wedding Present, Yeah Yeah Noh and even The Fall. City's gig was a six-aside competition taking place on a section of the Bangor City pitch, with smaller goals than normal and some unconventional rules. The tournament was completed in a single afternoon for the benefit of S4C (Welsh Channel Four), who managed to stretch the television coverage out for several weeks by showing one game at a time. Unfortunately for S4C, neither of the two Welsh teams competing for glory managed to win a single match. City and Villa comprised the English competitors, with Celtic and Hearts representing Scotland. Curiously enough, it was Hearts who boasted the most numerous and noisiest support. It was they who generated the only hint of atmosphere. Despite this, it was actually good entertainment – but then it wasn't really football. I wore my City shirt with pride as the Blues overcame Celtic in a tight group match. They were eventually eliminated by Villa. Both matches had ludicrous but exciting scorelines, like 7-6 or 8-7. Paul Simpson was particularly well suited to the format. The commentator probably referred to his low centre of gravity. I wouldn't know. The commentary was in Welsh.

As I recall, it was Villa, with Mark Walters and Paul Rideout looking impressive, who actually won the competition. This was football played for the benefit of television in front of a paltry crowd, a chilling insight into the future of football should present trends persist. You have been warned!

I moved back into the seething metropolis of Bangor; Bangor High Street to be precise. After the exertions of the season's climax, I could tuck into a pork chop and take a slurp of surprisingly good home-brew bitter, whilst listening to the excellent Meat Is Murder and contemplating the ultimate City triumph. I was also entertaining my first slivers of apprehension concerning my beloved team's ability to survive their first season back in the fold. Yes, it didn't take long for those negative thoughts to begin creeping to the fore, upsetting my, for once, cheerful disposition.

Whilst promotion with a low budget and a limited squad had been a considerable achievement by Billy McNeill, his real job was about to begin. I had invested much, emotionally and financially, in this promotion being a permanent arrangement. On the day after the glorious win against Charlton, I picked up the tab for a splendid meal for several people in a restaurant in Manchester's Chinatown, in recognition of City's success. I began to wish that I had retained the receipt and made it dependent on maintenance of First Division status for five years, at least. Spending the cash had been my offering to the gods of football for their generosity in allowing City back from the abyss. There was a strong possibility that more and bigger gifts would be required to ensure survival. After all, City had only just managed to sneak out of Division Two – on goal difference, and with two midfield players, Smith and Phillips, heading their goalscoring charts, with only 12 each. A regular supply of goals against the best defenders in the country was the priority if City were to be competitive. The City coffers were still not exactly bulging. McNeill's initial answer was to pay Huddersfield Town

£132,000 for the services of Mark Lillis, a Mancunian who had signed previously for City as a schoolboy. Lillis, with his shoulder-length blond hair, was a willing worker, but was he really the man to frighten First Division defences?

The other new signings were defender Nigel Johnson (£75,000 from Rotherham), whose City career never really emerged because of a propensity to suffer injuries, and Sammy McIlroy, on a free transfer from Stoke City. The arrival of McIlroy demonstrated a certain lack of understanding on McNeill's part. Anything suggesting, even remotely, that City were reduced to taking hand-me-downs from the football club purportedly located in the Trafford area of Greater Manchester, was to be avoided. McIlroy would have to play very well indeed to be accepted at Maine Road. He didn't even come close.

On a personal front, more changes were afoot as the new season began. After nine seasons in Block Y2, Row 24, Seat 4 of the Platt Lane Stand, I was forced to relocate to the North Stand. At the behest of James Anderton's barmy army, (aka police force) the powers that be had decided to allocate the whole of the Platt Lane Stand to visiting spectators, regardless of the opposition's level of support. This resulted in many matches being played with only a handful of people milling around in a largely deserted Platt Lane Stand.

The other change for me was that it was no longer easy to find places to stay in Manchester. Many of my friends had finished at university and moved to other areas of the country, although most eventually found their way back. For the next two seasons, this change of circumstances meant a number of long and lonely days travelling to and from Maine Road, usually on the train. With such expense and travel involved in attending home matches, visits to away games were necessarily infrequent.

The journey from Bangor to Manchester Victoria took a sluggish two hours and 50 minutes by rail, with the train stopping at Penmaenmawr, Llanfairfechan, Llandudno Junction, Colwyn Bay, Abergele, Prestatyn and Flint, before finally crossing the border and pulling in to Chester Station. When Chester was reached, I knew that the journey was, at last, nearing its end. The 09.10 train would finally pull into Manchester Victoria at noon, at which point I could emerge, slightly stupefied, into the rarefied atmosphere of the great city itself. The train offered the opportunity to read, and believe me, there were sufficient journeys for me to read some monster-sized books. Reading was also required as a defensive measure since I appeared to act as an unwilling and unintentional attractant to train loonies, who could make the journey even worse than it already was. I needed a legitimate distraction, entitling me to ignore them. For the same reason, I would always advise anyone waiting for a friend in a public house to carry a newspaper or other reading matter in order to avoid the pub loony, amongst whose numbers I also have many admirers.

It was often a touch on the cold side when I arrived at Victoria Station, but I was able to take refuge in the record shops on Market Street or the second-hand clothes shops of Afflecks Palace, hidden behind Piccadilly. Here I purchased an enormous second-hand coat that has served me well over the years and that, to the dismay of my mother, I still used regularly until quite recently, despite its fall to the Unibond League of fashion. Better warm than fashion victim, I say. That's because I'm getting old.

As an alternative, I sometimes hung around the library in my big coat, looking furtive, no doubt. It was quite warm in the library, and there didn't appear to be any library loonies. At least, if there were, they were the quiet type. For a while, I nurtured one of my minor rituals. This involved having a haircut in a particular barber's shop – or should that be hair design specialist's creative workspace – in Afflecks Palace. It was quite a costly habit because the price for the sheep shearer treatment I required – number one clippers all round – was far higher than the speedy but effective job available at the combined barber and fishing tackle shop in Bangor. I also tried haircuts as a source of team inspiration a few years later. This time the barber's shop was Sid's in Didsbury, where you could expect the usual friendly prattling from the proprietor, but the ceremonial aspect of payment was unique. In the corner of the shop, a mysterious old woman lurked in the shadows, behind a screen, like a priest in a confessional box. She didn't speak, and I never caught a glimpse of her face. Her existence was revealed only when she thrust out a hand to take money and deliver change.

I am not normally superstitious at all. In fact, I know it to be completely stupid and pointless, touch wood. However, when haircuts corresponded with wins over a period of time, I reasoned, why ask for trouble? Eventually, like all of these irrational little habits, the spell was broken and I had to look for another lucky omen. Over the years there have been quite a few, but none that managed to survive for long.

I always had a couple of hours to waste in central Manchester before meeting up with my dad in the Old Garrett at two o'clock. Having taken advantage of the records, books and clothes shops, I often wandered to the edge of Piccadilly and bought a dubious and excessively greasy beefburger from a man in a van. Having more than a passing knowledge of microbiology, this was not something that I did at any other time. If I develop CJD, the source can be traced directly to this unwholesome habit, and it will all be the fault of Manchester City Football Club.

There is little point in pretending that season 1985/6 was anything other than a dull season, with very few memorable matches. As it began, I was somewhere in central Europe on an Inter-Rail holiday. I found out about the opening match result, a 1-1 draw at Coventry City, from some obnoxious Chelsea fans on an overcrowded overnight train from Nice to Barcelona. I only discovered that they were obnoxious some time after receiving the football news. Surprisingly enough, their information proved to be accurate. McIlroy scored his only ever City goal in that match.

I was still endeavouring to make myself ill, with too much beer and too little sleep, when City drew their first home match, also 1-1, against Leicester City, and lost their second, 3-1 against Sheffield Wednesday. Lillis, with a penalty, and Simpson, scored the first City goals of the season at Maine Road. Luckily, I didn't learn of those results until after a 3-2 win at West Bromwich Albion.

Although in the country, I was, frustratingly, in completely the wrong part of it to make it to the next home match, against Spurs. I made a nervous phone call to my dad to find out what all the scores had been, and was reasonably relieved with the news of a relatively neutral start made by the Blues. My mother had the benefit of my new North Stand seat for the Spurs game, which City won 2-1. By all accounts this was slightly fortunate, but it enabled them to occupy a very secure looking ninth place in the Division One table.

Typically, as soon as I was able to keep track of all events, City began to slump, losing consecutive away matches at Birmingham and Southampton without scoring a goal. On 14 September 1985, I went to my first match of the season. It just happened to be against *The Nation's Team*, who had started the season in depressingly good form. They had won all seven of their League matches.

The one Mancunian in the visiting line-up was, gallingly, Peter Barnes. The match programme made a point of stressing all the locally-born City players: Williams, May, Wilson, Clements (surprisingly preferred to Reid), Lillis, Power and Kinsey. The other players lining up for City were McCarthy, Phillips, McIlroy and Simpson, the latter a product of our own youth system. The competition for 'most local players' was the only prize City took on this occasion. The match was effectively over with three-quarters of the time remaining. Referee George Tyson awarded an early penalty kick, penalising Alex Williams for an innocuous-looking challenge, and a freak 20-yard shot from Albiston made the score 2-0 before City had managed to get into the match at all. They never really did, eventually losing 3-0. I was beginning to wonder whether I should leave the country again to restore the team's fortunes.

Further calamity hit the Blues when Alex Williams suffered a serious back injury, from which he never fully recovered. The consolation was that Eric Nixon proved to be a perfectly adequate replacement. City seemed to find competent goalkeepers quite easily back then.

Billy McNeill began to swap the team around a little in an attempt to find a combination that might function tolerably well. Steve Kinsey was proving a little too frail for the rigours of the First Division. Jim Melrose was given a spell as Lillis's striking partner, and he managed to score three times in five matches, although two of them were against Bury in the incongruously named Milk Cup. (What next: Egg Cup? Butter Cup? Double D Cup?) Paul Power was switched to left-back to allow Clive Wilson into midfield at last. Eventually, Nicky Reid returned to the City defence as right-back, with Andy May making the majority of his appearances in midfield. Wilson and Baker had been quite a success at the heart of the City midfield in the promotion year, although the partnership rarely prospered long because of injuries to either or, more often than not, both. This time, Wilson lasted only a few matches before being injured and replaced by Baker, who in turn featured in a few matches before also getting injured. At least Neil McNab returned to the team as a replacement for McIlroy, who hardly played another match.

Three further League matches without a win, culminating in a dismal 1-0 defeat at home to Chelsea, sent City plunging into twentieth place. McNeill then paid out 3100,000 to Chelsea for moustachioed striker Gordon Davies, who took nearly two months to score a League goal. City continued a dreadful run of League matches, stretching to 11 without a win to firmly cement their position in the relegation zone.

Meanwhile, one of the brightest footballing ideas of the decade was being spectacularly put into practice: the Full Members Cup. The Full Members Cup was so popular that no First Division northern club, apart from City, deigned to take part. It should have been renamed the Few Members Cup. Whilst the Blues lurched dangerously downwards in the League, and exited the Milk Cup with a depressing 2-1 home defeat by Arsenal, they were able to bask in the glory of a magnificent Full Members Cup run. The Blues breezed through the Northern Section with victories over Leeds United, Sheffield United and Sunderland. In the regional final, City managed to lose 2-1 to Hull City in the first leg, before retrieving the situation with a 2-0 win at Maine Road. A measure of the esteem in which the competition was held by the footballing public can be judged by the fact that only 4,029 people turned up at Maine Road to see City beat Leeds United 6-1.

Midweek matches were not easy for me to attend. I therefore missed out on this momentous cup run. It's a pity. It would have really been something with which to impress people in later life. After all, what Manchester City fan does not still boast about the inspirational Full Members Cup run of 1985/86?

On 16 November 1985, City finally won a League match, achieving a surprising 2-0 victory away to Nottingham Forest. They were inspired by the return of Clive Wilson, who scored one of the goals. I remember toasting his return with a pint of disgusting bitter at the Bangor University Student Union disco that very evening. Nobody with me knew who Clive Wilson was. I had to toast alone. A few draws, and the inability of others to win their own matches, meant that City were still in touch with the teams above them. The win against Forest elevated the Blues to eighteenth position, and they rose one place higher at Maine Road the following Saturday, when, for the first time in season 1985/86, I was granted the privilege of witnessing a victory. The 1-0 win against Newcastle, courtesy of Mark Lillis's sixth League goal, attracted a crowd of only 25,179.

After scoring a long-awaited League goal in a drawn match at Leicester, Gordon Davies added two more in a 5-1 home victory over Coventry on 14 December 1985. The match programme featured a bizarre cover statement explaining that City would have to pay out £50,000 to erect fencing because in excess of 200 fans encroached on the playing area after the penalty shoot-out for the Full Members Cup win against Sunderland. This 'expression of jubilation' demonstrated a lack of perspective on the part of the fans concerned. Personally, I would have swapped a win in the final of the Full Members Cup for a single point in the League. I was beginning to realise that, with a new generation of fans, expectations were reducing. It was, after all, nearly 10 years since a Manchester City team had won a trophy.

The win over Coventry lifted City to fifteenth place, a position maintained despite a 3-2 defeat at Sheffield Wednesday. The Boxing Day match against Liverpool was one of the few memorable occasions of the whole season. Liverpool, with players like Lawrenson, Hansen, Paul Walsh, Skippy Johnston, Rush, Molby and McMahon, were lying second in the table, and everyone anticipated the usual Maine Road mauling. Indeed, Liverpool passed the ball amongst themselves with their customary disdain, occasionally deigning to have a shot at goal, but safe in the knowledge that comfortable victory would materialise, eventually. There was little evidence to the contrary. The Blues were unable to hold on to any significant amount of possession, and were reduced to chasing after the ball without ever actually touching it. As usual, Liverpool appeared to have more players on the pitch. Throughout the match, they were so far ahead on points, with bonus marks for artistic impression, that I had to keep reminding myself of the one rather significant detail still missing from the normal Liverpool visit to Maine Road. They hadn't scored.

To their credit, City ran around with as much enthusiasm as they could muster, and Liverpool may well have overdone the cultured football a little. Traditionally, Liverpool would at least take the lead before indulging themselves in a demonstration of their considerable passing ability. Despite the over-indulgence of the visiting team, there was a touch of the surreal about the moment when the ball sped across the Liverpool penalty area to the isolated figure of Clive Wilson. He calmly slotted it past Grobbelaar to give City the lead in front of a, for once, reasonably full, but entirely gob-smacked Platt Lane Stand.

Liverpool piled forward with more urgency. Shots peppered the City goal. But with the encouragement of a lead, City were able to overcome the fatigue induced by an afternoon spent chasing shadows. Miraculously, they held on for an unlikely win, and a considerable boost to morale.

After the Christmas miracle, a home draw against Birmingham City was a disappointment, but the Blues were in the midst of a run that rescued their season and ultimately saved them from an ignominious rapid return to Division Two. The cover of the match magazine for the Birmingham City game featured the City Youth team. Staring out from that photograph are many fresh faces belonging to players who later emerged to play significant roles for the City first team. Andy Hinchcliffe, Steve Redmond, Paul Lake, David White, Ian Brightwell and Paul Moulden are all there. The youth team was destined to provide City with their brightest moment of the season.

On New Year's Day I drove down the M6 to Villa Park with a fellow-sufferer. Arriving far too early, we took refuge in a rundown, but harmless, local hostelry – harmless, that is, apart from the pies. This match was the League debut of Paul Moulden, an 18-year-old striker who didn't look particularly strong, and wasn't especially quick, but whose goalscoring record at boys, youth and reserve team level merits the overused word 'phenomenal'. Indeed, Moulden made the *Guinness Book of Records* by scoring 289 goals in 40 matches for Bolton Lads' club. Regrettably, he was unable to quite maintain this scoring rate in the Manchester City first team.

Villa, under manager Graham Turner, were actually below City in the League. Goalkeeper Nigel Spink had to endure high-pitched, repetitive chanting of his name from the Faithful. For some reason, it seemed to tickle the collective funny bone, and it helped to warm the spirits on a cold day. Every time the ball came to him, the Villa goalkeeper was greeted with chants of 'Nigel, Nigel, Nigel' in an octave commonly used by Mavis from 'Coronation Street'. Spink's day was not improved by Mark Lillis, who steered the only goal of the game beyond *Nigel*'s reach. City were approaching respectability.

The improving League position and general form meant that the FA Cup could be welcomed with some optimism, and not just as a distraction from a relegation fight. The City defence of Eric Nixon in goal, along with Reid, Power, Clements and McCarthy, were enjoying a run of relatively Scrooge-like meanness. In nine matches, only four goals were scored against the Blues, which for this period of history was spectacular. The partnership of Lillis and Davies was also enjoying its most productive period, and although the midfield had been constantly disrupted because of injuries, Phillips, McNab and May, now rejoined by Paul Simpson, were able to offer some consistency for a reasonably lengthy spell in the early part of the new year.

The FA Cup draw obliged City to travel to Fellows Park on 4 January 1986, to take on Walsall, managed by Alan Buckley, and featuring none other than Steve Daley as their midfield general. As I drove down the M6 with a fellow-sufferer, there was snow, and I feared a late postponement or abandonment. During the match itself, there was a mini-blizzard, making the match somewhat farcical. The orange ball scuttled about as players sought to find a grip in a couple of inches of snow. It was all marvellous fun. Whilst the taller men struggled, Paul Simpson revelled in the conditions, scoring twice as City won 3-1 with surprising ease. We were also treated to Steve Daley blasting one of Walsall's best opportunities way over the crossbar. It was a good day out.

The Blues continued their rise to safety in Division One with a home win against Southampton, and an impressive 2-0 result away to Spurs, where Lillis and Davies both scored. The famous FA balls had, for once, been kind to the Blues. In the FA Cup fourth-round, City were drawn at home to Watford. The recent run of success suggested that there was a serious possibility of significant progress in the Cup: the *real* Cup.

The match against Watford included one of those distinctive turning points often referred to by the media. After an eventful but goalless first half, City, kicking towards the North Stand, took the lead with an acrobatic header by Gordon Davies, following a right-wing cross by Lillis. It was the contortion by Davies, twisting to divert the header in, that marked the goal out as a special one. It was indisputably the peak of his City career. The goal came eight minutes into the second half, and City looked in control. Another eight minutes further into the match, Mr Malcolm Heath, from Stoke-on-Trent, initiated the vital moment of the match and probably City's whole season. McCarthy headed clear a Watford cross. As in many incidents when central defenders challenge for the ball, McCarthy made some contact with an opponent, in this case John McClelland. Nobody claimed for a foul, but Mr Heath decided that Watford should have a penalty. Kenny Jackett scored to bring the visitors level. Seven minutes later, Mr Heath penalised a trip on Mark Lillis to offer City the chance of salvation. Agonisingly, Lillis spurned the offer by hitting his penalty kick against the post.

At the end of the match it seemed that the opportunity was lost, but in the replay City held out for a goalless draw after extra time, and a second replay, back at Maine Road, was required. That icy Thursday night at Maine Road was probably the peak of my stupidity as a Manchester City fan. Despite the foul and dangerous weather, I drove in my dad's green Mini, borrowed no doubt under false pretences, through the North Wales snow. I was urged on by my FA Cup obsession, despite the fact that I had already missed one match, the first replay. I made it to Manchester easily enough. The drive back, in freezing conditions, was always going to involve the largest risk, but I didn't care so long as City progressed. I paid my money and stood in the Kippax in expectation of reward for being so daft.

After twice playing splendidly, despite limited ability, City capitulated in calamitous fashion as John Barnes inspired Watford to a 3-1 win that never looked in doubt. The drive back to Bangor was an ordeal in more ways than one. When I eventually arrived, in no better mood than when the epic journey through snow showers and freezing fog had commenced, I was annoyed to see my drunken flatmates, recently returned from an enjoyable and warm night out. Their entirely innocent query as to the outcome of the game of football was not greeted with the courtesy it merited.

Two days later, with the need to return my dad's car, fortunately still in one piece, I was back at Maine Road to see a 2-0 win against QPR. The game featured an impressive debut by the youth team defender and captain, Steve Redmond. The Blues were sitting comfortably in eleventh place. That match took place on 8 February 1986. It proved to be a victory based on leftover adrenaline. The slide started on 11 February, and continued for the remainder of the season.

A run of four consecutive League defeats, with an aggregate score of 0-9, was not the best possible preparation for the Old Trafford derby encounter on 22 March 1986. Atkinson's Antichrist XI were placed third behind Everton and, inevitably, Liverpool, having suffered a reassuring slump, but their demise was nothing compared to the recent form demonstrated by the Blues. It was, therefore, with some trepidation that I made my way to the match, actually given a lift by a RAG. I would have happily settled for a draw to make the after-match journey tolerable. The important business of the day involved preventing the aberration of a League Championship for *The Nation's Team*, rather than any pressing requirement for points.

As the afternoon progressed, the prospect of double derby defeat loomed ever larger. Peter Barnes was again dressed incongruously in red as City defended the Stretford End in the first half. Colin Gibson scored following a free-kick to ensure a 1-0 half-time score, and things looked bleak indeed when, after Davenport had toppled over in the penalty area, the inevitable penalty was converted by Strachan. To be brutally honest, City did not really look capable of recovery, but a stooping header by Clive Wilson revived hopes late in the game, and a few minutes later City drew level. The equalising goal was something of a derby classic. With City players showing admirable determination, Strachan was pressurised into losing the ball in midfield, and with blue shirts converging on him at pace, Arthur Albiston planted a firm low shot beyond the reach of his own goalkeeper. Marvellous! I'm pretty sure that this was the season when Big Ron declared the Championship to be a two-horse race, between Liverpool and *The Nation's Team*. Ultimately, *The Nation's Team* finished fourth, which in a two-horse race is a unique achievement.

The following day Manchester City played at Wembley in the Full Members Cup Final against Chelsea. I still find the fact that 68,000 attended the game surprising. The thought of taking the trip myself never occurred to me. I had paid no attention to the competition previously, and I wasn't going to pay out for an expensive day-trip to a meaningless final. As far as I was concerned, a visit to Wembley Stadium was not sufficient incentive. Maybe that is because I had the luxury of three previous Wembley occasions to look back on, and I still hadn't given up the hope that City might make another genuine Cup Final. I listened to the match commentary on Piccadilly Radio as I drove back to Bangor. Steve Kinsey gave the Blues an early lead, but as the radio signal began to fade, so did City's hopes. I was out of range well before City slumped to 5-1 behind. Some late excitement, involving no fewer than three consolation goals, at least ensured respectability. Chelsea won the match 5-4, and Mark Lillis can recount the tale of how he scored a hat-trick in a Wembley Cup Final.

I had already forgotten that particular cup run by the following weekend, Easter 1986. A 2-2 draw against Aston Villa at Maine Road proved to be Eric Nixon's last match of the season in goal. It was a game where City trailed at half-time to a Steve Hodge goal, but recovered to lead following goals from McNab and Wilson, the latter aided by a deflection. With two minutes remaining, Simon Stainrod spoilt the day with an equaliser. It was most impolite of him.

On Easter Monday, at Anfield, Nixon was in the same stand as myself, having been omitted in favour of on-loan Barry Siddall, the now balding, ex-Bolton Wanderers goalkeeper, with whose earlier career I was most familiar. I went to and from Anfield in the company of some Liverpool fans, although I naturally sat amongst the City fans inside the stadium. My Liverpool friends would not believe me after the game, when I expressed myself relatively pleased with the 2-0 defeat. City not only managed a couple of attacks, but they avoided being humiliated. It was the best that could be expected. I was also relieved to have the opportunity to walk away from Anfield in the company of people wearing red scarves. The police policy still consisted of imprisoning all away fans after the final whistle, thus leaving nobody in any doubt as to their allegiances when they were eventually liberated.

The City slide down the table continued for the remainder of the season. The successful run of results either side of Christmas left the Blues with just sufficient points in hand to avoid serious relegation worries. When the final match kicked-off, ominously against Luton Town at Maine Road (a fact that had provoked shivers of anxiety throughout the season), City were in sixteenth position, five points clear of the relegation zone. After City's previous last day encounter with Luton, we were all very grateful for that. Despite the relative luxury of a worry-free final match, City fans were all too aware that, after finishing the season with a run of 13 League matches without a win, an improvement would be required if the team was to avoid a season of struggle in 1986/87.

I can now reveal the actual reason for City's dramatic decline in the latter stages of the 1985/86 season. It can be directly attributed to the theft, outside Anfield, of my favourite, old-fashioned, genuine sky blue and white City scarf from the back of my flatmate's 2CV. On the weekend in question, part of the deal for my lift back to Bangor from the North-West was that I go along to a televised encounter between Liverpool and *The Nation's Team*. Unfortunately, this entailed leaving my bag in a car boot about as secure as City fan Nick Leeson's bank. I also had to stand on the Kop with my gob firmly shut – not that I had any difficulty in associating myself with the all-embracing, vitriolic hatred effusing into the atmosphere. Liverpool didn't even win. They allowed *The Nation's Team* to escape with a 1-1 draw. From the moment that my scarf was stolen, City failed to win another match that season, and managed precious few victories in the whole of the following one.

Incidentally, the season tickets were also pilfered, causing considerable inconvenience for subsequent home matches. I know that the punchline should involve the thieves returning the season tickets, but unfortunately it wasn't a joke. My mother was more concerned with the loss of various edibles, kindly donated to my student survival fund. These were the only items that could have been of any conceivable use to the scallies who nicked them. I can't imagine what they would have done with a couple of Manchester City season tickets and a matching scarf. Well, maybe I can imagine, but I prefer not to.

The highlight of the season for Manchester City was provided by the youth team, which emerged victorious in the FA Youth Cup Final, with a 3-1 aggregate win over the Junior *Nation's Team*. Andy Hinchcliffe, Ian Brightwell, Steve Redmond, David White, Paul Moulden and Paul Lake all featured in the starting line-up for the 2-0 second leg victory at Maine Road. Indeed, Steve Redmond was released from first team duty to concentrate on completing the Youth Cup success. Paul Moulden scored the goal that confirmed City's win. The tragedy for City was that the youngsters were still just a little bit too young. Their services were required immediately.

Season 1986/87: Not with a Bang, but a Whimper

In the summer of 1986, as The Smiths, New Order, ACR, The The and James, amongst others, competed for my turntable, I could reflect on the ultimate achievement of the season. After all, survival was the aim, and survival was the outcome. The close season was a time for relaxing and putting aside consideration of possible traumas to come. The event of the year, for me, was the Festival of the Tenth Summer at Manchester's G-Mex, where The Smiths, New Order, The Fall, ACR, and Cabaret Voltaire were all scheduled to appear. It was unfortunate that The Cabs didn't perform, and that one or two of the lesser lights did, but this was a line-up from my dreams. It made me pine even more for a return to the great city, or at least somewhere closer to it. The Tenth Summer was not a reference to the last trophy won by Manchester City, but to the emergence of music that swept aside the aimless and pretentious nonsense prevalent in 1976. A few weeks later, The Smiths should have played Llandudno, but the show was cancelled due to some altercation between Mozzer and an audience at an earlier gig on the tour. That just about sums up my time in North Wales.

The 1986 World Cup was celebrated with much beer-swilling, and enlivened by some minor gambling. I had cash on Russia, Germany, and England, the latter simply because I ran out of ideas. My flatmate and I decided that we should back four teams each to add spark to our television viewing. I don't recall what my other team was, so they obviously made a deep impression. I regretted backing England as soon as I handed over the betting slip. The locals were quick to pounce, dismissing England's chances and ridiculing the bet. I didn't actually disagree with them, but there was little point in attempting an explanation. The Welsh like to get one over on the English, and they can't understand if some English, like me, are indifferent.

In the tournament itself, Russia, despite playing brilliant football, were given hardly any coverage. They should have gone much further than they did, but a bizarre match against Belgium ended in defeat, despite a hat-trick by Igor Belanov. In the group matches, the Russians scored a number of spectacular goals – I remember one long-range Vasily Rats shot in particular. England were awful until Bobby Robson's team selection was improved considerably by injury to Captain Marvel (Bryan Robson) and a suspension for Ray 'Butch?' Wilkins. Peter Reid, Steve Hodge and Peter Beardsley, none of whom were amongst Robson's original first-choice team, helped the cause considerably, and *the boy Lineker done well*. Dirty Diego finished England off. His second goal was a classic. His first provided England with something to moan about on the way home, and forever more.

The big clash at 364 High Street, Bangor, was in the semi-final, where the only two surviving bets met: Germany and France. With their customary efficiency, a very ordinary German side won to keep me in with a chance of financial gain. They even came from two goals behind in the final to raise my hopes, before going down 3-2 to Argentina. Because of the odds, there had been little point betting on Brazil or Argentina. All bets were wasted and the team with the best player won the Cup.

During the World Cup, we assembled, in our living room, a large, indeterminate construction referred to as The Kremlin, consisting of empty cans of Budweiser. The Kremlin was constructed beneath Slaphead's Corner, which consisted of lots of photographs of bald men but, curiously enough, was positioned in the middle of the wall and not in the corner at all. It would probably be superfluous at this point to emphasise that I was still a student.

The approach of the new domestic season was not accompanied by much transfer activity. The financial state of the club had still not recovered from earlier excesses. The signing of 20-year-old goalkeeper Perry Suckling ensured that it was no longer wise to derive too much amusement from opposing goalkeepers' names. The only other signing of note was Trevor Christie, a centre forward, and McNeill's replacement for Mark Lillis. Christie, purchased to form an unprecedented all-moustachioed attack – reminiscent of a good Saturday night out in Chorley – had scored a few goals for Notts County, but the signing did not exactly send the pulse racing. He didn't last long.

One notable departure was the long-serving Paul Power, who moved to Howard Kendall's Everton to pick up a Championship medal. The consequences of this were that the overall facial hair contingent remained at a steady level, and that Clive Wilson was destined to spend the whole season wasted at left-back. Kenny Clements, having established himself in the heart of the City defence in his second spell at Maine Road, was the new captain.

The 1986/87 season brought me into conflict with some of my new North Stand neighbours, and in particular two women who spent all match, every match, conversing behind my left shoulder with each other and with some younger men, namedropping at every opportunity. They were, apparently, close personal friends of all the players and the management, but they were particularly devoted to Mick McCarthy. Unfortunately, this was the season when McCarthy's limitations were exposed rather too frequently. Steve Redmond's pace often came to the rescue, but the clumsiness became too much to bear at times. In Division Two McCarthy had been very effective, but when faced with strikers of superior quality and speed, he found it difficult to cope. It didn't help that the whole season turned out to be dismal, virtually from start to finish. When the frustration becomes too much, there is a need to shout out. I became embroiled in an argument about the merits of Mr McCarthy. This sort of thing is always futile at a football match because everybody sees the match differently and we all have our favourites and villains. The argument didn't last long because one of the women called me four-eyes, temporarily throwing me off track since I hadn't anticipated having to combat the debating skills of a five-year-old. I don't wear glasses often, and had only been using them for driving and football games for a relatively short time. I'm not sure that it was an advantage to be able to see everything clearly in season 1986/87, but that was the effect that wearing spectacles had, so I wore them. This is the only time in my life that I have been called four-eyes. I treasure the moment. My adversary no doubt settled back in her seat feeling victorious, but I was more startled and amused than defeated. It emphasised the pointlessness of arguing with them, and enlivened an otherwise dreary and depressing afternoon's football. The correct rejoinder for this display of mental dexterity would have been to call them fish-faced old slappers. Isn't it irritating when you only come up with the pertinent debating point after the moment has passed?

In another captivating display of wit, my father also got called grandad by one of their young men friends, even though he had hardly spoken a word. Incidentally, this description was technically incorrect. We had to endure the relentless prattle for the remainder of the season, but I'm glad to say that they removed themselves elsewhere a couple of years later. No doubt, they were sitting with their famous acquaintances in the directors' box, or impersonating players' wives, a position in life to which they clearly aspired.

This kind of internecine bitching often occurs when things are going badly, which is most of the time at Maine Road. Many of the Faithful seem to attend with large helpings of retained anger and frustration loitering barely below the surface, just waiting for the opportunity to unleash it on one of their own players. Every so often somebody else defends a player and a slanging match, occasionally degenerating into near-fisticuffs, provides a distraction from the 22 men chasing after a ball. These disputes are seldom resolved and can fester for months, although I've never seen one result in a serious assault. Season ticket seats mean that you may be located near to people whose every loud and frequent utterances strike you as stupidity beyond words. It's tempting to get involved and offer your opinion, if only to gain a temporary respite. It is often difficult to restrain yourself from doing so, but it's best in the long run. Supporting the same club does not make you kindred spirits. Four-eyes and the fish-faced old slappers of the Mick McCarthy fan club did not see eye to eye.

The first match of the season resulted in a 3-1 win at Maine Road, against recently promoted Wimbledon. City really showed the new boys what a huge step up the First Division was. At least, that's what I thought at the time. Of course, Wimbledon are still in the top League, and have been ever since that day. Ian Brightwell was the latest City youngster to be given a debut, in a midfield also comprising Graham Baker, who scored twice, and Neil McNab. Steve Redmond switched between a position as extra defender and midfield. He should have been the main central defender all season, but it was primarily May, Wilson, Clements and McCarthy who formed the defence, with Gordon Davies partnered by Christie, a scorer on his debut, in attack. Paul Simpson actually replaced Brightwell early in the second half against Wimbledon, to spark City into some action.

On the following Monday, I was back working in the laboratory, massacring bacteria, and relying on sporadic reports from Anfield as City held out for a completely unexpected 0-0 draw against Liverpool. The promising start began to fade when the Blues lost 1-0 away to Spurs. A 2-2 home draw with Norwich didn't help, despite two goals from Christie, one a penalty. New arrival Robert Hopkins, from Birmingham City, made his debut in this game. Hopkins played as a wide midfield player. He lasted an even shorter time than Christie.

On Saturday, 6 September 1986, there was the opportunity to make progress up the table, with another home game against Coventry City. To attend this fixture I had to execute a cunning plan requiring military precision. The match coincided with a one-day conference taking place at Manchester University, in the Medical School on Oxford Road. Having commenced the journey at 0600 hours, following a rendezvous with my PhD supervisor, who was driving, we made our destination in good time for a light breakfast and a coffee in the refectory. At 0900, the conference got underway. What my supervisor didn't realise was that I was intending to go AWOL for the second half. After the lunch break, I had to extricate myself from earnest scientific discussions, sprint up Oxford Road – busily removing my tie and attempting to make myself more presentable for an afternoon at Maine Road – and rendezvous with my father at the Old Garrett public house. Having achieved this just within the time limit, progress was made through the slow-moving traffic and into Maine Road in time for kick-off. My reward for all this rushing around, and risking the wrath of an irate boss, was a performance of astonishing ineptitude from the Blues, who managed to lose 1-0 in an appalling match, Cyrille Regis taking advantage of one of a very limited number of scoring opportunities.

Two 0-0 draws and a 1-0 defeat at Luton, followed by a dispiriting 2-1 defeat at Maine Road against Leicester, where Hopkins scored his only ever City goal, sent the Blues plunging down the table to nineteenth. Further defeats at Newcastle and Chelsea left City propping up the First Division table. By that time big changes were afoot. Billy McNeill had decided to leave City for pastures new. He took the manager's job at Aston Villa, putting himself on a road that led to a peculiar double: the manager of two different First Division teams relegated in the same season – quite an achievement.

Jimmy Frizzell was put in charge of City, and his reaction was to speed up the introduction of the youth team players. David White, tall and unfeasibly fast, replaced Hopkins and began a long City career, initially as a right-winger. Hopkins returned to his beloved Midlands, to join West Bromwich Albion, in a deal which brought the exotically named Imre Varadi to City. Varadi, a striker, was one of those players who had always looked pretty good when playing *against* City. Varadi scored on his debut at Chelsea and further increased optimism about his prospects. The optimism proved ill-founded, but the Varadi deal did spell the end of Trevor Christie's brief Manchester City career. He was transferred to Walsall, just before he was due to complete a house move north. Frizzell's other new signings were an attempt to repeat the Gerry Gow/Bobby McDonald phenomenon of 1980/81. Tony Grealish, a strong contender for any Gow lookalike competition, was purchased as a grizzled midfield player, and John Gidman crossed the city for a modest fee to play at right-back. The debut match for both players was to be the Manchester derby game at Maine Road, on Sunday, 26 October 1986, in front of the live ITV cameras. Although City were bottom of the League, the enemy were only three places better off. Incidentally, Billy McNeill's Aston Villa were third from bottom.

The match was an ill-tempered affair, with skirmishes on and off the field, including some outbreaks quite close to my North Stand position. It was something of a baptism of fire for my girlfriend of the time, who had expressed an interest in attending instead of my father, who was away on holiday. The two goals came in quick succession. The City equaliser was Mick McCarthy's finest moment of the whole season, and probably his entire City career: a truly awesome header from the edge of the penalty area, following a left-wing corner in front of the North Stand. The ball simply thundered into the top corner. City rose to twenty-first place.

Three successive home wins in November lifted the spirits a little. Unfortunately, one of them was only in the Full Members Cup, another 3-1 win against Wimbledon, in front of 4,914 spectators. The match was significant for the fact that Paul Moulden was given the opportunity to play in attack alongside Varadi. He responded with two goals and was ensured selection for the grudge match against Villa, four days later. Moulden's precise finishing, leading to two more goals for the young striker, was the key factor in another 3-1 victory. Varadi contributed his first home goal. Perhaps Billy McNeill was wondering if he had made the right choice. No doubt McNeill felt badly let down by the lack of serious money to spend on players at City, but prospects at Villa looked no brighter.

A 2-1 win over Charlton, with Moulden again a goalscorer, completed a sequence that lifted the Blues out of the relegation zone, but only just, and not for long. A run of three successive League defeats sent City straight back to the bottom once more. The Full Members Cup win against Watford that interrupted this dismal little run was no consolation. Paul Moulden scored seven times in six matches before hitting a barren spell that lasted the same length. It is an unfortunate fact of life as a striker that chances are required before goals can be scored.

David White scored his first City goal in a 3-1 victory against West Ham at Maine Road on 13 December 1986, but City were still in serious trouble as Christmas approached. Nicky Reid made a return to the side for the trip to Coventry City on 21 December, my first away game of the season, but it was a muscular performance from Steve Redmond, in midfield, that rescued the Blues. Twice mid-table Coventry took the lead, and twice Steve Redmond equalised for City. He left the second quite late, and it was a considerable relief when it arrived. Coventry City was the home for David Phillips and Dave Bennett. Bennett was soon to gain some personal revenge against Spurs in his second FA Cup Final.

The Blues demonstrated good fighting spirit at Highfield Road, but I presume that this particular performance was not typical of the majority of away matches in season 1986/87. A 5-0 defeat at Charlton in the next away game confirms such a view. In between, a nervous Boxing Day crowd saw City edge a 1-0 home win against Sheffield Wednesday, with Paul Simpson scoring the only goal. A draw at Watford and another 1-0 home win against Oxford, courtesy of a rare penalty, converted by Neil McNab, lifted City to sixteenth place. It was then that things began to go horribly wrong. Paul Moulden suffered injury problems, which caused him to miss all but a few games at the end of the season, by which time it was too late. With Varadi proving inconsistent, and nobody else able to have much impact, the goals dried up.

The season began to turn sour early in the New Year. On 10 January 1987, City faced an FA Cup third-round tie at a bitterly cold Old Trafford. I sat high in J Stand, in the corner of the Scoreboard End, to witness a dour match played out on a frozen *Swamp*. City lost 1-0 in a game notable for a mysterious disallowed goal by Imre Varadi in the closing stages. I was at the right end of the ground to have a good view, and I watched it all again on 'Match of the Day'. Nobody came up with a plausible explanation for the decision.

Does there have to be one?

A week later, City's misfortune continued at home to Liverpool. The Blues played much better than they had when beating Liverpool at Maine Road in the previous season, but they couldn't score. Following a surprise return to the Academy, Peter Barnes was making his second debut, but it was youngster Darren Beckford, part of the prolific Beckford-Moulden partnership at reserve team level, who missed his chance for glory by squandering the best chance. As the match neared its conclusion, the decisive moment developed from an innocuous set of circumstances. The ball crossed the by-line in front of the North Stand for an obvious corner. Bruce Grobelaar grabbed the ball, as goalkeepers do, to prevent the corner from being taken quickly. City defenders moved forward. Suddenly, Grobelaar realised, before most others, that the referee had actually awarded a goal kick. Within a minute, the ball was whisked down to the other end of the pitch and Ian Rush steered the winning goal beyond a stranded Perry Suckling.

Paul Lake (aged 18) was the latest City youngster to make his debut, in a goalless draw at Wimbledon, and Ian Brightwell contributed his first goal in a 1-1 away draw against Norwich City. That result left City in eighteenth place. In between, City went out of the Full Members Cup, losing 3-2 at home to Ipswich.

Lack of goals and the inability to win a single match away from home all season led to City falling back into the relegation zone. They never recovered. The three points for a win system made winning essential, and City simply couldn't win. At the end of February I left Bangor to take up a job in Liverpool, which made the travelling to matches a whole lot easier. I was even getting paid a proper wage. Things were looking up, but not for City.

The League match at Old Trafford was a particular disappointment. I couldn't recall seeing such a lacklustre performance in a derby game. Even though Paul Moulden made a reappearance, City were comfortably beaten 2-0, and looking very much the part of a relegated team. The chant:

'We never win at home and we never win away,
We lost last week and we lost again today,
We don't give a fuck, 'cause we're all pissed up,
MCFC, OK,'

may lack a little in artistic merit, but sadly it was all too apt. Mind you, it scans better than most of Andrew Lloyd Webber's.

A home defeat at the hands of Chelsea returned City to the relegation zone. Although Jimmy Frizzell made the incredibly astute signing of Paul Stewart, for £200,000 from Blackpool, the momentum was all heading downwards. Stewart's debut was in a scoreless home draw against Newcastle, which was followed by a 4-0 defeat at Leicester City that sent the Blues to the foot of the table. Goals from Stewart and Moulden were not enough to prevent a 4-2 home defeat by Southampton, and we could all hear those nails being hammered into the City coffin. There was a much better performance in a 1-1 draw at home to Spurs, but single points were not sufficient.

On 25 April 1987, after a run of 14 League games without a win, Stewart was amongst the scorers as City thrashed Arsenal 3-0 in their penultimate home match – their best display of the whole season. This was closely followed by a 1-0 victory against Nottingham Forest in the final Maine Road game. Both of these opponents were highly placed. The belated improvement served merely to prolong the agony. The final match of the season, away to West Ham, kicked-off with City still harbouring remote mathematical hopes of survival. A 2-0 defeat ended all that, and the Blues were relegated, finishing in twenty-first position. The West Ham fans sang, 'We'll meet again.'

One curious fact about the 1986/87 season was that City comfortably won the Central League title. The youth team players were emerging, but they hadn't made it in time. I went to every home match in season 1986/87 which, considering my location for most of the season, and taking into account how poor City were for the majority of their matches, must say something. The Blues won only eight games at Maine Road, which is eight more than they managed on their travels. There are those who would accuse me of being a part-time supporter; after all, I didn't go to all of the away matches as well. Fair enough, I know that there are plenty of people who are even madder than me.

Season 1987/88: Remember When City Scored Ten!

Relegation was not so bad this time. It is possible, with practice, to grow accustomed to such things, and on this occasion it had looked inevitable for many weeks prior to the actual confirmation. Of course, it was not a pleasant experience, but at least *The Nation's Team* had failed, yet again, to win the trophy they most coveted, and I was now living far closer to the Academy. Although the traditional relationship with all things Mancunian is based on mutual distrust, contempt and hatred, Liverpool is rather a good place to be a Manchester City fan. One of Liverpool's main attractions is that no RAG dares to show their allegiance in public for fear of lynching – an admirable state of affairs, if you ask me. Liverpool and Manchester City fans have more in common than either group would care to acknowledge.

Contrary to popular belief, there is not a comedian on every corner, which is just as well. Imagine turning every corner with the threat of Jimmy Tarbuck looming. Liverpool is everything that Bangor isn't: a lively city, with plenty of good places to eat, drink, be merry, and regret it the day afterwards.

One of the few other consolations for relegation was that City would not be required to face Liverpool or Everton, thus saving me from potential embarrassment at my new workplace. At least, that was what I thought. City, of course, contrived not only to play the two Liverpool teams, but to lose comfortably on both occasions. Before the season began, I was much more concerned about the new play-off system. I was convinced that such a horrific method for denying the third-best team promotion could only have been devised to torment Manchester City fans. Surprisingly, it hasn't happened, yet.

I was a little disappointed and surprised to hear that Jimmy Frizzell was to be 'moved upstairs', as the phrase has it, to make way for a new team manager, Mel Machin. Frizzell had taken over a struggling team and adopted a brave and laudable survival strategy, giving several young players the opportunity to gain first team experience. It hadn't been enough to save the Blues, but there had been some promising signs, and the future looked reasonably rosy. Machin made little effort to endear himself to the Faithful. Initially, he put his name to the manager's notes in the match magazine, priced 60 pence for a second consecutive season, presumably as a consolation for relegation. After a while this chore was delegated to Jimmy Frizzell, officially the General Manager. It was this lack of rapport with the supporters that ultimately proved to be Machin's downfall. When he did eventually receive the Swales dispatch, Machin was just beginning to win me over. For much of his reign at Maine Road, however, I referred to him as Mad Mel, for reasons which will become apparent as the story unfolds.

The City team for the new season was an inexperienced one, containing a high proportion of home-grown talent. Eric Nixon was back in goal following the demotion of Perry Suckling, who didn't have a bad season in 1986/87, but did have his limitations.

In any case, I could never grow accustomed to his name. John Gidman, looking as though he would be very much at home swigging Newcastle Brown Ale at the UMIST Heavy Metal Disco, was at right-back, with Andy May somewhat cruelly discarded and sent to Huddersfield. My biggest disappointment was the departure to Chelsea of my favourite, Clive Wilson, whose talents had been completely wasted at left-back. His replacement, Andy Hinchcliffe, made his debut in the opening match of the new season and quickly established himself as the regular left-back; so much so that he was soon attracting unwanted attention from Division One vultures. Kenny Clements was still the captain, and with Mick McCarthy having departed following an unhappy season, Steve Redmond became the established partner for Clements in central defence. In fact, Steve Redmond rapidly became City's most important and consistent defender, exhibiting confidence and calmness way beyond his years. Mark Seagraves, who couldn't break into the Liverpool team, was bought to bring some extra competition for places in the City defence.

Neil McNab was to provide the necessary experience in midfield, to counter the youthful exuberance of the likes of Ian Brightwell. Brightwell was an energetic player who still looked very much at home in short trousers, but was soon to develop into an effective operator, defending well when needed, and possessing a useful knack of cropping up at the right moment in the opponent's penalty area to score some crucial goals. David White was continuing his development as a serious threat to the left flank of any defence, and another City youngster, Ian Scott, began the season with great promise, passing the ball with accuracy and contributing goals. Sadly, Scott, whose debut was also in City's first game of the season, failed to live up to the early promise. Paul Simpson began the season as substitute but soon regained a regular place on the left wing.

The forward line consisted of Imre Varadi, the man credited with inspiring the banana boom because of his exotic name – more of that later – and Paul Stewart. The latter had strength, determination and a considerable finishing repertoire, which included not only some very meaty efforts, but also a range of delicate curling shots that floated most pleasingly into the top corner. Stewart was the revelation of the season, terrorising unsuspecting Second Division defenders, and becoming the first City player for a decade to score 20 League goals, a feat achieved with a good deal to spare. Paul Moulden, still only 20 years old, suffered his fourth bone fracture, which meant that a Stewart-Moulden partnership was never really given a chance. Tony Adcock, a regular goalscorer in the lower divisions, was bought to provide some competition for the attacking positions.

Stewart and Varadi both scored in City's opening day 2-1 victory against Plymouth, in front of a paltry crowd of 20,046. A couple of draws away from Maine Road followed, but it was some time before the lengthy run of away games without a win was threatened. A 2-1 home defeat by Blackburn Rovers was a particularly traumatic experience. Indeed, the Blues sank to seventeenth place before eventually finding some acceptable form. A 4-0 win against Millwall and a 3-0 win against Stoke City, both at

Maine Road, in front of sub-20,000 crowds, came just in time to lift the spirits. Varadi scored all three goals against Stoke. Indeed, he outscored Paul Stewart to begin with.

The City season was one of irritating inconsistency from that moment onward. Depressing defeats would be followed by high-scoring victories. On 17 October 1987, after a 3-0 defeat at Ipswich, the Blues were languishing in fourteenth place. It was just after this match that the City youngsters began to demonstrate their considerable potential. Paul Stewart scored goals six and seven of the season as the Blues pulled off an emphatic, but surprising, 4-2 win away to League leaders Bradford City. This splendid midweek triumph ended the long search for a win away from Maine Road. Thankfully, I was within radio range again, and therefore able to listen to the Piccadilly Radio commentary. City surrendered a two-goal lead but fought back to restore it. Typically, back at Maine Road a few days later, City could only manage a 1-1 draw against Allan Clarke's Barnsley.

In the Littlewoods Cup (yet another name change) third-round tie at Maine Road on 27 October 1987, the City team were in the mood to prove their worth against First Division opponents, Nottingham Forest. Paul Stewart was the chief menace, although it was Varadi who scored twice as City took advantage of a nervous and tentative Forest to win 3-0, Stewart scoring the other goal. Only 15,168 witnessed this performance. City were going to have to work to bring back the missing thousands.

I was press-ganged into attending a wedding on the day of the next match, away to Swindon Town. I discovered that City were 2-0 ahead, but then lost contact with proceedings. I heard nothing of the intervening events until the game was over, at which point I awaited the final score expectantly, having managed to locate a television set displaying the BBC teleprinter. After seemingly endless non-league and Scottish results, the typewriter finally came up with *Swindon Town 3*.

I'm not sure whether the ensuing dramatic pause was genuine or imagined, but there was ample time for my heart to sink and a familiar sickening feeling to develop in the stomach, and then the rest emerged: *Man. City 4*. David White had contributed two of those goals.

Again the Blues failed to follow up an encouraging away win, drawing 1-1 at home to Middlesbrough, despite a fine goal by Andy Hinchcliffe. As a consequence of suffering injury in the Middlesbrough game, Varadi was unavailable for the visit of Huddersfield Town a few days later, on 7 November 1987. Varadi's absence meant that the ginger-haired Tony Adcock was offered a rare opportunity to start a match. On the face of it, a Second Division encounter with Huddersfield Town on a damp November day was not likely to set the heart racing with anticipation. Yet the crowd was close to 20,000, presumably because City were beginning to establish a reputation for high scoring. This was a match to justify the habitual attendance of those souls who turn out week after week to watch football matches, in the hope that something extraordinary might occur. Imagine the turmoil of the reasonably loyal fan who, for some reason, ended up missing this one. The game turned out to be one of the most memorable Manchester City matches in modern history.

Andy May returned to Maine Road as captain of Huddersfield, who were managed by the famous ex-Newcastle United hero, Malcolm MacDonald. In the opening exchanges the visitors had the more promising moments and the home crowd was subdued. There was no inkling of what was to come.

It was quite a relief when a left-footed drive by Neil McNab gave the Blues the lead, following the first meaningful City attack of the game. 1-0. With the Huddersfield defence offering the first indications of the debacle to come, Paul Stewart was left unmarked to fire in the second goal. 2-0. Andy Hinchcliffe's cross was headed in by the unmarked Adcock to give the stand-in striker his first goal for the club. 3-0. Four minutes before half-time, Paul Simpson broke clear down the left flank. Rather than crossing the ball, he decided to cut back and beat the defenders for a second time before presenting David White with a chance that would have been difficult to miss. 4-0 and half-time.

If Malcolm MacDonald gave his defence a severe reprimand during the interval, it did not have the intended effect. Kicking towards the North Stand End, City continued to threaten goals with virtually every attack. A Paul Simpson cross was misjudged by an increasingly distraught Brian Cox in the Hudderfield goal, and Tony Adcock scored with an emphatic volley. 5-0. Another Simpson cross caused similar uncertainty, and Paul Stewart was able to place his far-post header over the stranded Cox and into the net. 6-0. Huddersfield's resistance was becoming more feeble by the minute. When Adcock dispossessed the defender Webster and sprinted clear to complete his hat-trick, the match moved beyond the comprehensive slaughter stage and into the potential record-breaking stage. 7-0. I had never seen any team score seven goals in the same match previously. For the first time, a double figures score was beginning to look possible. Paul Stewart's tap-in from an Andy Hinchcliffe cross, to complete the second hat-trick of the match, emphasised the point. 8-0. Resistance was now virtually non-existent, but time was running out. McNab's through ball to Adcock inspired another City attack. Adcock's cross was inadvertently redirected into the path of David White, who thundered it into the net. 9-0. There could only be a couple of minutes remaining. The double figure scoreline was achievable, and the Faithful were willing it to happen. Everyone knew that the opportunity might never again arise. The City players became more anxious, despite the fact that the points were well and truly won. Huddersfield broke and were awarded a penalty kick. I hate to sound churlish, but I thought the decision harsh. More importantly, it looked likely to use up the remaining time and, therefore, prevent the tenth goal. Andy May stepped up to dispatch the penalty, subsequently performing a theatrical bow to the Kippax Stand fans, who were most amused and rewarded him with generous applause. 9-1. We were already into injury time when David White broke clear of the Huddersfield defence once more. He calmly skipped past the goalkeeper and fired the ball into the net to complete the incredible scoreline, and the third hat-trick of the match. 10-1. I do not ever expect to see the feat repeated.

After the match, Malcolm MacDonald questioned the last two City goals, suggesting a hint of offside. 8-1 would not have been much of an improvement, but let's face it, McDonald was brave to even attend the press conference. A couple of years later, I met a drunken Huddersfield fan in a pub in Liverpool. He was delighted to discover my allegiances and insisted on reminiscing. He was proud to have been at the match, and was most disappointed that I hadn't spotted him jumping up and down in the Platt Lane Stand in celebration of the Huddersfield goal.

This result inspired a formidable run of form, catapulting City into the promotion race as realistic contenders. The Simod Cup, the successor to the Full Members Cup, may still have been an exercise in futility, but it did provide City with the chance to continue their goalscoring feats with a 6-2 win at Plymouth, just three days after the Huddersfield massacre. Adcock again scored a hat-trick. The latest City youngster to make a real impression, the tall and elegant Paul Lake, playing alongside McNab in a central midfield role, was also amongst the scorers, as was Paul Stewart.

Stewart scored both goals in a far more important win, away to Reading, as City warmed up nicely for a Littlewoods Cup fourth-round tie at home to First Division Watford. In the Cup match, David White gave City the lead following a corner. The advantage was maintained until half-time, in front of a largely deserted Platt Lane Stand. The Watford equaliser, by Allen, was one of those shots off the underside of the crossbar that test the eyesight of the nearest linesman. This particular linesman decided that the ball had bounced down over the line, and it looked as though Watford might thwart the Blues once more in a Maine Road cup-tie. Instead, Paul Lake's nimble footwork took him past Tony Coton in the Watford goal, and David White swept City back into the lead. A fortunate penalty award for handball, somewhat belated compensation for the FA Cup penalty awarded against City a couple of years earlier, proved decisive. Although Coton saved the penalty kick, Paul Stewart still scored his goal, from the rebound.

Stewart completed a run of scoring in five successive matches, contributing a real screamer of a goal in a 3-0 win at home to Birmingham City, with David White adding two more to his tally. The match was all over by half-time. That made a total of eight Stewart goals and seven White goals in five matches. Adcock, lagging behind with a mere six, got the goal to earn City a 1-1 draw at West Bromwich Albion, a disappointing result after recent exploits. A goal each for White and Stewart at Bournemouth earned City a 2-0 win and sixth place in the League table, seven points adrift of leaders Middlesbrough, the highest position achieved so far that season.

Being back within Manchester local radio range, I was able to listen to the phone-ins and general football coverage concerning City. It was around this time that I recall driving back to Liverpool from a City match and hearing that virtuoso of footballing experts, Tommy Docherty, imparting his words of wisdom on Piccadilly Radio. Mystic Doc was offering his specialist opinions on the City youngsters. The Doc was replying to the general opinion of many that City's current crop of younger players promised riches, and that several of them were already valuable assets. Mr Docherty was emphatic that none of City's current team would ever command a fee of £1 million. Within 12 months, Paul Stewart alone had been transferred for more than twice that figure. White and Hinchcliffe also broke the Docherty limit, and there were some very serious money offers made for Paul Lake and Ian Brightwell over the ensuing couple of years. There can be no question that had Paul Lake's career not been seriously curtailed by injury, he would have been worth a minor fortune. Apart from that, Mr Docherty was, as always, spot on. His almost psychic abilities are positively spooky.

A crowd of 23,161 turned up at Maine Road to see the encounter with Crystal Palace on 5 December 1987, a match that contained one of the definitive moments of the whole season. With the momentum emphatically on City's side, following an unbeaten run of 12 matches in all competitions, there was every incentive for victory against a Palace side who were only below the Blues on goal difference. The Steve Coppell Palace side of the Wright and Bright era were, however, well organised and difficult to beat. As the match progressed, it became clear that this would not be a high-scoring encounter. Indeed, a goalless draw loomed large as approach play became bogged down in an overcrowded midfield. Palace, employing a classic Tommy Docherty-style offside-trap, virtually up to the halfway line, were getting the help they needed from overzealous linesmen, and City were having to work hard to create opportunities.

And then the Blues made a vital breakthrough. Paul Lake foiled the trap laid by the Palace defence, breaking clear with a run from deep. Showing typical confidence in possession, he calmly beat the Palace goalkeeper and City had the lead. With Palace now forced to be more adventurous, the match was there for the taking. The Blues had the players to exploit the new space created. I don't recall exactly what led to Eric Nixon's costly moment of madness, and I can't remember the Palace player involved, but the incident changed not only the course of this match, but the direction of the season as a whole. Nixon had the ball in his hands when he struck out at a Palace attacker in an ill-advised act of retribution. Had the outcome been a mere sending off, things may not have been so bad. There was only about a quarter of the match remaining. Unfortunately, when a goalkeeper commits such an act, the referee not only sends him off but also awards a penalty kick. City's hard-earned lead was thrown away.

We all love those momentous occasions when, in the face of adversity, an outfield player performs heroics in goal to lead his side to a famous victory. Well, this wasn't one of them. The unfortunate Steve Redmond was about to discover that he was not put on this planet to be a goalkeeper. Not only was the penalty converted, but Palace scored twice more to leave City's unbeaten run in tatters.

Eric Nixon was not a popular man that evening. It was an indiscretion that contributed much to his eventual demise as the City goalkeeper. The signing, on loan from Everton, of Bobby Mimms earlier in the season, for a less than successful three-game run, already suggested a lack of confidence in Eric. This proved to be his last season as the City number one.

A 1-0 win at Millwall, courtesy of Adcock's goal, suggested that the Palace defeat might be no more than a blip. City reached their peak position of fifth place. In fact, the City descent was merely delayed. I must have been very bored on Wednesday, 16 December 1987, because I attended my only ever Simod Cup (or Full Member Cup) match. It was at Maine Road and against Chelsea, who included my old favourite, Clive Wilson. I must say that the view from the Main Stand was extremely good. City lost 2-0.

The Simod Cup exit was practically to be welcomed, but a dreadful 2-1 defeat at home to Oldham, just before Christmas, was most definitely not. Perry Suckling did not exactly make the most of his opportunity to return to the first team because of Nixon's suspension. The City goalkeeper scored an early own goal, from which the Blues never really recovered. On Boxing Day, City's largest crowd of the season, 30,153, turned up at Maine Road for the visit of Leeds United. The Blues were in urgent need of a win. David White scored a breathtaking goal at the North Stand End, walloping the ball into the top corner of the net from distance, but City lost the match 2-1. Despite a 3-1 victory at Stoke, City's general decline continued with a fourth successive League defeat at the Academy, 3-1 against struggling Shrewsbury. The Blues were back down in tenth position and beginning to lose touch.

The FA Cup third-round draw offered me the chance of a trip to Huddersfield. With City having already beaten them 10-1, and the Yorkshire side propping up the Second Division table, this looked like an ideal opportunity to see an away win. Instead, Huddersfield exhibited admirable determination. It took a very late Gidman free-kick to earn City a 2-2 draw, with Ian Brightwell contributing the other goal. Three days later, the replay at Maine Road proved to be one of the dullest matches that I have ever had the misfortune to witness. Neither side managed a goal during 120 tortuous minutes.

Meanwhile, back in the League, City threw away a lead at Plymouth to lose 3-2 and consolidate their mid-table status. Current form did not suggest that the Blues were in any state to take on Everton at Goodison Park in the Littlewoods Cup quarter-final. The previous round had taken place a long time ago, during City's best spell of the season, but the whole mood was very different now. Adcock had stopped scoring and been replaced by Varadi, who fared little better. Paul Stewart was still contributing regularly, but when he missed a couple of matches, it merely served to emphasise the lack of firepower on offer in his absence. Mel Machin seemed reluctant to use the now fit Paul Moulden. This reluctance was to be a recurring theme throughout the remainder of City's time in the Second Division.

I went along to Goodison Park, for the first time in several seasons, still more than a little wary of the place. A couple of people from work came with me, and we arrived sufficiently early to enable discussions with stewards and police about the feasibility of being released before the end of the game, if we so desired. I was not confident about City's chances against an Everton side placed third in Division One and still pretty close to their peak. We were assured that our departure would be perfectly acceptable. City went behind early on, and rarely threatened to make an impact on the match. When an Adrian Heath goal put Everton two goals ahead with only about 15 minutes remaining, we decided to make good our escape plans. Of course, the police and stewards had now decided that everyone in the Manchester City end had to be kept behind until 10 minutes after the end of the match. Eventually, the police marched everyone out of the ground and towards the coaches, at a short distance from waiting and baiting Everton fans. As usual, I did not want to go in the direction of the coaches. I did, after all, live in Liverpool. I realise that the police wished me to go from Goodison Park to Newsham Park, only a couple of miles away, via Manchester. I hate to be awkward, but I didn't find that idea particularly appealing. We had all foreseen the problem, but for some reason the police simply could not allow for the possibility that some Manchester City supporters might not have travelled to the match on official coaches or trains. We had to break clear. Ironically, one of the lads I was with was an Everton fan. That wasn't about to save him now. By keeping heads down and plunging into the nearest crowd as soon as possible, we managed to avoid assault, but others were not so fortunate. I remained less than enthusiastic about visits to Goodison Park.

Rather than restore Paul Moulden to the side, Machin made the fateful signing from Northampton Town of Trevor Morley, a man with a horrible haircut, but another regular goalscorer in the lower leagues. Morley made his debut as Stewart's new striking partner in yet another home defeat, a painful 2-0 loss against Billy McNeill's Aston Villa, who were heading for promotion.

With City's League aspirations diminishing rapidly, attention returned to the FA Cup, and a Monday night, second replay in Huddersfield. City finally finished off their opponents with a 3-0 win, setting up a trip to the seaside in the next round. After the questionable safety associated with my previous visit to Bloomfield Road, there was no way that I was going back to Blackpool for a Cup match. In any case, I was in no position to queue for the limited supply of tickets so I had to listen to the encounter on Piccadilly Radio. It was a match that had me leaping around my flat like a deranged imbecile, firstly with agony as Blackpool took the lead, and then with ecstasy as Paul Lake equalised well into stoppage time, with virtually the last kick of the match.

In the replay, goals from Stewart, against his old club, and Simpson saw City through, and the season was still alive. Meanwhile, with Perry Suckling departing to Crystal Palace, Mike Stowell became the second Everton goalkeeper of the season to come on loan to City

After a 2-1 defeat at Blackburn, City at last managed a home win, against Bournemouth. That set the Blues up nicely for a 3-1 home win in the FA Cup fifth-round, against Plymouth, a match played in an excitable atmosphere. It may have required two last-gasp equalisers, but this now represented City's best FA Cup run since the 1981 final.

The magic balls had given City a home tie quarter-final against the all-conquering Liverpool. To make matters worse, the match was chosen for live nationwide television coverage. There was a full house at Maine Road on a memorable Sunday afternoon, as City's young team trotted out to take on the likes of Barnes and Rush. At the university, where I was working, there were plenty of Liverpool fans, both armchair and genuine. I didn't expect a win, but I was praying for respectability. My dad and I became embroiled in an argument close to kick-off because there were interlopers in our seats. The transgressors seemed unable to grasp the concept of seat numbers. I remember becoming a little agitated and mentioning that we came to every home game, and didn't see why we should be forced to move for this, the biggest match of the season. For some reason, the women from the Mick McCarthy Fan Club joined in, emphasising that they came to every game too, as if I was trying to move them. The argument had nothing whatsoever to do with them. Eventually, we managed to penetrate the grey matter of the individuals concerned, just in time for the kick-off.

For the opening quarter of the game, not much happened. City offered little threat, and Liverpool seemed content to play the ball amongst their defenders and back to the goalkeeper with monotonous regularity. Then Liverpool, attacking the North Stand End, advanced down the left wing. John Barnes used his arm to keep the ball in play. The referee didn't see it. The linesman didn't see it, and worst of all, the cameras were not at the right angle to pick it up, but it was totally blatant to anybody in the right-hand side of the North Stand. It was one of life's cruel little tricks. Ray Houghton volleyed the first goal from Barnes's cross.

Trailing 1-0 at half-time, there was still some hope on a muddy pitch, but Liverpool could now take as much time as they wished, and they were very good at that. The match was finished as a contest when the referee awarded a penalty kick for an alleged foul by Paul Lake, who slid in the mud to challenge Craig 'Skippy' Johnston. The penalty was dispatched, and it was no great surprise that Liverpool broke clear to take advantage of an under-staffed City defence to score twice more. I had to endure the expert comments from the armchair supporters in the tea room the following day, as they discussed the match in typically patronising and condescending fashion, as if I hadn't been the only one who was actually there. My excuses depended on the first two goals being dubious, but the cameras failed to back me up on the first one. In any case, 0-4 looks like a drubbing. In all honesty, City never threatened to score, and once they were behind, there was little hope of that changing.

Back in the League, City had at least rediscovered the ability to win at Maine Road, but the quest for away points was proving less fruitful. There was the occasional ray of hope, such as a 2-1 victory at Sheffield United, with Trevor Morley scoring the first following a corner, and David White bursting through in typical style to add the second, but the promotion challenge was stuttering to a halt. A Dave Bamber equaliser for Swindon, at Maine Road in a 1-1 draw, cancelled out Paul Stewart's twenty-fifth goal of the season, and left the Blues with little prospect of even a play-off place.

My dying hopes for the salvation of City's season evaporated during a depressing Easter afternoon spent on the large, open terraces behind the goal at Leeds Road, Huddersfield, when the Blues incredibly managed to lose 1-0 to the team which they had beaten 10-1 earlier in the season. You've got to laugh, haven't you? Haven't you?

The season petered out with City finishing in ninth position. Two Cup quarter-finals could not prevent it from being essentially a disappointing season. There had been moments of real promise, but they hadn't been sustained. It had to be promotion next season. Nothing less would do. This was particularly true following the departure of Paul Stewart to Spurs for £2.5 million. This was the second season in succession that had ended with my favourite being sold. It was becoming an unwelcome trend. In fact, Stewart never reproduced his devastating form elsewhere. I blame the appalling curly perm that he adopted on moving south. London can have a most distressing effect on people.

Part Three: A Temporary Respite

Ian Bishop brings The Nation's Team *to its knees.*

Season 1988/89: The Year of Paul Moulden and Yes! We Have Bananas

Looking back at 1988/89 makes me particularly nostalgic for those long-departed days when the future of football looked palatable and, whatever other calamity may be lurking, the Championship would not be won by *The Nation's Team*. I welcomed this season with impatience and high hopes. This was going to be my season. I had transport. I had enough money. I had contacts in the south for overnight residential facilities and post-match beer-assisted analysis. I was determined to get to as many matches, and particularly to as many new grounds, as I could. In addition, there was something inherently appealing about following a team consisting largely of the Youth Cup-winning side; the class of '86. It helped that City appeared to have a strong case as promotion candidates. Certainly, the pundits thought so. The general optimism was somewhat tempered by the knowledge that the pundits always think so, and that there were a number of questions as yet unanswered. Who was going to score all those goals that Paul Stewart might have contributed? Would Paul Moulden even be given the chance? Had Mad Mel spent the Stewart money wisely? Would the banana fad last? Was it possible that an album entitled Bummed could be so good? Did Mozzer really manage to come up with a solo LP much better than the final effort by The Smiths? What *is* the capital of Mauritius?

With the end of a decade once more sparking an explosion of excellent tunes, I finally deserted vinyl and bought my first-ever CDs: 'Gladsome', 'Humour and Blue' by Martin Stephenson and The Daintees and 'Life's Too Good' by The Sugarcubes. This was the era when bands like Happy Mondays and the Stone Roses, already famous in Manchester, became internationally renowed, along with the repetitive electronic dance music loosely referred to as House. The Hacienda was the place to be, particularly if you felt the need to relieve yourself of vast quantities of cash, but there were plenty of other options such as The Venue, if you were feeling young, or the PSV Club, for the more adventurous. I once more had friends in Manchester, and was able to spend many nights out, sampling the atmosphere and going to see all the bands. It was as if Bangor had never happened. Almost.

As season 1987/88 drew to a close, the inflatable banana craze became an increasingly prominent feature of terrace life. Initially, bananas had merely been waved by a few quirky individuals to coincide with the singing of 'Imre, Imre Banana' instead of 'Imre, Imre Varadi', but it soon became apparent that the banana phenomenon was gaining an unstoppable momentum. City were to play every game of the new season against the background of a mass of inflatable bananas, which were shaken vigorously to welcome the team on to the pitch or celebrate goals, and pointed to disarming effect as an accompaniment to chanting. There were big bananas or more sensibly sized bananas, and you could buy them outside Maine Road as easily as a burger of dubious origin or a ticket from a tout – tickets from the actual ticket office have rarely been so easy to obtain. Fyffes, big in the bananas business, were even moved to take advantage of the craze by sponsoring City. Manchester City went bananas, but not exclusively. Soon the inflatable bananas were joined by more esoteric inflatables, such as a paddling pool, a fried egg, Godzilla, Frankenstein's monster, a hammer, a dinosaur and a shark. Each was greeted with enthusiastic individual chants, and every time the fans were a little bored there came the rejoinder:

> *'We've got bananas,*
> *We've got bananas,*
> *You've not!'*

There really is no suitable reply!

So keen was I to see the start of the new season that I even contributed some of my hard-earned cash to Kevin Moran of *The Nation's Team*, by visiting *The Swamp* for a pre-season testimonial derby match. City's three new signings were all on display for our delectation. Andy Dibble (£240,000 from Luton), reasonably fresh from League Cup Final heroics against Arsenal, looked confident as the new City goalkeeper, and the modestly priced Nigel Gleghorn performed well as a left-sided midfield player. But Brian Gayle, the most expensive signing (£325,000 from Wimbledon), looked uncomfortable whenever the ball was lower than head height. On this occasion, first impressions were all too reliable; Steve Redmond, deservedly the new City captain, spent the whole season trying to cover for the inadequacies of Gayle.

The full-backs for the start of the season were Paul Lake, who could play virtually anywhere, and Andy Hinchcliffe. As the season progressed, Lake often featured in a midfield role, with Mark Seagraves playing at right-back. Stability and solidity in the City midfield was provided by Neil McNab, who was joined by the energetic Ian Brightwell for most of the season. David White provided the pace on the right, with Gleghorn proving to be an effective left-sided balance for much of the campaign. Gleghorn may not have had much pace, but his passing ability was good and he was an excellent team player. I was not terribly happy about Paul Simpson being sold off to Oxford United midway through the season, but Gleghorn did turn out to be an astute signing. The main problems for City were in attack. A combination of Trevor Morley and Wayne Biggins did not appear to be a terrifying prospect for Second Division defences. I wanted Paul Moulden in the side. In fact, virtually everyone wanted Paul Moulden in the side, except for Mad Mel.

In the testimonial match, a Trevor Morley diving header gave the Blues the lead, only for the obligatory dubious penalty decision to hand their multimillion pound opponents an equaliser. Yes, even in a testimonial game. McClair almost missed the penalty, but after striking the underside of the crossbar, the ball landed just over the goal line. The flimsy Jesper Olsen gave the home side the lead, but Morley scored a deserved equaliser for City, who were actually looking good. That is until the last 10 minutes, when they inexplicably and comprehensively collapsed, conceding three goals. Paul Moulden was the only City substitute who didn't get the opportunity to contribute.

It was only a testimonial match, I told myself, and in any case, the performance had not been so bad. I departed for a weekend in Hull in good heart, looking forward to the real start to the season, on Saturday, 27 August 1988. The Faithful were there in force to provide a spectacular banana greeting for the Blues and Hull City, contributing to a splendid opening match atmosphere. When the game began, City took immediate control. In the first half, the pick of the City chances fell to Morley, who missed them with considerable panache. Neil McNab struck a shot against the post, which was unfortunate, but it was surely just a matter of time before a dreadful-looking Hull side gave way to their superiors. There was, however, a shock in store at the beginning of the second half. Dibble blundered following one of Hull City's two corners, and Edwards scored to give the home side an unlikely lead. The crossbar was rattled twice as City endeavoured to rescue at least a point, but it was not to be. Despite their dominance, City went home with nothing.

It was only the first match of the season, I told myself, and in any case, the performance had not been so bad. This attitude prevailed for only two more days before giving way to despair. City's first home game of the season, against Oldham, was a complete nightmare. Machin had decided to leave out Gleghorn in favour of Varadi. It did not prove to be a wise decision. The strike force of Varadi, Morley and Biggins was little short of ludicrous. In defence, Brian Gayle seemed to be playing in super-slo-mo. Oldham could quite easily have been six goals ahead by half-time. They managed only two. Paul Lake missed a dubious penalty kick, although he did score later in the match, but not before Oldham's third goal. Five minutes from the end, ex-City striker Roger Palmer completed his hat-trick with an exquisite chip over City's star man, Andy Dibble. Had Dibble not been in top form, or had more of Oldham's chances fallen to Palmer, the final score could have been even worse than the utterly demoralising 1-4.

The home crowd were already jeering Trevor Morley in the next match, at home to Walsall, where he was partnered in attack by Varadi. Paul Moulden, a substitute, got to warm up on the touchline, to huge applause, but Mad Mel didn't bring him on until the eighty-first minute. Errors by Dibble and Gayle, interspersed by a Neil McNab penalty, left City trailing 2-1, and the crowd distinctly not amused. Trevor Morley equalised from a couple of inches, after McNab and Brightwell had combined to create the chance, but the Faithful were in no mood to forgive a number of earlier wasted opportunities. David White, also omitted from the starting line-up, got even less time on the pitch than Moulden. City had one point to show for their first three matches.

Mad Mel finally accepted the inevitable and chose Moulden for the next City game, away to Leeds United. It was my first visit to Elland Road for some time. Leeds, with Billy Bremner in charge, had also fallen on hard times, and had only acquired a single point from their opening two matches, which included a 4-0 thrashing at Portsmouth. This was a hard game, in every sense, but City performed better than in their previous two matches. They took a deserved lead with only 10 minutes remaining, when Neil McNab converted a penalty kick after Mervyn Day had brought Morley down. The Leeds goalkeeper might have been better advised to leave Morley alone. There was no guarantee that he would score. A much needed three points looked likely, but a free-kick two minutes from time allowed City to demonstrate how not to execute the offside-trap, and Noel Blake was left in glorious isolation to equalise. City remained in the relegation zone.

I had allowed myself to be talked into a holiday in the sun during this crucial period of the season. The home match against Brighton was to be my last prior to missing three games in succession, an agonising prospect, particularly with City in something of a pickle. My team needed me.

The pre-holiday game, on 17 September 1988, included the defining moment of the season. The match as a whole was distinctly ordinary. Ian Brightwell gave City the lead with a powerful volley, but a Brian Gayle gaffe allowed a Brighton equaliser, and with little over 20 minutes remaining, there were ominous movements on the City bench. My memory may be playing tricks, but I'm convinced that Paul Moulden's number was being prepared for a substitution, and the ball had merely to go out of play for Mad Mel to withdraw the City youngster. At that moment, Moulden, with his back to goal, received the ball 10 yards outside the Brighton penalty area, as City attacked the North Stand End. Moulden's turn bamboozled the defenders, and his right-foot shot was curled perfectly into the top corner of the Brighton net. It was the best goal of the season, and a solid metaphorical two-fingered salute to the management. What a hero!

At last, City had a victory, and I could go away in a better frame of mind. It would not be an exaggeration to say that I would much rather have been in Barnsley than in Bodrum. In fact, I would have preferred to be at all three matches that were played in my absence, and without my knowing the results of any until returning to Britain. The games were away to Chelsea and Barnsley, followed by a home match against Blackburn. The relationship with my girlfriend, the cause of this inconvenience, did not survive the season. The break-up was not due to my football obsession, but it freed me even more from any obligations that might prevent me from indulging it to the full.

As quickly as possible after landing back in the UK, I sought a newsagent's shop and nervously picked up a newspaper to flick through the back pages. Eventually, I found a League table. There was a moment of confusion as I looked for City's name, but it wasn't there. Naturally enough, I was searching from the bottom upwards. Suddenly, I located their position: **fifth**! I could hardly believe it. A quick calculation told me all that I needed to know. City had won all three matches! It may not be an original thought, but it was unavoidable. *Here we go*, I thought, or words to that effect.

In fact, a superb Paul Moulden goal, and two by Ian Brightwell, had secured a 3-1 win at Stamford Bridge. Morley and White had been the scorers in the 2-1 win at Oakwell, and a single Wayne Biggins goal had been enough to beat top-of-the-table Blackburn at Maine Road. City had also achieved a 1-0 win against Plymouth in the Littlewoods Cup for good measure. Even better, Imre Varadi had gone. Carl Bradshaw came from Sheffield Wednesday to City as part of an exchange deal.

I didn't have long to wait for the next match, at home to Portsmouth. Portsmouth were still managed by Alan Ball, and only one place below City. The seated Faithful barely had adequate time to manoeuvre their bottoms into optimal position before the Blues stormed into a 2-0 lead. David White lashed the ball in from a Moulden cross, and Moulden himself scored an admirable second goal, when there seemed little danger. A spectacular Biggins shot flew into the net after thirty minutes to complete City's dramatic opening. A Portsmouth goal, scored just before half-time, caused some concern, but a late Paul Lake goal, made by Moulden, settled matters comprehensively.

Five consecutive League victories had propelled City to fifth place, on equal points with their next opponents, Ipswich Town. This was my first opportunity to take advantage of a geographically-challenged fellow-sufferer, who lived in Hitchin, and could provide a convenient base for trips to grounds in the southern half of the country. We allowed a ridiculous amount of time to drive from Hitchin to Ipswich, with the intention of first meeting up with an Ipswich fan whom I knew from work in Liverpool. I had reckoned without the single lane roads and abundant tractors. We only just made it in time for kick-off. City had achieved no League victories at Portman Road for over 20 years, and they weren't about to start now. Jason Dozzell scored the only goal of the match from a free-kick after half-an-hour's play. The Blues created enough opportunities, but for once Paul Moulden was in a less than predatory mood.

The goals returned in abundance at Plymouth as City won the second leg of their Littlewoods Cup tie 6-3. Three days later, the Blues returned to Home Park to secure a 1-0 win in the League, thanks to a Brian Gayle goal. A very young Michael Hughes was a surprise Mad Mel selection for this match. This was one weekend spent visiting my girlfriend, who was now working in London, so I had to rely on very limited radio coverage.

Birmingham City breezed into Maine Road on 22 October 1988, displaying all the skill and imagination so typical of the team's great reputation for flare. Actually, I lie. Birmingham City came for and got a point in a goalless draw. Mad Mel's answer to City's lack of goals was to take off Paul Moulden and restore Trevor Morley to the attack, as a partner for Biggins. This appeared to most of us to be the footballing equivalent of throwing in the towel. After the match had been put out of its misery, for one horrible moment I thought that the Birmingham City team was going to perform a lap of honour. Thankfully, they thought better of it.

A 1-0 midweek defeat at West Bromwich Albion confirmed that City were struggling to maintain their forward momentum. Back at Maine Road, the Blues played out a bad-tempered match against Sunderland without the dropped Moulden, who wasn't even a substitute, or the injured Paul Lake. In a bizarre exhibition of tactical nous, recently signed Carl Bradshaw was chosen as a makeshift striker. Both goals came in the first half. Marco Gabbiadini headed Sunderland into the lead, but within four minutes Hinchcliffe blasted in the equaliser following a free-kick.

Paul Moulden was restored to the attack for the Littlewoods Cup third-round tie at Maine Road against Sheffield United, leaders of the Third Division. The young City striker, who clearly did not enjoy the confidence of Mr Machin, saved City from potential embarrassment against enthusiastic opponents by scoring a hat-trick. City won an open game 4-2.

After a goalless draw at Leicester, City played hosts to the League leaders, Watford, on 12 November 1988, and it turned out to be a memorable game. David White, City's unbelievably speedy winger, gave an awesome display of his talents in a match dominated by the Blues. White was prominent in the first half, when City attacked the Platt

Lane End, but the breakthrough didn't come. Just before half-time, Porter stunned the Faithful by curling a free-kick into the City net to give Watford the lead. Moulden was unable to convert a couple of chances early in the second half, and it began to look as if this wasn't City's day. The match was turned around when Moulden made amends for those misses by redirecting a Hinchcliffe shot beyond Tony Coton for the equaliser. That was the cue for some extraordinary wing-play by White. It seemed to everybody that the City winger had struck the ball too hard when he pushed it beyond the full-back and began to chase. White's remarkable pace, however, meant that not only did he reach the ball before it crossed the touchline, but he was able to deliver an excellent cross. Wayne Biggins, who had done well to anticipate, headed in at the near post. Inspired by that piece of action, City remained in the ascendancy, in an atmosphere of high excitement. There was more control about the next occasion requiring David White to demonstrate his speed, but the outcome was remarkably similar, a right-wing cross glance-headed in by Biggins. The 3-1 scoreline did not flatter City.

A Paul Moulden goal at Bournemouth was enough to earn the Blues three more points, and lift them to fourth, prior to the visit of Brian Horton's Oxford United, who included their recent signing, Paul Simpson. Horton had become the manager earlier in the season, following the removal of Mark Lawrenson, who had objected to the sale of Dean Saunders to Derby County. Oxford's Chairman was Maxwell Junior, Derby's was Maxwell Senior! An unstoppable shot by Richard Hill seemed likely to send Mr Horton away from Maine Road with a smile on his face. City struggled and Martin Foyle might well have increased Oxford's lead on a couple of occasions. With four minutes remaining, City were still trailing, but an incredible overhead kick by an improved Trevor Morley brought them level. The unfortunate Morley must have hoped for a reduction in his hate mail after that contribution.

Three minutes of panic ensued, amidst a cacophony of noise from a hitherto quiet crowd. A David White corner then provoked an almighty scramble in the Oxford penalty area. The ball broke to Biggins, who skied it to the edge of the penalty area. From there Steve Redmond planted an emphatic header into the Oxford net, provoking pandemonium on the terraces. Paul Simpson almost spoiled the great escape with a last-gasp solo run, but despite all their earlier efforts, Oxford departed with nothing to show for their afternoon's work. A somewhat fortunate City found themselves in third position, only a single point behind Watford, the leaders.

I managed to combine a visit to my girlfriend with City's next away fixture, against Crystal Palace. I tried very hard not to say I told you so, as we were searching in vain for somewhere to park her car, when a trip on the tube would have only taken a few minutes. These things must remain unsaid. We made it into the ground a couple of minutes late for the start, but in plenty of time to suffer an uncomfortable afternoon watching Andy Dibble perform heroics in the City goal, and Palace displaying an impressive repertoire of inept finishing. Dibble's best save was at point-blank range from Ian Wright. The Blues, like myself, must have been very grateful to escape with a goalless draw.

Back at Maine Road on 10 December 1988, three goals against Bradford City in nine minutes sent City to the top of the League for the first time. After an uneventful opening 40 minutes, Ian Brightwell burst through to lob City ahead at half-time. The real goal action began five minutes into the second half, when Brightwell steered in his second goal from a David White cross. Paul Moulden, demonstrating those admirable finishing skills, added two further goals to complete the scoring.

The approach of Christmas was the cue for the Maine Road panto, with the laughs all on City. They exited sheepishly at half-time in their next League match, trailing by two goals to a dreadful Shrewsbury Town side. Despite exerting plenty of pressure, City needed a generous penalty award, and a goal direct from a corner-kick, to rescue a point. Andy Hinchcliffe wasn't complaining; he was credited with two goals.

The weekend picked up significantly after the Shrewsbury match, with New Order, A Certain Ratio and Happy Mondays playing on the same bill at G-Mex on Saturday night. The following day, I was at the Royal Court Theatre in Liverpool for one of my many evenings in the company of The *mighty* Fall. This was a distinct improvement on the Bangor University Student Union disco.

On Boxing Day, at the away match against Stoke City, the teams ran on to the pitch to a splendidly colourful contrast of yellow bananas at one end, and pink panthers at the other. Many of the 12,000 City fans had also entered the festive spirit by sporting fancy dress. Quite a few lived to regret that decision. Some Stoke City fans were conspicuously lacking in the Christmas spirit department.

Mad Mel's selection suggested that the after-effects of Christmas Day had yet to clear. Paul Moulden, averaging a goal every two matches, and City's leading scorer by far, was omitted in favour of the notoriously impotent Morley-Biggins partnership. Despite this bemusing tactical manoeuvre, the City fans were able to maintain their jollity, thanks to an early goal by Nigel Gleghorn, who scored with a well-struck shot. Stoke City's new signing, the gangly Dave Bamber, seemed intent on adding to the general amusement amongst the Faithful by wasting the home side's few first-half opportunities in a most convincing manner. For City, 'Bertie' Biggins squandered two excellent chances to extend the lead. Just after half-time, the party mood began to dissipate. The home side scored three times in a ten-minute spell, as the City defence disintegrated. Kamara equalised from a corner, and added a second following a pinball-style scramble. The most poetic moment came when kindred spirits Brian Gayle and Dave Bamber collided. The resulting blatant penalty kick was converted, to leave City trailing 3-1 – and that was how it finished.

City ended the year with a much needed 2-1 victory at Swindon, where Jason Beckford celebrated a rare start with a goal. There were no goals for a bumper holiday crowd back at Maine Road on 2 January 1989, when Leeds United were the visitors. With Paul Moulden not even considered worth a place as substitute, City played out a sterile match. They dropped to fifth place, and were in danger of losing touch with the automatic promotion places.

The treatment of Paul Moulden by Mad Mel still rankles to this day. There appeared to be no logical explanation. Moulden was a good finisher, easily the best at the club, but he was also the most effective at feeding David White with the right kind of pass, the kind that went inside defenders and left them chasing White's shadow. Moulden himself did not have much pace, but he had good close control and clever skills, in addition to the goalscoring ability. In any case, whatever his personal merit, the fact was that City had nobody better. As far as strikers were concerned, Mad Mel was not exactly spoilt for choice. The seemingly unaccountable regular omission of Moulden prompted all manner of interesting theories. The dramatic decline in Moulden's subsequent career may lend credence to some, and legitimise Mad Mel's low opinion of him, but back in 1989, Moulden was *the* man.

Paul Moulden was restored to the side for the FA Cup third-round tie against Leicester City at Maine Road. He was only prevented from scoring by a handball. Neil McNab converted the resultant penalty kick, and it proved to be the winner.

With injuries and suspensions beginning to mount, Machin signed experienced midfielder Gary Megson. This was another player who had always looked quite good when playing for opposing teams, such as the Sheffield Wednesday promotion winning side during City's previous Division Two venture. Megson is a fine example of how misleading such impressions can be. His debut, at the expense of Ian Brightwell, who had been a resounding success in midfield, was made at a bitterly cold and windswept Boundary Park, against Joe Royle's Oldham Athletic. In the away supporters section there was no escaping the elements. The wind was heading full pelt into our faces and but for the opportunity to huddle together, there could have been cases of exposure or frost-bite. On that day, the main reason for waving a banana was to keep the circulation going, but it required a tight grip if irretrievable loss of the banana was to be avoided. The combination of a bitter wind and a plastic pitch resulted in a game resembling blow-football. Every goal kick or corner was reduced to high farce because of the refusal of the ball to stay still until kicked. City, with the substantial wind behind them in the first half, flattered to deceive. From David White's cross, a rather soppy Gary Megson header, straight at the Oldham goalkeeper, Rhodes, resulted in a soft debut goal. Nobody behind the goal was complaining. Mind you, we didn't realise that Megson's next goal would be two years away.

In the second half Oldham laid siege to the City penalty area. Heroics from Dibble and Redmond, coupled with profligate finishing by several Oldham players, including Roger Palmer, somehow maintained City's slender lead. Several minutes into injury time Oldham were still pressing, but after City's pathetic offside-trap had failed for the umpteenth time, Mike Milligan contrived to blast his shot over the bar. City escaped with three lucky points.

This fortunate victory prompted a run of impressive results that restored the Blues to a position of prominence, and confirmed them as serious promotion contenders. Three goals in rapid succession as half-time approached, two for Biggins and one for Moulden, put City in the ascendancy in their rematch against Hull City. White added the fourth goal in an emphatic 4-1 win. This was followed by an equally convincing 4-0 home victory against Ipswich Town, who were unable to cope with Brian Gayle's presence at corners. In between these home triumphs, Nigel Gleghorn had scored the only goal at Portsmouth, and City had exited the FA Cup, losing 3-1 at Brentford. This was a match of little importance for the Blues, although Brentford's Gary Blissett, scorer of two goals, no doubt enjoyed himself. I heard the result during a leisurely pub crawl in Liverpool. It was only a minor irritation, especially after several pints of bitter.

A 2-0 away win against struggling Birmingham City was notable for a splendid Neil McNab goal, and consolidated City's position in a breakaway group of two, with Chelsea. Since there were two automatic promotion places, it was all beginning to look rather cosy. On 25 February 1989, City managed a sixth consecutive League win, at home to Plymouth Argyle. Neil McNab was given the opportunity to take two penalties. He achieved a fifty per cent success rate. A scrappy second goal, which plopped into the net off the shoulder of Wayne Biggins, completed a 2-0 win. It could have been a greater margin of victory, but it was sufficient to send City back to the top of the table. A midweek home game against West Bromwich Albion offered the chance for further consolidation, but all was not going entirely smoothly. Irishman Gerry Taggart had been drafted in to replace Hinchcliffe, with Paul Lake reverting to right-back after injury to Seagraves. Having missed a couple of matches involuntarily, Paul Moulden was probably not surprised to find that he was not reinstated on becoming available once more. Unlike recent opponents, West Bromwich Albion proved to be a stern challenge for the Blues. After a goalless first half, Machin restored Hinchcliffe to the left-back position, but an increasingly confident Albion took the lead. Eventually, Mad Mel relented sufficiently to send substitute Moulden on to the field. City's attack improved instantly, and Moulden himself equalised at the third attempt, after having his first and second shots blocked.

City were lying in second place before the visit to fourth-placed Watford on the following Saturday. Using Hitchin as a base, I drove to Watford – only to discover that half the people there drive around in circles on a Saturday! The other half park their cars around Vicarage Road. Consequently, there is nowhere to park. Having successfully squeezed the Metro into a tiny space, I thought that we would make it with a good few minutes to spare. It was then that I discovered that Vicarage Road is surrounded by allotments. The several-mile allotment-circumference-run began, incorporating an exaggerated trip around the whole of the football stadium, which was visible but unapproachable.

Eventually, the correct entrance was located, but for the first 70 minutes of the match, there was little to merit our energetic arrival. The only incident of note came when Andy Dibble was caught in two minds, allowing Roberts to head the only goal, midway through the first half. Once more, Mad Mel had inexplicably omitted Moulden, and City lacked any attacking ideas. With 20 minutes remaining, Moulden was generously invited to partake, and the Watford goal was finally exposed to some threat. The main reason why City's late siege did not pay dividends was the goalkeeping of Tony Coton, who made several excellent saves, including a real heartbreaker to deflect a shot from Gayle, of all people, around the post. None of the goalmouth scrambles bore fruit and City were left pointless. Surely Mad Mel had learned his lesson?

He had, but only for one match. And what a bizarre match it was. The visit of Leicester City to Maine Road on 12 March 1989 was dominated by a near-tragedy, which occurred when the match was only five minutes old. An accidental clash of heads left Paul Lake unconscious and visibly twitching in a most alarming manner. For once, a referee acted swiftly and sensibly and the City physiotherapist was able rush on to the pitch and rearrange Lake's tongue, which had been swallowed. There were a lot of anxious-looking footballers on the field, and there was plenty of gesticulating to encourage the attention of a doctor located in the Main Stand. When Paul Lake was carried off on a stretcher, after a delay of about 10 minutes, nobody in the crowd could be sure that he was still alive. The atmosphere was decidedly eerie. Not surprisingly, the match itself failed to come alive before half-time, when better news of the patient was forthcoming. It would be charitable to assume that Neil McNab had other things on his mind when he spooned a penalty kick over the bar.

The goals came in two bursts of three in the second half. A City lead was cancelled out by a brilliant chipped goal from an impressive-looking midfield player called Gary McAllister. Trevor Morley scored with a neat curling shot to restore City's lead and, amazingly, Morley added two more goals before McAllister set up Mike Newell for Leicester's second in their 4-2 defeat. Like most of the crowd, I was somewhat stunned by Morley's sudden display of striking excellence. City returned to the top of the table.

Morley scored again in a midweek 4-2 win at Sunderland. This victory set City up for the real clash of the titans, against second-placed Chelsea on 18 March 1989. A crowd of 40,070 graced the Academy with their presence, in eager anticipation of a potentially decisive battle between the top two teams in Division Two. A significant proportion of the nation's attention was focused on Manchester City, and they responded by falling flat on their faces, in an almost literal sense. It was difficult to assess how good Chelsea were because they were not required to work for their victory. The crucial moments came midway through the opening half. The first cock-up was courtesy of Andy Dibble, who dropped the ball at the feet of Kerry Dixon. The second Chelsea goal was comical. Brian Gayle, given a six-yard start in a 10-yard race, was defeated by Dixon, a player not noted for excessive pace. Dixon dispossessed the wretched Gayle and presented Kevin Wilson with the easiest of scoring chances.

Paul Moulden was introduced for the second half, but this time City were beyond salvation. A Paul Lake error offered Kevin Wilson another scoring chance that he could not possibly miss. Of course, there is no such thing. He did miss. The Blues began to stage some kind of recovery, although strangely it was left-back Gerry Taggart who seemed to be on the end of most of their attacks. The portent of recovery was short-lived. Paul Lake was put in considerable trouble when he received a sharp pass near the halfway line. He was rapidly engulfed by Chelsea players, and lost out to Dorigo, who was left to race clear and score Chelsea's third goal.

A mystifying penalty decision enabled McNab to pull one goal back, and in injury time Taggart offered hope of a miracle by making the score 2-3. These barely deserved consolation goals were not sufficient to prevent Chelsea leaping above City to first place. After this result, there was never any doubt that Chelsea would win the Championship. The desperate City fight to hang on to the second automatic promotion place was about to commence in earnest.

The Chelsea game was the debut match for Machin's new signing, sort of striker and 'Neighbours' reject David Oldfield. This blond Australian was quite expensively acquired (£600,000) from Luton Town. Oldfield made no impression whatsoever in his debut appearance, but he was destined to play a prominent role in the outcome of City's next game, a memorable Easter trip to Walsall. This should have been a relatively straightforward match. Walsall were propping up the table, and the Faithful were expecting an enjoyable day out. In the event, City could not decide whether to opt for ignoble defeat or inspired victory.

As the teams made their appearance, Andy Dibble ran towards our end to receive the traditional banana greeting and a whole dollop of really quite sloppy affection and heart-warming goodwill. Such encouragement was far less evident, midway through the first half, after a couple of hopeful punts up the middle had caused panic in the City defence. Walsall scored twice, and only a fine example of the curiously described 'professional' foul, by Paul Lake, prevented a third. Luckily, the punishment for such an offence was not automatic dismissal in 1989. Andy Dibble, as the only City player who was actually within abuse range, was in receipt of a torrent of vitriol from the assembled mass behind his goal. Dibble's face was the embodiment of impotent rage as he came to retrieve the ball for a goal kick, a duty requiring that he wander right up to the less than happy City fans. There was little justice in the attack on Dibble since the City goalkeeper had not been to blame for either goal. He had his inadvertent revenge on the loud and abusive fans: the instant the goal kick was taken, he collapsed to the ground in agony, clutching his groin.

After half-an-hour's play, City were trailing 2-0 and Nigel Gleghorn was in goal. It didn't look good. The only saving grace was that Mad Mel had called a ceasefire with Moulden, who was leading the City attack, alongside new signing David Oldfield. This selection saved City from the ignoble defeat, and should have resulted in inspired victory. Moulden raced clear of the Walsall defenders, and fired a shot that the goalkeeper was unable to hold, enabling Oldfield to bring the score back to 2-1. In first-half stoppage time, David White's through-ball gave Moulden the chance to equalise, and equalise he did, with characteristic assurance. The second half was only seconds old when City launched another attack. Oldfield ran clear of Walsall's dithering defence. His shot rebounded at pace off the goalkeeper, but a brilliant reflex adjustment by Moulden enabled him to redirect the ball back into the roof of the net. Although City now had the lead, they continued to attack relentlessly. A defender handled, offering McNab the chance to increase City's lead from the penalty spot. Unfortunately, the Scot missed his third penalty in four. The Blues had other opportunities, but the lead remained slender. At the opposite end, Nigel Gleghorn was clearly enjoying his spell in goal. He dealt confidently with crosses, and managed to pull off one save, from point-blank range, that any goalkeeper would have been proud of, as City began to respond nervously to the approach of full-time. There was, however, nothing that

Gleghorn could do to prevent a galling equaliser four minutes from the end. David Oldfield directed a suicidal back-pass towards Gleghorn, but without the necessary pace. Gleghorn was committed to coming for the ball, and he managed to drive the Walsall player wide, but when the cross came over, City had no goalkeeper to prevent the headed equaliser from making the final score 3-3. It was the end of an incredible afternoon, but the result was not a good one for Manchester City.

At Maine Road two days later, the quest for three points at the expense of Stoke City was all that mattered. The Blues had a reasonable cushion in the League, and it would require another team to assemble an incredible run for City to be threatened, but such things mean little at the Academy. Apprehension is the natural state of the Maine Road crowd. Paul Moulden created an opening, enabling Oldfield to score for the first time at Maine Road and easing some of the early tension. Only minutes earlier, Dave Bamber had headed hopelessly wide from a good position; a warning that victory could most certainly not be taken for granted. Early in the second half, David White's pace induced a blatant trip, and Andy Hinchcliffe assumed responsibility to score the penalty. When Peter Beagrie limped off, leaving Stoke City a man short as they had already employed the permitted substitutions, it seemed plausible that the Faithful would be spared late alarms. This being Manchester City, such hopes were misplaced. Paul Cooper, the ex-Ipswich goalkeeper drafted in as Dibble's replacement, had been largely a spectator, but he was called into the action late on. Stoke pulled one goal back, but City held on to collect maximum points.

A few days later, the visit of City to Brighton was one of the lowlights of a distinctly unpleasant weekend. I finally split up with my girlfriend, who came up to Liverpool for the occasion. I recall straining to listen for news of the football on the radio during one of our earnest discussions. My priorities were no doubt all too clear. The home side's goals came from a twice-taken penalty and an emphatic Ian Brightwell own goal. City lost 2-1, and I was glad to see the end of that particular weekend.

Trevor Morley scored the winner in a tight scrap away to struggling Shrewsbury, increasing City's cushion to nine points. There should have been no need for the jitters displayed at the next home match, against Lou Macari's Swindon Town. City started brightly enough, with Moulden involved in most of their creative action, but a goal by Shearer (not *that* Shearer) after the failure of City's overused and incompetent offside-trap, brought the doubts to the surface. It took another penalty kick to pull City level at half-time, but the second half was played in an almost deathly silence. Paul Cooper came to the rescue on a couple of occasions, but a draw looked the likeliest outcome until Moulden set up a chance for Oldfield, who finished well. Moulden uncharacteristically wasted a couple of opportunities to make the game safe, and the sense of panic was such in the closing minutes that it required something of a miracle for the Blues to hold on. They did, and the cushion increased to 11 points. Surely it was time to relax?

City's performance at Blackburn Rovers could have been described as disastrous, but a sense of perspective is needed when viewing any match taking place on 15 April 1989, the day when a real tragedy occurred at Hillsborough. I was blissfully unaware of any events elsewhere as I witnessed City's worst display of the season, against the side nearest to them in the chasing pack. Blackburn's win was humiliatingly easy, and no doubt a source of considerable enjoyment for City old boy Nicky Reid. I drove to the match on my own from Chorley, where I was staying with my parents, and I had only just taken my place on the terrace, alongside the pitch, when the team announcement sent me into a pessimistic mood. Megson, Morley, Biggins and Oldfield were all chosen, and there was no place for Paul Moulden. Mad Mel simply would not give up on his determination to omit Moulden as often as possible. With City trailing 2-0, Moulden's appearance sparked a mini-revival midway through the second half, but Simon Garner scored twice more to complete an impressive hat-trick. The final score of 4-0 flattered City. The Blues were so bad that I tried to leave with more than 10 minutes remaining, but the local Constabulary were in sadistic mood and required me to stay until the bitter end.

The radio and television reports of Hillsborough were sobering and humbling. I was living only a short walk away from Anfield itself, and the mood of shock was tangible. I recalled my visit to Bloomfield Road, the worst crowd crush of my experience. It was not too difficult to imagine this minor incident amplified several-fold and leading to people being killed. The tragedy was a culmination of years of blinkered attitudes concerning crowd control. The object had been solely to keep the crowd away from the pitch area. It had not occurred to anybody in authority that, given the wrong circumstances, this could be akin to a death sentence. People in authority so seldom have any experience of the conditions faced by the average supporter. They view the match from the sanitised environment of executive boxes or, at best, the Directors' Box in the best stand. The Hillsborough incident led to the all-seater stadia that we now have for all teams in the Premier League, or those aspiring to it. It was not necessary to go this far, but the trend to sanitise football, and sell it as entertainment to a more up-market audience, appears to be irreversible. That is, at least until those involved realise that they are, as usual, totally ignoring the aspirations of those obsessed individuals who actually keep football alive, and who will remain to do so long after it has ceased to be an entertainment industry trend.

At 3.06 on 22 April 1989, a one-minute silence was respectfully observed at Maine Road, before the start of City's match against Barnsley. This game appeared to confirm City's single-minded determination to remain a Second Division club, against all the odds. There was an endearing hopelessness about this display, so typically City, that defeat was inevitable. After nine minutes, a shot crashed off the City crossbar and rebounded into the goal off the prostrate Paul Cooper. The infamous offside-trap failed once more, as Barnsley ended any hopes of a City revival, 10 minutes from time. Paul Lake scored for the Blues, but it failed to inspire any late recovery.

City's cushion was down to a mere six points. Crystal Palace could reduce that to three by winning a game in hand. Palace were in the midst of an awesome run, and their visit to Maine Road was imminent. It was perfectly conceivable that City's lead would evaporate totally over the next couple of weeks. With this thought firmly to the fore, I went to the away match against Brian Horton's Oxford United practically drunk with anxiety. In a perverse twist of logic, it required a quick pre-match pint in the local hostelry to sober up. The Blues had looked promotion certainties for so long that it was hard to come to terms with the possibility of failure. Yet that possibility seemed very real indeed during this, the ultimate game of two halves. Up to half-time against Oxford, City were a total shambles. They went behind to an early deflected free-kick, and old boy Paul Simpson added a second goal before half-time. Andy Dibble, making a surprisingly early return from his injury, had to face the wrath of the City fans once more.

Immediately after the half-time break, there were eight minutes of madness that changed everything. From a Hinchcliffe corner, Gleghorn hooked the ball in, after what looked suspiciously like a handball by Megson. A minute later, David White's shot flew into the corner of the net thanks to a glorious deflection, and seven minutes further on, after Paul Moulden had wriggled to the byline and crossed, Oxford defender Greenhall lashed the ball with gusto into his own net! I began to believe in the existence of God.

Memories of the Walsall match came flooding back as an under-hit back-pass by Paul Lake almost let Oxford snatch a couple of vital points away from City, but on this occasion, Dibble came to the rescue. With two minutes remaining, Ian Brightwell played the ball out to Morley, and raced into the penalty area to meet Morley's cross with a thunderous header right in front of the ecstatic City Faithful. The Blues had managed to turn 2-0 into 2-4. Surely nothing could stop us now.

Palace, City's only realistic rivals for that second promotion place, came to Maine Road on 1 May 1989 knowing that a win would close the gap to three points, and leave them with an extra match to play. The Blues started well, and David White sprinted down the right wing before firing a low cross that could have been turned in by any number of players. It evaded all but Nigel Gleghorn, who arrived at the far post to score.

It had been a surprise to see Andy Dibble back in the City goal so soon after the Walsall injury. It was noticeable that Dibble was not taking any goal kicks, which suggested that his fitness was not complete. There was certainly no need to rush his return. Paul Cooper had been an admirable stand-in. The decision to bring Dibble back proved to be a substantial, and almost very costly, error of judgement. Midway through the first half, after kicking downfield, Dibble was left doubled up in pain once more. He struggled on until half-time, but the goalscorer Gleghorn found himself in the City goal, once more, for the whole of the second half. Having looked in control, City began to surrender territory. The Blues might have extended their slender lead, but at the other end of the pitch, the crossbar, woeful finishing, and some heroic Gleghorn saves were required for its maintenance. It was difficult not to dwell on the previous Palace visit, when Nixon's madness had led to City surrendering all the points. They simply could not afford a repeat. Luckily, Gleghorn proved to be a far better goalkeeper than Redmond, and City almost held on for a win that would have virtually clinched promotion. A blistering late strike from Ian Wright prevented that, but City at least escaped with a draw. The Blues still needed one more win.

The match at home to Bournemouth, five days later, will live long in the memory of anybody unfortunate enough to have witnessed it. It is one of those unforgettable Academy experiences. The Blues required just three points to ensure promotion, and on a bright, sunny day, in front of a buoyant crowd, they duly swept into a three-goal lead. Paul Moulden, inevitably, scored the first goal, and both Morley and Brightwell came close to adding to it before Morley curled in a superb second on the half-hour. Four minutes later, Hinchcliffe's fiercely struck free-kick came back off the crossbar, and Moulden dispatched the rebound. 3-0. At half-time the crowd were jubilant. Everyone simply wanted full-time to come quickly, so that the celebrations could began in earnest. It was surely all over.

The only possible explanation for what followed was that City did not wish to be promoted. Morley and Moulden both wasted chances to add to the lead, but that was of little importance. Shearer (still not *that* one) headed a goal from a corner with fewer than 30 minutes remaining. That was enough to make some of us feel a little uncomfortable, and it would have been nice to see Moulden complete his hat-trick instead of heading wide. Yet, despite that miss, there seemed little to be concerned about. Bournemouth did not appear to be terribly interested in the match. But as City retreated, a long-haired Ian Bishop from Liverpool, began to exploit the gaps in midfield, and there were a number of corners for City to defend. With 10 minutes remaining, following one of these corners, the ball crept through a crowd of players and into the City net. To the dismay of the watching Faithful, City continued to sit back on their lead. It was an agonising finish, but the Blues held on well into injury time. I don't know from where the referee found six minutes of injury time, but he did. During the last of those minutes, Luther Blissett burst into the penalty area. Anxious to catch up, Andy Hinchcliffe chased hard after him. Blissett stopped, Hinchcliffe didn't, and following the inevitable collision, the referee pointed to the penalty spot. Blissett scored and the referee blew his whistle for full-time. Incredibly, City had wasted a three-goal lead. I could not help but blame Mad Mel for the defensive tactics that had led to the disappearance of that lead. Whether it was under instruction, or merely due to the players becoming overcautious, I can't say. The outcome of this match, however, is that I will never again be able to feel secure about even a three-goal lead. The Bournemouth match will haunt me forever.

The crowd was stunned. Some jeered and hurled abuse, others merely stared ahead in disbelief. I saw one grown man banging his head repeatedly against a concrete wall. I could understand how he felt. It looked rather tempting. The bananas had never been so deflated. When the trauma-induced haze had cleared, it emerged that results elsewhere had not been as bad as they might have been. City required a single point from their final game, and even if they failed, Crystal Palace would be required to make up a deficit in goal difference of six goals. That should have made us all feel safe, but after what we had just witnessed, anything seemed possible.

A few weeks previously, I had queued on a Saturday morning to secure tickets for the final match away, to Bradford City, expecting it to be a meaningless fixture but a good day out. The fixture was to be far from meaningless, and the jury was still out on whether the day would be good or not. I had a week to stew on the prospect.

Saturday, 13 May 1989 was the day of judgement. It is true that failure would have resulted in City entering the play-off lottery for a second chance, but few could have had much confidence of success should the Blues manage to blow automatic promotion, having been in a seemingly unassailable position. It was a crisp summer day, and the drive over the Pennines required constant use of shades, which gave an appearance of coolness that was not strictly reliable. Crystal Palace had considerable ground to make up, but they were at home to relegated Birmingham City, who had little incentive to put up much resistance. Bradford City, with a home crowd to keep happy, were likely to be stiffer opposition. Security around Valley Parade was tight, and only ticket-holders were allowed anywhere near the ground. I arrived with my comrade for much of the season's travels, and we took up our positions behind the goal, close to the tunnel through which the players made their entrance. Because of the heavy traffic, we did not have too long to contemplate the afternoon's possibilities before the teams appeared – to energetic banana-waving. I was pleased to see Lake, Hinchcliffe, Brightwell, Redmond, White and Moulden in the starting line-up. Paul Cooper was in the City goal and McNab, Gleghorn and Megson were also in the team. Moulden's striking partner was Trevor Morley, a man much maligned by City fans, including myself, because of Mad Mel's preference for him ahead of Paul Moulden.

City were nervous early on, although both Gleghorn and the inspirational McNab could have given them a reassuring lead. Bradford City had not looked particularly threatening, but they did manage to score the only first-half goal. A chap called Quinn swung his boot at the ball and failed utterly to make contact, but next in line was Ellis, whose low shot found the corner of the net behind which most of the assembled Faithful stood. It was a blow to our fragile morale.

There was a surreal atmosphere about the half-time break. In an extraordinarily crass display of thoughtlessness, Granada TV had chosen John Bond as their 'expert' commentator for the highlights programme. When Bond emerged from the tunnel for a half-time interview, there were immediate rumblings amongst the City fans. The disquiet swelled at an impressive rate, resulting in a crescendo of abuse directed against the ex-City manager. The baiting of Mr Bond continued for the whole of the half-time interval and, despite several attempts to record in the open, with the group shuffling furtively in and out of the tunnel, the half-time interview had to be conducted inside. The unifying vitriolic chants of 'Fuck off, Bondy', repeated ad nauseum, raised the spirits, and the team re-entered the stage to a raucous, if slightly desperate, welcome. These spirits were soon dampened, however, by alarming news filtering in from Selhurst Park. Crowd trouble had led to a delay, which meant that the two matches would no longer finish simultaneously. Palace would have about 20 minutes in which their exact requirements would be known because the City game would be finished. This might not have been so alarming had it not been for the supplementary information that Palace had scored four times in the first half. Rumours such as these always circulate at football matches, but there was an uneasiness amongst the fans that suggested legitimacy for this particular rumour, and on this occasion, the grapevine was not misleading. City were within one goal of the nightmare scenario: one more Crystal Palace goal or, heaven forbid, a second Bradford City goal, could spell the end of City's quest for automatic promotion. Memories of Bournemouth were far too fresh to discount the possibility. There was much fretfulness behind the goal. One long-haired fan ran on to the pitch to spread alarm amongst the players. Rumour has it that he reported Palace as 5-0 up.

Whether or not the Blues knew the full extent of their need for an equaliser, they performed admirably in the second half, playing some of their best football of the season. City totally dominated, creating a whole procession of opportunities, which they agonisingly failed to convert. Trevor Morley alone had three goalscoring chances, but having shot tamely twice, he blasted the third effort over the crossbar. Nigel Gleghorn also came desperately close with a superbly struck shot that narrowly flew over the bar and into the bananas. David White came even closer, when his powerful shot struck the foot of the post. Paul Moulden was often the provider for chances, but irritatingly none fell his way. The Blues continued to attack and threaten, but the all-important goal would not come. As the end became nigh, Bradford City broke clear, and Paul Cooper had to make a desperate save to prevent absolute calamity. Matters were, to say the least, delicately poised.

With three minutes of the City season remaining, Paul Cooper threw the ball out to Nigel Gleghorn, who helped it on to Paul Moulden on the halfway line. Moulden controlled the ball on his chest, swivelled and played a perfect pass into the path of David White. White's pace took him beyond the defender, and allowed him the space to direct the ball, left-footed, into the penalty area. Trevor Morley, the man who most of us had been determined to hate, was in front of his defender and first to the ball. Morley directed it beyond the goalkeeper's left hand, and at that point I lost sight of the ball altogether.

It didn't matter. I knew immediately where it had ended up: in the Bradford City net. There was the most incredible banana frenzy behind that goal. It didn't quite last for the whole of the remaining time. I, for one, regained sensibility just in time to begin worrying about the fact that the game was not yet over. The City players were, understandably, somewhat lacking in poise at this juncture, and they whacked the ball indiscriminately whenever it appeared within range. Eventually, the referee took pity and blew the final whistle. City were promoted, and there was a relatively orderly pitch invasion.

At five o'clock, I was taking a leisurely stroll across the turf, having secured my bit of souvenir grass, when a topless, fresh-faced Ian Brightwell suddenly whizzed by with a flag in one hand and a banana in the other. He was carried aloft amidst a sea of City fans on the Valley Parade pitch. That moment was a fitting epitaph for the season.

In fact, Birmingham City pulled a goal back at Selhurst Park and Crystal Palace had to settle for the play-offs, from which they deservedly emerged to be promoted alongside City. There was some sadness associated with the Valley Parade occasion. I knew that it would be Paul Moulden's last City appearance. Mr Machin had only selected him under sufferance. For the third season in succession my favourite would be sold off. The inexplicable decline in Moulden's career since leaving Maine Road has been dramatic. At Bournemouth he continued to score goals, and Joe Royle brought him back north to play for Oldham. On a couple of occasions when City didn't have a match, I went to Boundary Park to watch Paul Moulden play. There was no guarantee that Moulden would be in the team. It was strangely familiar: at one match the crowd was shouting for him to be brought on as substitute. On he came, with about 15 minutes remaining, and he duly scored the winning goal. That typified Paul Moulden as I remember him.

Moulden disappeared down the leagues after his short spell at Oldham, rarely playing for Birmingham City, turning up at Rochdale and then, the last I heard, Accrington Stanley, and a fish and chip shop in Bolton. Moulden may not have been the world's best striker, but surely he was better than that. Still, if there is one man I'd back to calmly dispatch mushy peas into the back of a carton, with ruthless precision and no spillage, it would be Paul Moulden.

For me the 1988/89 season will always be remembered fondly as the season of the City youngsters, the class of '86, and, in particular, Paul Moulden.

Season 1989/90: One-two, one-two-three, one-two-three-four, FIVE-ONE!

The approach of a new season at the Academy, after the ultimate achievement of promotion, provoked excitement and trepidation in more or less equal measure. I had visions of City prospering for many years to come from the precocious talents of the class of '86. In the short term, however, a few supplementary players were required to stabilise and consolidate. I had faith in the remaining youngsters, now sadly without Paul Moulden, but I wasn't so sure about the rest. Actually, that's not entirely true. I was pretty sure that Brian Gayle would prove a liability, and that City's lightweight attack required considerable reinforcement. As Moulden departed to Bournemouth, Scouser Ian Bishop made the opposite trip for a fee of £750,000. This link with Mad Mel's dastardly deed made me initially reluctant to welcome Bishop, but his midfield passing ability and general magnificence soon made him a favourite with everyone, including me. He even had the decency to crop his locks to a more acceptable length in recognition of the admirable haircut trend in the City ranks. Mad Mel's answer to the striking dearth was to acquire goal-machine Clive Allen from Bordeaux for £1.1 million. The Northern Ireland international and right-back Gary Fleming was the only other significant arrival for the new season. He most certainly was not the last.

I was at Old Trafford when City completed an impressive 2-0 victory over the enemy in a pre-season testimonial game. Unfortunately, I was at Old Trafford, home of Lancashire County Cricket Club. My ambition to see City victorious at *The Swamp* remains unfulfilled. I was watching cricket again when the real season began. One of the immediate consequences of the Hillsborough disaster was that ground improvements were leading to reduced capacity and, consequently, miserly ticket allocations for visiting fans. I hadn't realised that it would be necessary to camp outside Maine Road overnight to obtain a ticket for the opening match at Anfield. By the time that I arrived, it was clear that the couple of thousand tickets were already spoken for.

In fact, I didn't go to many away matches in season 1989-90, despite moving back to Manchester in December 1989. There were too many other distractions, such as band-watching and band practice. I was in Manchester, therefore I was in a band. It was 1989.

It was good to be back in the city, and there was plenty to keep the evenings occupied, with performances from the likes of Happy Mondays, Throwing Muses, Stone Roses, The Sundays, The Pixies, James, Martin Stephenson and still The *mighty* Fall. In fact, there was a short-lived but invigorating explosion of excellent music. As for the accompanying culture, I fiercely resisted any resurgence of flared trousers, but I did buy some of the T-shirts prevalent among the city's youth. I couldn't manage to use the word 'sweet' or the phrase 'top, pal, or what?' whilst keeping a straight face. I didn't buy the *Manchester: born in the north, live in the north, die in the north* T-shirt. I reckoned that the latter would severely restrict holiday plans. After all, you never know when your numbers up. I bought a *Pathetic Sharks* T-shirt instead.

The success of the Lancashire CCC season, in one-day competition at least, was pretty much assured as I sat in the member's enclosure on 19 August 1989, attempting to absorb the relatively tranquil atmosphere. Clutching a transistor radio to my ear, I was not so optimistic about City's opening day encounter with Liverpool. Indeed, I was shocked when Andy Hinchcliffe gave the Blues the lead from a deflected free-kick, provoking rumblings amongst the Lancashire supporters, indicating that I was not the only person whose mind was temporarily elsewhere. Liverpool came back to win 3-1, but at least we had put up a fight. Somehow that seemed enough for the first game; nothing more could have been expected. It was, however, vital to gain some points from the two home matches to follow. The last thing the Blues could afford was a poor start to the season and the consequent seepage of morale.

Bearing that in mind, it was almost inevitable that City had a poor start to the season. Nigel Gleghorn managed a goal for the Blues at home to Southampton, but the outcome was a demoralising 1-2 defeat. There was an improved display against Spurs, three days later, but David White's first goal of the season was only worth a point. City were already in the relegation zone, a sobering reality that was not improved by a 2-1 defeat at Highfield Road. The City youngsters seemed already to be lacking in confidence, and the season had hardly begun. There was much relief at Maine Road on 9 September 1989, when Clive Allen's first goal for the club secured a win against QPR. However, a 1-0 defeat at Wimbledon left City in eighteenth place. To add to the general woe, the Blues lost 2-1 at Brentford in the first leg of a Littlewoods Cup tie. That was the uninspiring build-up to 23 September 1989, and the ninety-ninth Manchester league derby.

It would be an understatement to say that I was not looking forward to this match with any relish. *The Nation's Team* had also started the season poorly, but their team was packed full of **very** expensive players, such as Paul Ince (already fine-tuning that trademark scowl), Danny Wallace (I think that they asked for the wrong Wallace),

Mike Phelan (a man who liked allotments), Brian McClair (sporting a ludicrous head-band), and the exorbitantly priced central defender, Gary Pallister. Just about wher-ever you looked in the enemy camp, there was a costly acquisition. I could virtually see the price tags. That in itself would not have been too dispiriting, had it not been for City's poor form, and the knowledge that Clive Allen would not be available.

The City line-up is well worth looking at. Paul Cooper was in goal as a replacement for the injured Dibble. Gary Fleming, Andy Hinchcliffe, Brian Gayle and Steve Red-mond formed the fragile defensive resistance. Ian Bishop was assisted at the centre of midfield by his athletic minder, Ian Brightwell, whilst White and Lake patrolled the flanks. City's strike force consisted of Trevor Morley and David Oldfield, which was more than a little worrying.

Surely, it was a mismatch. The only thing that City did have in their favour was a passionate belief in the cause. There were enough locals in the side to generate a healthy hatred for the opposition, and the players knew what this occasion meant to their supporters. The incentive was a massive one. So many other indiscretions could be forgiven in exchange for one momentous display. And a momentous display was precisely what we got.

Having reluctantly emerged to greet the day, and enjoyed a contemplative breakfast-cum-lunch nursing a mild hangover, I made my way to the Whitworth in search of the anaesthetising effects of Marston's Pedigree. There I sat, with a couple of pals, making myself even further depressed, in anticipation of a demoralising after-noon. Four pints later, it was time for the condemned to head for the scaffold. On en-tering the great arena, I became inspired by the occasion. The Faithful were in a state of some agitation about this fixture. There was an intoxicating atmosphere, and it wasn't merely the Pedigree. There were also early indications of crowd trouble to come. Violence can never be condoned, but it is fair to question the intelligence of anyone who purchases a ticket for a Manchester derby match from a tout, goes in amongst City fans, and then openly displays opposite allegiances. On this occasion, a number of such morons had assembled behind the goal in the North Stand, *our* Stand, in fact *my* Stand! Having presumably dislodged people with legitimate tickets for those seats, the intellectually-challenged tourists turned to face the City fans, not even adopting the pretence of interest in the match, which at this point had been underway for a few minutes. I became quite territorial and joined in the shouting, from a safe dis-tance naturally, for the intruders to be ejected, or words to that effect. I am happy to say that they were not ejected, but merely escorted to the Platt Lane End to join their kind. This was, without doubt, the most fitting punishment.

The match had started at a furious pace, with Ian Brightwell snapping at the highly paid celebrities in most entertaining fashion. During the disturbance behind the goal at the North Stand End, the players trooped off for a few minutes, but they soon returned to continue in much the same vane, with the Blues heading in our direction. David White smacked a shot unfeasibly wide following an early attack. The City players were in need of a little calming down.

Not long after the restart, during a hectic couple of minutes, the match took a dramatic turn in City's favour. A free-kick on the halfway line, in the left-back position, was struck long by Hinchcliffe across to David White on the opposite flank, and in a far more threatening location. White was able to pull the ball back across the penalty area, albeit with little pace. The trajectory seemed to be taking the ball within Pallister's range, but the gangly centre half displayed all the dexterity of a giraffe with one foot nailed to the ground in his attempts to turn and cut out the cross. He didn't make it, and the ball trickled on to David Oldfield, who swept it beyond the helpless Leighton and into the net. 1-0.

The visitors seemed stunned, and City continued to harass them pitilessly. As the enemy defence dithered, Morley won the ball in a dangerous position. Although Morley's shot was parried by Leighton, the rebound came to Paul Lake. He tormented a couple of defenders with a dribble into the penalty area, before crossing low. The television pictures of what followed never cease to be a comfort to me in times of stress. As the ball comes across the six-yard box, there are several defenders in the picture, all looking at each other, or the ball. Suddenly, Trevor Morley's boot appears in the frame to poke the ball past a bemused Leighton. Only 12 minutes had elapsed. It was 2-0.

After that stormy couple of minutes, the tempo of the match inevitably decreased, and *The Nation's Team* were able to keep the ball for longer periods. City fans were now left with sufficient time to contemplate the lead. I was probably not the only one already thinking about how depressing it would be to lose it. There were a couple of alarms in the City penalty area but, 35 minutes into the match, the Blues broke clear to score again. After intercepting near the edge of the City penalty area, Steve Redmond calmly brought the ball clear, before exchanging passes with White and playing a right-footed pass down the right wing. Pallister and Oldfield were left to chase. Pallister had a considerable start on Oldfield, and was the clear favourite to get there first. Once again he looked reassuringly sluggish and clumsy. It took him significant moments to set off. Oldfield narrowly beat Pallister to the ball, and headed off down the right wing into undefended space. Moments later, Oldfield looked up and crossed perfectly for the incoming Ian Bishop, who hurled himself full-length to score with a magnificent diving header. 3-0. Bishop's famous pose, in the shape of a cross, seemed most apt after that goal. Victory now really did seem possible.

The half-time break was ample time for thoughts of Bournemouth to creep into the mind, despite my best efforts. Unfortunately, I was now completely sober. When Hughes pulled a goal back early in the second half, the City fans went very quiet. We all knew that the Blues were quite capable of blowing a lead of 3-1, and that it would be most painful to witness it. Within eight minutes of that setback, a sudden burst forward took Paul Lake clear of the defence. His shot was blocked by Leighton, but as all enemy defenders in attendance overbalanced, Lake kept his feet and calmly squared the ball to Oldfield, who surely never scored an easier goal. 4-1. That seemed to take all the resistance out of the opposition, but the best was yet to come. Patrolling the centre circle with majestic control, Ian Bishop struck a tempting pass down the right wing for David White to pursue at speed. White reached the target and crossed first time. The ball arrived at precisely the same moment as Andy Hinchcliffe, who was running at full pelt into the penalty area. Without breaking stride, Hinchcliffe thundered a header into the top corner of the net for one of the best goals ever seen at Maine Road. 5-1. The RAGS behind the goal were stunned. Hinchcliffe wheeled round towards the Kippax, continually gesturing to them with five fingers outstretched, as if to reassure everyone that it was true; it wasn't a dream. There were still 28 minutes remaining, but the rest of the match was an irrelevance. It was amusing to see *The Nation's Team* failing in their attempts to make the final result more respectable. With some City players beginning to suffer the consequences of their exertions, the Faithful were quite happy to see the match end with the scoreline as it was. By the time that the referee had signalled full-time, there were plenty of open spaces in the Platt Lane Stand. This was City's day. The best ever day for many of their fans, myself included. I walked around in a daze for about a week afterwards.

The 'Manchester Evening News' Pink Finals were already spread out on the tables of the Grants public house in Hulme that evening, when I arrived to contemplate the day's proceedings with a number of other ecstatic Blues. This match didn't only make the whole season; it made the decade! Supporters of more successful clubs will no doubt think it sad that City fans still look back on this one day with such religious awe, but who cares? You have to cling to those moments of exceptional football bliss, espe-cially moments as unexpected as this one, and especially when they are so rare.

Mad Mel, or rather the honourable Mr Machin, was now accepted as a football gen-ius. Napoleon demanded that his generals be lucky; City fans demand that their man-agers preside over successful derby match encounters. Of course, there was still the little matter of First Division survival to be sorted out: a mere detail.

The Blues were operating on leftover adrenaline when they overcame Luton Town 3-1 at Maine Road the following Saturday, to rise to the reassuring heights of tenth place in the League. There was even sufficient left in the adrenaline tank to dismiss Brentford with a second leg 4-1 win that featured three second-half City goals in the space of five minutes. All seemed well with the world.

Reality reared its ugly head once more at Highbury, where City's defensive frailties were cruelly exposed in a 4-0 defeat. The last thing the Blues needed was for the live television cameras to appear at Maine Road for the visit of Aston Villa, but that's what happened. City responded by losing 2-0, with Tony Daley and Ian Olney scoring the goals. Trevor Morley getting himself sent off did not help the cause. Against Norwich City in the Littlewoods Cup three days later, City were back in confident mood. A close-range David White header was responsible for a half-time lead, which was stretched with goals from Ian Bishop and Clive Allen, on his return to the team. Robert Fleck's late goal was not sufficient to provoke any jitters.

City were trailing 1-0 at Stamford Bridge before a near-miraculous Clive Allen shot rescued a point in injury time. A win could have sent Chelsea to the top of the League. A 3-0 win at home to Crystal Palace, including another Allen goal, kept the Blues clear of trouble for the time being, but the sense of progression proved illusory. I was not amongst the unlucky ones who witnessed the 6-0 debacle at the Baseball Ground, on 11 November 1989. I did see the alarming capitulation to a Nigel Clough and Gary

Crosby-inspired Forest, 3-0 winners at Maine Road the following week. This was despite the fact that new signing Colin Hendry (£700,000 from Blackburn) had replaced Brian Gayle in defence. All of City's belief evaporated once more. Forest won with alarming ease. The Blues were back in nineteenth place.

Exit from the Littlewoods Cup followed, and despite a point-saving Clive Allen goal at Charlton, City were rooted in the relegation zone. The traditional Liverpool massacre at Maine Road was restored to the calendar, with a 1-4 result that sent City to the bottom of the table. The position was not improved by a 2-1 defeat at Southampton on 9 December 1989.

A few days later, Mel Machin was sacked as manager of Manchester City, and Howard Kendall returned from Spain to continue his managerial career in England, charged with the task of saving the Blues. I was not particularly upset at the demise of Mad Mel. In fact, I was strangely elated, for the simple reason that I could not forgive him for the treatment of Paul Moulden. It was as petty and personal as that. In addition, Kendall was a manager with a successful past. For once, City appeared to have improved on the manager's position. That was before Kendall embarked on his plans for an old boy's reunion, with emphasis on the *old*.

Kendall's impact was certainly immediate. The Maine Road pitch was narrowed, to prevent more skilful teams from having the space to play. City would not be required to operate in such a fashion. The new manager also got rid of the fan's favourite player, Ian Bishop, with indecent haste. Kendall and Bishop were previously acquainted from careers coinciding at Everton. Bishop, it seemed, was the one former Everton player that Howard Kendall did not wish to be at Maine Road: too young, I suppose.

Granada TV chose the wrong time to show a City away match live, when they covered Kendall's first match in charge, ironically at Goodison Park, against the club where Kendall had been so successful as player and manager. The latest City boss introduced new signings Peter Reid and Alan Harper and, alarmingly, restored Gary Megson to the starting line-up, in preference to Bishop. None of those players required any introductions at Goodison Park. I could see the logic of the experienced Reid being included, to add some grizzled steel and nous to the midfield. Reid was not the sprightly young thing that I had seen at Burnden Park, but City's youngsters were in dire need of some guidance, and at least he had been an exceptional player. Reid was also to join the management team. I was less convinced by the other decisions made in the early days of the Kendall regime. The tactics were also new. For most of the match at Goodison Park, David White was left to roam alone in the Everton half as City defended with 10, including Clive Allen. Allen was eventually taken off, presumably because he ventured too far forward. Kendall was nothing if not effective. The most negative City performance in living memory was rewarded with a point in a goalless draw. I was glad that I just watched on television. Most other viewers probably wished that they had done something else completely.

Clive Allen was omitted for Kendall's first home match, on Boxing Day, against Norwich City, but he emerged from the substitutes' bench to score the only goal. David White scored both goals as City overcame Millwall at Maine Road four days later. This victory took them out of the relegation zone. Mark Ward, yet another player with an Everton past, and Kendall's latest signing, made his debut in this match. Ward came as part of the £2 million deal that sent Trevor Morley and Ian Bishop to West Ham United. Ward was another of those players who looked pretty good playing for other teams. For the Blues, he didn't actually seem to do much, apart from fall over occasionally to win penalties, a useful skill, I admit. To make matters worse, Ward was something of a *me* lookalike!

Nevertheless, it was with cautious optimism that I drove across the Pennines on New Year's Day 1990, to see the new resolute City take on Ron Atkinson's Sheffield Wednesday at Hillsborough. I spent a crisp afternoon in the seats above the infamous and deserted Leppings Lane terraces, witnessing a dreadful City performance. It ended in a 2-0 defeat that might have been far worse had Dalian Atkinson, in particular, not suffered from serious operational defects in his shooting radar.

The Blues then embarked on something of an FA Cup marathon against Millwall. Episode One saw City unable to repeat their League victory of a week earlier; neither side managed a goal. Three days later, Colin Hendry scored his first City goal, a glancing header, to rescue a second draw in the replay, but the Blues capitulated back at the Den in Episode Three.

Meanwhile, back in the League, a 1-1 draw away to Spurs and a 1-0 win at home to Coventry, courtesy of a David White goal, had lifted City to fourteenth place. Yet another Everton old boy made his first appearance in the latter game: Wayne 'Sniffer' Clarke, a forward who was no more than a pale imitation of his famous brother. Mr Kendall was in danger of turning Maine Road into an Everton theme park.

When 3 February 1990 came around, all negative thoughts were put to one side as the Blues made the crucial journey to *The Swamp*, effectively defending a 5-1 first leg lead. The situation offered the rare opportunity for some really effective baiting. Before the match, the local constabulary were in edgy mood judging by the action of one police driver, who reversed a van into a supporter sporting allegiance to *The Nation's Team*. The driver may have been a closet Blue. If so, this is taking things a little too far.

The occasion was enjoyed by all of the City fans who, like me, had the pleasure to be there for the pre-match build-up. The Blues went into the match three places and two points better off than the enemy, and knowing that avoiding defeat would leave the Faithful free rein to continue basking in the glory of the first match. Ian Brightwell came in for the suspended Peter Reid, with Harper operating as a sort of sweeper, behind Hendry and Redmond. Paul Lake and Andy Hinchcliffe were the full-backs, with Brightwell joined in midfield by Megson and Ward, leaving Clarke to partner the roving White in attack.

City began the match in encouraging fashion. Clarke and White were almost able to take advantage of a terrible Pallister back-pass in the opening minutes. Wayne Clarke also had a good opportunity following a corner, but he headed wide. The Blues were having the better of the match, with Dibble only called upon once, to save from Beardsmore. The best chance of the half fell to Ian Brightwell, who won possession but didn't immediately seem to realise what a good opportunity it was. Jim Leighton was stranded, well off his line, when Brightwell lobbed the ball agonisingly wide of goal.

The Blues were playing towards the Faithful in the second half. There was some early pressure at the other end, but suddenly David White broke clear, heading towards us with the ball at his feet. For some reason, he hesitated when approaching the penalty area and eventually shot wide. It was another excellent chance wasted. This really did seem to be City's best opportunity to win at Old Trafford for many years. We could all sense it. Even I could sense it. Such positive thinking received its customary severe jolt when a rare attack led to a headed Blackmore goal at the other end. The gloom descended.

The misery was, thankfully, short-lived. A City attack broke down, and the ball came out to Ian Brightwell, some 15 yards outside the penalty area. The City youngster unleashed a left-foot shot that was a thing of rare beauty. I had a perfect view as the ball flew, with arrow-like precision, beyond Leighton's outstretched hand and into the top corner of the net, to trigger pandemonium behind the goal. It was awesome. One of the best goals I've ever seen. 'I just wellied it,' were Bob Brightwell's words after the match, and boy, did he welly it!

David White might have given City the lead, but as the match reached its closing stages, the Blues seemed to settle for a draw. The end of the game was bitter-sweet. Although a draw was perfectly acceptable, it seemed like an opportunity missed. Ferguson was very close to being sacked during this period, but a seemingly improbable FA Cup run, including a televised win at Newcastle in a game so bad that even Barry Davies was temporarily lost for words, rescued him. A City win would certainly have increased the pressure. Nevertheless, I could wear my maroon-striped away shirt with pride in the Venue that evening, and I wasn't the only one.

As if fatigued by their derby game exertions, City suffered another slump, with only a point to show for consecutive home matches against Wimbledon and struggling Charlton. Charlton won 2-1, in the match featuring the debut of the diminutive Adrian Heath, yet another ex-Evertonian. This was getting ridiculous.

Those results were compounded by an extraordinary 1-0 defeat at the City Ground. The winning goal was scored by Gary Crosby, who sneaked up behind Andy Dibble and headed the ball out of the goalkeeper's hands, before slotting it into an empty net. Apparently, because Dibble was not holding the ball with both hands, the goal was deemed legal. A different referee might well have booked Crosby.

On Friday, 9 March 1990, I made one of my rare nostalgic visits to Bangor, to see The Fall, who were, of course, first-rate. Somehow, my old North Wales stamping ground seemed much more attractive when I was safe in the knowledge that I could depart whenever I wished. The call, on this occasion, was soon. The Blues lured me back for the following day, when a David White goal was only enough to earn a point at home to Arsenal, and City were once more pushed into the relegation zone.

On 17 March 1990, the Blues made a visit to fellow-strugglers Luton Town, whose Chairman was the frankly bizarre David Evans. Because away fans were banned from

Kenilworth Road, my comrade in Hitchin became a member at Luton in order to pro-
cure tickets. Nobody was banning me from a football ground.

I watched the match, initially, with some uneasiness. After all, this was a vital occasion for both teams, and I was accustomed to segregation. Yet the home fans didn't
seem all that bothered, and there were, in fact, many City followers dotted around the
ground, particularly at the opposite end. The game itself was, unsurprisingly, rather
tense. With only about 15 minutes remaining, Luton took the lead from a penalty and
my heart sank. A defeat really was unthinkable. The Blues simply couldn't afford it.
Thankfully, the balance was redressed when Clive Allen equalised with a City penalty. I was glad when the final whistle had been blown and no more damage could be
done.

The following Wednesday was an important occasion all round. I had arrived at the
Academy fairly late because of the need to organise a first date, for the following evening, with my future wife. I was so hungry that I actually bought one of the City pies,
which had no mention of ingredients, they were simply referred to as 'pies'. Unfortunately, unbeknown to me, my mother had decided to make one of her very rare appearances at Maine Road with my dad, who had bought an extra ticket. I was, therefore,
caught red-handed with an inappropriate food source in my hand, and left open to accusations of not eating properly. Incidentally, even after eating the pie, I was no wiser
as to its contents.

The match was also the debut of Niall Quinn, whose signing, for £800,000 from Arsenal, had provoked a feeling of utter horror in me. Like most other people, I thought
he was just some big donkey with no skill. It seemed that Arsenal only wheeled him on
from the subs' bench when they were desperate, and that he was only good as a target
for balls which had been hoofed into the air. I am pleased to say that this misjudgement
of Niall served him, and City, well for a number of years. Deceptive skill with the ball
at his feet was Quinn's biggest asset. Defenders were continually surprised, even
when he had already demonstrated his ability earlier in the same match. The opponents on this occasion were Chelsea, who were well placed in the League. Big Niall
got the City goal in a 1-1 draw.

On Sunday, 1 April 1990, City played live on ITV, away to Aston Villa. So certain
was I of defeat against Graham Taylor's Championship-chasing side, that I didn't
even bung a video tape into the machine to record the match for posterity. Would that I
had. City were a revelation against a Villa side showing distinct signs of stress after a
long campaign trying to keep up with Liverpool. Despite falling behind to a Gordon
Cowans goal, the Blues played admirably and scored a deserved, if deflected, equaliser through Mark Ward. In the second half, the crucial moment came when David
White's pace took him clear of the Villa defence. His shot struck a post, and there were
agonising moments as the television viewer was treated to the sight of the ball in front
of an empty goal, with no indication as to who might be closest to it. The incredible
and unlikely solution to the conundrum was provided by the arrival into frame of the
grey-haired Peter Reid, who followed up to score City's winning goal. It was and re-

mained City's best live televised performance for an awfully long time; quite out of character.

The victory at Villa Park provided the impetus for City to haul themselves out of the relegation zone. Mark Ward completed a run of scoring in three consecutive matches by earning a point in a 1-1 draw at Millwall, and contributing to a 3-1 win at Loftus Road. The other goal-scorers were Clive Allen, against his old team, and Colin Hendry, whose partnership with Steve Redmond was looking increasingly secure. Gary Megson was sent off towards the end, but even City couldn't manage to make a mess of this match. Suitably inspired, 33,022 (including, for the first time, my future wife) were there to witness a 2-1 Easter win against plummeting Sheffield Wednesday. This was City's second largest home attendance of the season, and the late and fortunate winning goal was scored by substitute Adrian Heath. Heath's second Easter winner, at Norwich two days later, lifted the Blues to safety, and the comforting heights of fourteenth place. Harper, Reid, Ward, Heath, Megson and Clarke all played a part in the reunion with Everton at Maine Road on 21 April 1990. The Everton side, sitting pretty in the top five, were no doubt disorientated by so many familiar faces, and Niall Quinn's headed goal was enough for another City victory in an open and entertaining match, free from the tensions of recent weeks. Quinn had scored a goal in each of his first three Maine Road appearances. This was a man who knew how to ingratiate himself.

City's nine-match unbeaten run was ended by Derby County, whose 1-0 win in the final Maine Road match of the season ensured their safety. A draw in the last game of the season, at Crystal Palace, meant that City finished in fourteenth position, which, annoyingly, was one place below *The Nation's Team*, on goal difference. The satisfaction of City's final weeks of the season was soured by Palace's inability to win the FA Cup Final. It was the first FA Cup Final that I had deliberately avoided watching. The initial match draw lured me into viewing the replay which, of course, was a mistake. Ferguson managed to save his job, and the season finished on a bitter note.

I was not convinced about Howard Kendall, whose attention seemed to be drifting west on the M62. Niall Quinn was undoubtedly an excellent signing, but most of Kendall's other acquisitions looked short-term. The man was, however, clearly a good organiser, and the Blues had survived an eventful season. We also had a memorable Maine Road derby match to look back on. There has been nothing remotely like it since. There are no signs that anything remotely like it is imminent.

Season 1990/91: Howard's Way Out

The summer of 1990 was an eventful time. There was the excitement of Italia '90, and my incredibly astute and deliberately obtuse bet on West Germany, at ridiculously generous odds of eight-to-one. There was a particularly throbbing gig by the Charlatans at The Ritz – a venue described in a John Cooper Clarke poem as 'the mecca of the modern dance'. And who am I to argue? The seven live appearances of the band Biff! took place, featuring an earnest-looking yours truly concentrating hard on bass guitar. A hat-trick of performances at the Boardwalk, and four crushed into an unsuitable corner of Corbieres, were enough to confirm that another Manchester-based phenomenon was not about to take the music world by storm. One particularly ill-timed appearance at the Boardwalk, to which I had agreed most reluctantly, coincided in an act of fatalistic inevitability with England's match against Cameroon. Predictably, the game went into extra time to ensure that we played in front of virtually no audience, since anybody with any sense remained in the pub to see the outcome of the match. Even the sound engineer was straining to listen to the match commentary on the radio. We were virtually the only people in the world who didn't know what was going on in extra time. *Sod showbiz*, I thought. *Who needs it?*

The World Cup of 1990 was another to start well but fade away. The dreadful Argentineans managed one half-decent performance to oust Italy, but they cast a cynical shadow over much of the remaining proceedings, including the final. England supporters got carried away with a few fortunate results, particularly against Belgium and Cameroon. They were unlucky to lose in the semi-final, but the Germans had the best team that year and deserved to win. Especially when you consider that I backed them.

Mind you, I also backed Russia, who went out in the opening stages. England were, once more, much improved by injury to Bryan Robson. On this occasion it was David Platt who emerged as the more than adequate replacement. I was more interested in Ireland's progress, and was particularly pleased that Niall Quinn scored against Holland. No representative of *The Nation's Team* managed to register a goal in that World Cup. Any such minor victory is always gratefully received. Ultimately, the most surprising aspect of Italia '90 was the world's first good official football song, 'World In Motion', although its lyrical connection with the event was tenuous at best.

Howard Kendall's transfer dealings were a less comforting feature of the summer. The £1 million signing of Tony Coton looks good with hindsight, but it seemed wasteful at the time because Andy Dibble had performed well over the previous two seasons. The most alarming transfer activity concerned the sale of Andy Hinchcliffe to Everton. Neil Pointon, the Everton left-back valued at £400,000, came to City as part of the deal. In all honesty, I never rated Pointon, although I know that others did, and I couldn't help feeling that Mr Kendall had done his old team a considerable favour. Hinchcliffe went on to make full international status. There was an underlying disquiet amongst the Faithful. We did not want any more Everton rejects.

Mark Brennan (£400,000) was the only other signing of note at the start of the season, although Steve Redmond's replacement at the centre of defence and as captain, by Paul Lake, raised a few eyebrows. In fact, Lake looked just as comfortable as a central defender as he had in various other positions. It looked like an astute move, but it was short-lived. After only three matches, Lake suffered the cruciate ligament injury that prematurely terminated his extremely promising career.

Kendall began the season preferring the Little and Large double act of Heath and Quinn, considerably funnier than the real Little and Large, two of City's more embarrassing celebrity fans. As a result, Clive Allen was forced to start the first six matches from the substitutes' bench. The Blues began with a disappointing 3-1 defeat at Tottenham, but they built momentum gradually after that. At White Hart Lane, Niall Quinn equalised Lineker's opening goal with a header from a David White cross, and for a while an encouraging first result looked possible, but goals from Gascoigne and Lineker, again, finished them off. The media circus seeking to extend the reign of Gazzamania was placated.

After their fall guy role in the opening fixture, things improved for the Blues. Kendall had the knack of achieving narrow victories and, with three points for a win, those were certainly good enough. Heath scored what proved to be a rare goal in a 1-0 home win over Everton, whose poor start to the season was soon to have a significant bearing on events at Maine Road. In City's second home match of the season, the first of a surprisingly large number of penalties scored by Ward helped City to a 2-1 victory over Aston Villa, to leave the Blues occupying a very respectable League position. I missed that match, and Paul Lake's horrific injury, because of the opportunity to take a trip to Japan.

Luckily, the *South-East Asia Times* kept me fully informed of results. I arrived back in the country the day after a satisfactory 1-1 draw away to Sheffield United, with David White scoring his first of the season, and Steve Redmond restored as captain and partner for Hendry. Goals from Quinn and Brennan in another narrow win, this time 2-1 at home to Norwich, propelled City to fifth place in the table. The Blues maintained their solid start by earning draws away to Wimbledon and Derby County, and defeating Coventry at Maine Road by the unusually convincing scoreline of 2-0. In this game Niall Quinn added the comforting second goal with a only a few minutes remaining, following a real collector's item earlier in the half: a goal by Alan Harper. City came desperately close to winning at Wimbledon, thanks to a Clive Allen goal and Tony Coton's save from a Keith Curle penalty kick, but a last-minute equaliser ensured that the radio got a few stern looks and narrowly survived being tossed against a wall.

The basis for City's improved results was the defensive solidity offered by Tony Coton; a back-four featuring Ian Brightwell at right-back, in addition to Pointon, Hendry and Redmond; and an unadventurous midfield usually including two from Reid, Megson and Harper, all inclined to remain deep, more from necessity than choice. This made life for the opposition very difficult. With Ward and White also called upon to be disciplined, City became hard to score against. The pace of White, and the surprises offered by Niall Quinn, were employed to create the goals needed to win matches. Despite finding the net when chosen, Clive Allen was not integral to the Kendall/Reid plan, which relied upon the hard-working Adrian Heath to stifle opposition attacks early, despite the reduced offensive threat that such a policy entailed. City's other scoring possibilities came mainly from Mark Ward penalties. It was often pretty dull, but effective, particularly on the narrower Maine Road pitch.

My first view of the new City away from home came at the Baseball Ground, not a place with particularly happy memories for me. The Blues took an early lead, thanks to a penalty won and scored by Ward, and they rarely looked like either losing it or adding to it. It took a spectacular Dean Saunders goal to prevent City from taking all three points, but it was easy to see why the Blues were so much harder to beat. I was quite happy to settle for that after the traumas of the 1980s. Who cared about entertainment?

On 27 October 1990, *The Nation's Team* came to Maine Road for a derby match of quite different character to the encounter of the previous year. This time, both clubs had made reasonable starts to the season, with the Blues in fifth place, three points better off than their opponents. Because of the crowd disturbances of the 5-1 match, an earlier kick-off time was imposed. It was not a great inconvenience. I didn't require the Marston's Pedigree quite so much on this occasion. I walked to the Academy in a mood as close to optimism as I can manage.

The Blues kicked towards the Platt Lane End in the first half, with Kendall preferring Harper to Brightwell, much to my disgust. In fact, there were only two Manchester City players amongst those starting who had also played in the 5-1 win: David White and Steve Redmond. Things went well for City in the first half, after a typically frantic start. I didn't know at the time, but it was David White who fired City in front after 21 minutes, when the ball broke to him in a crowded penalty area. White scored again five minutes later, after latching on to a flick by Heath and using his pace to sprint clear. Our esteemed visitors were hesitant and nervous. Another emphatic win seemed possible. Unfortunately, a header by Hughes just before half-time brought the Faithful back down to planet earth, and there were some awkward moments to endure in the second half. David White could have eased our anxiety by completing a hat-trick instead of placing his header against the crossbar, but a tremendous goal by Colin Hendry, scored with 12 minutes remaining, following a neat exchange with Quinn, looked to have put us on the way to another night of ecstasy. It all seemed too good to be true. It was.

The media made much of the replacement of Peter Reid with Ian Brightwell soon after the Hendry goal, because it was Brightwell's mistake that led to McClair breaking clear to score after 81 minutes. Three minutes later, a header by Bruce, following a corner, was deflected in by McClair from close-range, for a sickening equaliser. The match ended with a massive feeling of anticlimax and disappointment. It was as if City had lost.

A typical stifling performance by Arsenal, who were far better at that sort of thing than City, led to a Littlewoods Cup exit a few days later, thanks to a couple of smart breakaway goals, and despite Clive Allen coming on as a substitute to score. It hadn't been a good few days, but after a 1-1 draw at Sunderland on 3 November 1990, City were still occupying fifth place in the table.

Soon after that match, Howard Kendall ensured that City were the talk of the back pages once again. Mr Kendall decided to leave City for his first love, Everton, a team struggling to escape the lower reaches of Division One. It might be assumed that City fans would be demoralised by the departure of a man who, on the face of it, was something of a saviour; the results certainly indicated so. In fact, although everybody was taken by surprise, few were disappointed to see Kendall leave, and most were quick to back caretaker manager Peter Reid for the manager's job.

Kendall departed, making some garbled remarks that could be interpreted as him viewing Manchester City as a bit on the side, and Everton as his true love. Personally, I felt used and no, I did not respect him in the morning. I was hoping that he would return for his old belongings, particularly those belonging at Goodison Park. He didn't, at least not for a while, and even then, not for all of them. Men!

Peter Reid's first game in charge, on Sunday, 11 November 1990, was, unfortunately, chosen by ITV for live coverage, with the usual consequences. City were awarded two penalties, the second dispatched by Ward after the other had been spectacularly missed by Harper, but the Blues went down 3-2 to Leeds United. To make matters worse, the winner was scored by Gordon Strachan, who looked suspiciously offside when he received the ball just inside the City half, but somehow managed to keep clear of the chasing defenders before sliding the ball beyond Tony Coton. Despite this result, Peter Reid was still very much the choice of the fans, and it wasn't too long before Mr Swales decided, for once, to do something sensible and appoint him in the interests of stability, a rare commodity at Maine Road.

A draw at Luton Town was followed by the supreme test, a trip to Anfield, where no visiting side had won for over a year. It was seven months since anyone had departed with so much as a point. Liverpool had conceded only a single goal at Anfield all season. The signs were, therefore, none too promising. I didn't obtain a ticket for the match and wasn't even following the radio commentary. There was little reason to expect anything except defeat. But Manchester City are nothing if not occasionally unpredictable and, after holding Liverpool in a goalless first half, City twice came close to taking the lead. Firstly, Quinn shot narrowly wide of the post and then he forced Grobbelaar to save acrobatically following a header. On the latter occasion the ball remained in the Liverpool penalty area, and Mark Ward was clumsily felled by Ronnie Whelan. Ward dispatched the penalty himself, just, and after 63 minutes, City had the lead. They held on until eight minutes from the end. By now I was paying attention to the latest scores on 'Grandstand'. As far as I was aware, the Blues led with just a couple of minutes to go, and then the scoreline flashed up: 2-1. I couldn't believe it. What happened to 1-1?

An Ian Rush equaliser had been followed within a few minutes by substitute Ronnie Rosenthal's goal. With two minutes left, Clive Allen came on for Adrian Heath and won City a free-kick, which Ward struck surprisingly well, but Grobbelaar diverted wide. From the corner, taken by Ward, Niall Quinn equalised with a sensational header directed into the smallest of gaps above the head of a defender on the line and into the top corner. The goal came a minute into injury time. It was a real boost for the Blues, and an indication of genuine fighting spirit. I was left wishing that I *had* queued all night for one of the few tickets available for visiting fans.

Peter Reid's first signing as manager was Sam Ellis, who became the first team coach, and ultimately the target for much criticism. Ellis had been a City fan, watching from the Kippax terraces in his youth, but that didn't save him.

Reid's first victory as player-manager of Manchester City came at Maine Road against QPR, on 1 December 1990. A goal in each half, both from the trusty boots of Niall Quinn, left City in a comfortable position before the obligatory late goal, a rather good one by Sinton, made us sweat a little. There was further evidence of Reid-inspired battling qualities in the next match, at home to Spurs, who were third in the table, and still even more fashionable than usual because of the presence of Gascoigne and Lineker. At the behest of the referee, who reckoned he couldn't see blue in the fog, City played at Maine Road in their all-maroon away strip. A typical Gazza dribble, encompassing a Lineker touch and a slice of fortune, ended with Spurs taking a first-half lead in front of the North Stand. The Blues fought gallantly to rescue the game and, with 15 minutes remaining, Steve Redmond diverted a Wayne Clarke shot into the net for an equaliser. Amidst a cacophony of noise, a most generous penalty award, for handball against Paul Walsh, offered Ward the opportunity to put City ahead, and this he did emphatically. It proved to be the winner.

Approaching Christmas, City were in a position of prominence not experienced in over a decade. The thought of being as high as sixth place caused some temporary trauma, resulting in consecutive defeats against Crystal Palace and Southampton. However, there was a happy post-Christmas day out for those of us visiting the City Ground on 29 December 1990. The Blues took control with a couple of first-half Niall Quinn goals in front of the assembled Faithful, and it was a surprisingly comfortable afternoon against a lethargic Forest side. Although a Jemson goal provoked familiar feelings of unease, a David White cross headed in by Clarke provided a reassuring cushion.

City's 1991 unbeaten run did not stretch to a single match or day as on New Year's Day, whilst many a hangover was nursed, Arsenal repeated their Littlewoods Cup stifling of the Blues. Arsenal, battling for the Championship, managed to scrape a 1-0 victory at Maine Road. With the European ban only partially and selectively lifted, in order to allow the Nation's and World's favourite team in, qualification for exotic foreign travel was not a realistic aspiration for City. Attention, therefore, turned to the FA Cup, which surely represented a genuinely attainable target for a team now quite difficult to beat, and capable of being at least competitive – given a following wind, some luck, and the correct alignment of the constellations. It was at this point that my addled brain turned to the invention of the Five Year Rule.

Let's consider the evidence. The Blues were at Wembley in 1976 for their last real triumph. The next Wembley trip was for the 1981 FA Cup Final which, by my calculations, was five years later. The clinching piece of evidence was provided by the invention of a stupid competition that hardly anybody entered. This allowed City a trip to Wembley for the final of the Full Members Cup in 1986, despite the team being distinctly ordinary. Now, there had to be some divine intervention in that!

It was 1991, five years further on! To make matters worse, I was suffering under the illusion that the Blues had a League Cup triumph in 1971, rather than 1970.

It could all have ended at Turf Moor against Fourth Division Burnley, a club that had fallen considerably in stature since my last visit. There was a new motorway to help me get to the town, but the ground had changed little, and the big, old shed that was my home for this Sunday afternoon had certainly seen better days. The home side put up plucky resistance, as expected, but Colin Hendry smacked in the only goal, after

White's header had been saved. This was much to the chagrin of the locals, who disliked anyone with the slightest Blackburn association, past, present or, in Hendry's case, future. The goal, which came as the result of Pointon's passable impersonation of a winger, meant that we could all relax a little. Despite Burnley's best efforts, they were able to make little real headway, although Tony Coton did have to make a few saves, including one from City old boy Ron 'the other' Futcher.

Sunday, 13 January 1991 provided the opportunity for another relaxing day out. By this time, I had actually moved back to Liverpool to share a house with my future wife, who had the pleasure of accompanying me to Goodison Park. The frosty afternoon was warmed by lashings of unbridled hatred and vitriol aimed at Howard 'Judas' Kendall, the Everton manager. There was an eager desperation for revenge and the Faithful worked themselves up into a frenzy of indignation. Unfortunately, the live ITV coverage ensured that such yearning would be in vain. Megson could have given City the lead in the thirteenth minute, but two minutes later events deteriorated at the other end, our end. There was a general consensus that Pat Nevin was offside in the build-up to the opening goal. Peter Beagrie's volley and subsequent acrobatics, which alternate between infuriating and inspiring depending on which side he's on, and a second goal by Sheedy, ensured that City left Liverpool pointless. This was despite an impressive overhead kick by substitute Clive Allen, which would have given City a chance had it not been for an overeager linesman who decided that the preceding cross had been struck from beyond the touchline.

Those dreaded numbered balls matched the Blues with Second Division Port Vale, a side with a reputation for giant-killing, in the FA Cup fourth-round. Before that important event could take place, City played host to one of the few surviving matches on a weather-affected Saturday, 19 January 1991. The visitors, Dave Basset's Sheffield United, included a certain Vincent Jones in their side. Vinny did not disappoint. He earned a booking after approximately four seconds, following an ugly lunge at the City player-manager. When he repeated the act in the second half, Jones succeeded in what appeared to be his aim: he got sent off. It was a match in which Mark Ward made rare significant contributions, turning in White's cross to give City the lead, and curling an impressive second goal near the end. Strangely enough, Ward repeated the feat of scoring twice against the same opposition three days later. This second match was in the Zenith Data Systems Cup, a competition in which I took no interest whatsoever.

It was dry for the trip to Vale Park on 26 January 1991. Everyone expected the game to be rather tricky. Brennan and Harper were drafted in for Reid and Hendry. Hovering like vultures, the 'Match of the Day' team were on the lookout for an upset, but this time they were to be disappointed. There had been growing agitation about the continuing preference for Heath rather than Allen, and 'Inchy' was once more preferred in attack. Allen's minimal recent contributions had been put down to slow recovery from illness, but it later transpired that he and the manager did not exactly see eye to eye. Allen was, at least, on the substitutes' bench, along with David Brightwell, Ian's younger brother.

The match kicked-off, and I braced myself for an uncomfortable afternoon. Initially, at least, it didn't transpire. An excellent piece of finishing by Niall Quinn gave City an early lead, and David White might have added a second. Port Vale looked strangely subdued. It all changed when City-reject Darren Beckford extracted some revenge with a well-taken equaliser, blasting his shot through a crowd and into the roof of the net. We had all been standing behind that net, feeling fairly smug. The feeling dissipated as Vale proceeded to take charge in the second half, wasting several excellent chances. Coton's save from Robbie Earle was particularly impressive, but the Blues were looking vulnerable and the Five Year Rule seemed a bit silly. With 20 minutes remaining, City made a rare foray towards us and won a corner. Peter Reid decided, at last, to remove Heath and bring on Clive Allen. Allen strolled casually into the penalty area, just in time to nonchalantly score the winning goal with his first touch. Ward's left-wing corner had been flicked on at the near post by a combination of Quinn and a defender. It required only a simple header from Allen. Not surprisingly, this took the momentum away from Vale, and City held on to the 2-1 lead with no undue alarms. The Five Year Rule was looking more sensible by the minute.

Those cruel balls again sent City on their travels for the fifth-round. Their opponents were to be Notts County, who were in the higher echelons of Division Two. Before that, the Blues notched up a couple more League victories. At Norwich, a White cross headed in by Quinn, and a Quinn header volleyed in by White, gave the Blues a 2-0 first-half lead which they only half surrendered. At home to Chelsea, in a game rescued from the snow by the under-soil heating, Gary Megson stunned everyone by taking a Quinn headed pass on the chest, and smacking the ball into the net right-footed; his first goal for two years! A slip by Dorigo let White in for the second goal, a lob over the stranded Beasant, with only 20 minutes gone. Again the Blues allowed the opposition back. This time Dennis Wise was the beneficiary, but an embarrassing dismissal for Steve Clarke, after he had been outpaced by Neil Pointon, made the City task more comfortable. This rare home victory against Chelsea embroiled my future wife in another mythical rule. Her attendance at Maine Road coincided with victories. This one lasted for quite a while before going the way of all such rules. Incidentally, she worked the other way around away from Maine Road.

It was an impressive and confident build-up to the Meadow Lane trip and the quest for an FA Cup quarter-final place. At no time during this match did I feel that City would lose it. The Blues played far better that they had at either Burnley or Port Vale, dominating the game and creating chances. Steve Cherry, in the County goal, was in stubbornly brilliant form throughout. Clive Allen, in from the start, came closest in the first half, when his shot struck the post, but there were other opportunities. The second half continued in much the same fashion, but City were unable to apply the finishing touch. A long-range shot by Harper smashed against the woodwork, but County held on. It looked as though the Blues would have to settle for a replay. It was with utter disbelief that I saw City's season fall apart in the final minute. The winner by Gary Lund was a messy and unexpected affair, with a suspicion of offside about it, but it counted, which was all that mattered. Having been unusually calm and confident, I was shattered by this blow. City had time to attack our end again, and Niall Quinn became yet another City player to divert the ball against the frame of the goal. I felt as unwell as a brightly plumaged, talkative tropical bird suffering from a touch of psittacosis. The Five Year Rule was in tatters.

County went on to play far better and lose against Spurs in the quarter-final. That was certainly no consolation. I wanted them to win that one. Having convinced myself that City were going to make something of this season and get to the Cup Final, this result, and particularly the manner of it, was hard to swallow, and I was reduced to surly sulking for a couple of days.

The Blues attempted to placate me on 5 March 1991, in a midweek match at home to Luton. It coincided with a Throwing Muses gig at Liverpool Polytechnic. Instead of simply not going to the match, I decided to drive over and watch the first half. Incredibly, City won 3-0 and scored all the goals before I had to leave. I still can't quite get over this unprecedented display of co-operation, the chief architect of which was Niall Quinn, who burst clear to score one goal, and headed David White's cross home for another. City again found themselves in fifth place.

A few days later, the Blues were back at Maine Road, against Liverpool, for the second of three consecutive League home matches. This was not the Liverpool of old. On this occasion, Dalglish's men required considerable assistance in order to achieve the traditional convincing scoreline. It came courtesy of referee George Courteney, who endeared himself forever to Manchester City fans by awarding Liverpool two penalties, both of which were converted. Twice, Peter Beardsley was faced by Tony Coton. Twice Coton dived at Beardsley's feet. Twice, the City goalkeeper appeared to make some contact with the ball – at least, to me he did. Twice Beardsley collapsed into an imploring heap. Twice Mr Courteney of Spennymoor pointed to the penalty spot. City went on to lose 3-0.

An uninspiring home draw against Wimbledon, and a 3-1 defeat at Coventry, then well into their annual survival fight, suggested that City were about to slide into mid-table obscurity, ending the season with disappointing anticlimax. April Fool's Day sparked an improvement. Away to Crystal Palace, who were third in the table, Niall Quinn scored with two first-half shots, the second a precise volley, and completed a hat-trick with a header.

In fact, City finished the season well. There was another unexpected away win at Leeds, with Quinn heading the winner, and the Blues even fought back from a two-goal deficit away to title-chasing Arsenal. They needed the help of an improbable penalty, converted by Ward, but City's equaliser was down to David White's pace. With the Arsenal defence adopting their familiar synchronised offside salute formation, White sprinted clear from within his own half to bring City level before half-time, and there were no further goals. After that, the Blues had the dubious pleasure of relegating a couple of teams at Maine Road. The first victims were Derby County. When Quinn volleyed his twentieth goal of the season, the outcome did not seem in doubt, but after Dean Saunders was brought down by Coton, City found themselves reduced to 10 men and facing a penalty kick. By the processes of selection that operate in every school yard up and down the land, Niall Quinn emerged as the man to take over in goal, a decision he fully justified by diving to his left and saving Dean Saunders' penalty kick. A defensive cock-up allowed David White in to score an emphatic second after half-time and, despite their numerical advantage, Derby looked like a doomed side. Harford's late header spoilt Quinn's perfect day, but City held on for a 2-1 win.

I wish that I could claim to have been at Villa Park three days later for one of City's most spectacular away wins in modern history, but I had to settle for the radio coverage and television highlights, which are poor substitutes. It was probably David White's finest match, a game in which he demonstrated what an awesome chap he could be. White was always a moody character, who attracted critics because of his tendency to appear disinterested, but even the most ardent of detractors would have been hard pushed to criticise this display – mind you, that wouldn't have prevented them from trying. I was always a fan. As one of the original class of '86, who won the Youth Cup and swept the Blues to promotion, he was guaranteed my absolute devotion. On this particular occasion, blind faith was handsomely repaid.

After just five minutes, White fired in his first goal left-footed after a neat through-ball by Brennan. He added a second after a Niall Quinn flicked header had inspired a race that White was always going to win. It was a neat finish; lobbed first time over the stranded Nigel Spink. In the second half, Ward smashed a shot against the post before White's cross provided a simple chance for Brennan to extend City's lead to 3-0. A fortunate penalty award gave David Platt the opportunity to narrow that lead before White demonstrated a couple of touches of refreshing arrogance. His hat-trick was the result of an almost casual curling shot beyond Spink. A less confident White would have taken the ball much closer. It seemed the obvious thing to do. He didn't feel the need, and that was why it was so impressive. White's fourth goal was equally outrageous. Cutting inside on his right foot, White had several options to pass the ball and, clearly, that's what he should have done. But not on this night. Instead he fired a right-foot shot through the tiniest of gaps betwixt Spink and his right-hand post. The final score was an awesome 5-1, a scoreline already awash with religious connotations.

There was a real purpose to City's late run of form, and the prospect of finishing above *The Nation's Team*, for the first time in over a decade, provided a target that was virtually achieved following the exploits at Villa Park. There were only two matches remaining, and one of them was at *The Swamp*. A draw would have been sufficient to leave City confident of winning the battle to finish highest but, on a rather depressing afternoon, they didn't succeed. The only goal was mysteriously credited to an unknown debutant named Giggs, who was about as close to the ball as I was when Colin Hendry deflected it into his own net.

I think it was during this game that I heard a most interesting line of abuse, aimed at Mark Hughes, a player whom I have always detested. The insult was not of the 'Fuck off, Hughes, you long-haired Welsh git,' or, 'Fuck off, Hughes, you fat, ugly git,' or even, 'Fuck off, Hughes, you contrary-to-the-spirit-of-the-beautiful-game-dirty git,' variety. No, it was, 'Fuck off, Hughes, you spectacular-goalscoring git.' The main criticism was that the despised one scored only spectacular goals. This is not a line of abuse often directed at City players.

I felt a bit gloomy after the derby match. Having missed the fun at Villa, I was expecting more than the laboured performance at Old Trafford. Luckily, City could still finish above *The Nation's Team*, and in an incredible fifth position by winning their final match at home to Sunderland. Niall Quinn's neat finish for the first goal indicated that things were going to plan, but goals from Marco Gabbiadini and Gary Bennett gave the lead to a spirited Sunderland team, who were still clinging to mathematical chances of avoiding the drop. Quinn took advantage of defensive frailty to bring the Blues level before the break. The second half was not quite so frenetic. David White's headed goal proved to be the winner, and the end of Sunderland's battle against relegation. The Sunderland fans were in admirable form, using the chant 'Always look on the bright side of life' in exactly the right context. Others later stole the idea, but demonstrated a flimsy grasp on the intended irony. The Monty Python film obviously went above *their* heads.

The result meant that City did finish in fifth place, their highest position since season 1977/78, and three points ahead of *The Nation's Team*. Back in 1977/78, fifth position was seen as evidence of a decline. How times had changed. It was almost the perfect end to the season. Unfortunately, the European Cup Winners Cup competition beggared belief in 1990/91. *The Nation's Team*, having disposed of a tremendously obscure Hungarian team, faced the might of Wrexham in the second-round. Somehow they overcame that stern challenge to face an atrocious Montpellier team, featuring the Columbian Jim Tolmie lookalike. Montpellier would have been better with the real Jim Tolmie.

Having scraped through that tie, and a semi-final against Widzew Lodz, only an under-strength Barcelona prevented them from actually winning a European trophy. An under-strength Barcelona should have been more than sufficient, and I will never forgive them for their pathetic display in the final. Even the 4-0 thrashing, a few years later, fails to compensate. They saved Ferguson's job. There was no excuse for that. And they spoilt what had otherwise been a perfectly acceptable season – and there haven't been many of those. How dare they!

Season 1991/92: David White and Niall Quinn

The relative progress achieved in season 1990/91 came as something of a surprise. The defence had its shortcomings, and the midfield lacked creativity. To be perfectly honest, there were a number of players that I didn't think were up to it at all. And yet the proof was in the final League table. This modest but welcome success was based on the Reid ethic of hard work and organisation; at least as close to organisation as a Manchester City team ever gets. There was an additional factor marking out this team from those spanning the previous decade. We had players worthy of the opposition's fear: David White, with his scary pace and occasionally ruthless finishing; and Niall Quinn, strong, always surprisingly adept with his feet, and a player whose awesome size made him impossible to mark. Seldom did Manchester City score a goal during this era that did not involve either White or Quinn, and usually both. Niall Quinn ended the 1990/91 season with 20 League goals from his 38 appearances, and David

White contributed a further 16, despite only rarely being employed as a striker. The combination of a White cross and Quinn header was the archetypal City goal, but this belies the truth. City goals were constructed in many different ways but, other than the often dubious penalties finished off by Mark Ward, you could be fairly sure of involvement by the tall, slim, moody one, or the even taller, affable Irishman. At the time, I got the impression that many of the City fans failed to appreciate their fortune, judging by the abuse often hurled at the two men in question. It no longer amazes me that you can find spectators who are adamant in their misguided criticism of even the best players representing *their* team. The more vociferous critics tend to choose an individual and construct a mindset dictating that every little thing that goes wrong is the fault of that single player. Few players, apart from those who seldom make any impression at all, have escaped this treatment, particularly at Maine Road. If a pass goes astray, it's because the player in question didn't anticipate. If the other side scores, then the guilty party should have been marking the goalscorer. Even when the target smacks the ball into the back of the net, a respite is only temporary. It could drive those within hearing range to distraction, if it were not for the fact that they are openly, or secretly, blaming a different individual for the same misdemeanours. Most of us do it. I would quite happily blame Neil Pointon, Mark Ward, Gary Megson, Alan Harper or Adrian Heath for anything; it's just that I didn't do it as loudly as some, and I had more variety.

City were fortunate that neither White nor Quinn had missed a League game in 1990/91, an astonishing record considering Quinn's constant physical battles, and the tendency for defenders to curtail White's bursts of pace by desperate means. Both would be essential to the success of a new campaign. I had hoped, during the close season, for some spectacular signings. Finishing fifth might have been enough to persuade a really class midfield player, a tough but skilful, goalscoring, play-making mega-hero preferably, to come to Maine Road. A younger Peter Reid would have fitted the bill perfectly. If only Gio Kinkladze had arrived at this juncture. That would have done very nicely too.

There was talk of a return for Paul Stewart, whose initial years at Spurs had been less than distinguished, despite his winning FA Cup Final goal. This was in the match where Gazza most emphatically demonstrated his tendency to be barmy. I was driving along the M62 when the news came on the radio of City's big new signing, and I was convinced it was Stewart. The announcer introduced the subject and spoke of City spending £2.5 million, but still hadn't mentioned a name. At the moment when I expected the words 'Paul Stewart' to appear, the voice said 'Keith Curle' instead. I didn't know who Keith Curle was. When I found out his position, I could hardly believe that City had spent so much money on another centre half. It was a British record fee for a defender. I thought it was stupid. Mind you, I was wrong.

Curle was an excellent player: a good tackler and, at last, a defender with pace. He was made captain, which must have irritated Steve Redmond, who had lost the captaincy at the beginning of the season for the second time, having been replaced previously by the unfortunate Lake.

The other transfer activity involved the departure of Mark Ward and Alan Harper, whom I saw several months later in our local pub, the Rose of Mossley – I did not rush to get a beer mat autographed. Howard Kendall bought them both. Good for him! Ashley Ward, who had made only rare first team appearances was transferred to Leicester City.

The fixture list hadn't been terribly kind to the Blues. A trip to Coventry, not often a happy ground for Manchester City teams, was followed by consecutive home matches against two of the previous season's top three sides, Liverpool and Crystal Palace. With such tough matches to follow, it was a matter for some celebration that City managed to win 1-0 at Highfield Road. The winning goal was described by Bob Greaves on 'Granada Goals Extra',

> *'Right, what happened was, Micky Gynn side-footed...here it comes...and it's in...over the hands and the head...oh!... that was Niall Quinn, that was Niall Quinn...I beg your pardon...that was Niall Quinn's goal.'*

You can always rely on ITV for succinct, quality coverage.

My mood was, therefore, considerably lifted for the Maine Road midweek clash with Graeme Souness's Liverpool. My dad had finally given up on City; my future wife therefore had the honour of accompanying me to this highly charged and emotional occasion. The ladies of the Mick McCarthy fan club were no more, but we found ourselves in the vicinity of the Pie Men, so-called because of their tendency to arrive just after kick-off with pie and chips. These they consumed with relish before operating on a short fuse, with plenty of leaping up and finger pointing to accompany their abuse. They have mellowed somewhat in recent years and, sadly, the pie and chips are not such a frequent feature as they once were. I mention the Pie Men only because my future wife was granted the pleasure of a hug from the largest of the two during this very match. I escaped unmolested.

The game against Liverpool raised all of our expectations. It was the first occasion for many, many years when a Manchester City side defeated the mighty Liverpool totally on merit. As it turns out, Liverpool were not so mighty this season, but that isn't the point. We all thought that they were.

A crowd of 37,322, as near as damn it to capacity, was packed into the Academy on a balmy and barmy August night. Keith Curle found himself matched against the visitors' big-news signing, Dean Saunders. Curle had a brilliant home debut, removing all doubts instantly. Andy Hill, a modest signing from Bury, who had bided his time on the fringes of the side, was promoted to right-back, allowing Ian Brightwell into a right-sided midfield position, with Mark Brennan playing on the left. The centre midfield of Megson and Reid was not brimming with vitality. Once more, therefore, City were relying heavily on Niall Quinn, who would battle, almost literally, with Mark Wright, and David White, operating as a striker. Steve Redmond was chosen as Curle's partner, leaving Colin Hendry on the bench. It wasn't long before Hendry returned to Blackburn. At the time this appeared to be a downward career move.

White looked in belligerent mood from the beginning, forcing Grobbelaar into an early save from an unusual angle. City actually looked threatening, a rarity against

Liverpool, and Ian Brightwell came close to scoring following a corner, but a goal line block prevented him. On 29 minutes, Quinn's pass set White on the gallop down the right wing. Sheer pace took White clear and allowed him to cut inside, making a more promising angle for the shot, which flew past Grobbelaar's right hand and just inside the post. It was impressive and precise finishing. White almost added to his goal with a snap shot, but we were all more than happy with the outcome of the first half. Liverpool had looked tentative.

The visitors emerged from an interval earbashing to offer a greater threat. Coton foiled Houghton at point-blank range to maintain City's lead. After 64 minutes, Niall Quinn's header found the hyperactive White, who burst into the penalty area before unleashing a left-foot shot. The sheer pace defeated Grobbelaar. The ball thundered against the underside of the crossbar and downward before spinning away from goal and landing conveniently in the hands of the Liverpool goalkeeper, just as he turned to face his own goal. It all happened quickly, but I had a good view from the North Stand and my immediate impression was that the ball had crossed the line before spin took it out on the bounce. My second thought was that, of course, the match officials had missed it and the goal would not be given, and City would go on to lose. This would set off a disastrous run of form resulting in several consecutive relegations and a place in whatever equivalent of the Unibond League was in existence. After many years of watching the Blues, that's the way I think.

There was a delay, and plenty of confusion, but it suddenly became clear to us and to White, who was obviously convinced he had scored, that the goal had been given. It was 2-0. There were arguments, of course, but the television replay from the side of the goal suggested that the ball did bounce over the line. Professor Elton Welsby claimed that the better camera angle was from just below the roof of the Main Stand, because it was above the pitch. Welsby's theorem suggested that if the ball landed over the line, a camera from above should have revealed space betwixt ball and line. You saw no space, therefore there was no goal. *Ipso facto.* Welsby's theorem had one minor flaw. As Pythagoras, a man who knew his angles, might have said, 'It was a bag of shite.' He would have said it in Greek, naturally.

The camera was not directly above the goal; it was at an angle of about 45 degrees to the goal line. Might I suggest that the camera along the goal line was just a little better placed? Professor Welsby would not let it lie. It dragged on in the Granada TV football coverage for weeks. The Professor had, of course, been the Radio City man at Anfield for a number of years.

Back to Maine Road on 21 August 1991, at approximately 20.50 hours: the goal had been awarded and my future wife was being hugged by a Pie Man. An impudent curler by an inspired White almost completed a heroic hat-trick, but Grobbelaar recovered from the shock just in time to tip it over the bar. With 20 minutes remaining, Mike Marsh came on as a Liverpool substitute and, along with Steve McManaman, sparked a youth-led Liverpool revival that threatened to spoil everything. With 75 minutes of the match expired, a cross by Marsh was headed in by MacManaman. I blamed Pointon, who was the wrong side of the goalscorer. There was probably somebody in the ground who blamed White.

The goal changed everything. City lost their earlier control as Liverpool began to dominate possession for the first time in the match. I made regular anxious glances at my genuine mock-Rolex watch from Thailand. Unfortunately, it kept time brilliantly, and there was no comfort to be had. With eight minutes remaining, Dean Saunders crumpled under challenge from Hill, and referee Paul Vanes from the West Midlands awarded a penalty kick. Hearts sank on all sides, bar that behind the goal faced by Dean Saunders, who elected to take the penalty kick himself. Saunders was the man whose penalty for Derby County had been saved by Niall Quinn in front of the very same goal, four months previously. On this occasion, his penalty was not saved by Tony Coton. Instead, the ball crashed against the crossbar, came straight out into the mêlée, and was cleared to safety. It is at times like these when I could be convinced of the existence of a higher being. Unfortunately, such times are vastly outnumbered. At least they are if you support Manchester City. Mercilessly, the referee played three minutes of injury time, but the Blues held on for their first win against Liverpool in nearly eight years.

The match three days later, against Crystal Palace, always had too much to live up to. Geoff Thomas gave the visitors the lead, but a generous penalty award allowed City to draw level. Mark Brennan succeeded in his effort to kick the football into the same net that Dean Saunders had been unable to disturb. Actually, I cannot be sure that the net was identical, but the frame of the goal almost certainly was. Just before half-time, the positively predatory White turned in Brennan's cross to put City ahead. The lead did not last long into the second period, as the Blues struggled to reproduce the heights of their midweek special. If anything, it was Steve Coppell's team who looked the more likely winners. With three minutes to go, divine intervention struck Palace defender Richard Shaw for the second time in the match and there was another harsh penalty award. Everyone was a little stunned, but Brennan kept his cool and made the most of the windfall. City won 3-2 to complete their first three-win start to the season since 1982/83: the season when they were relegated. City were also top of the table, just as they were in 1982/83.

The Blues lost top place after a midweek goalless draw at Norwich. At Highbury, three days later, the Blues held a half-time lead against the reigning Champions, Arsenal. Ian Brightwell had headed the ball as David Seaman punched fresh air. A victory at Highbury would have everyone taking City seriously. Unfortunately, it all fell apart with Arsenal scoring two second-half goals, but the Blues were at least proving competitive. There was still a mood of relative optimism for the midweek home match against Nottingham Forest. This would be a battle to decide who should occupy second place, behind *The Nation's Team*, whose unbeaten start to the season was already putting a bit of a dampener on things.

Clough, Keane, and the rest started the brighter, and there were early Forest chances before City got into the swing of things. The Blues broke through six minutes before half-time, following a Brennan corner. Quinn and Curle had a quick game of head-tennis before Quinn struck a volley through the crowd. The ball rebounded off the post and in off a bemused Scott Gemmill. City began to take control in the second half, with a White volley and a Quinn header coming close to extending their slender lead. Forest equalised when they least looked likely to. One of those typical sophisticated passing moves was initially thwarted by Coton, but persistence paid off, and Clough's cross was turned in by Teddy Sheringham. With Forest looking lively on the counter-attack, the match was delicately poised. A David White header would have restored City's lead, had Niall Quinn not inadvertently blocked it. The game was drifting towards a draw when a touch of adventurous spirit from City full-back Andy Hill inspired another home win. With four minutes left, Hill ventured forward and planted a header beyond Crossley, to send the Blues into second place in the table. It was a tremendous City start to the season. The matches at Maine Road had been both inspiring and entertaining. It didn't last.

The Blues lost 3-0 at Elland Road. A penalty award gave City an inkling of a way back into the match, but with Brennan having been taken off, Peter Reid struck it against the post and followed up the rebound himself. You can't do that. Had Reid left the ball alone, somebody else might have scored.

Worse was to follow with a frustrating 1-0 home defeat by Sheffield Wednesday, followed by an even more frustrating 1-0 home defeat by Howard Kendall's Everton. The latter match marked the appearance of tricky winger Michael Hughes, and the debut as substitute of the enthusiastic Mike Sheron. When another penalty kick offered the Blues the hope of late salvation, or at least a point, Hughes, who had had a fine game, shamed his more experienced colleagues by being the only one willing to take it. The deserved fairy tale ending was not forthcoming. The penalty sailed over the bar, and City dropped to tenth place.

The slump was arrested at Upton Park. With 15 minutes remaining, Steve Redmond became the latest City player to volunteer for penalty-taking duty. This was one of the finest moments of Piccadilly Radio's Brian Clarke. It was clear that Redmond had struck the penalty kick, but from Clarke's commentary it was far from obvious what the outcome was. Clarke was so upset by the fact that Redmond had miskicked the ball that he forgot, for a ludicrously long time, to mention that the goalkeeper had dived completely the wrong way, and that the ball had still found its way into the goal. City led 1-0. Five minutes from the end, the Blues surrendered their lead over West Ham, but a dramatic late winner by substitute Colin Hendry, playing as a striker, restored it. Back at Maine Road, wins were proving harder to come by. Despite taking the lead following an impressive build-up and excellent David White finish, City lost 2-1 to Oldham.

Away to Notts County, promoted for a one-off season, City fell behind but equalised from a corner: Mike Sheron's first goal for the club. The real significance of this match was the return from obscurity of Clive Allen, who clearly felt that he had something to prove. When Allen's shot was handled on the line, he took and scored the penalty himself. He later volleyed a superb City third, after which he pointedly refused to accept the congratulations of the player-manager. According to Allen, not only was he forced to train with the juniors, but he had not spoken to Reid for 10 weeks. This was clearly not a case of happy families. Two days later, Allen was granted the honour of a start against Chester City, in a Rumbelows League Cup match played at Stockport County's Edgeley Park, my only ever visit, and a wet evening out. Allen scored an immaculate striker's goal to add to earlier efforts by Sheron and Brennan, making the final aggregate score a comfortable 6-1. The match also featured a compact, as in small, on-loan Dutchman called Danny Hoekman. He made a couple of appearances as substitute and looked quite skilful, but he wasn't signed permanently. Clive Allen didn't start another City match. Personalities were given prominence over the best interests of the team.

A spectacular, late, left-foot shot by Niall Quinn brought City a win at Tottenham and sent the Blues back up to third place in the table. The position was maintained with a 3-2 home victory over Sheffield United, on the same day that *The Nation's Team* surrendered a two-goal lead to lose their unbeaten run against Sheffield Wednesday. City's winner was smashed in by Michael Hughes, following up after a Quinn shot had struck the post. City's impressive run of League form continued at Southampton, where Quinn and Sheron both scored neat goals, and Gittons helped out by steering the ball past his own goalkeeper. Sheron was making quite an impression standing in for the injured White, and Michael Hughes was a permanent feature on the left wing.

White returned for the crucial Maine Road derby match which, unusually, featured two of the top three teams in the First Division, with City three points adrift of the enemy. White and Ian Brightwell were the only two Mancunians on show. It was not a pretty match. Right from the start, Reid and Brightwell snapped at their illustrious opponents in a most pleasing manner. Steve Bruce replied by physically assaulting Heath. No caution was administered. It was Heath who wasted City's best first-half opportunity, although a dreadful Pallister back-pass almost allowed Michael Hughes in. With Schmeichel missing the ball – one of those rather frequent rare mistakes – Hughes dabbed it towards goal, but with insufficient power.

The Blues attacked the North Stand in the second half. There was a rare moment of anxiety at the opposite end when Blackmore's shot warmed Tony Coton's hands. Generally, City had the better chances. Sheron might have scored with his first touch after coming on as substitute; but he fired straight at the Blonde One. In the interests of fairness, I should point out that Heath did well to create that opportunity. He did not, however, do well to scoop the best chance of the match into the North Stand, after Sheron had returned the compliment. Heath had not scored a goal for over a year which, considering that he was most often used as an attacker, is quite an achievement. Two minutes from the end, another grotesque challenge by Bruce, leading to broken ribs for the City player-manager, was still not sufficient to prompt Mr Hackett to produce the yellow card. City should have been grateful for even being awarded a free-kick. The challenge may have been enjoyed by one person in a blue shirt; Clive Allen was the substitute who came on to replace Reid. The match ended goalless.

After both sides had failed to score at Maine Road, City and QPR tried again in a Rumbelows Cup third-round replay at Loftus Road. This proved to be a momentous occasion. City fell behind after seven minutes, but a thrusting run by Neil Pointon resulted in a chance for Adrian Heath that was, astonishingly, converted. It would be churlish to suggest that he was aiming for the opposite corner of the net. The score was 1-1, after 10 minutes. In the second half, everything went City's way. A Heath shot was deflected into his own net by the balding Butch Wilkins, Penrice had what would have been his second goal of the night mysteriously disallowed, Quinn scored a City third goal after splendid work by the tricky Hughes, and Tony Coton contributed a couple of spectacular saves. It was yet another away win: 3-1.

I was out of the country when the Blues came back from behind twice to draw with Luton, but I saw the result on French television and was a bit disappointed. A Curle header and a rasping right-foot Quinn volley earned City a point, despite an unfortunate afternoon for Steve Redmond, who was sent off near the end. The Blues then suffered a minor wobble. In the League, there was a tortuous goalless draw at Maine Road against Wimbledon, followed by an emphatic defeat, 3-1 at Villa Park. Regis with a header, Yorke from a corner and Daley, with an eye-catching volley, scored the Villa goals. David White brought City only briefly into contention, at 2-1, when he headed a goal from an unlikely angle. In between those two games, a 2-1 defeat on a foggy night in Middlesbrough ended City's interest in the Rumbelows Cup. White scored again.

The crowd was down to a meagre 21,437 for the visit of QPR on 14 December 1991, despite City's high standing in the League table. The Faithful were in need of a bit of inspiration at Maine Road, where the Blues hadn't won a League match since September. The criticism of the City side during this period was that they had very little flair and struggled to break down well-organised defences. Away from home, with more space to operate in, City were finding it easier. The criticism isn't entirely fair. Against QPR, Michael Hughes lifted the spirits with a performance exuding flair from every available orifice. White had already given City the lead when a Kinkladze-style jinking run by Hughes won the Blues a clear penalty kick. Although Redmond's penalty was saved, Curle followed up to score. City led 2-0 after 25 minutes. Unfortunately, it all went awry in the second half. Roy Wegerle's excellent finish brought the City nerves to the surface, and a dubious penalty award in the last few minutes looked certain to thwart any hopes of a home win. What joy it was, therefore, when Coton saved Wegerle's penalty and the ball was hacked to safety. Well, not quite safety. From the resulting corner, Dennis Bailey scrambled a QPR equaliser. That's football for you. One minute you're down and the next minute you're down again.

On 21 December 1991, the Blues travelled to Anfield, without me, to take on a Liverpool side that was, by their standards, struggling. It proved to be the inspiration needed to kick some life back into City's season. It certainly confirmed David White as a man to cause stressful times for Liverpool fans. Reid returned from his rib injury to replace Megson, who was, in any case, becoming an increasingly peripheral figure, thank goodness. Steve McMahon played for the home side amidst talk that his transfer to City was imminent, and so it proved. After nine minutes, Saunders shot from outside the penalty area straight at Coton, who somehow managed to let the ball beat him. It was a rare error from a goalkeeper having an excellent season, and eventually voted as goalkeeper in the PFA First Division team. I expected it to be a costly error, but events turned dramatically at the start of the second half. After 48 minutes, a long ball headed on by Quinn provided the chance for White to sneak between two defenders and neatly lob the ball over Grobbelaar. Yes, it was route one, but it was also a move against which there was virtually no defence. Seven minutes later, White lobbed Grobbelaar again, this time from a quite incredible angle. Liverpool were stunned. I, only listening on the radio, was stunned. City's first League double over Liverpool since the war was conceivable. Set up by the substitute Marsh, Nicol spoilt that particular dream by sweeping in the equaliser with eight minutes remaining, but it was still a City performance to take pride in, and I could go to work with a feeling approaching smugness.

On Boxing Day, City unveiled the ultimate in grizzled midfields: Reid and McMahon (purchased for £900,000). They were both beyond their prime, and neither was inclined to venture much distance away from the centre circle, for fear of having to make it back again. After falling behind to an early Norwich goal, City recovered in textbook style; White's cross was headed in by Quinn, and White added the second before half-time. A couple of days later, there was a typically miserly encounter with Arsenal at the Academy, but for once the Blues emerged with the points. A nimble run by Michael Hughes provided the only moment of quality excitement, but the most telling contribution was the seventy-first-minute goal. This was dispatched by White, after the ball had made untidy progress to his feet. It was the sixth scoring game in a row for Mr White. Hughes might have added a second had Linighan not scythed him down and earned a sending off near the end, but 1-0 was quite sufficient. On New Year's Day 1992, Clive Allen found the back of the net once more. Unfortunately, he was now playing for Chelsea. A last-minute deflected shot by Mike Sheron rescued a point for the Blues.

We had arrived at that time of the season once more. I was cautious about City's chances of an FA Cup run, but there did seem some justification for hope. The Blues had been amongst the top five for most of the season, and could, on their day, compete with anyone. Yet it so seldom was their day on the big occasion. The FA Cup draw once more forced City to travel for the third-round, this time to Middlesbrough, promotion contenders in Division Two and the side responsible for City's Rumbelows Cup exit earlier in the season. I arrived in Middlesbrough early, and admired the beautiful backdrop of the ICI site, belching out its fumes. It was my only ever visit to Ayrsome Park, one of those ancient northern grounds from another era. The Blues coped surprisingly well in the first half, defending competently and looking the more likely scorers. When it did come, the goal was from a very unlikely source: Peter Reid, finding himself in the penalty area with the ball at his feet, managed to summon the memory of what to do, and shot beyond the goalkeeper.

There was no noticeable barrage from the home side as the second half progressed, until the approach of the closing stages. City seemed inclined to hold on to their narrow lead, rather than seek to increase it, and a threat emerged from the blond-haired Stuart Ripley, who was receiving plenty of possession, and attacking with pace down the right flank. The whole day fell apart in the space of a couple of minutes, as the finishing line came into sight. In the Rumbelows Cup match, Boro had scored twice in quick succession. They did the same again, and although the Blues had several minutes to attempt a recovery, the momentum was all against them. The Cup dream expired for yet another year.

My future wife feared a repeat of the previous season's distress, having discovered that an FA Cup exit was one of my annual low points. This time around, however, there was no Five Year Rule, and the tortuous journey back was sufficiently long for sanity to be restored.

It was only the fourth of January, but there seemed little point in continuing with the season. The Blues were out of all Cup competitions, not good enough to challenge for the League title or one of the still miserly number of European places, and not bad enough to contest relegation. To make things worse, the unthinkable seemed likely: *The Nation's Team*, after all those years of hype and throwing money around, looked set to win the Championship. This was the one thing that I could not tolerate. This was the worst thing that could possibly happen, or so I thought. My imagination wasn't up to contemplating the *actual* horrors in store.

A combination of foul weather, causing cancellations elsewhere, and some good results, allowed City to toy with the idea of threatening the leading clubs in the early part of 1992. Deep down, I knew that it wasn't a realistic possibility. The City squad was flimsy, unable to tolerate the absence of a couple of individuals. Keith Curle was the latest volunteer penalty-taker, and he earned City a point in a 1-1 draw at Crystal Palace. At the Academy, David White's header from a curling Michael Hughes free-kick was enough to secure all the points against Spurs. It was a good display, and there should have been more goals, but somehow it was hard to be too excited, even about a win against Spurs.

Some cheery news emerged in midweek, when Southampton dumped *The Nation's Team* out of the Cup in a penalty shoot-out at Old Trafford. Neil Webb skied one over the bar. Even better, Giggs, having looked the picture of arrogance when he approached the penalty spot, juggling the ball from foot to foot, shot straight at Tim Flowers for the decisive moment.

It was back to normal on a cold Saturday, 8 February 1992, when I had the pleasure of standing in a bitter wind, queuing for one of a miserly allocation of Manchester derby tickets for the forthcoming attraction at *The Swamp*. My future wife had the honour of accompanying me in the queue, although there would be no ticket for her. I know how to show a girl a good time. She still married me! Having gradually shuffled closer to the ticket office over a tedious three hours, we were within about 20 people of achieving our objective, when the announcement was made that all tickets were sold. We had already been monitoring the time because the plan was to drive over the Pennines to see the afternoon game at Bramall Lane. Because of the agonisingly slow progress of the queue, we were in danger of missing the start, and considering whether to abort the ticket mission. The announcement made the decision for us.

I felt strange, leaving the queue without tickets. The whole point of having regular seat season tickets was to ensure that tickets were obtainable, on the understanding

that some discomfort must be endured in a queue in order to earn that right. The consequence was that I was about to miss my first Manchester derby match in nearly 15
years. It had been one of my initial ambitions, still unfulfilled, to see City victorious in
a derby game at Old Trafford. I would now have mixed feelings about the encounter.
Of course, I would desperately wish a City win, but should they achieve it on the first
occasion when I was prevented from attending, I would take it extremely personally.
Of course, my worries were ill-founded. I haven't been back to *The Swamp* since and,
to be quite honest, I don't wish to. I discovered that I can live without it.

The business at hand was a trip to Sheffield where, having attracted the wrath of
some moronic locals for obeying speed limits because I didn't know where precisely I
was going, I stood with my future wife atop a slightly exposed corner of the ground. It
was still cold, but the wind was less cruel, and if the match should prove boring, there
was a lovely view of beautiful Sheffield behind us. The game could not be described as
boring but, for City, it was dreadful. Dave Bassett's team knew how to apply pressure,
particularly with corner-kicks, which were emerging as a particular concern for the
City defence. With the likes of Brians Gayle and Deane, and some excellent delivery
into the most dangerous areas, Sheffield United looked likely to score every time a
corner was taken; and there were plenty of such occasions, particularly in the first half.
City were always struggling to stay in the match, and although a Curle penalty, and a
neat Andy Hill goal, early in the second half, offered hope, City never caught up. The
home side won 4-2. It was not, all things taken into account, one of my better days as a
City fan.

Yet, because of postponements and Cup matches elsewhere, a home win over Luton
Town was enough to propel City into third place. This was achieved with some ease,
White scoring twice, Hill firing a goal from the edge of the penalty area, and Heath
shocking everyone by scoring with a delicate chip near the end. The highlight was
White's second (City's third) goal at the North Stand End after 48 minutes. When the
ball was over-hit towards the Luton goalkeeper, Steve Sutton, a linesman's flag was
raised for offside. The referee waved play on, but for some reason Sutton thought that
a free-kick had been awarded. He casually strolled over to the ball, and gently side-
footed it towards the area from which he expected the free-kick to be taken. David
White came haring in like a well-directed Scud missile, and smacked the ball from
some distance into the empty net. I thought it was funny. For some reason, Sutton
didn't.

The Blues remained in third place, despite succumbing to the aerial threat of Wimbledon in a 2-1 defeat. Fashanu and Earle, again following a corner, put the match beyond City before half-time. A neat goal by City substitute Mike Sheron raised hopes
near the end, but it was insufficient. At Maine Road on 29 February 1992, the Blues
took a third-minute lead when Quinn volleyed a goal against Aston Villa. They then
spent most of the match admiring the play of the opposition, and particularly the
speedy Tony Daley, who was really rather scary in an ebony-David White kind of
way. Thankfully, his finishing didn't match White's on this occasion. With 15 minutes left, White scored with the most delicate of finishes, sliding the ball through a tiny

gap beyond the goalkeeper and just inside the post. Somehow, City emerged as 2-0 winners.

As teams began to cash in their games in hand, City slumped and reality was restored to the League table. A 4-0 thrashing at QPR was followed by a dire live televised home defeat by fourth-from-bottom Southampton, with Iain Dowie scoring the only goal. After another defeat, at Nottingham Forest, and a goalless home draw against Chelsea, City were down to sixth place, and the end of the season simply couldn't come soon enough.

Peter Reid introduced a couple of modest pre-deadline signings during this period. Fitzroy Simpson, a central midfield player, was another in the Reid-McMahon mould, although younger. The skill and variety offered by Michael Hughes was sacrificed. Dutch footballers are renowned for being delicate and inventive on the ball, versatile, interactive, sophisticated, bright and skilful. Michel Vonk was Dutch. He had a savage haircut and a basic approach to the game. I rather liked the idea of him, despite the fact that I suspected his arrival might mark the end for another of the class of '86. Steve Redmond was the scapegoat for City's inability to defend aerial assaults, particularly from corners. I suppose that Redmond and Curle were too similar, and the arrival of City's new captain at the start of the season had already undermined Redmond's position and confidence. Vonk was bought at a cost of £500,000 to sort out the aerial problems, and Redmond's time was up. Incidentally, Reidy considered the prospect of having a defender called Michel an affront, and insisted on mutation of the name to Michael.

On 4 April 1992, I was faced with a serious dilemma. There was only one team that could prevent the unthinkable from happening in season 1991/92, and that team was Leeds United, the visitors to Maine Road. I took my usual position in the North Stand but, for the first time ever, I was hoping for City to do the decent thing, in the interests of a higher cause. I hoped they would lose, not heavily, but nonetheless lose. Within the space of three days, the Blues were set to take on both Championship contenders. The nightmare scenario was victory over Leeds and defeat at *The Swamp*, virtually handing over the Championship in the process. City's build-up to this match had been appalling, but they couldn't be trusted. The Blues took the lead in front of the North Stand, when Andy Hill headed in Brennan's corner after only 11 minutes. I honestly didn't know whether to celebrate or not. I don't think I did; at least not with any enthusiasm.

Leeds really needed the points, but it was hard to tell. The revered Cantona was virtually anonymous. His one contribution, a header, was directed straight at Tony Coton. The Leeds defence, particularly Whyte and Fairclough, behaved as though they had never played together before. Some impressive approach-play was finished by Sheron nipping in ahead of Lukic after 33 minutes, and the Blues went in at half-time leading 2-0. Howard Wilkinson must have offered a few words of advice during the interval, but it didn't have much effect. When Rod Wallace whacked the best Leeds chance to date into the North Stand, I was on the verge of saying, 'Stuff it! If they're that bad, they don't deserve anything.' When Quinn scored City's third, with an exceptional delicate chip from just inside the penalty area after 62 minutes, I was fully committed to the cause. I now wanted City to punish Leeds for being so poor, since there was obviously no way that *they* were going to win the League title. Further punishment did come near the end, when Brennan beat a flimsy offside-trap to complete a 4-0 rout – indisputably City's best result of the season. When I had time to reflect on it, I was depressed.

When City visited *The Swamp,* I was forced to suffer the torture of derby match radio commentary for the first time since the mid-seventies. There were television highlights to come later, which is why I know that *The Swamp* has never been more aptly named. The quagmire of a pitch was more suited to hippos or warthogs than footballers. Still, Steve Bruce was playing.

After 20 minutes, 'the boy wonder', Ryan Giggs, gave *Satan's Spawn* the lead. This time, at least, he did actually score the goal. City trailed 1-0 at half-time. *The chosen one* was involved in a less savoury incident in the second half, when he floored Neil Pointon with a tackle so late that it was positively deceased. Joe Worrall didn't see fit to brandish a yellow card. A couple of minutes later, Pointon extracted his own revenge and was sent off, which all seemed very fair, I must say. Prospects did not seem encouraging.

Luckily, Steve Bruce came to the rescue with a marvellously clumsy challenge on David White, who had just nipped the ball past him. Even so, it was astonishing that the Blues were actually awarded a penalty kick at Old Trafford. I still find difficulty in grasping the concept. It was completely blatant, so much so that there was no argument. This is almost incredible from a team including a couple of players whose main function seemed to involve following the referee around and giving him constant earache. Despite all that, it was still a shock. Keith Curle converted the penalty by blasting it into the top corner, to the delight of those assembled behind the goal. And not only did City hang on, they wasted the best remaining chance: a Bruce miscue fell into the path of White, but the City enigma, in one of his non-scoring runs, smacked it just wide.

With five games remaining, there was not much to be achieved. Defeat at Sheffield Wednesday was followed by victory at home against doomed West Ham. A Quinn double completed a happy Easter by enabling a 2-1 win at Everton. In both matches City struck early. Against West Ham, Neil Pointon scored spectacularly in the opening minute. Sniffer Clarke emerged from beyond the grave to score City's second. The Blues also managed to relegate Notts County, by beating them 2-0 at the Academy. Fitzroy Simpson scored his first City goal, with a left-foot shot that flashed inside the post, and a David White cross was headed home by Quinn, in front of the rubble that used to be the Platt Lane Stand. Plans were underway for the Umbro Stand, with its 48 executive boxes promising, according to the match magazine, 'superb foods and wines and the finest facilities for businessmen (women were not mentioned) wishing to sample the exciting atmosphere of top football action in luxury and style.' Oh, and by the way, there will be one or two seats for football fans, maybe. This was the future of the game. The pressure was supposed to be pushing clubs towards all-seater stadiums. If so, then why rebuild the Platt Lane Stand whilst the Kippax remained? I do know the answer, and it has nothing to do with the comfort of fans and everything to do with corporate hospitality.

I didn't go to the final match of the season, at Boundary Park against Oldham, because when the tickets were on sale, I was still a bit depressed about the title edging its way to Old Trafford. It's a pity. The Blues finished the season in style. David White ended a mini-goal drought by scoring a hat-trick. Adie Mike scored a senior goal, with the aid of a deflection, and Sheron added to his tally, as City ended 5-2 winners. Oldham's second goal was scored near the end by one of their substitutes, a certain Paul Moulden.

The season did not finish as badly as anticipated, thanks to the heroics of Brian Gayle. His superb own goal at Bramall Lane, against Leeds, clinched the title for Howard Wilkinson's team. The way that Gayle teed up by kneeing the ball, before heading neatly over his own goalkeeper, lives in the memory, and compensates for any negative recollections I have of him as a City player. Brian Gayle, I salute you.

Thanks almost entirely to White (18 goals) and Quinn (12 goals), the Blues finished in a comfortable fifth place for the second season in succession, but it had not been an enjoyable experience. The threat of a Championship title for *The Nation's Team*, although ultimately and spectacularly thwarted, hung over the season like an impending death. I hoped that this was a temporary phenomenon. I wanted back the security of someone like Liverpool winning the Championship, year after year. Unfortunately, just as the hype was poised to go into orbit, standards were plummeting. We were entering the nightmare nineties in earnest, and football was about to alter irrevocably. The forthcoming years were not for the faint-hearted.

Part Four:
The Nightmare Nineties

King-kladze: spicy chicken and walnuts amidst so much dodgy pie and soggy chips.

Season 1992/93: Happy Days Aren't Here Again

In 1992, football sold its soul to Rupert Murdoch. He already owns most of the press, and now he's set to own the biggest slice of football. There was a certain inevitability about it. The idea of football as a community-based spectator sport, in the traditional sense, has been gradually replaced by football as a multimedia entertainment industry for those who can afford it. It is centred on television coverage, but encompasses all aspects of the media, corporate hospitality, fashion and, ultimately, the Stock Exchange. Football results are no longer merely the concern of dedicated fans and those employed by a club; they are now a contributory factor in the accumulation of vast quantities of wealth and power.

The *so-called* Premier League was invented. I tried to ignore it. After all, it was, in fact, only the First Division, and a pretty poor First Division at that. But style had already triumphed emphatically over content in most other areas of life, so why not football? The major consequence of the financial dealing was that the wealthiest, most media-attractive clubs would prosper, receiving millions of pounds of extra cash, plus free marketing and publicity, courtesy of the press and television. This would ensure that their positions of prominence were inviolable for the foreseeable future. There was also the very real prospect that pressure would be applied to ensure their success because of the threat that failure might pose to the value of shares, not only in the clubs, but in the corporations controlling the media.

The spectators who actually attend matches were once the major source of income and, as such, of primary importance. Now they are more peripheral figures, at best tolerated, but at worst merely extras for the television show. For the Big Boys, the serious money now comes via income from television, corporate hospitality, and the sale of replica shirts and other merchandise to people who have never attended a football match, and have no actual connection with the club they purport to support.

To me, the idea of a marriage between Murdoch and *The Nation's Team* is a match made in heaven. They deserve each other. Stepping briefly off my soapbox, I have to admit that I wasn't so appalled back in 1992, at the start of the new season. The renaming just seemed plain silly, and I was grateful for the return of 'Match of the Day' to save me from the incompetence of ITV. I could hardly have cared less for live television coverage. If I wanted to see a whole game, I went to a match. In fact, often even if I didn't want to see a whole game, I went. That is what real football fans do. I had no desire to see *The Nation's Team* play Liverpool, and I certainly had no intention of paying Mr Murdoch for the privilege. The only inconvenience back then was that News International determined when matches should be played, and the length of the half-time break, which became far too long. I was reasonably confident, and certainly hopeful, that Sky TV would stay away from Maine Road. Our record on live television made that rather important.

In fact, City were one of the first victims of the new television powers. The opening match against QPR was put back to Monday, 17 August 1992, which meant that City were required to play on both Monday and Wednesday of the opening week. Yet, I was still quite cheerful about prospects for the new campaign. Peter Reid had made a few changes. The unfortunate Redmond was followed to Oldham by Neil Pointon, with the Latics' left-winger Rick Holden making the opposite journey. Megson and Heath had also disappeared into the sunset, but the most surprising departure was that of Michael Hughes. He had clearly not been happy with the general outlook on football at the club, and emigrated to Strasbourg for less of a transfer fee than I would have hoped for. In fact, I would have hoped that he didn't depart at all. The most encouraging news was that, after an absence approaching two years, Paul Lake was fit for the new season.

Over the summer, there had been an international cap for Keith Curle during England's ill-fated contribution to the European Championship finals in Sweden. Curle was a good marking central defender, with the kind of pace needed to keep up with nippy continental strikers. Bizarrely, he was played against the Danes, as a right-back, for his one cap. He ended up being the spare man, who seemed to be getting most of the possession. A nation watched expectantly to see what he would create with it. Even his biggest fans would not claim Curle's primary asset to be his distribution. It was a strange managerial decision. It is worth remembering that Peter Swales played a prominent role in Graham Taylor's appointment. Still, even though Keith Curle's brief England career was not terribly successful, there was a positive side. After all, it had been a long time since any City player was deemed good enough to play for England.

There were other reasons for my relatively cheerful mood as I went to the opening match at Maine Road. City had a nice new away strip of purple with thin white stripes, and *The Nation's Team* had lost their opening match, away to Sheffield United. The game was chosen, inevitably, by 'Match of the Day'.

The match against QPR was Sky TV's first live Monday game. I knew that there was to be some sort of pre-match, showbiz, American-style razzmatazz: such as fireworks, or parachutists, or skateboarding dolphins, or unemployed actors, dressed as Mickey Mouse, break-dancing. Consequently, I deliberately arrived as late as possible in order to avoid any attempts to subject me to such entertainment. Football grounds are not places for enjoyment, at least not the infantile and trite enjoyment peddled at mass events over the pond, but losing all in the translation over here. By the time I entered the arena, there was little remaining of the hype, bar the massive speakers at the deserted building site of the Platt Lane End. They were blasting out music that was actually distinguishable, which was something of a novelty. The tinny mess emerging from the normal Maine Road sound system rarely hits a range audible to humans, and when it does the response is one of pain. Mind you, the local canine population no doubt has a thoroughly invigorating time.

When the hype was cleared away, all that we had was a football match. It's tempting to say that City's season peaked at half-time in the opening game, against QPR. In the first half, Paul Lake, playing in a forward position, showed great touch and awareness. City looked quite impressive, with Quinn and White both lively, and Fitzroy Simpson continuing the encouraging form shown at the end of the previous season, as a midfield player with bite, but also some skill. City scored eight minutes before the interval. Holden's cross was neatly turned by Lake into the path of Niall Quinn. Quinn's shot was blocked, but White followed in to score. Half-time came and City's peak was over.

In fact, half-time rapidly degenerated as a makeshift centre circle stage was erected to allow Gerry Rafferty and his band the opportunity to perform 'Baker Street'. I have hated this tune since the days when I had to travel on the bus to sixth form college in Leyland, in the company of some RAGS, one of whom was always ranting on about how good the saxophone bit was. I was determined to dislike the whole thing, and I succeeded. As always happens on such occasions, when the performance finished it was greeted with apologetic applause from a disinterested audience, which quite cheered me up. What we actually want is a large electronic scoreboard replaying incidents from the current or other matches. People go to football matches to see football. This rather simple concept does not seem to have penetrated the relevant marketing circles.

Half-time dragged on for about 18 minutes because of the need to squeeze in some more advertisements on Sky, and dismantle the stage. Within two minutes of the restart, Andy Sinton drove a long-range shot into City's net, and although Fitzroy Simpson struck a blistering shot against the crossbar, the Blues had to settle for a disappointing point.

Two evenings later, I must have been so engrossed in 'Coronation Street' that I forgot about the kick-off in City's match away to newly promoted Middlesbrough. By the time I switched on the radio, City's whole season had fallen apart. They trailed 2-0, which was bad. Niall Quinn had been sent off, which was worse. And poor Paul Lake had been carried off in agony with a repeat of his dreadful ligament injury, which was unbelievable. The game was fewer than 15 minutes old. The score remained 2-0, and a shell-shocked City lost again, 1-0 at Blackburn, three days later. This result left them occupying twentieth place in the first published League table.

The news that Peter Reid had decided to spend £2.5 million pounds on a left-back shocked most of the fans. Terry Phelan was a good attacking full-back, with exceptional pace, but surely the Blues were looking for some creativity in midfield, or a top-name striker, particularly for such a large sum of money. When Coton, Curle, Phelan and Vonk were all in the team, City's defence was now the most costly in the country; even more costly than Mr Ferguson's expensively assembled entourage. It had been an unnerving start to the new season.

A form of sanity was restored in Terry Phelan's home debut. This was against Norwich City, who almost always seem to let City win, bless 'em. The Quinn-flick / White-finish combination sent City in leading at half-time. Norwich equalised in the second half when two City rejects combined. David Phillips took the corner from which, gallingly, Gary Megson scored with a header. Prolific marksman Megson had managed such a feat only twice in his entire City career. Fortunately, the Blues responded. Quinn set up White for a second goal, and McMahon struck the third near the end. We all knew that Steve McMahon had a dangerous shot, and expected many such displays of this finishing prowess. We were to be sadly disappointed. Normally, the only danger was of damage to the roof of the stand, the windows of the executive boxes, or the unsuspecting occupants of Row Z.

The visit of Oldham a few days later confirmed that City were still struggling to come to terms with the new season. On this occasion, the weather played an interesting role in a six-goal first half that included a mini-typhoon. Michel Vonk's presence in the Oldham penalty area, at the North Stand End of the pitch, led to City taking a two-goal lead in the opening eight minutes. Vonk's header set up Niall Quinn for the first goal, and Vonk himself followed up to score, after a David White header had rebounded off the crossbar. Although Vonk was credited with this goal, the final touch actually came off old boy Neil Pointon. As gale-force winds and torrential rain swept over the ground, Jobson headed Oldham back to 2-1, but White sped clear to restore City's two-goal advantage. The weather relented, and goals from Mike Milligan, with a cheeky flick, and Halle, brought the score back to 3-3. City pressed in the second half, but to no avail. It proved to be a satisfying return to Maine Road for the recently departed Redmond and Pointon.

In amongst the general mess of City's start to the season, David White was again making an impression. White became the latest to join the growing ranks of players called up to the England squad by Graham Taylor, and he celebrated by cashing in on a rare forward venture by Reid to score the only goal at Wimbledon. At Hillsborough, White was again the key City figure. Sheffield Wednesday fell victim to the new pass-back rule, which was harshly interpreted to give City a free-kick inside the Wednesday penalty area. The ball was touched to White, who smacked it through the wall for the opening goal. I was surprised that the first significant incident involving the new rule had gone in City's favour. The Blues defenders, particularly Curle and Phelan, seemed determined to put Tony Coton under continual pressure with persistent and unnecessary back-passes, as if the rule had not been introduced at all. Coton's kicking proved to be remarkably resilient. In the second half at Hillsborough, Vonk headed City further ahead, and White added another with a cool finish. City seemed to be back on track, having risen to sixth in the League.

White's only ever England cap was won in a friendly encounter with Spain in Santander, coinciding with a trip I took to Barcelona. Graham Taylor must have made a deep impression on David White. After scoring seven times in seven matches before joining up with England, the City striker went nine matches without scoring again! I remember wandering around the bars of Barcelona with my future wife, trying to find somewhere with a television so that we could watch the game. Eventually, we gave up and settled for the other attractions that bars have to offer. At about 11 o'clock, whilst wandering past a small local café, we spotted a television showing football. The start of the game must have been 10 o'clock in the evening. Obviously, they do things differently over there.

We went in and managed to establish that England were losing 1-0, and White was playing. I didn't know then that White had a chance for glory in the opening minutes, when his pace took him clear. Unfortunately, he was coming in from the left, and his left-foot finish failed to beat the goalkeeper. It was probably the turning point of his whole career. From what I saw, David White didn't fare too badly. Yet, after England's 1-0 defeat in Spain, Taylor declined to pick him again, even for a squad.

White's finishing was often criticised, but people rarely considered the fact that, because of his pace, White got into scoring positions that other players were incapable of aspiring to. Therefore, even if he missed half of those chances, White still ended up scoring more goals than another player would have. His biggest problem with the fans was that he was capable of awesome form, and the supporters expected a demonstration every week. The other constant perplexity with White was whether he was best played as a winger or a striker. This was never really resolved. When he was in goalscoring mode, he was better as a striker. Otherwise, he was probably more effective as a supplier of chances for others. Unfortunately, nobody could tell what mood he was going to be in from one week to the next. His goals usually came in bursts, but you couldn't predict when one of those goalscoring runs was about to begin.

On the plane back from Catalonia, I discovered from a complimentary newspaper/comic that City had lost 1-0 at home to Middlesbrough. This confirmed Boro's status as an official bogey side. I was at Maine Road to see the same scoreline repeated against Chelsea. The only bright spot was the emergence of young midfielder Garry Flitcroft, who had an attacking instinct when he first broke into the team and provided City with options not available from Reid and McMahon. Flitcroft had energy and skill. A couple of seasons alongside McMahon, and injury problems, combined to dampen his impact on the team, which was initially considerable.

City's dismal run continued with a goalless draw against Bristol Rovers in a Coca-Cola Cup first leg tie at Maine Road, followed by defeat at Highbury, sending the Blues back down the table to fifteenth. The Arsenal match should have been one of those occasions when the Sky TV deal might come in useful, but I trailed around several pubs in Liverpool, vainly trying to locate one that was showing the game. I gave up at about half-time.

Some consolation was derived from watching *The Nation's Team* being defeated by Torpedo, the fourth-best team from Moscow, in a penalty shoot-out. The defeat ended their European hopes for another season; this despite leading 2-0 after both sides had taken two penalties. It was a sign of things to come. Taking pleasure in the downfall of others became as rewarding as basking in the success of City, and about as frequent – not very.

Rick Holden was making little impression as City's big attacking signing of the summer. When playing at Oldham he was renowned for providing an excellent supply from the left wing, but most of the time for City he looked lethargic and isolated. At first, I thought that he was unfit, and awaited developments with some patience. Over time it became clear that this was as quick as he got. It was quite a disappointment.

Meanwhile, injury to Vonk meant that Andy Hill had been restored to the side, this time as a central defender, and he made quite a good job of it. Injuries were to become something of a recurring theme over the next few seasons.

The Blues were still searching for some form when struggling Nottingham Forest visited Maine Road on 3 October 1992. Rick Holden scored his first City goal, thanks to some woeful defending, and Fitzroy Simpson scored his first goal of the season, but Forest equalised twice. Stuart Pearce had the final say late in the match. City only just edged past Bristol Rovers at Twerton Park, thanks to an own goal, extra time, a Holden shot that crept just inside the post in the last minute, and some excellent goal-keeping by Coton. Rovers included Chorley's second-biggest footballing export, defender Geoff Twentyman. He did not quite achieve the heights of the first, Paul Mariner, but no doubt tried his best. The full-time score of 1-1 would have been enough for City to progress on away goals, but the strange competition rules determined that extra time should take place. In effect, Holden's goal was superfluous. ITV, with only the Coca-Cola Cup left to cover, tried to make it seem exciting, but even the use of a Northside tune for their incidental music wasn't enough to make El-ton Welsby palatable.

On 24 October 1992, at Maine Road, City achieved their first League win since early September by defeating Southampton 1-0. With Quinn having scored only once in the League, and White suffering his post-Graham Taylor trauma, it was left to Mike Sheron to score the winner. A 1-0 midweek home defeat by Spurs led to City's Coca-Cola Cup demise for another season and, to be honest, things appeared a bit bleak generally.

I was in amongst the Faithful at Goodison Park for the beginning of a startling week when City suddenly looked like a good football team again. Although Everton were struggling, and Howard Kendall's return had most certainly not gone as planned, there seemed little reason for much optimism about City's chances, with both Quinn and White suffering barren spells. On this occasion, Mike Sheron was given the opportunity to show what he could do in attack alongside Quinn, with White playing deeper. The tactics worked perfectly. White gave a demonstration of his abilities as a right-winger. His cross gave Sheron the opportunity to score the first goal, which he did with a delicate glance off his knee. City struck again before 20 minutes had elapsed. This time David White ended his goal drought in remarkable fashion, cutting in from the left to unleash a long-range dipping shot over Southall's head. Kicking towards the Faithful in the second half, the Blues extended their lead further when Terry Phelan sprinted down the left flank like a greyhound responding to a strategically placed red-hot poker. His cross was delicately jinked over the diving Southall's body by Sheron, to complete a fine afternoon's work for him back in his native city. The Blues tried their best to mess up an unassailable position. Ian Brightwell somehow managed to direct a header into his own net, and the home side were awarded a penalty kick. Luckily, Stuart Barlow struck it against the post, which was considerably closer than he had achieved with a couple of other good opportunities. There was a suggestion that 'Barn-Door' might be more appropriate than Barlow.

The match finished 3-1 and represented the best City away display witnessed by me for a very long time. A week later the mood was retained for the visit of Leeds. This time I had no qualms about hoping for victory, and City obliged with a repeat of the previous season's exploits. When Chris Fairclough's poor back-header left Mervyn Day in the lurch, Mike Sheron nipped in to head City into an early lead. Sheron turned provider for David White to score the second before half-time. Andy Hill added to an impressive scoring record against his home-town team, but the best goal was the last. Ian Brightwell, playing at right-back during this part of his career, began the move from deep inside his own half. Niall Quinn and Mike Sheron were both involved, but it was Brightwell himself who applied the finishing touch, making the final score an impressive 4-0.

In their next match, away to Coventry City, the improved form seemed to have dissipated as quickly as it had arrived. Two goals from the highly tuned athlete, Micky Quinn, ensured that the home side led 2-0 early in the second half. However, City replied with three goals in a 25-minute spell, to turn the match around in dramatic fashion. A Sheron header, a scrambled equaliser from Niall Quinn, and a Keith Curle penalty, won by the City captain himself after an impressive attacking run, left City with a 3-2 away win and sixth place in the League table.

City's topsy-turvy season took another downwards plunge with a 1-0 home defeat by Spurs in the build-up to the Old Trafford derby game on 6 December 1992. It was to be covered live by Sky, and after the events of the previous season, I didn't even try to obtain one of the paltry number of tickets available for City fans. Instead, I stayed over with City pals and paid a modest fee to watch the match live in the City Social Club. It was not a pleasant experience. The Blues were poor and trailing 2-0 before they made any real contribution. A late Niall Quinn goal revived hope, inspired by memories of previous recoveries, but it was not to be. The most astonishing event of the afternoon was provoked by the presence, in the Manchester City Social Club, of someone overtly supporting the opposition. If that isn't the definition of imbecilic, I don't know what is.

City lost again at Ipswich, despite taking the lead with a goal from Garry Flitcroft, who had been restored to the team ahead of the fading Fitzroy Simpson. City took on title-chasing Villa at Maine Road on 19 December 1992. The match is notable for a fine Garry Parker volley, although Dalian Atkinson was clearly offside twice during the move. On the second occasion, he was right in front of Coton, blocking his view. City's second-half reply was a Flitcroft header from Brightwell's cross.

That respectable draw was followed by a 2-0 home win over Sheffield United on Boxing Day. David White scored both the goals, the first being a typical White goal, a lob over the goalkeeper after his pace had taken him clear. Two days later, the Blues achieved a third successive draw at Anfield, although it could have been even better. The floppy-haired Flitcroft caused havoc with his runs from deep, and he should have given City the lead from one of these breaks. Quinn also came close with a header, and White scored only for a linesman to rule that Flitcroft, whose run inspired the goal, had been offside. The linesman was wrong. City got their deserved lead when Quinn headed home from a Brightwell cross, but they couldn't hold on to it in the second half. It took a spectacular Rush volley to earn Liverpool a point. The Liverpool of old might have stolen all three points. John Barnes should have headed a winner, but he didn't.

The football year of 1993 did not mess around. It was straight into the serious business. The only salvation for City's erratic season was represented by the FA Cup, which began for the Blues on 2 January1993, at Maine Road, against Second Division Reading, managed by Mark McGee. The rare luxury of a home tie should have augured well for a comfortable passage, but the Blues, and Reading, had other ideas. I made one of my infrequent forays into the Kippax on a cold and windy afternoon, to witness a Scott Taylor shot whizzing into the City net at the deserted Platt Lane End. With the Blues struggling for any kind of cohesion, an early exit looked quite conceivable, but Mike Sheron popped up with a second-half equaliser, after good work by Flitcroft. By now City had an epidemic of injuries to defenders. Joining Vonk and the ubiquitous Lake on the casualty list were Andy Hill and Ian Brightwell, which meant another opportunity for David Brightwell, and the surprise return on loan of City's 1981 FA Cup Final right-back, Ray Ranson.

It was fortunate for City that they regained some form before the replay at Reading. The Blues won 4-2 at Chelsea, surging ahead with two goals in a minute midway through the first half. These goals were scored by White and Sheron, and a deflected Phelan cross extended that lead to 3-0. But City again did their best to throw it all away. With 12 minutes to go, Graham Stuart pulled one goal back and John Spencer added a second. Fortunately, Sheron popped up to head Quinn's cross into the Chelsea net.

Sheron was enjoying an excellent spell of form, and demonstrating his eye for goals. His reward was a call-up for the England Under-21 side. With Flitcroft also looking impressive and in line for a similar call-up, the Blues seemed to have hope for the future. Such hope, as usual, was not solidly based.

The FA Cup replay against Reading attracted the television cameras in search of an upset, and put the new 'Match of the Day' housewives' pin-up, Alan Hansen, on the spot because he tipped City to win the Cup. Despite all this, the Blues were in no mood to go out just yet. Even a last-minute switch by Sky TV to cover the game live did not prompt disaster, suggesting that City were not quite their usual shy selves when only the modest satellite television audience might be watching. Their capacity for being embarrassing on terrestrial live television remained undiminished. They proved that emphatically later in the season.

Mike Sheron's headed goal settled the nerves after a mere three minutes, and a bumbling run by Rick Holden, culminating in a shot that took the goalkeeper by surprise, put City 2-0 ahead. Reading had opportunities but were rather wasteful, and second-half goals by Flitcroft and Quinn saw City comfortably through to a fourth-round tie at Loftus Road.

I made my way to the QPR match on the train, along with a fellow-sufferer. A little inside knowledge allowed us to avoid the busiest tube station and make stress-free progress to Loftus Road, a ground very close to its community. Some of the surrounding houses seem almost to merge with the stadium itself. The Faithful were massed behind one goal, hoping for a sign that Alan Hansen's wisdom was inviolable. With Hill, Brightwell and Curle all unavailable, the return of Michel Vonk was particularly welcome. The small City squad was being stretched to the limit. Garry Flitcroft was playing as a makeshift centre half. Actually, he was reassuringly good at it.

In the first half, QPR advanced towards us with some purpose, and there were some worrying scrambles in the City penalty area. The narrowest escape came just before half-time, when Les Ferdinand failed to make contact as the ball flew across the face of an open goal. The Blues were struggling to make any impression on the match.

After the interval, it was a case of *new* City, *new* danger. The revival was sparked by a Mike Sheron chip that bounced off the top of the crossbar with the goalkeeper well beaten. The main action came with two City goals in the space of four frantic minutes, midway through the half. Niall Quinn demonstrated exceptional skill to control a long Coton goal kick. Quinn found Sheron, who in turn played the ball into the path of David White, steaming in from the right. White hammered his shot into the top corner, defeating the goalkeeper with the pace of the strike. Inspired, the Blues piled forward mercilessly, causing pandemonium in the Rangers defence. Holden's right-wing corner, flicked on by Quinn, caused a desperate goalmouth scramble before the ball was poked into the net by Vonk, who headed straight towards me in celebration. There were obstacles of a small fence and several ecstatic Mancunians blocking his path, so he didn't make it all the way. There was sufficient time remaining to mess things up, and an injury time goal by Holloway had the Faithful screaming at the referee to end the game. City held on, and we all began to believe in Alan Hansen's magical powers. The unheard-of luxury of another home draw, this time against Barnsley, seemed to confirm it.

In the meantime, City returned to League duty. It was hard to concentrate on such trivia, especially since *The Nation's Team* were knocked out of the Cup by a splendid Sheffield United, whose sheer determination carried them through after going behind. It came as no surprise when the referee gave *The Nation's Team* the chance to sneak a draw with a late penalty award, but Bruce made a hash of it. I had long since given up following the ranting of the tabloid comics, but their reaction to this result was illuminating. I was in Terry's barber's shop on the Monday, waiting for my Vonk-esque haircut, which gave me the chance to peruse the comics. The headline news on the back pages concerned the fact that there may have been a Sheffield United player encroaching in the penalty area when Bruce took the penalty kick. There was nothing about Sheffield United having earned their win and no mention that the penalty was decidedly soft. These were articles written by blinkered fans. Of course there was someone encroaching in the penalty area. Watch any penalty kick. There's always somebody encroaching, usually from both sides. It was such a trivial cause for complaint. They weren't content with the penalty. They wanted the penalty taken until it was scored. The alleged offence couldn't possibly have made any difference to the botched kick. The media was clearly desperate to see *them* win everything, and somehow it was becoming inevitable. This was a sobering prospect to contemplate whilst the unsubtle Terry did his worst. Terry, I'm pleased to say, was not a chatty barber. Contemplation was permitted.

City's League form remained erratic. A home defeat by Arsenal, just prior to the QPR cup-tie, was followed up by a 1-0 victory at Oldham, who were struggling. Oldham old boy, Rick Holden, contributed the cross for Niall Quinn's header. Blackburn

Rovers had, much to my chagrin, been reinvented as a significant force, thanks to Jack Walker's millions. At school I had always been able to look down on Blackburn fans, safe in the knowledge that they were unlikely to be able to retaliate, much as RAGS do with everyone: that's why they become RAGS. No doubt I deserved my comeuppance. City had encountered Blackburn with variable success in the old Division Two, but this was the first Maine Road meeting in living memory in the top flight, and City had a 1-0 defeat earlier in the season to revenge. When a fourth-minute goal from Mike Newell and an own goal by Terry Phelan propelled the visitors into a 2-0 lead, the prognosis did not look good. City responded with a Sheron header before half-time, and completed an unlikely and fortunate comeback in the second half. When Sheron was felled by Kevin Moran, Curle converted the penalty with ease. Within three minutes, a deflected White shot had given City a 3-2 lead, which they maintained.

This match saw the first appearance, as substitute, of Reid's latest recruit, the Norwegian international Kåre Ingebrigtsen, signed for £600,000 from Rosenborg. Ingebrigtsen no doubt regretted the move. He made little impression at Maine Road, and lost his place in the national team.

The Blues returned to Loftus Road and picked up a point with another Sheron headed goal, after City old boy Clive Wilson had given the home side the lead from the penalty spot. City, forced to field a much depleted side, were quite happy with a draw.

At last 13 February 1993 came around, and Mad Mel returned to Maine Road with his Barnsley team, including City old boys Gerry Taggart, Wayne Biggins and Gary Fleming. With MacMahon and Ranson added to the growing injury list, Fitzroy Simpson and Peter Reid had to fill in. I was about to invent another of my stupid rules, this time concerning transport to the match. Every time I had borrowed my dad's car to drive to a game, usually because my own was being tampered with, City won. The run had only stretched to three matches, and all at Maine Road, but it was a run nonetheless. The Barnsley game fell into this category, and the outcome speaks for itself.

With the Umbro Stand still empty, I watched from the Kippax as Tony Coton made an excellent save from David Currie, and Niall Quinn put a good heading chance wide of the goal. City were attacking the deserted end of the ground when the breakthrough was achieved, just before half-time. Terry Phelan provided the cross, and although David White's header was saved, White followed up himself to score. In the second half, White was initially denied a second goal by Lee Butler's fine save, but from the resulting corner by Holden, Sheron's flick caused havoc. White scrambled the ball over the line to make it 2-0. Rick Holden struck a shot against the post and Sheron's follow-up was impressively saved by Butler. In addition, an offside decision dubiously robbed Flitcroft of a goal, but City were more than happy with the final score.

The following Saturday, City lost 2-1 at Norwich. The last time that happened, in the 1980/81 season, the Blues went all the way to the FA Cup Final. There had to be an omen in that, didn't there? A home defeat by Sheffield Wednesday followed, but goals by White and Flitcroft in a 2-0 win at Nottingham Forest provided a reasonable precursor to the biggest match at Maine Road since the 1988 FA Cup quarter-final humiliation by Liverpool. Things were very different now. City and their opponents in this quarter-final, Spurs, were separated by only a point. When the Blues took on Liverpool, the difference was not merely a division, Liverpool were clearly the best side in the country. Yet some things were alarmingly familiar. The BBC had chosen the match for live Sunday coverage. City had a live television ghost to bury. In fact, against Spurs they had many ghosts to bury, including their exit from the Coca-Cola Cup earlier in the season.

One thing that was decidedly new was that this match represented the grand opening of the new Umbro Stand, in all its glory. Greater Manchester Police and FA rules had determined that I should not be allowed to take my place in the North Stand, which was given over in its entirety to Tottenham fans. In fact, I was up for a change generally. Along with a pal, I had decided to move to the new Umbro Stand, taking up an offer of swapping ends for a handful of games towards the end of the season, as well as a permanent move. My time in the North Stand had not been a success, and I imagined that a new stand might be better all round. OK, so I was wrong.

I drove to the game in my dad's car, having pathetically borrowed it on a flimsy pretext just in case it could produce magical effects. I was not the only one in this kind of mood. As Alan Hansen made his way towards the corner commentary position at the junction of the Umbro and Kippax Stands, people rushed forward to touch the hem of his coat in awe. This was the man whose very word had offered City the prospect of Cup triumph.

The Umbro Stand was not a pleasant experience. The corridors may be heated and there may be a greater choice of burgers, but the facilities are cramped, and unless you're on the back row or high up in one of the corners, the view is terrible. The Stand was clearly built primarily for executive boxes. Our alternative to the excellent season ticket view in the North Stand was to watch the game through the goalkeeper's legs, hoping that he might occasionally go walkies. Our seats for the following season, already determined, were not much better. It was the back row or nothing. I couldn't argue that the PA facilities were less effective in the Umbro Stand. You could certainly hear the music. Unfortunately, it was so loud that I had to cower in the heated corridors until kick-off to prevent my ears from bleeding. It was nice that City had bought a new record – 'Regret' by New Order – but even that lost its appeal when causing actual pain. We tolerated the Umbro Stand for the rest of the season, but quickly made arrangements for a return to the North Stand for the following season.

I wasn't particularly happy, therefore, as the start of the match approached, but that sickening feeling in the stomach soon took the place of minor irritation at the view. This was surely it. After 12 years of trying, the Blues had been offered a quarter-final home tie against a side of similar ability, and with most of the first-choice players available. The match began with City kicking towards the North Stand. They made a sensational start. Terry Phelan broke down the left wing, and his cross was headed in by Mike Sheron: 1-0, and only a few minutes played. I expected City to be nervous, but surely this was just the tonic they needed, that we all needed.

It was a tremendous beginning. I even managed to glimpse the goal between Tony

Coton's legs. The match restarted and then nothing. City stopped competing alto-gether. They retreated as though losing, not winning, and as though away from home, not at home. They were tentative, indecisive, generally clueless and downright embar-rassing, and by half-time they were losing; Tony Coton was forced to turn and face me twice, in order to retrieve the ball. My heart had already sunk, but we all hoped for a second-half improvement. Instead, City got worse, degenerating into a complete shambles. Tottenham scored twice more, the lightweight Nayim completing a hat-trick, as the City defence lapsed into whimsical mood. Sheringham missed a penalty. The Faithful were stunned; the players were zombie-like; even Spurs seemed taken aback at the ease of their win.

We decided to leave.

As I was walking out through the heated corridors, past the stalls offering unrivalled selections of fast food, I caught a glimpse on one of the numerous television sets of Terry Phelan running through the entire Spurs defence to score what might have been, on another occasion, one of the best City goals ever. We instinctively went back into the stadium, as if Phelan would be re-enacting his run in a real-life action replay. In-stead, a number of City fans in the Umbro Stand, chiefly of the urchin variety, decided to get themselves on television and invaded the pitch, in a fairly unthreatening man-ner, intent on jumping about for the cameras. This made it easy for those in authority to identify and ban them subsequently. It also gave the media something about which to foam at the mouth indignantly. It all looked a bit silly to me. We turned and left again. The match finished 2-4. It was as bad a City performance as I can recall, and I have no explanation for it. The players let everybody down in a massive way on that Sunday afternoon. It was also a general turning point. City never truly recovered from that day, and matters elsewhere also degenerated, with the imminent triumph of *The Nation's Team*. In fact, a big, gloomy cloud parked itself above Maine Road, and I do believe that it is there still. I decided that maybe the lucky car rule was a load of crap.

A measure of the disillusionment can be gauged from the turnout, three days later, for a League clash with Coventry City: 20,092. Garry Flitcroft scored the only goal with a bit of a mishit. Nobody really cared much either way. City followed that with a 1-0 defeat at Leeds, thanks to an early David Rocastle goal.

There was considerably more interest in the Manchester derby match, on 20 March1993. Kick-off was brought forward to 11 o'clock in the morning because of the mood of disquiet around Maine Road. City had the opportunity to redeem themselves. They seemed instead to be trying to make matters worse. Twice in the first half, City defenders set up good scoring chances for Giggs, who twice made a mess of them, hit-ting one shot well over the bar and the other comfortably wide of the post. One of the culprits, Andy Hill, came closest for City with a shot that skimmed the post. Back at the North Stand End, it took an excellent save from Coton to keep *the French one* out. Things continued along the same lines after half-time, with a Vonk error offering Mr Cantona another opportunity. Again, Tony Coton produced the required heroics. If only City could curtail their inclination to offer easy chances to the opposition, there was still the opportunity to send their fans home considerably more cheerful than of late. Indeed, Niall Quinn's fifty-eighth-minute headed goal, from a Rick Holden cross, raised morale considerably. The lead only lasted 11 minutes. Cantona equalised with an unchallenged header, and although Mike Sheron came close with a good shot that struck the foot of the post, City had to settle for a draw. That wasn't good enough. There have been occasions since when a draw would have been greeted with far greater enthusiasm.

City still had five League home matches to complete. Their only victory was against Ipswich Town, and it was the one occasion when I saw the Blues win a game from the Umbro Stand. Even then, Ipswich took an early lead, but three second-half City goals provided some cheer. There were 1-1 draws against Liverpool and Wimbledon. In fact, the Blues played quite well against Liverpool, taking the lead when David James misjudged a cross, allowing Flitcroft to head his fifth League goal of the season. Neither side had much to play for, but Liverpool managed a second-half equaliser. A messy late equaliser by Holden was required to rescue a point in a dire encounter with Wimbledon. Sandwiched between those two home games was a rather more important encounter with Aston Villa at Villa Park. It was imperative that City should lose this game. Villa were the only team who could prevent the unthinkable from happening. Obtusely, City decided to play well, and Niall Quinn headed them into the lead after 34 minutes. Dean Saunders, now a Villa player, equalised just after half-time, but it took a penalty to resolve matters in Villa's favour. Keith Curle handled the ball for no apparent reason. I, for one, was not inclined to criticise. I was also glad that Dean Saunders didn't take the penalty kick. Parker scored and Villa went on to win 3-1.

Astonishingly, a David White header, enough for three points at Southampton, left City in fifth place with two games remaining, both at home. However, on 5 May 1993, the Blues could only manage a goalless draw against Crystal Palace, and there was a foul mood for Howard Kendall's return three days later. The mood was entirely due to events elsewhere. Villa's challenge had failed; *The Nation's Team* had fittingly won the first Premier League, and there had been celebrations in the streets of Milton Keynes, Basingstoke, Coventry, London, Buenos Aires, Brussels, Vladivostok etc...

Nobody paid much attention to Mr Kendall this time. City were still in fifth place, and victory might have enabled them to hold on to it. Psychologically, that could have made a difference. The fans, including myself, were in irrational mood, and Mr Swales was seldom anything else. The season seemed catastrophic. The collective desire for recriminations was insatiable. Martyn Margetsen had made four competent previous appearances for City, but none had been at Maine Road. His introduction to the home crowd, in this ugly mood, proved to be a mistake. He, amongst others, had a nightmare, as City were trounced 5-2. Poor Margetsen must have felt as vulnerable as an unfamiliar member of a 'Star Trek' landing party. Reidy beamed him up at half-time. In amongst the debris, David White headed his sixteenth League goal of the season, and Everton scored a couple of crackers, including one particularly memorable shot by Preki, a Slav import.

When the fixtures had all been completed, the Blues slumped to a final ninth position. A measure of the paucity of City's resources can be seen from the fact that their reserve team was relegated from the Pontins Central League. Meanwhile I was engaged in a failed attempt at a total media blackout, avoiding all newspapers, all radio sports news, and all television sports programmes. *They*, the media, had their desired result, but I didn't wish to know anything about it. It was impossible to achieve this desire, since even non-sports programmes contrived to slip in references to the Premier League Champions, with the flimsiest of excuses, and the shortest of warnings. I considered emigration, but that would have been no use. I've been to plenty of foreign countries, and the first mention of English football is almost always a mistake. The media web stretches far and wide. It's just like the 'Invasion of the Body-Snatchers': *The Nation's Team* are everywhere. In fact, Liverpool was just about the best place to lie low.

I was distraught. I did not think that things could get worse than this. Not for the first time, I was completely and utterly wrong. This was merely the beginning.

Season 1993/94: Brian who?

The denizens of Maine Road were in psychological turmoil during the summer of 1993, and the hangover lasted through to the beginning of the new season. After successfully hovering in the background for a few years, Peter Swales once more became the focus of discontent. He reacted in the only way that he knew. He blamed somebody else.

I was engaged in my own unwelcome transfer dealings. My contract was up and there was no queue of Premier League employers wishing to secure my services. I ended up being forced to the very limits of acceptable distance from Maine Road. I was sent to Coventry, where I spent a particularly miserable 1993/94, alone in a virtually unfurnished rented house, with a jungle where the garden should have been. I relied on Radio Five Live and weekend trips north to maintain my sanity. Before the day of my departure, scheduled for 1 September 1993, there was plenty of time for the Maine Road story to take a new twist.

There was little activity to excite over the summer. The Faithful were in desperate need of some encouraging signs of enterprise and ambition. New players were required. The Blues began the season with long-term injuries to Paul Lake and Ian Brightwell, and every indication that Peter Reid had all but given up as a player. However, the only new man to arrive was Dutchman Alfons Groenendijk, signed from Ajax for a fee of £500,000. He was more typically Dutch than Mr Vonk, and had skill and poise. However, he hadn't got the slightest idea what he was getting into. After a couple of months Groenendijk joined the expanding list of injured players, and by the time he recovered, the world had moved on.

The maxim 'American is Best' was again followed blindly by those in charge of marketing football, and the stupid squad numbering system was introduced. With over 30 players representing Manchester City in the turmoil of the 1993/94 season, the Blues made full use of the numbers and names. These were hardly visible to spectators but, and this was the point, could be seen on television.

Seldom can a season have started in an atmosphere of so little cheer. The opening match of the season, against Leeds United at Maine Road on 14 August 1993, still attracted a crowd of 32,366. This was close to the new capacity, but not a full house. My future wife and I needed to leave the match early in order to beat the traffic and make it to a wedding reception in Bangor. It was no hardship. City were awful, and had the Leeds finishing not bordered on the incompetent, the Blues would have been facing a first defeat. As we left the ground with a few minutes remaining, there was a big cheer. Garry Flitcroft appeared to have stolen an undeserved win for City. A couple of minutes into our car journey, Brian Deane equalised to restore some credibility to the final score: 1-1.

The City team for the opening games had changed little from the previous season. Tony Coton was probably the best goalkeeper in the country. The full-backs were Andy Hill and Terry Phelan, who was regularly one of City's best attackers, scurrying down the left flank. Curle and Vonk comprised the centre of defence, with McMahon, Flitcroft, White and Holden forming a midfield that occasionally involved Simpson, Groenendijk or Reid. With Quinn initially absent, Sheron and White were the strikers for the first three matches. David Brightwell was the main defensive back-up and, thanks to the accumulation of injuries, he started about half the matches in season 1993/94.

Brightwell Junior was playing alongside Vonk for the trip to Goodison Park on 17 August. I remember standing amidst an abnormally subdued set of City fans, watching Everton make and miss plenty of chances. They took one. It was certainly sufficient to beat City in this mood. The Blues lost by the same scoreline at Spurs to complete a dismal start to the new campaign.

Nobody could argue that things did not look bleak, but sober reflection might have been advisable. After all, the previous season also began with only one point to show from the opening three matches. If it had not been for the outcome of the Premier League title race, I doubt that the pressure would have built so quickly and so intensely. Some City fans will argue that Peter Reid deserved to follow Sam Ellis, who had been sacked earlier, because City were not entertaining, preferring to use long-ball tactics. I would argue that the tactics to use are those best suited to the available players. The major fault lay in the inability to attract creative midfield players to the club, to allow more options. The accusations about City's style of play were often exaggerated. *The Nation's Team* had won a Championship with their game based largely on the use of the long ball, particularly away from home, with players whose main asset was pace chasing after those long kicks or throws from *the blond one*. Since Reid's involvement, City had finished fifth, twice in succession, and but for the result of the last match, they could have finished fifth again in 1992/93. This record compares well with that of all predecessors back to Tony Book in the mid – to late 1970s. It also compares well with all who followed Peter Reid, although we could not know that at the time. Reid was still learning his trade. Turning around a seemingly demoralised side was his first real test. Unfortunately, we were not about to discover how he would cope. The real heat from supporters was directed at Peter Swales, whose overall record was far less impressive. The Swales response was to sack Peter Reid, even if he did bring in a chap called John Maddock to do the deed.

A sacking always promotes a giddy feeling of anticipation. The fact that a manager who had fared reasonably well was sacked inspired feelings of optimism, based on the premise that such a manager would not be removed unless somebody far better was poised to take over. Meanwhile, Tony Book, the reserve-team manager, stepped into the limelight once more as caretaker manager, and the Blues suffered a comfortable home defeat at the hands of Blackburn Rovers. City sank into twentieth place, and there was a worrying delay in the announcement of the identity of the knight in shining armour. I began to suspect that there was no significant figure about to be revealed. Surely, even Peter Swales wouldn't sack a manager merely to divert attention.

It quickly became clear that he had done exactly that. There were rumours floating around about City representatives driving down the motorway for intense negotiations with big-name managers. The length of the journey was used to calculate the possible locations. Speculation was rife. Everyone expected Joe Royle, again, but that possibility soon elapsed. There were southern-based managers to consider, such as Gerry Francis. A whole host of names were mentioned. One was conspicuous by its absence: Brian Horton. Brian who?

This was the name of the new City manager. He watched from the stands as the Blues took on Coventry City at Maine Road on 27 August 1993, my last match before departure to live in Coventry. With Tony Book still in charge, the rumours of Horton's imminent arrival actually made things worse for Swales. The traditional chants of 'Swales Out' were taking on a more menacing, expectant resonance. City quelled the chants to some extent, but not entirely, by performing far better than in previous matches. Mike Sheron played an excellent one-two with Niall Quinn, and lobbed the ball over the goalkeeper to give the Blues a deserved lead. This lasted until the eighty-fifth minute, when a McMahon blunder let in Roy Wegerle to equalise. The late goal was to become a familiar theme in encounters with Coventry City. There was a big demonstration outside Maine Road after the match, a show of dissatisfaction that would have taken place regardless of the match result. The newspapers had told everyone what they needed to know. Horton, the Oxford United manager, had no real track record. Even worse, he was in the Luton Town team that relegated City in 1983.

The media spent the remainder of the season, and the following one, continually expressing their sorrow at Horton's plight. I agree, it probably wasn't a pleasant experience for him, but from the beginning he should have been in no doubt as to what he was taking on. The only surprise element was that the Swales trick was to backfire. There was no escape for him this time.

City still had some good players. And, so we are frequently told, good players do not become bad players overnight – mind you, quite often merely putting on a City shirt seems to do the trick. It was, therefore, no surprise that they eventually won a match, away to Swindon, who struggled all season after being deserted by Glenn Hoddle following their promotion. City had their fair share of fortune in this game. Curle brought down Nicky Summerbee to give Swindon a first-half penalty opportunity, but Coton saved the kick. In the second half, City did fall behind when a Summerbee free-kick was deflected past Coton. A scrambled equaliser by Vonk, a fine goal from Quinn, and another by Adie Mike in the last minute, looking suspiciously offside, secured the points for City in Horton's first game.

Horton's home debut went spectacularly well, on the field. QPR's finishing was erratic, Coton was in fine form, and the woodwork did sterling work. At the other end, Quinn followed up to score after a Sheron shot had struck the post, and Sheron scored following a poorly defended corner. City's 2-0 half-time lead was extended to 3-0, courtesy of a deflected Flitcroft shot, and the scoreline might have been even better had Adie Mike not spurned an excellent chance.

You might think, therefore, that the crowd was in the mood for celebration. The presence in the Main Stand of Francis Lee and Colin Barlow, and the growing media coverage of a takeover bid ensured otherwise. There was a demonstration before the match and loud and repetitive chants could be heard during the game. The final whistle provoked mass outbursts of 'Swales out' and 'We want Franny', with many people remaining in the stadium longer than normal. There was another demonstration outside the ground. The general message was the polite suggestion that Mr Swales might wish to reconsider his position as Chairman.

Gradually, Horton began to introduce a few changes. Another long-term injury to Andy Hill was initially covered by playing Flitcroft at full-back, but eventually the solution was found by promoting the impressive Richard Edghill (aged 19) to the first team. With Edghill, Phelan and Curle in the back four, City could not be accused of lacking pace at the back. In a clear attempt to rectify this, Horton signed Alan Kernaghan for £1.5 million, a move spelling the ultimate demise of Michel Vonk. Horton was clearly not too impressed with the contribution of Rick Holden, who soon lost his place and moved back to Oldham. It is difficult to criticise that particular decision.

Edghill and Kernaghan made their debuts at Wimbledon in a 1-0 defeat. An untimely injury to David White meant that there was a debut for Steve Lomas at Bramall Lane. A goal from close-range by Mike Sheron gave City a 1-0 win against Sheffield United, and a hike up to fourteenth place in the table. Sheron scored a late equaliser in a dire Monday night Sky TV spectacular, a 1-1 home draw against Oldham. Meanwhile, the power struggle continued unabated at Maine Road, with Peter Swales stubbornly refusing to give way. I didn't go to this match because it was moved to a workday evening, which makes it tricky when you live the wrong side of the M6-M5 interchange. I really love Sky TV. Actually, for once, they did me a favour.

After drawing 1-1 in the first leg at Maine Road, City looked vulnerable on their trip to Reading in the Coca-Cola Cup, but Simpson and Lomas both had good first-half chances. Lomas took one of his well. Standing in for Coton, Dibble went on an ill-advised walkabout just after half-time, and there was no goalkeeper around when Jimmy Quinn headed the equaliser. With nine minutes remaining, a typical burst forward by Terry Phelan resulted in Niall Quinn restoring City's lead, and the Blues clung on.

After missing four matches, David White looked all set to embark on a much needed scoring run. He latched on to Flitcroft's through ball to give City the lead at home to Liverpool. Quinn should have extended the lead but he shot straight at Grobbelaar, after White's cross had created the opportunity. The Blues were made to regret that miss when Liverpool equalised.

Despite a round trip in excess of 200 miles, I left work sufficiently early to drive to the Coca-Cola Cup fourth-round tie against Hoddle's Chelsea, three days later. I tried to locate some pals in the Kippax Stand, but despite the meagre midweek attendance of 16,713, I failed. The match was tedious, with the only excitement generated by the arrival, as substitute and centre forward, of Michel Vonk, in the eighty-first minute. A minute later, after a Phelan surge and cross from the left, Vonk's far-post header back across goal was turned in by David White for the winner, prompting chants of 'Oooh! Vonky, Vonky'.

The return journey from the Academy to Coventry took two hours, but could be extended to three by being marooned in post-match traffic. From the North Stand, I had this operation well under control. With a couple of minutes of a match remaining, I hovered by an exit, often waiting right up to the final whistle before making my energetic sprint, Phelan-esque, down the stairs, through the ambling crowds and to the car. This performance became a regular occurrence when, at the end of the season, my future wife joined me in my new, bleak, midlands home city.

The Horton honeymoon period was brief and unenthusiastic. On a black November Sunday at Maine Road, it disintegrated in humiliating fashion. The script could have been written by Sky TV to maximise the enjoyment of the armchair audience, and particularly the army of TV Reds. The Blues took the field against the Premier League Champions in seemingly determined mood. Kicking towards the Umbro Stand in the first period, City harassed their illustrious opponents, revealing hitherto unseen cracks in the defence. *The Nation's Team* were, without doubt, rattled by City's determination and vigour. Niall Quinn's header from a Sheron cross gave City the lead. A left-wing cross curled in by McMahon induced another of those rare mistakes by *the blond one*, and Quinn headed City 2-0 ahead. Quinn and White both threatened additional goals. *The Nation's Team* were in distress.

Brian Horton does not have the voice of an inspirational leader. The pitch is just a little too high, and he ends most statements with a question, as if seeking reassurance, doesn't he? This is, of course, trashy amateur psychology. What cannot be disputed is that Mr Horton's half-time team talk was less than entirely effective. It is difficult for me to adequately describe City's second-half performance on 7 November 1993. It was the worst ever 45-minute display by a Manchester City side that I have seen. Words such as cowering, submissive, pathetic, servile, scraping, pitiful, feeble and many more spring to mind – particularly with the aid of a thesaurus. Yet, somehow they fail to convey adequately City's retreat, first to the edge of their own penalty area, and then into it. This left Sharpe, in particular, free to pepper them unmolested with crosses that were bound eventually, despite his erratic delivery, to lead to goals. The trigger for the Blues' sudden retreat in search of mother's apron was a mistake by Vonk, which allowed *the French one* a clear run at goal to make the score 2-1. The young man on my right, who had been rather quiet up until that point, decided to leap to his feet in celebration, and was instantly set upon by several men. After a brief fracas, with many fans around us attempting to becalm the situation, the threat subsided, but it did not go away. I offered friendly advice suggesting that it might not be a good idea for him to stay. After a while, he came to the same conclusion, which is just as well, considering the events that followed.

Many City fans perversely chose to blame David White, who spurned City's only second-half chance from virtually their only venture into the North Stand half of the pitch. The real fault seemed to lie with the collective psychology of the team. They expected to lose, and their expectations were realised. The equaliser was scored near the end and the winner even nearer. I left in a daze, astonished at how bad City could be, so soon after playing well. It was unforgivable. Not least because it set *The Nation's Team* back on track after a stutter that included a 3-3 draw at home to Galatasaray. City fans taunted them about this before the match,

'Galatasaray, Galatasaray,
2-0 up when you fucked it up,
Galatasaray.'

The irony of this chant is self-explanatory.

The big gloomy cloud was darkening above Maine Road, but Mr Swales was nothing if not dogged. Brian Horton's latest signing was forward Carl Griffiths (£500,000 from Shrewsbury), a player recommended by no less an authority than John Bond. Griffiths ran around a lot, often to no perceivable purpose, although his chasing should have earned him a winning goal at Norwich. There he seemed to beat Bryan Gunn to the ball, only for the referee to rule that Griffiths had kicked the ball out of the goalkeeper's hands. Earlier, a Quinn header had cancelled out a goal by Ruel Fox.

The season drifted on with the occasional draw and a couple more defeats, including 3-1 at home to Sheffield Wednesday, and 3-2 at Leeds, after City had recovered from 2-0 behind to draw level. Sheron scored in both matches, and Griffiths' chasing got him City's equaliser at Leeds, following an inadequate Fairclough back-header. During this spell, City lost the services of Niall Quinn with an injury that kept him out for the remainder of the season.

On 8 December 1993, Everton, manager-less after the resignation of Howard Kendall, were defeated at Maine Road. A tenth-minute Griffiths header proved to be the only goal. Everton's Peter Beagrie had a goal dubiously disallowed, and smashed a late chance over the crossbar when he should have scored, but City held on to actually win a match. They then went on to lose at home to Tottenham, to First Division Nottingham Forest in the Coca-Cola Cup, despite taking the lead, and to Blackburn (2-0).

The Ewood Park match proved to be the final Manchester City appearance of David White, a player who had contributed around 20 goals in each of the three previous seasons. Brian Horton decided to swap White for David Rocastle, who looked overweight, and whose career was floundering at Leeds United. To me, David White virtually *was* Manchester City. With Moulden, Hinchcliffe, Redmond and now White sold, and Paul Lake permanently injured, only Ian Brightwell remained from the class of '86, and even he was currently absent due to long-term injury. White had failed to score in a run of 11 matches, but that was the way he operated. He was just as likely to set off on a run of 10 goals in his next 11 matches. I resented that an interloper like Horton could make such a change. He had no right. He wasn't going to be connected to City for long. I was.

The reaction of many City fans to this move also irritated me. Rocastle, a midfield player clearly past his best, was welcomed as some kind of saviour. Such sentiments were even recorded for posterity on the otherwise excellent 'Middle Class Revolt' album by The Fall. There's a snippet of John Peel interviewing a band member. I think that it is Craig Scanlon, whom I saw quite often in queues for tickets or away-match toilet facilities – it's a glamorous life being a City fan; always mixing with the stars.

It seemed at the time that I was in a minority in coveting the presence of some home-produced players in the team. I had nothing against Rocastle. His signing may have been worth a gamble, but not when the gamble included selling our leading goalscorer, at the very time when the other regular source of goals, Quinn, was out injured for the remainder of the season. Mike Sheron, still only 21, could hardly be expected to shoulder all the responsibility himself. Nobody seemed to notice, but City were deeply involved in a relegation battle.

On Boxing Day, Rocastle made his debut in a match at Maine Road against Southampton. Horton played Vonk as makeshift striker, and moved Phelan into a midfield role. Dowie, as usual, scored against City, with a header after 27 minutes. A minute later, Richard Edghill's cross made it all the way over to Phelan, who fired in the equaliser. David Brightwell headed against the crossbar in the second half, but the crowd departed in sombre mood. On New Year's Day, at Newcastle, injuries forced Horton into playing another youngster, John Foster, in defence, and giving a debut to Carl Shutt, on loan from Birmingham City. A 2-0 defeat was the best we could hope for. City were nineteenth.

Instead of White and Quinn, City's strike force was now Griffiths and Shutt, both of whom were battlers, but I don't think that many defences were shivering with fear. Occasionally, Vonk was played up front to add some of that Dutch sophistication to proceedings. Indeed, on 3 January 1994, City stormed into a 2-0 lead against Ipswich on a sodden Maine Road pitch. Michel Vonk was like the proverbial pig-in-shit, thoroughly enjoying hurling himself about in the water. Vonk it was who chased after a ball that looked beyond reach until it stuck in a puddle. The Dutchman hammered it past the goalkeeper to make the score 2-0. It was entertaining, it didn't look particularly dangerous, and City, in desperate need of points, were winning. After 39 minutes, therefore, the match was abandoned by referee David Elleray.

On 8 January 1994, there was a temporary respite from the League struggle as City played host to First Division Leicester City in the FA Cup third round. I had no FA Cup aspirations whatsoever this season, but City progressed comfortably, thanks to an unexpected and fruitful appearance by Ingebrigtsen, who profited from the service of Our Terry, playing pretty much as a left-winger.

Phelan's abilities can be best summed up by this chant, to the tune of 'You've Lost that Lovin' Feeling':

> *'We've got that Terry Phelan*
> *Wo, that Terry Phelan,*
> *We've got that Terry Phelan*

and he's fast, fast, fast... wo-oh-oh-wo.'

That's about the size of it.

After a goalless first half, twice in the space of a couple of minutes, Ingebrigtsen headed Phelan crosses into the net. An astonishing 40-yard shot from Alan Kernaghan added to the general air of unreality, and Ingebrigtsen scored from the edge of the penalty area to complete a hat-trick. A David Oldfield goal for Leicester, from some distance, rounded a surreal occasion off nicely.

Back in the real world, City fans were treated to a goalless draw against Arsenal. I made the trip to Anfield on 22 January 1994, to see the Blues totally outplayed, after taking the lead with an early Carl Griffiths goal. Liverpool left their winning goal irritatingly late, just at the moment when I thought that maybe City would escape with a fortunate point. I'm sure that the Anfield Faithful were very happy not to see David White in the City team.

The journey to Cardiff, the following week, was a late decision. My future wife offered me an excuse to go and, as usual, I stupidly grabbed it. The lucky woman also got to come with me on a wet and dismal afternoon. After losing our way a little, we spotted and subsequently followed the City team coach to Ninian Park; there was no mistaking that window-seat Vonk haircut amongst a group of card-players. We parked in the middle of a sodden field and edged our way to the ground gingerly. Thankfully, we arrived quite early, and were safely inside whilst the running battles were taking place outside the old stadium. There was no welcome in this hillside. Maybe that's because there were no hills.

Despite the sustenance of some hot chocolate, we were cold and damp as we took our places in a roofless, exposed stand and awaited the thrills and spills of an FA Cup fourth-round tie. It was a romantic clash of Premier League giants and Division Two hopefuls so the cameras were poised to record the almost inevitable upset. I'm told that Welsh television covered the match live. The writing was on the wall.

Wellies might have been more effective than boots. Groenendijk was no doubt wishing himself back at Ajax, as he forlornly attempted to thread passes through the mud. Keith Curle scored a neat goal for City, timing his run well. At least, he should have done. A ludicrous offside decision prevented it. The referee almost made amends, but not before an impressive strike by Nathan Blake, Cardiff's powerful centre forward, had given the home side the lead. City's chance for redemption came when Rocastle went over in the mud, and Curle stepped up to take a penalty. Unfortunately, he missed.

FA Cup exit was a minor concern. City were twentieth in the League table and desperately short on goalscoring potential. After personal abuse and threats to his family, Peter Swales finally gave up his battle to stay as City Chairman. Francis Lee and his entourage assumed control amidst euphoric optimism.

Chairman Lee's home debut was the re-scheduled match against Ipswich Town, and 28,188 turned out to see the dawn of a new era. Ingebrigtsen and Groenendijk were made the scapegoats for City's FA Cup demise, rather unjustly, particularly in the case of the Dutchman. Both were pointedly ignored for the rest of the season. Carl Griffiths, Carl Shutt and Mike Sheron formed the attack. With so many changes around him, Sheron was understandably struggling to reproduce the form of the previous season, but he would still be the leading League goalscorer, albeit with only six goals.

Despite themselves, City won the match against Ipswich. Carl Griffiths missed a golden opportunity after John Wark had fluffed a back-pass. When Garry Flitcroft made a similar defensive error, Ian Marshall, a man whose hair made Neil Pointon's seem acceptable, punished it to the full. City trailed after 16 minutes. Some 15 minutes later, David Rocastle, performing for the 'Match of the Day' cameras, did his famous touchline trick to deceive two defenders, and Carl Griffiths directed Rocastle's cross into the net. City's increasingly anxious attacks culminated in a second-half winner, bundled over the line by Flitcroft after Vonk's header across goal. Carl Griffiths took the ball off Forrest, the Ipswich goalkeeper, but somehow failed to extend City's lead, leaving us all with stressful closing minutes to endure. City held on. Chairman Lee had cast his magic spell. This was the road to recovery. Possibly.

City drew 0-0 at home to West Ham the following week and returned to the relegation zone. A visit to Phil Neal's mid-table Coventry City offered them the chance to demonstrate an improvement, and me the opportunity to walk to a Premier League match involving the Blues. The atmosphere within Highfield Road was, as always, contributed entirely by the visiting fans, here occupying one length of the ground rather than one end behind the goal. The team were not suitably inspired. This was the performance of players expecting to be relegated. Kernaghan and Vonk were constantly exposed by the pace of N'dlovu and Williams, and the Blues had no attacking ideas whatsoever. Coventry won 4-0, but could easily have scored twice as many. Manchester City looked doomed.

Dean Saunders completed a spectacular treble three days later by missing a penalty kick against City for a third club, this time Aston Villa. That late reprieve enabled City to escape with a point, and offered pub-quiz question writers all over the country an idea for a darn good question. Back at the Academy, the Blues had a showdown against bottom-of-the-table Swindon Town. Fjortoft not only gave Swindon the lead, but was very unfortunate to have a second goal disallowed. An own goal by Kevin Horlock enabled City to draw level before half-time, and David Rocastle threaded in a neat winning goal in the second half. It seemed that Chairman Lee's magic was working, just. City were hovering one place above the relegation positions.

The magic proved less effective away from Maine Road. At Loftus Road, two goalkeeping howlers cancelled each other out. In the first half, Andy Dibble smacked the ball in-off Penrice after a poor McMahon back-pass. In the second half, a tame Rocastle shot somehow found its way to goal, rescuing a point.

With Garry Flitcroft, and later Richard Edghill, adding to City's mounting injury list, action was required. Chairman Lee's overseas connections secured the services on loan of Dynamo Dresden striker Uwé Rösler, as the time for pre-deadline panic buying approached. The German was thrown straight into the QPR match. It was this move, ultimately completed for a fee of £300,000, and the subsequent arrivals of Paul Walsh (for £750,000 from Portsmouth) and Peter Beagrie (£1.1 million from Everton), that saved the Blues from relegation. After some brief impact, Rocastle became a peripheral figure. City's need for goals was adequately demonstrated by three consecutive goalless matches: a 0-1 defeat at home to Wimbledon, when Walsh made his first appearance, and 0-0 draws at home to Sheffield United and at Oldham, both clubs down in the mire along with the Blues.

The recovery began at Portman Road. The additional ingredients were the return of Ian Brightwell and Andy Hill, and the signing of another German, Steffan Karl, on loan. Although David Linighan gave Ipswich the lead, Walsh followed up to score after a Beagrie shot had rebounded from the post, and then set up a second-half chance for Rösler to score his first goal for the club. Unfortunately, the City lead lasted only five minutes because of an ill-advised challenge by Vonk, which led to an Ipswich penalty. The significance of this match was that at least the Blues had scored some goals.

The two Easter matches proved to be central to City's escape. At home to Aston Villa, City struggled to get the ball, but when they did, it was used to good effect. After 39 minutes, Peter Beagrie's shot was deflected into the Villa net. Before half-time, Paul Walsh headed a second City goal from Ian Brightwell's cross. In the second half, Rösler scored a third City goal with an emphatic header. Villa, despite looking quite good, made no impression on the scoreline.

The Blues were still just one place above the relegation zone when they visited Southampton for an Easter Monday relegation dogfight, without the dogs. Steffan Karl was not at the club for long and didn't play many matches, but he will be remembered as the man who cracked the eighty-eighth minute winner with considerable force. An impudent Le Tissier free-kick, struck against the post, almost brought Southampton level, but the victory lifted City to fifteenth place.

On 7 April 1994, at Maine Road, the Blues took on Kevin Keegan's Newcastle United, still in need of points. In the first half we had to endure a wave of Newcastle attacks towards the North Stand. Scott Sellars crept in behind Andy Hill to give the visitors the lead, and the afternoon had an ominous look about it. Sheer determination led to Rösler directing a shot against the Newcastle post to raise hopes, and Beagrie skipped past a couple of defenders before crossing for Paul Walsh to equalise with a header. That provoked a serious response. Beardsley scuffed a chance, falling over when faced with Dibble. I would not dare to suggest that such an esteemed, nay saintly, player, was halfway to the floor anticipating a contact from Dibble that never came. It isn't as if he has any track record of such behaviour at Maine Road, in the penalty area in front of the North Stand.

In addition to Beardsley's miss, Dibble saved well from Robert Lee, and Andy Cole shot against the underside of the City crossbar when clean through. In the second half, the Blues cashed in on those misses, when a loose ball was lashed home by the taller and younger Brightwell, his first goal for the club. A terrific piece of skill by the lively Walsh, who scooped the ball through to Beagrie, should have led to a security goal, but Srnicek made a good save. Nevertheless, City held on for an unlikely win.

With Walsh proving tricky and elusive, Beagrie capable of beating defenders on the wing and striking accurate corners and crosses, and Rösler strong and direct, Horton's panic buys saved the day. Another point was earned by a Rösler header from Beagrie's cross in the game away to Norwich. This stretched City's unbeaten run to seven matches. Inevitably, it all came unstuck at *The Swamp*, where despite some promising moments, the Blues lost 2-0. On this occasion, Rösler's finishing let him down when he struck a shot against the post, with the score still 0-0. At least one of the goals, both scored late in the first half, was offside, but that hardly merits a mention. Horton's decision to counter the pace of Kanchelskis by assigning David Brightwell to the full-back slot was, to say the least, eccentric.

Chelsea came to Maine Road as FA Cup finalists, blissfully unaware that David Ellaray would scupper their hopes by awarding two penalty kicks to *The Nation's Team*, and thus ensure the double. This match, played on 30 April 1994, represented the last for the Kippax Stand as a wide open standing area. The Taylor report had recommended all-seater stadiums and City had to comply. I wasn't a Kippax regular, and had few happy memories of the stand. Mind you, I had few happy memories of any Maine Road stand. I know that many people did have fond memories of the Kippax: it was always a safe, large terracing with plenty of exits. The capacity at Maine Road was certainly about to suffer a permanent drop.

Chelsea tried to spoil the occasion by taking a 2-0 lead. The goalscorers, Fleck and Cascarino, wanted FA Cup places. City were level before half-time, with Rösler and Walsh profiting from Beagrie crosses to score headed goals. The match ended 2-2, which meant that there was still a contrived, remote mathematical possibility that City could be relegated. It was highly unlikely, and another Rösler header in a 1-1 draw at Sheffield Wednesday made sure that it didn't happen. In fact, City finished in the relatively elevated position of sixteenth place. The real final-day escape was performed by Everton.

So let's recap on 1993/94. A successful season? I think not. A narrowly escaped relegation, two derby defeats, and a *Nation's Team* Cup and League double – surely it couldn't get *much* worse than this, could it?

Season 1994/95: Uwé Rösler's Grandad

The summer of 1994 was a welcome relief from the English football season. I got married, thus inducing my wife to accompany me to the seething metropolis and cosmopolitan melting pot that is Coventry, and we were able to fit in a few fjords during a quick jaunt around Norway, with only occasional exposure to one of the myriad of shirts marketed by *The Nation's Team*. Prior to that escapade was the World Cup, which took place, quite disgracefully, in the USA, a country with little or no interest in proper football. My money was on Italy – literally. The Italians fortuitously progressed all the way to the final, where they took on the, as usual, over-hyped Brazilians. 'The Divine Ponytail', who had virtually single-handedly taken Italy to the final, eventually cost me my stake. In the penalty shoot-out he struck the kind of penalty kick that your granny might manage on a bad day. City had some interest in the competition, with Our Terry scampering up and down the left flank for Ireland, who once again did as well as could possibly be expected, even without the injured Niall Quinn.

There was continual speculation about Brian Horton's position as manager, but he was still in place as the new season reared its ugly head. In the first match magazine of the new season Horton wrote that, 'the start of the League season fills everyone with enthusiasm for the months ahead.' You could have fooled me.

Brian Horton managed to get on my good side in one respect. The Maine Road pitch was widened, reversing the decision of Howard Kendall, in the interests of City's new attacking strategy of playing two wingers. Peter Beagrie, on the left, but comfortable with the use of either foot for purposes other than merely standing, had been a revelation, with his excellent supply to the forwards, and his ability to actually take on and beat defenders. The other flank was to be patrolled by City's only notable summer signing, 22-year-old Nicky Summerbee (£1.5 million from relegated Swindon), son of City legend Mike. A consistent supply from that flank was not to be quite so forthcoming. The major departure, that of Rocastle to Chelsea for £1.25 million, provoked little dissent. In effect, Horton had sold David White for a sum of approximately £1.5 million, which, considering the player's goalscoring record, did appear on the Margaret Thatcher side of barmy. More money was lost with the cut-price sale of Groenendijk to Sparta Rotterdam. The return of Neil McNab, appointed as Youth Team Coach, was to be welcomed as a response to the general demise of the club – attracting and developing young players were to be given priority. One of the few successes, Richard Edghill, was chosen to play for the England Under-21 team over the summer. Another, Mike Sheron, was sold to Norwich City for a mere £800,000 in the first two weeks of the new season. Brian Horton was an awfully generous chap.

Although Niall Quinn was fit enough to be named as substitute in City's opening fixture, Horton was relying on his successful late buys, Walsh and Rösler, to supply the goals. Walsh, along with Beagrie, added a refreshingly creative dimension to City's play. His long, flowing locks and nimble turns had changed little during a lengthy career, and he enjoyed a brief but impressive swansong at Maine Road. So much so that I could forgive him for his part in the 1983 relegation match against Luton Town.

Uwé Rösler's biggest asset as a potential City folk hero was the fact that his name fitted perfectly into the football fans' new and rapidly ubiquitous anthem, based on the song 'Go West', as performed by those rugged Village People and the equally butch Pet Shop Boys. The irony of macho football fans chanting to the tune of such a song requires little expansion from me. The fact that Rösler was German provoked some ill-founded speculation on the possibility of Rösler's grandad's involvement in the bombing of Old Trafford earlier in the century.

The Blues lost 3-0 at Highbury in the opening match of the new season, with Rösler's first significant contribution being to get himself sent off. Two consecutive home matches gave City the chance to rescue the first week of their campaign, and this they achieved in surprisingly impressive style. The demolition of the Kippax Stand revealed a hitherto concealed view of Rusholme and beyond. It's not exactly the Grand Canyon, but it beats the half-time entertainment. Work was under way on the main structure, but meanwhile there was some exposed seating available, with complimentary rain protection provided in the form of white, plastic covers for the punters. Luckily, it rarely rains in Manchester.

Visiting fans were initially barred because of the lack of space. An attendance of fewer than 20,000 for both of City's first two home games and the failure to fill the Kippax seating suggests a waning in interest, but the customary confusion concerning membership cards and the requirement to purchase tickets in advance were the main contributory factors.

The Blues won 3-0 against a West Ham team featuring both Trevor Morley and Ian Bishop, the erstwhile darling of a bygone age. Walsh scored early with a header, and the first acrobatics of the season were prompted by a Beagrie shot that deceived Miklosko and gave the Blues a comfortable half-time lead. Rösler registered his first goal to round off a stress-free evening. City followed that heartening win with an even more rousing victory over Everton. After a goal-free first-half, Rösler headed City into the lead from a Walsh cross. Within a few minutes, the Blues led 2-0, after a neat build-up involving Rösler and McMahon, and a pleasing finish by Walsh. City scored their third goal following an Everton corner. The rapid break ended with Summerbee sliding the ball into the path of Walsh, who placed it beyond Southall. City's fourth was the result of a through-ball by Flitcroft to the unmarked Rösler, who confidently lifted the ball over Southall to provoke further raucous chanting of his name to the tune of 'Go West'. It took a remarkable save by Neville Southall to prevent a first League goal by Nicky Summerbee. We were to have a long wait for that momentous event, but the Faithful departed ecstatic, and with considerably raised levels of expectation, after a 4-0 rout.

The City system relied on a lightweight midfield of, initially, McMahon and Flitcroft, with a player on either wing. Later, Lomas replaced McMahon, who left to become player-manager at Swindon Town. The tactics were quite successful at home, but away from Maine Road things were not running so smoothly. Another 3-0 defeat, this time at Chelsea, left City in comfortable mid-table.

The increased goal action still failed to tempt a crowd in excess of 20,000 for the visit of Crystal Palace. Although Walsh scored early with a header from Summerbee's cross, Dyer equalised before the break, and the Blues had to settle for one point. A welcome first point and goal away from home came at Hillsborough. Peter Beagrie's corners, particularly those swinging into the near-post, were a recurring danger to opposition defences. It was from one such corner that Paul Walsh scored City's goal in a 1-1 draw with Sheffield Wednesday.

After an embarrassing 1-0 defeat at Barnet in the first leg of the Coca-Cola Cup second-round, when Dougie Freedman scored after only 27 seconds, Horton decided to play Niall Quinn in the starting line-up for the first time in 10 months. This was to be for Norwich City's visit to Maine Road on 24 September 1994. Quinn, Walsh and Rösler were competing for two places. It proved a difficult decision for Horton all season, but on this occasion all three played, and the outcome was more than satisfactory. Quinn marked his full return with a headed goal and played a significant role in City's second, scored by Rösler. When Mike Milligan scythed down Rösler, Peter Beagrie assumed penalty kick duty in the absence of the injured Curle. Although the penalty was quite well struck, Gunn made a good save in the Norwich goal to keep the score down to 2-0. Defeat at Leeds by the same scoreline ensured that City remained doggedly in mid-table.

Injuries were beginning, once again, to cause serious problems, particularly in City's defence. Keith Curle recovered, but Horton was constantly forced to tamper with the centre of defence, with Kernaghan, Foster and later Edghill suffering injuries of varying severity. The latest addition to the injured was Tony Coton, whose absence due to a troublesome shoulder injury acquired at Leeds provided Andy Dibble with the opportunity to resume duties as the City goalkeeper.

The Blues managed to overcome Third Division Barnet, 4-2 on aggregate, and attracted a more respectable Maine Road crowd for the visit of Frank Clark's Nottingham Forest, who were seeking a win to put themselves top of the Premier League table. It proved to be a traumatic day for Andy Dibble, who inadvertently directed into goal a Stan Collymore shot that was clearly going wide. A Niall Quinn volley brought City level before half-time, but Forest restored their lead when Collymore gave chase to a long ball and somehow cracked a shot between Dibble and his post. The City goalkeeper appeared to dive out of the way. Dibble clearly blamed his post, which he kicked in retribution. When a Beagrie corner led to a chaotic scramble, Niall Quinn brought City level again. A demonstration of excellent chest work by Quinn gave Steve Lomas the opportunity to fire City ahead. In the dying seconds, after Dibble had ventured from his line, a speculative lob into the penalty area by Ian Woan rescued a point for Forest in a 3-3 draw.

The Blues edged into eighth position after their first away victory, in an eventful game at Loftus Road. Garry Flitcroft headed City into the lead, and within two minutes the QPR goalkeeper, Tony Roberts, in his attempts to clear, struck the ball against the head of the energetic Walsh. The ball rebounded into an empty net to give City a two-goal half-time cushion. In the second half, Andy Dibble was again the central figure. When he ventured just a fraction too far to punch the ball clear, the home fans were baying for a red card. It was such a marginal offence that only a harsh referee, or a QPR fan, could have interpreted the handball as deliberate. City received their punishment when old boy Clive Wilson scored from the free-kick, but Dibble's afternoon was far from over. With 20 minutes still remaining, he rushed out of the penalty area to take the ball off Ferdinand with a sliding tackle. The referee objected to this and sent Dibble off.

This did not prevent irate QPR fans from phoning in to the dreadful Mr Mellor's 'Six-O-Six' on Radio Five Live, complaining that Dibble should have been sent off earlier. This despite the fact that the initial decision had only extended Dibble's contribution by a few minutes and QPR scored from the free-kick.

With 17 minutes remaining, the baying fans had more blood when Richard Edghill was sent off for a second offence deemed worthy of a yellow card. Despite having only nine men on the pitch, City held on to win 2-1.

On 22 October 1994, there was a sell-out crowd of 25,473 for the visit of Spurs to Maine Road, for one of the most open matches I have ever seen. My count of grudges held against Spurs was mounting. The four defeats suffered in one season, including a live FA Cup humiliation, was one of the more recent to spring to mind. Spurs, managed by Ossie Ardiles, boasted an array of World Cup talent, notably the Romanians Dumitrescu and Popescu, and the German Klinsmann, whose conversion from tabloid *ultimate cheating villain* to *super-mega nice-guy hero* had astounded even cynical paranoiacs like myself. Spurs were attired in Scottish Blue, and their fans in cheap white plastic as the rain poured on the unprotected and minimalist Kippax seating. Spurs passed the ball around admirably all afternoon, with intricate little exchanges and delicate flicks, particularly by Klinsmann. Dumitrescu looked like the best player on the pitch, despite attracting the wrath of City fans, for a reason which escaped me. Mind you, as far as I'm concerned, playing for Spurs is sufficient reason.

Barmby had two early chances, one missed, one saved by Dibble, as Spurs assumed total control. Fortunately, the Ossie Ardiles Spurs side was not so adept at defending as they were at attracting the drooling admiration of John Motson, amongst others, for their passing moves. After 15 minutes, ex-Spurs player Paul Walsh took advantage of a Campbell error to fire City into the lead with a left-footed strike.

Spurs appeared unaffected, and Klinsmann was twice through on goal. The first chance he put wide. On the second occasion, he advanced on Dibble, who dived at the feet of the megastar to induce a classic triple axle with twist. David Ellaray pointed to the penalty spot and Dumitrescu scored the goal. With City struggling to either win or keep possession, I was in a glum mood. A brilliant Dumitrescu chip beat Dibble but rebounded off the crossbar to Sheringham, who wasted the chance. City made the most of the lack of end product to the Spurs pretty patterns. Four minutes before half-time, Summerbee broke clear on the right wing and crossed. The header by Walsh was saved by Ian Walker, but Quinn followed up with a diving header to score. Just before half-time, Peter Beagrie, starting from within his own half, executed a notable escape from a tight situation near the touchline, leaving two defenders in his wake. Beagrie found Quinn, and Quinn crossed for Walsh, whose first-time shot was generously allowed in by Walker, who was clearly admiring the aesthetic qualities of the City build-up. The Blues led 3-1 at half-time.

In the opening minute of the second half, Dumintrescu halved City's lead with a deflected shot, after a Klinsmann back heel had given him the chance to strike at goal. City, however, continued to make good use of their limited possession. An example of their directness came when Walsh ran forward, taking the ball with him, as Spurs defenders backed away in confusion. Walsh gave the ball to Beagrie, who skipped past a defender and crossed perfectly for Steve Lomas to score with a header. There was still plenty of Spurs possession, but with just over 10 minutes remaining, Walsh again caused panic by running straight at the Spurs defence. He set up Garry Flitcroft for a shooting chance which was well converted and made the final score a shocking 5-2. Neither side had shown much concern for defending, which made for great entertainment. Somehow, 2-5 would not have been so enjoyable. The failure of Spurs players to track their opponents into the penalty area was positively negligent. Such an approach won't prosper in these competitive days. Ossie Ardiles didn't last long.

City followed up with another spectacular goal-fest, a 4-3 Coca-Cola Cup triumph at QPR, featuring a first City goal for Summerbee. My first view of City away from home in the 1994/95 season came at Highfield Road, on 29 October 1994. The Blues were lying in seventh place and attracting attention for their goalscoring exploits. A couple of fellow-sufferers were sufficiently inspired to visit me in order to sample the delights of Coventry, take in the match, and help me finish off a duty-free bottle of Slivovice. The latter task, after a number of pints earlier in the evening, was ill-advised.

The Faithful were out in number and in ebullient mood, and City responded by dominating the match. Peter Beagrie was on fine form, performing my particular favourite trick, which was to induce a defender to fall over, just by the slightest of implied movements. With Coton injured and both Dibble and Margetson suspended, Simon Tracey had arrived on loan from Sheffield United as a stand-in. Ian Brightwell, demonstrating his often unappreciated versatility, was playing particularly well at the centre of the City defence, on this occasion partnered by Vonk. The Blues looked in control, but they failed to convert any of the chances made. In the last few minutes, Dion Dublin snatched an undeserved winning goal for Coventry City, who were beginning to annoy me. Like most football fans, I had hardly noticed the existence of Coventry City previously, apart from their one notable triumph in 1987. Living in Coventry made me pay more attention. They never go down. They never get near the top. Nothing much happens. Their World Cup import was Coby Jones, which just about sums it up.

Back at the Academy, City rediscovered their goal touch in a 3-3 draw against Southampton, for whom Matthew Le Tissier was outstanding. He was involved in the build-up to the only first-half goal, and twice provided the pass for on-loan Ronnie Ekelund to score in the second half, but not before City had taken a 2-1 lead. This was thanks to two Walsh goals, the first of which may not have crossed the line. The best City goal was reserved until the end, when Peter Beagrie wove his way into the penalty area, finished with a left-footed shot, and performed the traditional somersault in celebration.

When everything was taken into account, the season was progressing better than expected. At least, it was until 10 November 1994, when the Blues were required by Sky TV to play against *The Nation's Team* at *The Swamp* on a Thursday night. I made no attempt to get a ticket. I would have found it difficult to make the match, but having been forced to miss one Old Trafford derby game, I had lost all desire to visit that place ever again. I was, at least, hopeful that the Blues might manage a respectable showing. After all, City's form had been quite good of late. It might not be unreasonable to expect, for instance, that they might score a goal.

I dragged my wife – not literally, I hasten to add – along to a public house in Coventry, to watch proceedings unfold on a very small and distant television screen. There were, as anticipated, a number of local and student TV Reds in residence. The prevalence of people modelling fashion accessories reflecting allegiance to *The Nation's*

Team had prepared me for that. The Blues seemed to be putting up some sort of a fight for the first 20 minutes or so. Then a goal was scored, to the delight of the TV Reds, who were suffering under the misapprehension that it had anything whatsoever to do with them. Before half-time, a second goal added to my discomfort and we decided to leave. By the time the bus had carried us home, Ceefax revealed that City were trailing 4-0. They waited until I was paying attention before adding the fifth goal, thus wiping out any lingering defence that City fans could extract from the 5-1 triumph of 1989. I don't know who scored the goals. In fact, I don't care. It was November and I was wishing an end to the season.

I already had tickets for the away trip to Leicester City, which was scheduled on a Sunday to suit Sky TV. The natives were restless due to the impending departure of Brian Little, and their mood was not improved by the afternoon's match. I went with my wife who, thanks to a smartly dispatched Niall Quinn goal, broke her away match duck as City took all three points. I tried to feel enthusiastic about it. I failed.

A rare 2-0 home triumph against Wimbledon followed, and by 30 November 1994 I was sufficiently recovered to make the tortuous midweek trip to the Academy for a Coca-Cola Cup fourth-round match against Newcastle. Being just the wrong side of Birmingham ensured that the car journey to Maine Road, requiring as it did passage through the M6 car park, was tedious and unpredictable in duration. I did, however, gain an intimate knowledge of several motorway service stations, especially Knutsford, from where the comforting tones of GMR's Jimmy Wagg could, at last, be picked up by car radio. I can also advise you that should you want to buy throat-soothing double action Lockets, you shouldn't stop at Knutsford.

Having missed several matches with injury, Rösler had to be content with being a substitute, but for the second successive match he came on to score, this time with a second-half header that cancelled out an early Newcastle goal. The match ended 1-1, which seemed to spell the end of City's hopes for that competition.

Rösler was in the starting line-up at Portman Road a few days later. This time he scored what proved to be the winning goal, a volley adding to an earlier strike by Flitcroft. It was City's first League win at Ipswich in 33 years. The home side pulled a goal back in the second half, but City's 2-1 win lifted them to sixth position in the League table. That was as high as they got.

Sky TV again caused me major problems by moving City's home game against Arsenal to Monday, 12 December 1994. My reward for managing to get there was for the Blues to concede two first-half goals. There was a rare appearance by Fitzroy Simpson, who came on as substitute and scored a late goal, but City still lost.

Francis Lee's German connections secured the services, on loan from Eintracht Frankfurt for the remainder of the season, of Maurizio Gaudino, at a cost of £200,000. The long-haired, unshaven Gaudino, a man with a shady past and a court case looming, was a mysterious, elusive figure. He had an uncanny ability to drift unnoticed into threatening central positions. Regrettably, he was as likely to be unnoticed by colleagues as by opponents. As a member of Germany's 1994 World Cup squad, Gaudino's talent was in no doubt. There was a deftness of touch and awareness that made a refreshing change for the centre of City's often workman-like midfield. Drifting around like a misunderstood revolutionary or fugitive from justice, Dino also rejoiced in a splendidly exotic-sounding name that fitted nicely into a song to the tune of 'The Red Flag':

> *'Maurizio,*
> *Maurizio,*
> *Maurizio, Gaudino.'*

Imagine a ruddy-faced, obese man, with trousers creeping down at the back, standing to chant this in a lusty monotone. Picture a programme in one outstretched hand and a pie in the other, and the romance is complete.

Gaudino made his debut on 20 December 1994, at St James's Park, in the Coca-Cola Cup fourth-round replay against Newcastle. An assortment of defensive injuries led to the pairing of Kernaghan and Ian Brightwell at the centre of the City defence, with Lomas and John Foster completing a busy back four. On a night when City progressed against all expectations, Ian Brightwell was in particularly resolute form as City hung on to a lead given them by Rösler. Newcastle, who unforgivably featured the hair of Barry Vennison and Darren Peacock *in the same team*, came close on numerous occasions, but Dibble performed well. Andy Cole kept just missing, and to the frustration of the home fans, and the amazement of the Faithful, City broke clear to secure a 2-0 win late in the match. It was one of Nicky Summerbee's finest moments of the season, which, admittedly, is not saying a great deal. Summerbee advanced down the right wing, looking every bit the effective professional football player. He made a bit of a mess of the cross, but headed back into the penalty area at the second attempt. Niall Quinn, on as substitute for Gaudino, who was already tired by half-time, completely missed the ball, which fooled everyone. Paul Walsh was first to react when the ball fell kindly at his feet.

This surprising success proved to be a lonely one. The Blues last tasted League triumph on 3 December 1994. It was to be 22 February 1995, against the same struggling opponents, Ipswich Town, before they did so again. Christmas defeats by Blackburn and Liverpool were followed by a Maine Road encounter with Aston Villa, on the last day of 1994. A goal in each half by Rösler seemed to have put City in a strong position, but within a minute of Rösler's second, the ball bounced into the City net off the head of Ian Brightwell. Four minutes later, Dean Saunders ended a messy scramble by bringing Villa level.

City returned to frustrate Newcastle once more on 2 January 1995, in a goalless draw that was the precursor to an important couple of Cup matches. The outcome of the whole season now depended on these games. My return to Meadow Lane, on Sunday, 8 January 1995, for the FA Cup third-round tie, was not so demoralising as the previous visit. On this occasion, County were propping up the Endsleigh League Division One; that's the Second Division to those of us wishing to maintain our sense of reality. Meadow Lane was considerably improved, with some perfectly adequate seating on which to perch in anticipation. Despite the home side's modest League form, City might easily have been dumped out of the Cup at the first hurdle. Rob Matthews scored the opening goal with a neat, close-range volley to provoke mutterings amongst the Faithful. Cheeriness was resumed with the equaliser from Beagrie, whose shot somehow squeezed between Cherry and his post. The County goalkeeper, whose form had been on the miraculous side of perfect in the 1991 cup-tie, seemed rooted to the spot. Just before half-time, County regained the lead when Dibble fumbled a shot from Matthews and Devon White followed up to score. Attacking towards the increasingly disgruntled City fans, the Blues applied earnest second-half pressure, without looking terribly convincing. The day was rescued when David Brightwell headed City level to force a replay. He was later rather close to turning from hero to villain when he inadvertently directed the ball, via his head, on to the City crossbar.

Three days later, Manchester City appeared in their first quarter-final since the Spurs debacle at Maine Road. This time there were no live television cameras, but the Blues exited the Coca-Cola Cup pathetically, beaten 4-0 at Selhurst Park by Crystal Palace, a team several places lower in the League table. To add to the unadulterated joy of the occasion, Lomas joined the long-term-casualty list.

Notts County arrived at Maine Road for the FA Cup replay with the recently appointed Howard Kendall as manager, which added much needed spice to the occasion. Only 14,261 could find the motivation necessary for attendance. I made the trip out of habit and a curiously undimmed expectation that one day my efforts might be rewarded with an FA Cup triumph. It proved to be one of City's better 1995 matches, and a personal demonstration of finishing ability by Uwé Rösler, who scored four times in an eventful 5-2 win. The other City goal was headed home by Maurizio Gaudino, much to the delight of all concerned.

City's hopes for another season rested on a fourth-round home tie against Aston Villa. With increasingly poor results at home matching those achieved on their travels, City's form was less than encouraging. However, on a heavy pitch and after a generous first-minute miss by Dwight Yorke, City took a seventh-minute lead, when Paul Walsh applied the finishing touch to Ian Brightwell's penetrating through-ball. Gaudino was twice spotted by colleagues after ghosting through the Villa defence, but he was unable to make the most of the opportunities. There were some insistent late Villa attacks and, in the dying seconds, the recalled Tony Coton saved from Johnson, with Staunton disturbing the post from the follow-up. The final whistle was a charitable act of liberation for us all.

City's reward for their FA Cup win was a trip to Newcastle, and the opportunity to demonstrate that lightning can strike twice. The Blues faced two League matches between the two cup-ties. In the first, City rescued a creditable 2-2 draw at Southampton, thanks to a late Flitcroft goal. In the second, the Blues capitulated to *The Nation's Team* at the Academy. They did so in distressingly feeble fashion, to complete a 0-8 aggregate derby score that should be sufficient by itself to seal the fate of any Manchester City manager.

This inauspicious preparation for the live televised Newcastle match meant that the long drive north was undertaken with little or no expectation of City survival. It was a pleasant enough Sunday afternoon, and St James's Park was looking splendid from both the inside and outside. The way that the stands appeared to be coordinated, with similar roofing and matching styles, was most unnerving for somebody accustomed to Maine Road and the intermittent, always curtailed, efforts to build the stadium anew.

Under Kevin Keegan, Newcastle United were now a force to be reckoned with. For many years, when seeking consolation in the worse plight of others, I could look to Newcastle for comfort, but not any more. The Blues did manage to rise to the occasion and perform creditably, but unlike the Coca-Cola Cup Tie earlier in the season, nothing went their way. The first goal no doubt provided a moment of light relief for the subscribers to Sky TV, but seemed less amusing to those of us who had invested more time and money into the event. With both linesmen waving their flags, and everyone expecting a free-kick of some sort, referee Gerald Ashby decided to make no decision. The ball had drifted towards Andy Dibble from the head of a defender. Dibble looked at the ball and at the referee, thought about it, had a cup of tea, considered the plight of the Amazon jungles and the philosophical nuances of being, and then, too late, noticed Gillespie rushing towards him. Despite Dibble's late reaction, Gillespie easily relieved him of the ball and scored.

The Blues responded courtesy of a mistake by Srnicek, who failed to catch a Beagrie corner. He was left to rue the error when Rösler deposited the ball into the Newcastle net. Rösler then whipped off his shirt to reveal a black T-shirt, and ran about like a recently decapitated chicken. City looked all set to reach half-time on level terms, and deservedly so, when a cross by John Beresford – a former City player released by Billy McNeill – drifted over Dibble's head and into the net. With David Brightwell unaccountably dozing by the post, Gillespie nipped in to increase the home side's lead after the break. Garry Flitcroft wasted a good chance to make the last few minutes more agonising for the locals, and it all ended tamely. I was clinging to the hope that a draw away to Leeds United might end the Cup hopes of *The Nation's Team*, but by the time I had reached the car and turned on the radio, Leeds were already trailing 2-0 with the match barely started. What a splendid day out!

City ended a dismal run of 10 League games without a win thanks to a goal from substitute Niall Quinn, 20 minutes from the end of a home match against Ipswich. A few minutes later, Rösler added a second. In a goalless Maine Road encounter with Leeds, the transfer-listed Terry Phelan had the best opportunities, and Keith Curle came closest of all, striking a post after an impressive surge forward.

On 4 March 1995, I was huddled in a seat at a breezy Carrow Road as the Blues fought out the battle of the plungers with Norwich City. Both sides had begun the season well then fallen away dramatically. Although Norwich were in fourteenth place, with the Blues just one place lower, neither could consider themselves unaffected by the relegation fight below. This was my first visit to Norwich, despite at least two family holidays at Great Yarmouth. The journey was one of frightening length and complexity back then. The roads from Coventry to East Anglia have barely improved now, but my wife and I decided to make a weekend of it, which proved to be a good idea, despite the cold.

The match was the most uninteresting and uncomfortable part of the trip. Too many team changes had left City looking disjointed, and with the home side, including old boys Mike Sheron and Ashley Ward, equally demoralised by a poor run of results, the game was never likely to be inspiring. The Blues have rarely lost to Norwich. When they fell behind well into the second half, I was beginning to feel personally responsible. Fitzroy Simpson rescued us all by blasting the equaliser following a free-kick, but the highlight of the match was the final whistle.

City's relatively long Cup runs had left them with a backlog of midweek fixtures. It was hard for me to find either the time or the motivation to attend all of these games. The decision to avoid the home match against Chelsea proved well founded. Despite a smooth strike from Gaudino giving City the lead, the Blues lost 2-1. Gaudino scored another fine goal at Everton, but some odd refereeing sent City's evening downhill. Phelan was sent off for kicking the ball away, when it seemed clear that he had not heard a whistle. After Limpar had hurled himself horizontally in the general vicinity of Vonk, referee Willard adjudged that a penalty kick was a sane response, and City had to settle for a 1-1 draw.

Now reduced to sixteenth place, with the points gap to purgatory narrowing, the Blues played host to fellow-strugglers Sheffield Wednesday on 18 March 1995. Midway through the first half, City trailed 2-0, courtesy of goals from Whittingham and Hyde, the second following an undignified scramble prompted by Waddle's cross. Relegation seemed more than a remote possibility in the moments leading up to a Rösler header that raised spirits before half-time. In the second half, Paul Walsh headed a City equaliser from Beagrie's cross, and with seven minutes remaining, a telling pass by Simpson led to a winning goal by Rösler. Rösler's sharpness remained relatively undiminished, contrasting with the stark drop in form exhibited by others, and the inadequate consistency of Summerbee.

The Blues leapt to twelfth place, but doggedly returned to the relegation fight by losing three consecutive matches in London, at Wimbledon, Crystal Palace and Spurs. Rösler scored the only two City goals in those defeats. The Blues were back in sixteenth position at the start of a tough-looking Easter weekend.

Liverpool were the visitors to Maine Road on a bright Easter Saturday. The Blues found some of their earlier form, taking the lead after Gaudino's flick found Summerbee, who, to everyone's surprise, struck the ball perfectly. He scored his first City League goal with a low shot into the corner of the net, in front of the North Stand. Because of a neat individual effort by McManaman, the City lead lasted only five minutes, and the teams departed level at half-time. In the second half, the Blues always looked the more determined side. The winner came with 17 minutes remaining, when Maurizio Gaudino headed just inside the post from a Rösler cross, and followed through to become embroiled with some eager admirers at the front of the Umbro Stand. Strangely, Liverpool did not seriously threaten City's lead, but that didn't prevent the latter stages from being traumatic.

Thanks to the intervention of Murdoch's News International Corporation, the Ewood Park encounter with Blackburn Rovers was shifted to Tuesday, making it more difficult for me to attend. I could still have gone, but decided against it because, partly at least, of considerable feelings of ambivalence. Rovers, a team that had been so inferior to City for most of my time as a football fan, were now the only side capable of preventing yet another Championship success for *The Nation's Team*. Despite my horror at finding them in such a prominent position, I wished them to do so. I very much wished them to do so.

My paranoia had been particularly active after seeing highly dubious refereeing decisions prove to be crucial in both encounters between the two sides contesting the Championship. At *The Swamp*, Shearer's late equaliser, the kind of goal scored every week by a strong striker attacking the ball with his head, was disallowed. At Ewood Park, with Rovers leading 1-0, a quite extraordinary decision had led to Berg being sent off and a penalty kick awarded, after what looked remarkably like a rather good and very clean tackle. Had it not been for those two decisions, Blackburn would have been clear at the top, and a City win would have caused little concern. There was another aspect to consider: City still required points to remain in the Premier League.

The match was played on a heavy surface, with plenty of rain to continually top up the mud. The surface may have been partially responsible for the Coton kicking error that led to Blackburn's first goal, after seven minutes. If you were going to miskick against the Blackburn of this era, you didn't want the ball to go straight to Alan Shearer. That's what happened, and Shearer returned it directly into the empty net. After half an hour, referee Keith Cooper awarded City a mysterious penalty and Keith Curle equalised. Before half-time, City old boy Colin Hendry restored the Blackburn lead with a shot that found its way through a crowd of players, and deflected in off Coton. This should have given heart to Rovers, but in the second half, City took complete control. As the Blues began to cut through the hesitant home defence, Rösler stroked in a second equaliser with a careful side-foot shot from outside the penalty area. Flowers was able to deny Flitcroft, but after Summerbee's shot was saved, Walsh followed up to put City ahead for the first time. After a Quinn header had released him, Flitcroft scored what should have been City's fourth, but a bizarre refereeing decision prevented it. Mr Cooper blew his whistle just before Flitcroft's strike in order to book a Rovers player. Flitcroft again found the net with a header, only for a marginal offside decision to deny him once more. Rösler struck the crossbar after finding himself clear, and Blackburn simply fell apart. Not only did City hold on for a 3-2 win, but they should really have won more emphatically.

City's impressive Easter proved to be their salvation. A goalless home draw with Newcastle was followed by a 1-1 result at Aston Villa, where Ehiogu got away with a goal scored with the hand, but Rösler equalised. With the Blues suffering a goalkeeping crisis, the 42-year-old John Burridge, he of the astonishing pre-match hyperactive warm-up, played in the last three matches of the season. The draw at Villa was followed by a 1-0 defeat at Forest, but City were mathematically safe from relegation before their final League game of the season, at home to QPR on Sunday, 14 May 1995. For the benefit of Sky TV, all of the Premier League matches were moved to Sunday.

City's final League match was a strange occasion because practically everybody's attention was elsewhere. It was the day when Blackburn won the Premier League title, despite losing at Anfield, because West Ham United had the audacity to get a draw against *The Nation's Team*.

It was a quiet Maine Road crowd, not helped by a less than emphatic kick by Burridge that led to an opening goal for Ferdinand. Quinn scored, following a neat turn, to make the half-time score level. This added to the improvement in the atmosphere, which had been prompted by news of a West Ham goal and a lead for Blackburn. Things took a turn for the worse in the second half as Dichio restored the QPR lead and *The Nation's Team* equalised.

When Gaudino toppled over with 10 minutes of the match remaining, Keith Curle was able to make the score at Maine Road 2-2 from a fortunate penalty kick. An eerie silence descended in the closing stages: a late Liverpool goal meant that Blackburn were now losing, and just one more goal at Upton Park could deny them a deserved Championship. There were many surrogate Blackburn fans in Maine Road, and an eighty-ninth minute winner by Ferdinand seemed of little importance to many of them, including me. The City match finished with the teams trailing off largely ignored. After a pause, with no further information coming through, I decided to leave, and it was outside the ground that I heard the loudest cheer of the afternoon. Ian Bishop, Trevor Morley and their pals had managed to deny Mr Ferguson his Championship. The cheery Scot took the setback with his customary grace and humility.

There was some consolation to be gleaned from the fact that *The Nation's Team* had fallen at the last hurdle in both the League and the FA Cup, but this hardly made amends for yet another season of almost relentless gloom. City's Premier League survival had been only narrowly achieved. The Blues finished in seventeenth place, with just Aston Villa between them and the four relegated teams. Survival was largely due to the 15 League goals of Uwé Rösler. The Francis Lee revival bandwagon was stalled. It was about to shoot off in reverse and plunge over a cliff.

Season 1995/96: *Maybe You're Gonna be the one that Saves Me, or maybe not*

The traditional Manchester City song, with its player promise to 'carry on the glory of the City, keeping City in first place', and its claim that City players are 'the boys who are playing to win', and that 'the boys in blue never give in', clearly no longer stood up to scrutiny. Under the Francis Lee regime, we were in for a spot of modernising. It was *New Franny, New City*.

For a while, the teams made their dramatic entrance to the accompaniment of 'Also Sprach Zarathustra', the theme for '2001: A Space Odyssey'. If the date was a reference to the estimated time of arrival of City's next trophy, it was wildly optimistic. Eventually, this too was dumped in favour of the most famous musical connection to Manchester City. Yes, the Blues decided to make their entrance to 'Eat Y'self Fitter' by The Fall.

Sadly, this is not true. Noel and Liam Gallagher were the latest in a long line of Blue double acts, and their tunes were earmarked for use as team inspiration. 'Wonderwall' was given a brief spell as the actual running out song, but the more rousing 'Roll With

It' was ultimately adopted. The consolation prize for 'Wonderwall' was to be chosen by the Faithful as the tune for a new song that epitomised season 1995/96. The words were:

'Maybe, you're gonna be the one that saves me,
And after all, you're my Alan Ball.'

The mere thought of large, tuneless men striving to attain and hold the notes, veins bulging from temples and neck muscles strained to bursting, brings tears to the eyes. In retrospect, the comic value could have much the same effect. This was to be the most important City season of the decade, and it all went horribly wrong.

The summer of 1995 actually began quite well. It was amusing to hear the RAGS in and out of the media establishment bemoaning the way that Blackburn Rovers had *bought* the League title, and suggesting that it was terrible how Newcastle were attempting to do the same, as if Old Trafford were the last bastion of the Corinthian spirit. What really upset them was that Blackburn's return on their massive investment had been so much quicker than *The Nation's Team* could manage. Mr Ferguson's prolonged and gargantuan spending spree took several years to yield rewards. His predecessors had achieved little return on their considerable outlay. Kenny Dalglish landed a League Championship within a couple of seasons. RAGS assume that the League itself only exists for the greater glorification of their club, and that it is tantamount to treason for upstarts like Blackburn to usurp their rightful place in the European Cup. The standing of this competition, now called the Champion's League, has been considerably diminished by the dubious attempts to favour teams from those nations with the greatest televisual value, such as England. UEFA appears to be edging towards a media-inspired league, exclusive to clubs which are considered attractive. They haven't quite worked out how to completely remove the threat of teams like Spartak Moscow – who comfortably saw off Blackburn Rovers – but they are working on it. The Russian winter league break, during which time western clubs can sign all of the best players, certainly helps in this respect.

I have always thought that there are Eastern European bargains to be had, particularly in view of the astronomical fees being paid for rather mediocre home-grown talent. I was hoping that City would have the foresight to make a modest investment into scouting in some of the less exotic areas of Europe, prompted by recollection of Kaziu Deyna, the 1986 Russian World Cup team, and a memorable Dynamo Tblisi side that once ripped an English team to shreds. I forget which team – West Ham? I dreamed of some young, hidden gem being discovered, brought to Maine Road to grace the sacred turf, and leading us into the promised land. In 1995 the chance was there. A 22-year-old Georgian playing for Dynamo Tblisi was spotted by the Blues and brought to Maine Road for a fee of £2 million. His name was, of course, Georgiou Kinkladze, and his favourite dish, so we are told, is spicy chicken and walnuts, which as a devotee of chilli peppers, sounds pretty good to me. Kinkladze was virtually unheard of in this country, with only a tasty goal scored in Georgia's 5-0 win against Wales to offer a hint of his ability. This chapter should be all about the incredible talent possessed by Kinkladze: the way he could exert control over the ball whilst twisting and turning in the tightest of situations; the penchant for mesmeric runs, leaving confusion in his wake; the way that opponents and, alas, colleagues alike, were induced into a near-hypnotic state, rooted to the spot in awe. The reason why the story of season 1995/96 is not entirely about Gio Kinkladze is because, unfortunately, football is a team game. For exceptional individuals to flourish there must be some rudimentary organisation to the rest of the team. It is a lasting testament to Alan Ball's ability as a coach and manager that, despite having at his disposal the most gifted player to wear a Manchester City shirt in at least 20 years, he managed to preside over City's worst start to a season in all that time. He ultimately cost the Blues a place in the Premier League, just when such a place was financially at its most crucial. I wonder if there is anybody still getting wear out of their *Alan Ball is a football genius* T-shirts?

I'm digressing into a rant. I'm afraid that Mr Ball can have that effect. Let's get back to the beginning. The other reason why the summer of 1995 began quite well was that Brian Horton's association with the club ended. I had not been in favour of his appointment, and I was not in any way disappointed to see him leave. Contrary to the general impression created in the media, Horton was given a reasonable amount of time to demonstrate his abilities. Two consecutive narrow escapes from relegation were the result.

I awaited the appointment of somebody with a proven track record. The summer stretched on. The Test Matches against the West Indies were top quality, with a particularly splendid one at Old Trafford. There were plenty of distractions, and I enjoyed not having a constant football-associated gloom surrounding my waking moments. But in the meantime there was no news from Maine Road. Transfers were taking place elsewhere. Others were making plans but Manchester City were drifting towards the start of a new season with no manager and, apart from the little-known Kinkladze, no new players. It started to get a little worrying. I followed events on the Manchester City Supporters world wide web page (accessible at work) and some of the suggestions were disturbing. Having said that, none were as alarming as the actual choice. It became apparent that nobody wanted the job. I was in favour of Martin O'Neill. Honestly. But nobody asked me.

The announcement came, with the pre-season already upon us: Alan Ball. *Alan Ball!* I couldn't believe it. I could have accepted a young manager of limited or even no experience, although I would have preferred an experienced man of proven abilities. Instead we got an experienced man who, despite ample opportunity, had precious little to show for it. His supporters, if there are any, point to the fact that Southampton survived relegation after Ball's mid-season arrival in the previous season. There was also a short-lived promotion for Portsmouth. That was the best case to be made. Even worse, City had to pay Southampton compensation. I am not being wise after the event. I was utterly disheartened that Francis Lee appointed one of his old pals as manager rather than trying to be more forward-looking. I hoped to be proved wrong. Ball had been a good footballer, but we needed a good manager, not a good ex-footballer.

In his defence, Ball had little time to make an impact on the playing staff. Welsh international Kit Symons came to Maine Road from Portsmouth as part of a £1.5 million deal involving the opposite trip for Carl Griffiths and Fitzroy Simpson. Somewhat stranger was the deal early in the season to send Paul Walsh and £400,000 to Portsmouth, in order to secure the services of Gerry Creaney. With Tony Coton being a long-term casualty, German ex-international Eike Immel was acquired for a modest fee. We all assumed that Immel, who was a good shot stopper but ill-suited to deal with either crosses or repeated back-passes, was a temporary cover for Coton, but when Coton recovered, Ball stuck with Immel. Eventually, Coton moved across to *The Nation's Team* for a derisory sum, with a view to keeping their bench warm, despite protestations about wanting first team football. It was no great surprise that another German, Gaudino, did not return for the new season.

On the positive side, I was pleased to see Asa Hartford back at Maine Road, as Ball's assistant. He was one of my favourite City players, and although I know that doesn't necessarily make him good management material, I would rather see a good ex-City player than a good ex-elsewhere player given a chance.

Not surprisingly, most pundits included City amongst their three teams for the drop before a ball had been kicked in earnest. A studious analysis of the fixture list suggested to me that the first three games were of prime importance for the Blues. After that, things became considerably tougher. The first opponents were Tottenham, splendidly dumped by Klinsmann. Following on were trips to Coventry and QPR, both likely strugglers. The Blues needed early points before encountering the likes of Arsenal and Newcastle. We badly needed to hit the ground running. Instead, we just hit the ground.

Ball's team selection for his Maine Road debut, on 19 August 1995, was further hampered by injury to Keith Curle, but a rusty Steve Lomas was fit to make a welcome return to the side. I travelled to Maine Road with low expectations, and came away no clearer as to City's likely fate for the season. Sheringham gave Spurs a first-half lead, heading in from a position of some isolation. The City defenders were far too polite to intrude on his personal space.

Soon after half-time, Lomas drifted a high ball into the Spurs penalty area. Whilst Walker busied himself with an attempt to capture an imaginary ball, Rösler was free to head the real one into an empty net. The final score was an inconclusive 1-1. I was not too disappointed because of the instant impression made by Kinkladze, who broke all recent tradition at Maine Road by playing the entire match without once giving away possession to the opposing team. It was unheard of.

The show moved on to Highfield Road, where a large and expectant contingent of the Faithful awaited, still clutching their pink tickets. An early match against Coventry City is a good barometer for the season. If you are worse than Coventry City, then you know it's going to be a long, hard season, because finishing below Coventry usually means relegation. Over the summer, Ron Atkinson had amply demonstrated his ability for reducing the size of a Chairman's wad, and there were Coventry hopes for better than the usual one place above relegation. By the end of the evening, those hopes had been encouraged by a feeble City display. The Blues should have been trailing by more than new signing Paul Telfer's early goal, but when, with eight minutes to go,

Rösler headed in Summerbee's teasing cross, it seemed that a fortunate point might be rescued. Of course, it wasn't. The traditional late Dion Dublin goal saw to that.

Three days later, City completed a poor first week by losing 1-0 at Loftus Road. The combative young midfield player, Michael Brown, made a mark on his debut by getting sent off after coming on as a substitute. Up and down the land, referees could be seen brandishing red cards like deranged poker players, amidst claims that they were only obeying orders. I seem to have heard that excuse before somewhere. I doubt that there was really a FIFA directive instructing referees to behave as if incapable of rational thought. I could be wrong.

Meanwhile, Alan Ball was already in the midst of an early crisis. His response was to bring Brown and young defender Rae Ingram in from the start of the next game, which was at home to Everton. Walsh was omitted and sold, and Quinn was chosen to partner Rösler. Another youngster, David Kerr, also made an appearance as substitute. It made no difference. City lost 2-0, with Kanchelskis enjoying an evening of unimpeded freedom down the right flank.

Ball seemed to have acquired the knack of getting the worst out of his players. Flitcroft looked a pale imitation of his former self, Rösler was beginning to assume a sulky look and concentrate his efforts on falling over, and the City defence played as if they had not been introduced. In amongst the debris was a bemused Kinkladze, who had yet to realise that his colleagues had not a fraction of his close control and could not fathom his requirements. City looked as though they did not train. There were no apparent plans at set pieces, which were generally taken by Kinkladze, with nobody else seemingly able to communicate with him. It took the Georgian maestro some time to adjust to the limitations of his colleagues, and to realise that the best option was usually the solo one. He kept on trying to play neat little one-twos, but they generally ended up as mere ones.

The next match was moved to a Sunday by Sky TV, which meant that I could not attend it. I had to settle for watching in a nearly deserted London public house as City took on Arsenal at Maine Road. Again the Blues seemed bereft of any ideas or strategy. Arsenal simply lacked ambition. The game was heading for a dull draw until Ian Wright's last-minute winning goal. After four consecutive defeats, and only one point and two goals to show from their first five outings, City were already beginning to lose touch at the foot of the table. A trip to Newcastle was not helpful. Creaney scored a debut headed goal, but by then the Blues were trailing 3-0 and down to 10 men after the dismissal of Edghill, who was more than a little unlucky. The second bookable offence, a challenge on Gillespie adjudged as a penalty, looked pretty benign to me.

After a morale-boosting 0-0 draw at Wycombe in the Coca-Cola Cup, City played host to bogey-team Middlesbrough and their popular manager, Bryan Robson. The outcome was another dreadful afternoon's football and a 1-0 defeat. This was followed by a trip to Nottingham to take on Frank Clark's Forest. City lost 3-0, with Ian Brightwell being bizarrely sent off for two yellow cards in quick succession. The second offence was to kick the ball away approximately as far as he could comfortably spit.

By now Beagrie had made a brief but unsuccessful attempt to return from injury. City were soon to lose his services for the rest of this and most of the following season. It wasn't too long before Richard Edghill went the same way. Keith Curle had returned to the centre of the City defence, but injuries and suspensions were making for a highly variable back four. The midfield of Lomas and Flitcroft seemed unable to cope, and Summerbee's inconsistency had earned him the honour of personally directed booing at home matches, and temporary omission from the team. City were a laughing-stock.

Only 11,474 turned up for the return match with Wycombe Wanderers, when the Blues registered their first win of the season, a resounding 4-0 victory. But things were so bad that most City fans would probably have settled for the 1-0 defeat at *The Swamp*, a few days later. In fact, Niall Quinn had chances to improve on that. Needless to say, he didn't take them. After nine League matches, the Blues still had only one point. This magnificent return was doubled in a goalless draw at Maine Road against Leeds United, who seemed to be suffering from the same lethargy.

As October drew to a close, the Blues faced the prospect of two consecutive trips to Anfield. In the Coca-Cola Cup game, City were thrashed 4-0. At least, I thought, they could do no worse in the League match three days later. As usual, I underestimated them. Liverpool won the second game 6-0. I attended neither match. For some reason my enthusiasm for away matches was waning.

Terry Phelan became the latest City player to be transferred. He moved to Chelsea for £750,000, leaving City without any player happy to be operating on the left side of the pitch. It would be superfluous to point out that the Blues once more lost a considerable amount of money on the deal.

On 4 November 1995, the team nearest to the Blues, newly promoted Bolton Wanderers, came to Maine Road. It represented a last realistic chance for City to kick-start their season into action. A couple of points from their first 11 League matches represented the worst start to a season in the club's history. A home defeat by one of the teams closest to touching distance would surely have induced a rapid end to Alan Ball's spell at City. He had certainly made a most dramatic impact on the players, and it is hard to see how anybody could conceivably have done much worse.

City earned a reprieve by a first League win, against a team who were also somewhat demoralised. The only goal, from an unlikely source, was the result of some silky touchline skills demonstrated by Niall Quinn, who found Kinkladze in space. The Georgian, in turn, laid on the opportunity for Summerbee to score a very similar goal to his only previous Maine Road effort, a shot struck hard and low into the corner of the net, in front of the North Stand.

Further encouraging signs were provided by the first point achieved away from home, at Sheffield Wednesday. This was despite a harsh penalty award against Keith Curle, who was punished for close contact with a forward. Nobody appealed, but the referee saw fit to give a penalty, and City were trailing until a second-half header by Steve Lomas rescued a point. After that match the Blues were still propping up the table, but a midweek 1-0 home win against Wimbledon, courtesy of a last-gasp deflected winner by Niall Quinn, was enough to take City up to eighteenth place.

Three days later the Blues were back at Maine Road to face a resurgent Aston Villa. There was some optimism in the air. Before the kick-off, the legendary Bert Trautmann, a man who didn't let a trivial thing like a broken neck get in the way of his goalkeeping duties, officially opened the new Kippax Stand. The City players must still have been admiring the new stand when Villa burst through in the first minute, but Tommy Johnson couldn't apply the finish, despite getting round Immel. The Blues were, however, improving, and Kinkladze was beginning to make opposing teams suffer. The distraction of a Kinkladze run created an opportunity for Flitcroft, but the shot was saved by Bosnich, and the follow-up shot by Rösler was deflected against the post. Another Kinkladze run won a rare City penalty, but Keith Curle struck his shot comfortably wide. The crowd were in a relatively forgiving mood as City were certainly matching their higher-placed opponents.

Immel was forced into a good save by Milosovic as the second half progressed, and it looked as though we would have to settle for a point. With five minutes remaining, there was one of those rare moments when supporting Manchester City seems like a sane thing to do. Kinkladze played the ball to the feet of Quinn, who held on to it for precious moments as Kinkladze made his run into the penalty area. At precisely the right time, Quinn executed a brilliant back flick into the path of Kinkladze, who beat Bosnich with a cross shot, and found himself embroiled in a small gathering of manic Mancunians.

This was still Manchester City. There was, therefore, sufficient time remaining for Immel to flap fruitlessly at the ball, providing the opportunity for McGrath to direct a shot goalwards. Fortunately, Ian Brightwell saved the day with a header that redirected the ball over the bar to safety. City were out of the relegation zone for the first time, and Alan Ball was named Manager of the Month for November. The spectacular recovery even stretched into the start of December. City took advantage of an out of sorts Leeds United to secure their first away win of the season. Rösler struck the crossbar with a first-half header, but substitute Gerry Creaney was more successful with the second-half opportunity provided by a Steve Lomas cross. Manchester City leapt to fifteenth position, and that was as high as they managed all season.

At Middlesbrough, a brilliant individual goal by Kinkladze seemed set to maintain the City momentum, but by half-time the home side had scored three times, and the Blues went on to lose 4-1. Reality had re-emerged. Sky TV caused me the inconvenience of a Monday night trip for the next home match – against Nottingham Forest, whose European successes were all the rage. I was rewarded for my efforts by the first Rösler goal in sixteen Premier League matches, but this was a patchy display by the Blues. Quite how Jason Lee contrived not to score, only he will know. I did not realise that it was possible to miss in so many different ways in the same match. One wasted opportunity, after Immel had mistakenly kicked the ball straight to him, was particularly impressive. In the second half, Stuart Pearce struck a shot against the City post to confirm the Forest reluctance to actually score, but the inevitable equaliser was eventually scrambled in by Kevin Campbell.

The Blues were again in disappointing form when Chelsea came to Maine Road on

23 December 1995. City were still finding goals extremely difficult to come by, and the one goal by Chelsea was sufficient for all the points. The Dane Ronnie Eklund made his debut on-loan appearance in this match, as a substitute. Eklund had been crucial to Southampton's survival in the previous season, during a similar loan spell. Indeed, he had scored twice at Maine Road. The City loan period was far less successful. It did not seem to be the same player.

A dismal Christmas was confirmed by a 2-0 defeat at Blackburn where, just to rub it in, David Batty scored a rare goal with an unstoppable long-range shot. City sank back into the relegation zone.

City's inability to persuade a football into the opponents' goal led to a series of anxiety-ridden matches at home and on their travels. They were incapable of making any game safe until the referee had decided to put everybody out of their misery by blowing the whistle for full-time. A typical example was on New Year's Day 1996, at home to West Ham United. Niall Quinn profited from a Rösler flick to score the opening goal, but with 15 minutes remaining, Iain Dowie, a man who has taken a liking to Manchester City defences over the years, grabbed an equaliser that the Blues could ill-afford. On this occasion, City responded to retake the lead with a scrambled Quinn goal. They earned the precious three points, but nobody could claim to have enjoyed the experience.

Given the perilous League situation, the FA Cup could be little more than a distraction. City were drawn away to First Division Leicester City in the third round, and I took the opportunity to revisit Filbert Street, entering through what looked uncannily like someone's house, and leaving totally disorientated. The match itself was poor, and City were grateful for wasteful finishing by Iwan Roberts, who squandered the best chance late in the game.

Before the replay, City suffered another away defeat in the League, this time 1-0 at White Hart Lane. There was an unseemly scramble for points developing at the foot of the Premier League table. Only three points separated five teams, including City, who were still just within the relegation zone, and the Blues faced three consecutive matches against relegation rivals. The FA Cup replay was therefore a welcome relief from more stressful matches, and it proved to be City's biggest win of the season. The new Leicester manager, Martin O'Neill, was facing increasing pressure already from disgruntled fans, and his team's performance at Maine Road did little to improve his standing. Having said that, Kinkladze was in such inspired form that there was nothing Leicester could do to stop him. It might have been a good idea for someone to challenge Rösler, who opened the scoring with a header from Kinkladze's free-kick, but the Georgian's solo goal, following a run beginning from deep within his own half, was clearly something beyond the experience of most mortal football players. A succession of defenders were so hypnotised that they failed to make a challenge until it was too late. Kinkladze calmly side-footed the ball into the corner of the net, and City had the rare luxury of a two-goal lead, after only 18 minutes play. In the second half, Niall Quinn scored a third City goal from close-range, and Lomas added the fourth with a formidable strike, after another Kinkladze run. Near the end, Kinkladze again bamboozled the Leicester defence and set up an opportunity for substitute Creaney to score the fifth City goal. Gerry Creaney, who could well have the same dietician as Gazza, did not look capable of lasting for a whole match, or running about for very long, but when the ball came to him in the penalty area, he seemed to have a happy knack of re-directing it into goal. The game finished 5-0.

The serious business resumed on 20 January 1996, with a fateful match against Coventry. Despite their big-spending and glamorous management team, Coventry were, as usual, down with the strugglers. It was a match that City needed to win. Quite how much they needed to win did not become fully apparent until May. The two sides had been drawn together in the FA Cup fourth round, but there was no doubting which match was of the greater importance. It was this one.

'Match of the Day' sent the cameras in order to allow Barry Davies free range to bemoan his lot and complain about the lack of entertainment for the neutral. A neutral had no business at Maine Road on that day. Two teams were playing for their clubs' survival. The result was all-important. Twice in the first half, Niall Quinn wasted good chances. Temporarily at least, the goalscoring knack had completely deserted Quinn. The touch was still there, and he was creating opportunities for others, but the goals would not come. Already a popular figure at Maine Road, Gordon Strachan endeared himself further to the crowd by abusing his position as substitute to issue management instructions up and down the touchline. The half ended without a goal.

At half-time, Ball introduced new signing Martin 'Buster' Phillips into the action. Demonstrating an eccentric sense of perspective, Ball had greeted the arrival of Phillips, signed for £500,000 from Exeter, with the claim that the youngster would be the first £10 million player. Phillips did liven things up moderately on the left wing by running at defenders, but the breakthrough came when Quinn controlled the ball on his chest, and crossed overhead for Rösler to score with a glancing header. The German considered the goal so important that in his celebratory run he took two shirts off, his sky-blue top and the black T-shirt underneath. The business of re-clothing seemed to take some time.

The goal prompted a previously apathetic Coventry to attack. Whelan should have equalised but missed. Unfortunately, the irritating Dublin did level the scores with a header after 66 minutes, considerably earlier than usual. City had the better late chances, but failed to take them. It was an ominously poor result for the Blues.

Some compensation was obtained from a trip to Southampton, where City went behind to a skimmer by Shipperley in another relegation battle. The match featured the debut of Nigel Clough, signed for City from Liverpool for a fee of £1.5 million. I always liked Clough as a player, and this looked liked a good signing to me. It just goes to show.

Clough was involved in the late City attack that led to a vital Rösler equaliser at The Dell, and he squeezed a shot in to give the Blues the lead in the third of their relegation showdowns, at Maine Road against QPR. A second-half Symons header earned City a two-goal lead which, unusually, they maintained. Despite the fact that there was hardly a bad tackle in the game, referee Graham Poll booked six Rangers players and sent one off late in the match. The balding German left-back Michael Frontzeck had a relatively uneventful but impressive debut for City.

The FA Cup fourth-round tie at Highfield Road, on 7 February 1996, had already been called off once because of a frozen pitch. I was, therefore, a little surprised to learn that it was to take place on a bitterly cold evening, when a trudge through considerable quantities of snow was required to get to the ground. This was one of the few matches of recent years when I was totally convinced that City would not lose. The reason for this is quite straightforward. The fifth-round draw had already been made, offering the winners the prospect of a trip to *The Swamp* as guests of *The Nation's Team*. The tie had already been chosen for live coverage by the BBC. I knew that City would be unable to resist the opportunity of again humiliating themselves, and me, in front of the nation's terrestrial television viewers. The Blues were going to win through this tie. There was no doubt about it.

It was somewhat contrary to expectation, therefore, when Noel Whelan, keeping his feet on the frozen swamp of Highfield Road, scored after only two minutes. However, Busst contrived to direct a Rösler cross into his own net for City's equalising goal, and the teams reached half-time on level terms. Just about everyone seemed to be fair game for the snowball bombardment maintained by the Faithful, although Gordon Strachan attracted particular attention. With nine minutes remaining, City took the lead for the first time. Steve Lomas had three attempts at a cross. His final effort was deflected into the path of Flitcroft, who volleyed through a narrow gap, beating Ogrizovic. Incredibly, City nursed their lead with maturity and composure, maintaining possession and denying the home side any opportunity for salvation. With no alarms whatsoever, injury time was reached. Coventry were awarded possession by referee Gerald Ashby, who penalised Flitcroft for seeking to shield the ball near one of the corner flags, in precisely the manner that is seen up and down the country every week. City were taken aback by the apparent emergence of a new rule, and Coventry took the free-kick quickly. The home side managed to mount only one attack after Flitcroft's goal, but that was enough. Much to the delight of Barry Davies, who commentated on the highlights, Strachan played his part in setting up the goal scored, inevitably, by Dublin. There was just enough time for Rösler to get through on goal at the other end, at which point the final whistle was blown. I knew that City would win the replay. The whole charade was simply to force me into another midweek motorway trip.

I was barred from the North Stand for the replay because of the anticipated hordes of Coventry City fans. Instead, I sat for the first time in the new Kippax Stand. Although the seat, right in the Umbro Stand corner, offered a poor view, it was good enough to see that there were no Coventry fans in M-Block of the North Stand, or in N-Block, or indeed in the majority of the North Stand. In fact, the entire contingent was huddled into half a block.

Clough gave City a first-half lead from close-range, and Niall Quinn added a neat second goal, finding the corner of the net with a low shot, early in the second half. I knew that City would win, but I hoped to be spared extra time, penalties, and arriving home in the middle of the night. When Dion Dublin scooped an easy chance against the bar things looked promising. Unfortunately, the rebound came straight back to him, and he scored to set up some fretful closing minutes. For once, City spared me the full act, and held on to win 2-1. Habit meant that I was tempted to make an attempt to get to the fifth-round game, but it simply wasn't possible. The queues were long and early, and I had to go to work the following day, 105 miles away.

The televised FA Cup derby match was only four days later. I expected City to lose, and braced myself for the televisual torture in a calm and relaxed state. *The Nation's Team* didn't look terribly impressive in the early stages, but I have learnt from bitter experience to take little notice of such details. After 12 minutes, a goal kick by Immel was instantly controlled by Kinkladze, who delivered a perfect ball through to Rösler. *The blond one* rushed out of goal, but Rösler scored with a delightful chip, and City had the lead. The Blues looked refreshingly organised and determined, whilst their opponents seemed rather aimless and confused, as if disorientated by a change in the script. There was some pressure applied leading up to half-time, but nothing terribly serious. And then, after 39 minutes, referee Alan Wilkie took it upon himself to re-shape the afternoon's proceedings. A left-wing corner flew over everybody in the penalty area and away to safety. I knew instantly exactly what had happened. The referee had awarded a penalty. I couldn't see any reason for it; there didn't have to be a reason. This was a Manchester derby match.

I have come to expect this sort of occurrence. In fact, instead of prompting me to rage at the television and bemoan the ill-fortune of my team, it was strangely comforting. It is reassuring for paranoid cynics like myself to have such incidents laid bare to the scrutiny of millions of television viewers. The replay revealed that two players, Frontzeck and *the French one*, had made some sort of physical contact prior to the ball disappearing way over their heads. This was the cause of Mr Wilkie's decision. Nobody else noticed anything amiss, and no member of the home side appealed for anything. That says it all.

The consequences of this decision should have been sweeping. An average of at least five penalty kicks for each side in every subsequent match could be anticipated. For some reason, this has not occurred. I cannot imagine why. *The French one* scored the penalty kick, and it was a different match. Everyone now *knew* who would win. The actual winning goal, by Sharpe, was late in arriving, but it was no less inevitable for that. *The Nation's Team* surprised nobody by appearing in the FA Cup Final once again.

City emerged from their little Cup run with credit, but running out of League matches to secure their future. In amongst the FA Cup activity, there was another away defeat, 2-0 at Everton, featuring a sending off for Frontzeck. He was having a strange couple of weeks.

On 24 February 1996, League-leaders Newcastle United brought their six points lead, with a game in hand, to Maine Road. City required the points at least as urgently as Keegan's team. It turned out to be a thriller for the neutral, but of little value to either team.

Scott Hiley, a player who actually looked like he belonged at left-back, made an impressive debut in this match. He barely managed another couple of appearances before joining the lengthy long-term injury list. The goals began to arrive after 15 minutes, when Nigel Clough's shot was inadvertently deflected in by Niall Quinn. This prompted City into believing that a win was possible, and Kinkladze began to work his magic. He made a number of captivating runs, one of which was finished off with a shot fired over Srnicek and into the North Stand, flicking the crossbar on its way. Newcastle, of course, had opportunities. Several times, Ginola cut in from the left wing to shoot right-footed. Every time the manoeuvre seemed to catch the City defence by surprise, despite its repetitiveness. City looked set for a half-time lead, but just before the break, Newcastle's recent Columbian signing, Faustino Asprilla, accepted the ball from Albert and found the Belgian defender with a return pass that split the City defence asunder. Albert finished the move with a first-time shot that Immel could not reach.

City began the second half reasonably well. There was an astonishing run by Kinkladze, but after outwitting three defenders, he was foiled by a fourth. A running battle between wrestling fan Keith Curle and the scowling Asprilla culminated in the Columbian quite blatantly felling Curle, with an emphatic swing of his elbow into the City captain's face. It was a clear red-card offence. Referee Martin Bodenham either didn't see it or thought otherwise. The presence of the 'Match of the Day' cameras ensured that Asprilla received his punishment later, but City's cause would have been much better served by an earlier response from the match referee.

Kinkladze took off towards the Umbro Stand on another of his runs, emerging in the penalty area. At first Srnicek was able to thwart him, but Kinkladze crossed to the far post, where Quinn found the net with a header from the narrowest of angles. In a frenzied atmosphere, it was central defender Albert who again played a prominent role in the second Newcastle equaliser. His shot was blocked by Immel, but Asprilla, who should not have been on the pitch, followed up to score his first goal for Newcastle, with 20 minutes of the match remaining. The pessimists amongst us suspected the worst, but within six minutes City regained the lead when the famous Newcastle defensive frailty was demonstrated to the full. Lomas struck his shot across goal, and the Newcastle defenders simply watched as Rösler, lurking at the far post, sneaked in to score. Unfortunately, this lead lasted only four minutes. An Albert shot deflected in off Quinn for the final equaliser.

Quinn finished 1-1 on deflections.

We were denied a perfect finale, and goal of the century contender when Kinkladze shot over the Newcastle crossbar after extracting himself from a posse of defenders. The match ended in chaos as Newcastle survived a possible Peacock handball in their penalty area, and play continued beyond the final whistle. Asprilla and Curle failed to hear the whistle and engaged in another touching dance routine, which was somewhat petulantly ended by a mini-head-butt by Asprilla. His fuse appeared far too short for the English Premier League, or, indeed, any kind of physical contact sport. Thanks to the three points for a win system, intended to encourage attacking play, a final score of 3-3 was of little use to either camp. The Blues remained in the relegation zone.

City edged out of the bottom three with a 1-1 home draw against Blackburn Rovers, despite falling behind to a second-half Shearer goal. Rösler contrived to miss a heading chance that appeared easier to score. The ball struck the inside of the post, ran along the line, and popped out off Tim Flowers' knee, much to his and everyone's amazement. To their credit, City continued to press, and an equaliser came via the head of Steve Lomas, following a cross by Rösler.

The Blues were still proving a soft touch far too frequently on their travels. At Highbury, Arsenal were completely dominant. The scoreline of 3-1 flattered City, who gained a possible lifeline when Creaney brought the score back to 2-1, but there was no real threat of a recovery. A midweek trip to Chelsea proved slightly more profitable. Gullit fired Chelsea ahead midway through the first half, with a shot from outside the penalty area, and it looked like business as usual. City battled back to score through Nigel Clough before half-time, and the match ended in a 1-1 draw.

The home game against Southampton, on 16 March 1996, could hardly have been more important. With QPR looking set to join struggling Bolton amongst the relegated, City were fighting primarily against Southampton and Coventry City to avoid occupation of the third place. There were other possible contenders, but both teams knew that a win in this game would be a significant boost to their chances. The match was won by Kinkladze in the first half. The warm-up was a shot full against the Southampton crossbar. The Georgian genius then gave City the lead with a rare tap-in, after a Clough shot had been saved by Beasant. But the real moment to treasure was yet to come. Picking the ball up well outside the Saints penalty area, with the defence all back in position, Kinkladze ran straight for goal. He managed to pass inside one defender and between two others before executing an exquisite flick over the prostrate and bemused Beasant, who had been induced to go to ground prematurely. I don't think that I have ever seen a better goal. Surely it had to be worthy of three points. City led 2-0 at half-time.

The second half increased in tension as the Blues failed to make much of an impression attacking the North Stand goal, and the Southampton substitute, Gordon Watson, began to make an impact at the other end. Everyone's hopes sank when Watson laid on a goal chance for Tisdale, inducing panic late on. In an increasingly ragged and desperate, not to say seemingly endless, period of injury time, Dodd's cross carried through to Robinson, who controlled the ball well and struck a shot into the City net. Luckily for City, another player had been offside from the initial cross, and a reprieve was at hand. The importance of the result can be demonstrated by the fact that Watson was sent off for disputing the decision, and Le Tissier became the ninth player to receive a yellow card. It was an anxious afternoon that should have been remembered for a moment of footballing beauty, but ended up being yet another vital but narrow victory, greeted with much relief.

The win against Southampton lifted City into the apparent comfort of fifteenth position in the table and made other teams look far more at risk, but there were difficult matches ahead for the Blues. The visit to Upton Park, on 23 March 1996, did not go well. Iain Dowie scored two more goals against City. In between, Keith Curle missed a penalty won by Kinkladze and Steve Lomas was sent off following fouls on Ian Bishop and Julian Dicks. Quinn pulled one goal back after following up from a Hiley shot. This lifting of City hopes proved transitory. A Dicks thunderbolt, and a goal squeezed in by Dani, left City well beaten. This despite a superb turn and shot by Quinn in the last minute, which made the final score 4-2.

Alan Ball's final transfer activity of the season led to the departure of Flitcroft to Blackburn Rovers for £3.2 million. The deal seemed quite good financially. I know that many people were upset by Flitcroft's departure, but he had rarely been able to re-capture the form shown prior to injury. The wisdom of selling when City were in something of a crisis could certainly be questioned. A second Georgian, Mikhail Kavelashvili, was signed from Spartak Vladikavkaz for £1.4 million, after the personal recommendation of Georgiou Kinkladze. I had high hopes of Kavelashvili, a prolific goalscorer in the Russian league. I didn't realise that he would never be given a realistic chance to demonstrate his ability.

The visit to Burnden Park, to face bottom-of-the-table Bolton, was never likely to be a comfortable one. Bolton, staging a belated recovery, had won three of their previous four matches. I faced an agonising afternoon trying to keep informed on proceedings. For this, I decided to rely on Ceefax In-Vision, which promised to display latest scores at the bottom of the screen. I had tried everything to find a method that would lead to a win, but City's away form remained largely calamitous. This seemed to be working. Niall Quinn headed the Blues in front in the first minute. According to Ceefax In-Vision, City held that lead right until the 'Grandstand' final scores were emerging. The final score came through: Bolton 1, City 1. I kicked something, but I cannot remember what.

In fact, McGinlay had equalised as early as the seventy-third minute. So much for Ceefax In-Vision! In between, as I later discovered, Summerbee and, most spectacularly, Clough from only a few yards out, had wasted chances to extend City's lead. After the equaliser and a dismissal for Summerbee, it took some acrobatic saves from Immel to save even a point, but one was not sufficient.

The Easter programme was going to be vital to the outcome of City's season. City simply could not afford to lose both of their matches. That, therefore, is precisely what they did. The third Manchester derby game of the season took place at Maine Road on 6 April 1996, and seemed all set to proceed in the now customary manner when a stupid challenge by Summerbee led to a blatant early penalty kick that even I could not dispute. The City response was mildly encouraging, and Kavelashvili scored on his debut to bring City level, after Niall Quinn's header had created the chance. Whilst City were still congratulating themselves, *The Nation's Team* advanced unchallenged to restore their lead. In the second half, City continued to show spirit. Rösler, deservedly omitted from the starting line-up, came on as substitute and scored his finest ever City goal, cutting in from the left and firing emphatically past *the blond one*. It seemed that City would gain a point, which was the very least they merited. But in the last minute, a sickening long-range shot by Giggs flew into the top corner of the City net to provide absolute proof that if there is a God, then he (or she) wears, in rotation, all of the strips ever modelled by *The Nation's Team*, even the grey one.

Before the game there had been an ugly mood prevailing around Rusholme. There had been trouble in The Clarence, and when I was, unwisely, standing outside The Albert, with a number of City fans, mostly sporting colours, the police escorted a substantial number of ugly-looking tourists in red regalia right past us. There were stern and challenging looks, but nothing more serious on this occasion. A few minutes later, a dishevelled and bewildered middle-aged man sauntered by wearing only pyjamas, not even any shoes. Care in the community, I thought.

Two days later, City collapsed horribly at Wimbledon, losing 3-0 and relinquishing control over their own destiny. Even worse, City's season lay largely in the hands of Coventry City, who duly scavenged a point away to Nottingham Forest in their game in hand. They had now caught City on points and overtaken on goal difference.

With three matches remaining, City were level on points with both Coventry City and Southampton, but because of their awful goal difference, the Blues were the ones in the relegation zone. A frightened crowd assembled at Maine Road for the visit of Sheffield Wednesday. Not only did City have to win, but they needed one of the other teams to slip up. It was a scrappy match. Blinker looked the best player on view and he set up the first half's most prominent chance. This was for David Hirst, who blasted his shot over the crossbar, much to everyone's relief. In the second half, City's attacks became increasingly desperate. With 20 minutes remaining, Quinn and Phillips were sent on as substitutes. Within a minute, Quinn's cross found Rösler, who fired City ahead. Somehow, the Blues hung on to their lead, although had Pembridge squared the ball to Hirst, there would have been a simple tap-in for a Wednesday equaliser. In the closing minutes, Kinkladze, at last finding some freedom, set up a chance for Phillips, who should have eased all the tension by scoring, but instead struck his shot against the post.

The final whistle was greeted with huge relief, but any celebration was short-lived. Victories for both Southampton and Coventry saw to that. City looked to be in desperate trouble. Their penultimate match was away to Aston Villa, one of the top five sides. I know that I should have gone, but I simply could not face it. In any case, obtaining tickets when you live over a hundred miles away is far from a simple matter. The decision was flawed: listening to the commentary on Radio Five Live was far worse.

Midway through the second half, the Blues looked relegated, but a Lomas header, in-off McGrath, gave them a lead, and they were able to hold on for an unlikely and spirited win. Unfortunately, the other two sides also won. Everything would now depend on the final game of the season. City had to gain more points than either Southampton or Coventry, otherwise they were relegated. The final game for City was at home to Cup finalists Liverpool, whilst Coventry played hosts to Leeds, and Southampton to Wimbledon. The Blues looked to have the hardest task, but they did have memories of recent home wins against Liverpool to cling to. Whatever the outcome, it was always going to be a difficult Sunday afternoon.

The gods of football were frowning on City in a first half that could hardly have turned out worse. Liverpool, without really trying, took a two-goal lead that looked to have finished City off by half-time. The tone was set early on, when a McManaman cross into a City penalty area bereft of any Liverpool players, bounced into the goal off

Steve Lomas. The second goal came from a quick break. Ian Rush, playing his final League match for Liverpool, hit a shot that lacked conviction, but a truly sadistic deflection, off Keith Curle, took the ball into one corner of the City net, whilst Immel studiously guarded the other. Meanwhile, David James had been doing the hokey-cokey at regular intervals: out to claim a cross, back in having missed it. The only thing lacking was the shaking it all about. Each time, he escaped unpunished. In between the Liverpool goals, City created more chances than they normally managed in several matches. Niall Quinn directed a header off the post and James saved the follow up. Another Quinn effort flew, via the body of James, up on to the crossbar and over. The best opportunity of all was spurned by Rösler, who must have been confused by the absence of a goalkeeper. He headed wide from Quinn's cross. When Summerbee was fouled by Ruddock, it looked as though some help was at hand, but instead of a penalty, the referee decided to award a free-kick on the very edge of the penalty area. It was a typical referee's compromise decision.

At half-time most of us were willing to accept that City would be relegated. As the second half progressed, the Blues threw caution to the wind, and might well have been further punished on the break by a more motivated Liverpool team. Rösler had a shot saved and Kinkladze fired over the crossbar, but time was running out. Just when there seemed little hope remaining, the gods of football appeared to have a change of heart. Midway through the half, rumours began to circulate about scores from other matches. Wimbledon were ahead at Southampton, according to a most reliable source, presumably some bloke who couldn't hear his radio properly. With 20 minutes left, a typical Kinkladze run ended with a Ruddock challenge that the referee, somewhat charitably, interpreted as worth a penalty kick. It was about the first dubious penalty in City's favour all season. It seemed too late to matter, but Rösler converted the kick to liven up the crowd. The rumours concerning matters elsewhere were gathering momentum. I began to hope that one more City goal may yet rescue them. It wasn't long in coming. Substitute Martin Phillips crossed from the left wing, and the ball found its way through to Symons, who lashed in the equaliser. Suddenly, Maine Road was a sea of optimism. So much so that I really believed that events elsewhere must truly be in our favour. The players seemed to think so. Liverpool were generously wasteful with their opportunities as City appeared to settle for what they had. The clinching confirmation that one of our competitors for relegation must be losing came when Steve Lomas took the ball into the corner of the pitch to waste time. He successfully passed a couple of minutes. Unfortunately, I was making a crucial false assumption: that Manchester City, being an organisation with a multimillion pound turnover, was run with a modicum of professionalism. What followed from this assumption was that somebody connected with the management of the team knew the scores from The Dell and Highfield Road, since City's whole future hung on those outcomes. Surely, somebody was listening to a radio. Was that too much to ask?

In subsequent interviews Ball seemed to be encouraging us not to blame Steve Lomas. We didn't. We blamed Alan Ball. What other multimillion-pound business would have deemed it unnecessary to be in possession of such a vital piece of information? In fact, the management seemed to be oblivious to the fact that Lomas was wasting time whilst the cause was virtually lost. A lull in the noise enabled a truly reliable source, my wife, who was next to me and struggling to hear the radio, to pass the shocking news that both of the other matches remained goalless. I cannot forgive Alan Ball for this. What possible excuse could he have?

In the last few minutes, more accurate counter-rumours seemed to penetrate and the crowd sought to urge City on for the winning goal that really was required. It didn't come, and the match ended in a deathly silence. The City players trudged off the pitch knowing from the eerie quiet that all was lost. A final whistle blown elsewhere sealed City's fate. On 'Match of the Day,' Niall Quinn made a rather touching apology on behalf of the players, but they could not be faulted for the final few performances. The damage was done in the first couple of months of the season. The Blues were relegated on goal difference, whilst having the same number of points as both Southampton and Coventry City. When Manchester City go into the final game with a real chance of being relegated, they grab that chance.

Season 1995/96: a good season for City? Let's consider the evidence. Three derby defeats (making it seven in succession), relegation and a League and FA Cup double for *The Nation's Team*. I hesitated to think that things could get any worse, because they always had in the past, but I dreaded to think how.

Season 1996/97: Can you Manage?

The Faithful, particularly the younger devotees at the Academy, appeared genuinely optimistic about the new season. It was seen as an opportunity to visit strange and exotic new grounds, to see City play and defeat teams of lesser stature, emerging triumphant as runaway Champions. Quite what such optimists are doing at Maine Road, I don't know. The bookies also seemed quite upbeat about City's prospects. We were, as usual, installed as favourites. This meant very little, yet there did seem to be some logic justifying a positive view of City's prospects. The Blues had only narrowly failed to remain in the Premier League and there was, so we were told, a large gap between the Premier League and the Nationwide League. In fact, the gap was between the top Premier League clubs and everybody else. As time goes by and the money seeps in, the gap may well be sinking further down.

The other argument in City's favour was that survival would have been achieved quite comfortably had it not been for that disastrous start to the season. In other words, our exit velocity was encouraging. In addition, Kinkladze remained. Indeed, no player had departed without the express wishes of Mr Ball. Having wished away our best goalkeeper in the previous season, Mr Ball wished away our best defender, Keith Curle (£650,000 to Wolves), and our best striker, Niall Quinn, who was reunited with Peter Reid at newly promoted Sunderland for £1.3 million, only to suffer an injury-ruined season and a relegation repeat.

I was not as optimistic as most, although even I expected that City would be in contention somewhere near the top of the table. This hope was based on the assumption that the City players would be prepared to try their hardest in order to make amends for the previous season's disappointments. It did not take into account that several players would respond to having to play in a lower league by sulking.

The timing of City's exit from the financially lucrative Premier League was, to say the least, unfortunate, but I did have three consolations for relegation. Firstly, Sky TV would no longer be dictating when I should go to watch City play. Unfortunately, this consolation was removed during the summer when Mr Murdoch bought the TV rights to the Nationwide League, presumably just to annoy me. My other consolations were that I need not go to Highfield Road to see yet another last-minute Dion Dublin goal, and that there would be no Manchester derby matches.

The summer began with Euro '96, which was something of a success, apart from the poor attendance at some matches. I saw two games live. At Anfield, Italy played Russia in what looked like a potentially decisive first game. In fact, neither side progressed. It was a good match, but I found life as a neutral a bit dull. I was just beginning to wish that the unglamorous Russian team would go on to win when Italy scored the second and winning goal, which proved that I hadn't lost my touch. My other match was the quarter-final, at Villa Park, between the often aimless but talented Portugese and the hard-working Czechs. Rui Costa and friends looked extremely impressive in terms of close control and comfort on the ball, but they lacked bite near goal. The Czech Republic stole the match 1-0. I took a dislike to Poborsky, whose scooped winning goal was either a work of genius or a fluke. Posterity suggests that the latter is nearer the truth.

Other notable events of the summer included an England Under-21 cap for Michael Brown, one of the undoubted City successes of an otherwise dismal season, and the surprising appointment of Kevin Bond as reserve-team trainer. The return of a Bond to Maine Road certainly caused a few raised eyebrows. City's pre-season tour of China indicated that their jinx extends far and wide. After one drawn match, the tour had to be cancelled because of floods.

Sky TV got their claws into City in the very first game of the season, at home to Ipswich Town. They shifted the fixture to a warm Friday evening, prior to all the other matches. City, therefore, had the opportunity to leap to the top of the League, and they took it, albeit without much conviction. The first half was fairly reassuring, with Kinkladze doing sufficient to suggest that he would be too good for the Nationwide League defenders to cope with, and Kavelashvili linking well with his compatriot and almost matching his skill. Inevitably, Kinkladze played the major role in City's goal, which was headed in by Lomas. Early in the second half, Kavelashvili should have added to the lead, after seemingly doing the hard part of skipping around the goalkeeper. He failed to finish, and Ipswich Town began to force their way into the match. Frontzeck was rightly sent off for physically assaulting an opponent, although the challenge owed more to buffoonish clumsiness than malice, and the defending became increasingly desperate. In a late Ipswich assault, the frame of the City goal was disturbed twice, but the Blues clung on to win 1-0. I had plenty of time to reflect on the schizophrenic display, thanks to a truly monumental traffic jam caused by the closure of the M56. I once more had reason to be grateful to Sky TV.

The key question to be answered concerned City's ability to compete away from Maine Road, a quality conspicuous by its absence throughout the previous season. Two consecutive away matches suggested that there was no improvement. A 1-0 defeat at Burnden Park should, by all accounts, have been more emphatic, and the Blues fell 2-0 behind before half-time against Stoke City, the second goal being bundled somewhat fortuitously in by Mike Sheron. Rösler took advantage of some lax defending to pull a goal back, but the Blues got what they deserved: nothing. After two dismal away defeats, the tide turned quickly against the retention of Alan Ball, who had received quite staggering levels of support throughout the traumas of the previous season. Ball resigned, setting in motion one of the most laughable periods in City's tortured recent history.

Asa Hartford was given temporary charge over first team affairs, and his first game, at home to Charlton, seemed to suggest that he was blessed with a magic touch. City were utterly dreadful and deservedly trailing 1-0. Then late in the match, new signing Paul Dickov fell over in a rather unconvincing fashion, after executing a quick turn. The referee awarded a penalty kick and Rösler scored. This party trick proved to be a common occurrence with Dickov, who cost Alan Ball £1 million from Arsenal. Worse followed for Charlton when substitute Gerry Creaney curled in a peach of a goal, direct from a last-minute free-kick. Despite being awful, City stole all three points.

Jeff Whitley made an impressive debut at home to Barnsley a few days later, but that was the only bright aspect to another poor performance. Unfortunately, Whitley made the mistake that led to Barnsley's winner late in the match, and City lost 2-1. Rösler and Dickov both scored in a 2-0 win at Port Vale, suggesting the possibility of brighter things to come, but such optimism proved premature. The seventh position, occupied after that victory, was the highest achieved all season, apart from immediately following City's first match, before anybody else had played!

Meanwhile, City were finding it embarrassingly difficult to attract a manager. George Graham made much of his interest on the radio, and then publicly rejected City after discussions with the club. This little cameo had all the charm of someone inviting a member of the opposite sex out for a date on the basis of their photograph, only to reject them as too ugly when they showed up. Dave Bassett was the next to follow suit. Maybe City's poor performance against his Crystal Palace team influenced that decision. As the Faithful taunted the home side with open invitations to their manager, Palace scored three times, helped considerably by some woeful defending, and a half-hearted non-save by Dibble, who had replaced Immel in the City goal. To complete a splendid afternoon's work, the lack of pace exhibited by City's new captain, Kit Symons, resulted in a sending off. Kavelashvili, reduced to substitute after playing the first three games, finished off a splendid City move for a goal of little consolation in a 3-1 defeat.

Worse was to follow in the Coca-Cola Cup when, despite Rösler scoring in the first minute against Lincoln, the Blues collapsed to a 4-1 defeat, following up with a 1-0 second leg loss at Maine Road. After that fiasco, I skipped the home match against Birmingham City. This was won 1-0 with a late, fortunate Kinkladze penalty, following an earlier penalty miss by Rösler. The first penalty was the result of a Bruce challenge on Dickov that was milked to the full. It was a game in which Eddie McGoldrick, signed from Arsenal for £300,000, made his first City appearance. My reason for not attending was straightforward. I simply couldn't be bothered to drive up the motorway for the sake of watching the current crop of Manchester City players. It has not happened often before, and I managed to recover later in the season, but this is as close as I have ever been to giving up. I was asking myself awkward questions like *Why? What's the point? What do you actually get out of it?* There are no reassuring answers.

A comfortable 2-0 League defeat, away to Sheffield United, followed. When the home fans chanted 'We hate Wednesday,' the Faithful were moved to respond, 'We hate Saturday.' These were dreadful times for Manchester City.

Eventually, after 42 days of uncertainty, Francis Lee found somebody willing to become manager of the club on a permanent basis, or so we thought. Steve Coppell was installed in the job. The unfortunate playing connections with another club were tempered by the relief at finding anyone at all, and at least Coppell had some sort of pedigree, as a reasonably successful manager of Crystal Palace. There was some disquiet when Coppell decided that Phil Neal should be induced away from Cardiff City to become his assistant, but Coppell said all the right things and sounded like a plausible choice. The City team responded to his first match in charge by earning a point away to QPR. As usual, City went 2-0 behind, but with an uncharacteristic display of resistance, they fought back. Kinkladze earned and converted a penalty kick, and a spectacular Ian Brightwell goal secured the point. Coppell's first home match, against Norwich City, also went well, although it has to be said that Norwich City's record at Maine Road would make them anybody's first choice for a debut match. In fact, Norwich looked the better team for much of the time, but a deflected Clough shot gave the Blues a half-time lead, which was increased when Dickov took advantage of an under-hit back-pass. The visitors finally scored with two minutes remaining, but City held on.

A week later, the Blues played far better at home to Wolves, but they failed to take their chances. Lomas missed what was remarkably close to an open goal, and Whitley struck a shot against the crossbar. The 17-year-old Whitley was proving to be one of the season's few successes. For Wolves, Steve Bull had two chances, both in the second half. The first was hardly a chance at all, but he only just sent his shot over the goal. The second came late in the match, after a horrible misjudgement by Symons. Having used the opening opportunity to find his range, Bull dispatched the second for the winning goal.

A couple of days later, the Blues managed a second away victory at Southend, although a 3-0 lead was cut to 3-2 with a late rally by the home side. Kinkladze scored twice, including yet another penalty – penalties certainly seemed to be far more plentiful in the Nationwide League. My first away game of the season was less encouraging. It was my only ever visit to the home of Swindon Town, managed by Steve McMahon and coached by none other than Mike Walsh, whose own brief City career had been memorable, although not for the right reasons. I arrived too early, casting anxious glances at the sky and the lack of roofing in our section of the ground. I gambled on entering the stadium in order to partake of the culinary delights, and to buy and read the match magazine in the comfort of a seat. As soon as I appeared on the other side of the turnstile, the heavens opened, and they remained open for the rest of the day, drenching both me and my soggy match magazine, which was converted into papier-mâché.

It can be best described as a game of two halves. In the first half, City were poor and the rain was persistent. Swindon missed a penalty after a foul on Wayne Allison. In the second half, City were even poorer, the rain was persistent, and Allison scored twice. It was the wettest match I have ever been to. The City display matched the weather perfectly. The defence included Darren Wassall and Simon Rodger, both on loan, in preference to Ian Brightwell. If you add Frontzeck and Symons to that, you have a recipe for disaster. Too many experienced players, such as Clough, Rösler and McGoldrick, did not look sufficiently interested in proceedings. Even Kinkladze seemed to be losing heart, leaving Whitley to contribute the enthusiasm for virtually the whole team apart from Dickov, who ran around a lot, but to little discernible effect.

City had fallen to seventeenth position in the League, but it was still a shock to find that the Swindon Town match was Steve Coppell's final one in charge. On Friday, 8 November 1996, after only 33 days in the job, Coppell resigned, giving obscure reasons vaguely connected with the good of his health. City were in the mire, and on the back pages, once more. Remarkably, the Lazarus-like Coppell recovered sufficiently to become the manager of Crystal Palace later in the season, miraculously leading them to promotion. Hallelujah!

Phil Neal, whose splendid nodding donkey, to Graham Taylor's tortured clown, had captured the hearts of a nation in a television documentary, was left in charge. The Blues lost 3-2 at home to Oxford United, in a midweek match that would have required some enthusiasm on my part to attend. I couldn't muster any. Andy Dibble suffered a nightmare match as City relinquished a 2-1 lead. A 2-1 defeat at Portsmouth followed, despite the fact that the Blues took an early lead through Rodger. Fitzroy Simpson scored the winning goal direct from a free-kick. I missed another midweek home match, a goalless draw against Brian Horton's Huddersfield Town. This wasn't entirely my own fault – so few of City's home matches were actually being played on a Saturday. If it wasn't the work of Sky TV, it was due to postponements because of City's numerous illustrious international players.

The home match against Tranmere, on 23 November 1996, was the second of three consecutive Maine Road games for the Blues, and it actually took place on a Saturday. I attended and was rewarded with a pitiful performance, with all the goals coming in the second half. Dave Higgins was left alone to score from a corner flicked on by John Aldridge, but the generosity of Eric Nixon allowed Summerbee to equalise. Some more inept defending allowed Tranmere to restore their lead. Ian Brightwell could do little other than turn an awkward cross into his own net. The Blues had fallen to twenty-first place. I was already in transit by the time that the demonstration outside Maine Road had reached its peak. The target of people's anger was more obscure than usual. There was no Peter Swales, and the manager had been in control for only a short time. The message was simply a plea for something to be done by somebody to stop City from looking so ridiculous.

Having won my personal battle against a tendency to be sensible, I was back at Maine Road for the midweek match against West Bromwich Albion. Neil Heaney, signed from Southampton for £500,000, made his debut for City. He did a passable impersonation of a left-winger, winning a penalty that Kinkladze converted, to add to an early headed goal by Rösler. Albion pulled one goal back, but a second Kinkladze penalty, induced by Dickov, restored City's two-goal lead before half-time. Despite conceding another Albion goal, City were able to win under Phil Neal for the first time.

The Blues slumped 3-0 at Wolves to confirm that there was no real improvement. We were all most grateful for a fortunate 3-2 home win over Bradford City, including another Kinkladze penalty kick. In a desperate finale, the City crossbar was twice rattled. Following the Bradford match there was a welcome respite in proceedings, during which time Frank Clark resigned as manager of Nottingham Forest (19 December 1996) and the disappointing Clough went to the City Ground on loan, at the request of Stuart Pearce.

Meanwhile, City's mission to be the butt of all the football jokes continued unabated. There were certainly plenty of them to chose from. There was the one about Francis Lee, who spots an old lady carrying heavy bags with some difficulty. Chairman Lee approaches to offer assistance. 'Can you manage?' he enquires. The old lady turns and recognises him, which prompts the reply, 'Bugger off, I'm not doing it. Find somebody else!'

There's another one when Francis Lee has a funny turn passing a large, Manchester city centre hotel, which is hosting a conference. The doorman spots the fainting Lee, brings him inside, and seats him within one of the conference rooms to give him time to recover. Lee eventually awakes and asks, 'Where am I?' Somebody replies, 'You're in the conference.' 'Bloody 'ell!' says Lee. 'What happened to Divisions Two and Three?' Ho, ho, ho.

'Have a Merry Christmas with Latics,' announced the programme for the Oldham Athletic match against City at Boundary Park, on 21 December 1996. There was even snow atop the word 'Latics', which for Boundary Park, feels just about right. On this occasion, however, the sun shone so brightly into the eyes of those of us in the Lookers Stand, that the lookers amongst us had to shade our eyes. Even then, we had considerable difficulty in distinguishing the hideous maroon and white mishmash of City's strip from the red and blue, horizontal rugby-shirt stripes of Oldham, for the first half at least. I was amongst Oldham fans, along with quite a few other Blues, having acquired my ticket via a friend of a friend of an Oldham supporter. It hardly mattered. For much of the game there was an unofficial love-in, or rather hate-in, between the rival supporters, as they backed up each others claims of detestation for *The Nation's Team*.

The match itself was typical of City's pitiful season. Georgiou Kinkladze shone, like the star of Bethlehem itself, way above the heads of the other players. With a closer view than normal, the difference in skill became even more apparent to me: a Prokofiev amongst Andrew Lloyd Webbers; Johnny Marr jamming with *The Wombles*; Laurence Olivier appearing in an episode of 145Neighbours'; an eminent philosopher invited to partake in an earnest debate on ethical and moral issues, on a panel also consisting of Sue Pollard, Mr Blobby, and a can of Boddingtons draught with a defective widget.

It was only my second away match of a season where enthusiasm for long drives and M6 traffic jams was hard to find, when the prospect of watching a feeble and listless City was the only reward. Yet, I'm sure, it was fairly representative of Manchester City on their travels circa 1996. Oldham were three points behind the Blues before the start of the match, and were basing much of their game on the punt up to the giraffe-like Ormonroyd. In a lively first half, the crossbar was induced to wobble at both ends. Rösler's effort for City was one of his brightest moments for some time. It stood out because of its novelty value.

The referee then generously awarded City yet another penalty kick, after Dickov's usual party-trick of a rapid turn and fall had cajoled the former City captain, Steve Redmond, into making some contact. Kinkladze, however, placed his kick too close to Kelly. The City star made up for it, scoring with a glorious chip over Kelly after some defensive dithering by Oldham had presented him with the chance. Had Rösler been of an earlier vintage, the Blues might even have increased their half-time lead.

Whether it was the half-time team talks or merely habit, I cannot say, but in the second half City were back to their submissive and spineless worst. The blond-haired Simon Rodger was suffering an individual crisis at left-back, and this was admirably exploited by Oldham. The hard-working Latics had already wasted a couple of good opportunities to profit down the right wing when Henry crossed for Ormonroyd to head the equaliser. This was a real test of City's character, and somehow we all knew that they would fail it. The substitute, Banger, added Oldham's second goal with 15 minutes remaining, following pitiful defending from a corner.

If we had all been at Maine Road with City leading 2-1 and 15 minutes to go, there is little doubt that, regardless of the opposition, be it Oldham, Liverpool, or a Dagenham Girl-Pipers Eleven, the match would have been played out in the City penalty area, with the Blues hanging on desperately. At Boundary Park, there was hardly a whimper of resistance as the remaining time elapsed, and City had yet another defeat to ponder.

It was rather easy to have a merry Christmas with Latics when the opposition is as soft as Manchester City were. The small lad next to me was particularly delighted, but there were a lot of tell-tale glum faces dotted around the stand. I left about four minutes before the end, safe in the knowledge that City did not have it in them to come back. Manchester City sank to fifth from bottom, with relegation looking increasingly possible.

Kinkladze's goal proved to be the highlight of a grim festive season for an increasingly inept and dispirited – I'm running out of adjectives – Manchester City. The fact that more than 30,000 people were on hand to witness Port Vale's 1-0 win, at Maine Road on Boxing Day, was a testament either to dogged loyalty or desperation to escape the family bosom at Yuletide. This was the first time in season 1996/97 that a crowd in excess of 30,000 had attended any Nationwide League match. They were not treated to a Christmas spectacular. Vale crowded the midfield, stifling Kinkladze, and thus thwarting City's only perceptible game plan. The goal came just before half-time, bundled over the line by Martin Foyle, following a corner. Vale had just failed to convert their only other opportunity of the match. Symons and Rösler were amongst the guilty who could and probably should have equalised, but the inevitability of defeat cast a gloomy shadow over a frustrating second half. Like the Blues, a fan band, making an appearance at the rear of K-block in the North Stand, had a very limited repertoire.

A couple of days later, City suffered another predictable defeat at Barnsley. At one time such a defeat would at least have been a surprise. A ludicrous penalty decision hardly helped, but like so many of City's away games, the match was already over as a contest by half-time. Just prior to the Barnsley match, Phil Neal had issued a 'back me or sack me' ultimatum to the Board. Now, considering the team's record since Neal took control, that was a tricky choice, wasn't it? City, fourth from bottom of the League table, were occupying the worst position in the club's history. On 30 December 1996, following Neal's resignation, Frank Clark was appointed as City's fifth manager of the season. It's just as well that replica shirts with the manager's name on the back are not a popular line.

Tony Book also lost his battle to stay at the club. After 30 years, he was sacked as first team coach to allow Clark complete control. It was rumoured that Howard Wilkinson was Franny Lee's preferred choice. If this were true, I was inclined to agree with him at the time. Lee did not, however, have a good track-record in the choice of managers.

The Faithful, assembled in force at Barnsley, were chanting, 'I'd rather be in Barnsley than Barbados.' This was a reference to Chairman Lee's inexplicable preference for spending the festive season in the Caribbean. I'm sure that this was a considerable fillip for those involved in the promotion of tourism in the Barnsley area. Jill Dando will be on her way soon, no doubt.

City's opening two matches of 1997, away to Birmingham City on New Year's Day, and away to Brentford in the FA Cup, were a considerable improvement. Both fell victim to the weather. The first actual game of the Frank Clark era did not suggest that a miraculous transformation was imminent. Against Crystal Palace, City did at least manage to sustain a spell of pressure early in the second half. At least, I think that's what it was. It had been so long since such an occurrence at Maine Road that I may have mistaken it for something else. Whatever it was, the culmination was an emphatic sixty-fourth minute own goal, headed in by Tuttle in the Palace defence. It followed a wicked free-kick by a limping Kinkladze. The Blues actually looked likely winners, until George Nda took advantage of enough room in the City penalty area to swing a very large cat and headed the equaliser from another free-kick, with seven minutes remaining.

The Frank Clark unbeaten run was extended by yet another postponement of the Brentford FA Cup tie. I did not particularly enjoy my early evening 180-mile round trip to a roundabout in Maidenhead. Others travelled even further. The game was only called off two hours before the scheduled kick-off.

A 1-1 draw at Huddersfield completed an awesome two-match unbeaten run, unprecedented in season 1996/97. The match provided the on-loan Northern Ireland goalkeeper, Tommy Wright, with his first experience of life in the Manchester City goal. He was not available for the FA Cup match against Brentford, clear leaders of the Second Division, that took place, finally, at Griffin Park on 25 January 1997. The sun was shining, the cheerleader/acrobats were enthusiastic, the giant bee mascot was greeted cordially, and the choice of pies proved too exotic for one fan, who demanded a meat pie and didn't care for the more specific choice of steak and kidney or chicken and mushroom. The kick-off was delayed, probably because of there being virtually nowhere to park a car and only one entrance to the away-end shed. The result was a shock for everyone. City won.

Rösler tried his best for Brentford, particularly early on when, after latching on to Rae Ingram's pass, he dragged the final shot horribly wide. Indeed the Blues shooting in the first half was so lamentable that a goal seemed out of the question. The home side came to life early in the second half, and quite how they contrived not to score, I don't know, although Margetson deserves some credit for a couple of good saves. In the second half, City were supposed to be attacking the goal behind which the Faithful were assembled. On the first occasion that they managed to do so, on the hour, they unexpectedly took the lead. The scorer was Summerbee, who had been receiving constant abuse from the assembled City fans. It was an impressive flowing move, suggesting that City were capable of playing football, occasionally. Lomas played an important part in the build-up, before finding Kinkladze, who for once was not immediately felled, presumably because he was in the penalty area. Kinkladze's subtle pass into the path of Summerbee was perfection, and Buzzer blasted the ball past Kevin Dearden, the Brentford goalkeeper. The goal did not save Summerbee from further abuse, although there were some stunted attempts to chant his name. This was asking a lot. There were far too many offences to take into account. Surprisingly, Brentford did not equalise, and the City fans amused themselves by persistently drawing attention to the rotund nature of Kevin Dearden, who took it all in good heart.

With the Blues having slipped into the relegation zone, the Faithful were rather hoping for a home win against Howard Kendall's third-placed Sheffield United, four days later. Instead, we were treated to a monotonous stalemate. Rösler was bundling around in attack for City, desperately and often vainly seeking support, and an excitable former City hero, David White, was a lone figure darting around up front for the visitors, eagerly awaiting those rare moments when the ball might be encouraged in his direction. It wasn't that City played badly. Summerbee and Lomas had their best matches for some considerable time, and Peter Beagrie showed the odd flash of skill during his all too brief reappearance as substitute after a long, injury-induced absence. There was, however, very little to show for the promising approach play. Kinkladze wasted the best chance of the match late on, blasting wide with his right foot, after a Rösler header had put the Georgian genius clear. It would not be an exaggeration to say that, in footballing terms, Kinkladze's right foot is not as good as his left foot.

Tommy Wright had little to do on his home debut, but what he had to do, he did badly, exhibiting a textbook case of the goalkeeping Maine Road jitters prevalent during this painful phase in the club's history. Wright was responsible for the visitors' most dangerous moments, but he survived to fight another day. The fans were left hoping that his performance was a mere one-off: first night nerves. Fortunately, it proved to be so; for a while, at least.

City had managed an unbeaten January, but they still languished fourth from bottom of the Nationwide League Division One. On the following Sunday, the Blues defied the presence of live terrestrial television cameras to give their best display of the season, and register their most emphatic win ever in front of a live television audience. The victims, Oxford United, contributed splendidly with a headed own goal by Gilchrist from Kinkladze's corner, before the Georgian magician scored two brilliant goals. Latching on to a clever back-flick by a more animated Rösler, Kinkladze bamboozled two defenders before dispatching the first goal. City could have added a couple more before Gio's second, following a splendid run and a devastating turn of pace. Oxford pulled a goal back with 10 minutes remaining, but Rösler scored a deserved fourth goal near the finish, to finally arrest the doubts of even the most pessimistic of City fans, for example, myself. Wright played well in the City goal, and Kevin Horlock (signed from Swindon Town for £1.5 million) had an exceptional debut in midfield. The ITV viewers must have been left wondering what on earth City were doing lurking just above the relegation zone.

Four days later, City won their first Maine Road match of the new year in an FA Cup fourth-round tie against Second Division Watford. A scrambled Heaney goal was all that they had to show for a first-half performance that suggested much improved levels of confidence. In the second half, Kinkladze's shadow, Steve Palmer, took exception to Steve Lomas standing between him and his prey, and received marching orders for a blatant punch. Admirably, Lomas made no fuss about it at all, but the incident took place right in front of the referee, who had little choice but to send the player off. The Watford equaliser came as a bit of a surprise, and it looked as though sourness would once again be the order of the day. This time, however, a bit of spirit, and a touch of brilliance from a quiet Kinkladze, led to Summerbee restoring City's lead. The Faithful even had the luxury of a two-goal cushion for the final 12 minutes, after the hard-working Rösler had sprinted clear to make it 3-1.

The visit of Southend to Maine Road gave the Blues the opportunity to put some distance between themselves and fellow strugglers. The first half was a dour affair, with the visitors getting everyone behind the ball as often as possible, and City's new defender, Paul Beesley, a £500,000 signing from Leeds, enjoying the luxury of a very comfortable afternoon. Rösler made the breakthrough early in the second half, bursting clear to score with his old assurance. That was the cue for the Georgiou Kinkladze show to commence. He curled a free-kick against the crossbar as an appetizer, but the main course came following a typical burst into the penalty area, to the right of goal. Kinkladze stopped, switching direction, and turned to face two seemingly mesmerised defenders, just a few yards away. After a pause, Kinkladze bisected the two bemused Southend players with a shot that curled inside the far post from an unlikely angle. For dessert, Kinkladze jinked past several defenders before setting up a chance for Rösler to score his second goal of the game. The Georgian genius also sent Summerbee clear with an audacious flicked pass. Summerbee, virtually unrecognisable from the hesitant shambles of a player of only a few matches ago, struck his shot against the inside of the post. Somehow it stayed out of the net. A 3-0 win was more than satisfactory, and some of the skills displayed by Kinkladze during the second half defy description.

There was an optimistic full house for the FA Cup fifth-round visit of Bryan Robson's Premiership strugglers, Middlesbrough. The pre-match hype concentrated predictably on the Kinkladze versus Juninho angle. Both responded by giving largely anonymous performances, their skills stifled in an overcrowded and often bad-tempered midfield war of attrition. In a tight match, either team might have scored and, in fact, both did. City had the better moments of the first half, but they badly needed a goal to force Middlesbrough into committing more players to attack, thus leaving the space for Kinkladze to exploit. Commentators are always happy to inform us that just before half-time is a good time to score a goal. Ian Brightwell steered the ball inside the post during this allegedly psychologically important period, only for a linesman's flag to spoil the moment. The cameras, which never lie, suggested that City were hard done by. Brightwell himself was certainly not offside. Rösler, who was running away from goal, in an area well clear from the action, may have been, but there is little doubt that the linesman flagged for Brightwell.

In the second half, another expensive Middlesbrough import, the Italian defender Festa, flattened Steve Lomas with a blow to the head, in a fit of petulance and in much the same fashion as Watford's Steve Palmer in the previous round – Lomas did not appear to be terribly popular with opposition players. The referee had no alternative but to send Festa off. It was, therefore, no surprise to see the Italian escape with a yellow card and play a prominent role in the visitors' late winner. This was scored by Juninho who had, for once, been given plenty of time and space. Earlier, Kinkladze had departed after one kick too many, and with him went most of City's realistic hopes of scoring. After falling behind, it was City who had to commit players to attack, and it was Middlesbrough who might have benefited further on the break. The other famous foreigner, Ravanelli, spent most of the match whining at his colleagues, or the referee, or both. This endearing act was occasionally further embellished with theatrical diving. When he did have opportunities, he made a complete mess of them. It made no difference. Frank Clark's unbeaten run was over.

The Blues confirmed their much improved status with a comfortable home victory over Swindon Town, achieved notably without the injured Kinkladze. In the absence of the wizard, players such as Heaney and McGoldrick demonstrated previously hidden talents. Swindon old boy Kevin Horlock scored the opening City goal, before Holcroft successfully got himself dismissed for throwing a punch at Dickov. Lomas may well have been disappointed to have his role in the team usurped.

Ten-man Swindon deteriorated badly, and City might easily have approached double figures had their finishing not bordered on woeful. Summerbee and Rösler completed the scoring. Unaccustomed to the luxury of a comfortable lead, the crowd didn't seem to know how to behave towards the end. The closing stages were enlivened by the appearance of young striker Chris Greenacre, who made an enthusiastic impact as substitute, and might easily have marked it with a debut goal.

The Bradford City goalkeeper, Jonathan Gould, made City's fourth successive League win considerably easier by simultaneously conceding a penalty and getting himself dismissed. Rösler scored twice, including the penalty kick, as City won 3-1 at Valley Parade. A late equaliser, scored by old boy Fitzroy Simpson, cost City two valuable points back at Maine Road, on a night when FC Porto came bearing gifts across the city. We should have swapped opposition. At least Portsmouth put up a fight at Maine Road. The Blues followed that result with an unconvincing 1-0 win over Oldham, in front of the biggest Maine Road crowd of the season. So pleased was Uwé Rösler with his winning goal that he set off on an elaborate celebratory run, hurdling the fence at the North Stand End to embark on a whirlwind handshaking tour with the fans in the front row of the North and Main Stands. When he eventually reappeared on the field of play, Rösler was greeted by a yellow card brandished by a typically humourless referee.

With the optimists already beginning to talk in terms of play-offs, despite City's position in the lower half of the table, an unbeaten League run of nine matches since the arrival of Frank Clark came to an end. After two emphatic away victories, the City team were obviously awaiting my presence before achieving their worst result under the new management. A midweek rearranged game at St Andrews, against a truly appalling Birmingham City team, whose manager, Tricky Trevor, was under mounting pressure, did not appear to be the perfect opportunity for failure. The Blues achieved it nonetheless. The continuing absence of Kinkladze was, no doubt, a contributory factor, but I blame myself mainly. After two previous unfruitful visits to that ground, I should have stayed well clear. The stadium may have changed since my last visit, but the outcome did not. The home crowd watched a dreadful first half in absolute silence, but despite Birmingham City's obvious lack of belief, City were unable to make much of their possession. Rösler and Dickov were particularly ineffective, falling foul to a Steve Bruce-inspired offside-trap.

The ex-*Nation's Team* defender had not lost his knack with referees. Nothing short of murder would provoke the award of a free-kick for one of his famous barging challenges from behind. Mr Kirkby, the esteemed silver-haired referee, evidently decided that the match required enlivening. He awarded the home side a typical Nationwide League penalty early in the second half. Furlong scored, and the giraffe-like Kevin Francis, whose long topple to the floor led to the first goal, headed the second direct from a corner, always the most likely source of a goal. City sent on forgotten man Kavelashvili, who once more looked skilful, but he could not inspire a goal. City played quite nicely, but with insufficient threat. Even so, quite how they managed to lose 2-0, I do not know. The play-offs were looking a long way off.

A couple of away draws followed. The 1-1 draw at Grimsby was notable only for a rare start by Kavelashvili, who headed the City equaliser. It took a late own goal to earn the Blues the same result at Tranmere. Back at Maine Road, against Stoke City, the Blues included home debutants Ged Brannan (from Tranmere) and Dalian Atkinson, whose Fenerbache transfer saga was temporarily resolved with a loan spell.

At three o'clock on a Saturday afternoon of a home match, I was in the penalty area, just, at the North Stand End, and I was awake! As I had arrived quite early, I was already in the ground when a strange, coded message over the PA system – 'Mister

Banks is in the North Stand' – led to some unfamiliar and furtive manoeuvring amongst the stewards. The fans occupying a couple of blocks in the North Stand were evacuated on to the pitch. There was no explanation at the time, but later reports blamed a fire alarm; either that or Mr Banks was an escaped psychopath in search of a spiritual home. No fire alarm was audible from inside the ground. This was my first-ever foray on to the Maine Road pitch, and I took advantage of the opportunity to make sure that I stepped completely on to the playing area, albeit briefly, and touched a sacred goalpost. It's all rather pathetic, I know, but there were plenty of others doing exactly the same thing, and many were even older than me. Some of the more obvious tampering with the net brought out the latent sergeant major tendencies of the chief stewards. In all, the start of the game was delayed for 45 minutes.

Stoke came as the side with real prospects of a play-off place, but City dominated totally, rattling the frame of the goal twice, in addition to scoring twice in the second half. The goals were from headers by Atkinson and Lomas, the latter executed from a position remarkably close to where I had been standing earlier, the ball skimming the very post that I had touched. It proved to be the last significant contribution by Steve Lomas as a City player. On transfer deadline day, his on-off move to West Ham was resolved in the on position, for a fee of £2 million. He seemed reluctant to move. The wisdom of selling yet another young player was, to say the least, questionable.

Despite the tendency of Manchester City to virtually always let their supporters down, there are a surprisingly high number of optimists who make the regular pilgrimage to Maine Road. There was still much talk of a possible play-off place, notwithstanding a double figure points gap to close, and matches running out. Optimism was dented by a 1-1 draw at Charlton – clearly wins were required. Even those exhibiting optimism to the verge of insanity must have been shaken from their belief by the visit of Bolton Wanderers, on the night when a severely depleted Borrusia Dortmund established a 1-0 lead against *The Nation's Team*.

After 20 years of mostly depressing attachment to the Blues, I could detect the work of forces beyond our comprehension in the timing of the Maine Road encounter with runaway leaders Bolton Wanderers, the team I had rejected in favour of City. Bolton required only a point to clinch the Championship and return to the Premier League, to join up with Blackburn Rovers, the other side I could have chosen to support as a youngster. There was something inevitable about the outcome, despite City's impressive first-half performance, a goal by Kinkladze direct from a free-kick, and John McGinley, football's answer to Jocky Wilson, departing with an early injury. Bolton equalised just before half-time, and exploited the lamentably slow defensive pairing of Kernaghan and Symons to secure a 2-1 win, thanks to a well-struck goal by Scott Sellars. Bolton were Champions, and City's play-off dreams were finished.

There was still an impressive turnout of the Faithful on my first visit to the home of West Bromwich Albion a few days later, and the bright sunshine encouraged a carnival atmosphere. So rapt in their sunbathing were some City fans, that the PA announcer had to remind them that a football game was about to commence, and ask them whether they would mind taking their places in the ground. Leaving the stunning view of a shimmering, picturesque Birmingham behind was, no doubt, a wrench. My view, from inside a compact and neat ground, rather unfairly criticised with the traditional chant of 'shit ground, no fans', was excellent, and for the first 35 minutes of the game, City made football look surprisingly easy. They were helped by Albion's seeming reluctance to keep tabs on the whereabouts of Uwé Rösler, who headed Kinkladze's curling cross into the net after three minutes, and would have added a second had not Miller pulled off a quite exceptional reflex save. On 23 minutes, an impressive build-up involving the Georgian genius culminated in a Horlock headed goal from a splendid Brightwell cross. Ten minutes before half-time, City again prospered down the right flank, and the otherwise woeful Summerbee squared the ball for Rösler, again unhindered, to put City 3-0 ahead. My biggest ever away win looked a distinct possibility, until Murphy headed a goal back just before half-time. In the second half, despite a couple of close calls for the home side, and a curling Kinkladze shot that narrowly failed to find the smallest of gaps, there were no further goals.

There were still some die-hard optimists amongst the Faithful, and a 3-1 home win against Grimsby had them perusing the League tables to confirm that City's play-off chances were still in theoretical existence, despite their inability to reach the top half of the table. The visit of QPR to Maine Road finally ended all such nonsense. With Kinkladze comprehensively man-marked by Brevitt, City lacked ideas, and Rangers won with three second-half goals, two scored by John Spencer. Assists by Alan Kernaghan, on goals number two and three, earned him the familiar sound of resounding boos whenever he touched the ball. Quite how this helps the cause, I fail to see. I prefer, on the whole, to seethe inwardly. No doubt the limitations of a Symons/Kernaghan central pairing were duly noted by the management.

The season drifted to its dull conclusion, with a 1-0 defeat at Ipswich followed by a goalless draw at Norwich, leading to the final match of the season, at home to Reading. The Faithful were in a strangely high-spirited mood for this final, largely meaningless fixture. I was reasonably cheerful myself, two days on from the landslide humiliation of Dismal Johnny's Tory Party. Like many others, I was more delighted by the downfall of those I despised than optimistic of improvement. As it turns out, this is just as well. Changing governments has been remarkably similar to City's more recent experiences of changing managers: new regime, same old rubbish.

I overheard a topical debate outside the ground, where one fan was explaining to another the reason why he had previously voted Tory: because they were associated with the colour blue. As an Italian football club Chairman once remarked, 'The mother of the stupid is always pregnant.' Mind you, with British politics in its current state, this may prove as good a way of deciding as any.

I found it difficult to be terribly enthusiastic about the match, particularly because an injury suffered in Georgia's international game against England had left Kinkladze unable to play. Reading took the lead in the first few minutes with a deflected goal, which was mildly irritating. They extended their lead as the City defence slumbered in the sunshine, Symons applying the final touch. The hi-tech Maine Road scoreboard registered the score as 0-3, which demonstrated a discouraging lack of confidence in our blue-shirted heroes. Dickov hooked the ball in to bring the half-time score back to a more respectable 1-2. I was still having difficulty caring much about the proceedings, but I appeared to be in a minority. The schizophrenic chap next to me was in emotional turmoil, switching constantly between loud declarations of undying love for his team, and randomly directed personal abuse of the players in that same beloved team. The only player who seemed exempt was Paul Dickov, who rewarded his fan by missing a couple of golden chances, one by such a distance that, in cricket, it would have merited a wide. Eventually Rösler, who had also spurned two excellent opportunities, equalised from close-range, after a Brannan shot had been parried. The winning goal was knocked in by substitute Heaney, after the Reading offside-trap had failed miserably, leaving their beleaguered goalkeeper alone to face four City players – it still took rather a long time to beat him. It was a modestly rousing comeback. The Blues celebrated their impressive fourteenth position in the Nationwide League Division One with a lap of honour, and virtually the whole crowd stayed behind, concentrating all their efforts on a desperate plea to the besuited Kinkladze to stay for another season. It looked like a goodbye. It was a sad occasion. In fact, City couldn't even get their fond farewells right. Much to everyone's surprise, Kinkladze didn't leave.

I wanted City to mark my twentieth year as a season ticket holder with a successful season, and they didn't let me down. The Blues secured promotion to the Pontins League Division One, finishing second to the mighty Grimsby Town. This success did not save Kevin Bond from the chop.

Season 1997-98: City's Touching Tribute to Titanic

After a largely futile attempt to rid themselves of a juggernaut-load of unwanted personnel, Manchester City embarked on the challenge of a second season in the Nationwide League carrying the undaunted optimism of a record number of season ticket holders, and wearing their new Kappa turquoise pyjama tops. This capacity for blind faith suggests that many of the Faithful suffer from selective memory loss that relents, for brief moments only, when the goals fly into the City net, and even then is circumvented by thoughts of mathematically possible but implausible achievements. Kappa demonstrated a clear marketing trend when they added City to a list of clubs that includes Juventus, Red Star Belgrade and Barcelona. Well, I'm sure that it's clear to someone.

The only City player to attract an acceptable bid was Peter Beagrie, who departed for Bradford, which, by a strange quirk of fate, was precisely what I was about to do. After four years in the city of the perennial unworthy survivors, I was poised to make good my escape north. It wasn't Manchester, but it was close.

Frank Clark's summer acquisitions were the blond Dutchman Gerard Wiekens, defender Tony Vaughan (£1.35 million from Ipswich Town) and the new record City signing, ex-serviceman Lee Bradbury (a whacking great £3 million from Portsmouth). The latter fee surpassed the previous record held equally by Curle and Phelan, bringing City in line with the conventional notion of the most expensive player being a striker. The new League season and Bradbury's debut, against his old club Portsmouth, came along abnormally early because of the requirements of a congested fixture list in the build-up to the World Cup Finals. The one major encouragement came in the decision of the Georgian genius, Gio Kinkladze, to remain at the club. His compatriot, Kavelashvili, who had provided Kinkladze with a family home, was loaned to Grasshoppers Zurich after failing to meet the requirements of a British work permit. There were other attempts to find a Georgian playmate, but for some bizarre reason the favoured Arveladze brother preferred Ajax of Amsterdam. The pundits judged City amongst the favourites, as usual, although the glamour side was Middlesbrough, who boasted the finest collection of overpaid prima donnas ever to venture into the lower leagues. At least, to begin with they did.

A sultry Maine Road embraced the opening match as a follow-up to a pitch appearance by the Gallagher brothers, with Liam clearly misinterpreting the weather forecast, judging by his winter apparel. The ever-hopeful Faithful, expectant of a comfortable win as a precursor to an all-conquering season, were in buoyant mood. Within five minutes, the Blues were behind. Kinkladze, attracting the usual close attention, was involved with Brannan in the build-up to Rösler's equaliser, after which both sides seemed to be hankering for a siesta.

The joy at the initial omission of Nicky Summerbee was tempered by his introduction as a replacement for the injured Beesley at half-time. Horlock moved to left-back and Brannan to centre midfield, where he formed an almost convincing partnership with Wiekens during City's best spell of the game. Summerbee's cross, headed back across goal, led to the Wiekens goal that gave the Blues the lead. With Portsmouth visibly flagging in the heat and carrying an injured goalkeeper, all should have been well. Most fans seemed to believe that the game was already won – that memory loss affliction once again. With 10 minutes left, City surrendered the lead and with it two points. It was evident that their penchant for the massive anticlimax remained undiminished.

It was a disappointing performance, made worse by the lack of faith shown by Frank Clark in the club's younger players. The genuine claims of Jeff Whitley, Lee Crooks and Michael Brown, in particular, were unjustifiably ignored. Of the starting line-up, only Ian Brightwell and Martyn Margetson, standing in for the injured Tommy Wright, were genuine Manchester City products. This was a very different approach to the 1988/89 promotion campaign, and it was much less attractive because of it.

A disappointing start to the new season worsened just three days later, in City's inaugural Coca-Cola Cup first-round first leg encounter. Although the 1-0 defeat by Blackpool was an improvement on the previous season's visit to Lincoln in the same competition, the headlines describing the result as a shock must have been written by more memory-loss sufferers.

A few years ago, a Niall Quinn goal in the Stadium of Light would have been the stuff of dreams. The reality on Friday, 15 August 1997 was less palatable. Sunderland must have been ecstatic that Manchester City were the guests to their big opening night for the successor to Roker Park. No team are less likely to be party-poopers. Quinninho gave Peter Reid's Sunderland the lead in their new stadium, and Alan

Kernaghan celebrated his return to League football by getting sent off with three-quarters of the match remaining. Georgiou Kinkladze won and converted a penalty, to earn City a surprise equaliser with 15 minutes remaining. Listening to the radio commentary, I, for one, was not taken in by the thought that a point could be rescued in adversity. I expected a Sunderland goal within two minutes. Demonstrating uncharacteristic resilience, City held out for four. The match ended 3-1 to complete a miserable first week to the new season.

Sky TV are no great respecters of Friday night M6 traffic, or indeed anything else. Their choice of City's next home match for a live screening made me reliant on Radio Five Live commentary because, unfortunately, I had yet to escape Coventry. If I am honest, the excuse came as a welcome relief. The sinking feeling was already upon me. In the event, I missed little. Tranmere were unfortunate to be merely level at half-time. Kevin Horlock surprised everyone with a long-range shot to give City the lead 11 seconds into the second half, but the visitors cancelled it out 15 minutes later. After another home draw, the Blues exited the pitch to much booing and wailing.

Around 12,000 stalwarts turned out on the following Tuesday night to see City mark their first-ever Coca-Cola Cup first-round tie with ignoble defeat. Horlock scored with two minutes of normal time remaining and took the game into extra time, but his aim in the eventual penalty shoot-out was less assured. City's other failure from the spot was Lee Bradbury, who had been starved of opportunities to score in a City shirt, but could no longer claim to have had none. The comic element was provided by the name of the taker of the decisive penalty kick: Micky Mellon. During my long vigil as a fan, it was City's first-ever meaningful penalty shoot-out at Maine Road, and their first anywhere for well over a decade. Kinkladze, the only City player worth backing to score, was unable to take a kick because of retirement due to injury. There are seldom half measures with City, and this had all the makings of yet another crisis.

A first-half Wiekens goal at Charlton gave the hint of recovery, but midway through the second half, the home side scored twice in as many minutes. The first was an own goal by another recent signing, Australian defender Jason Van Blerk, his first in City colours. The hint of recovery receded to a distant memory in record time.

As City prepared to visit the Division pace-setters, Nottingham Forest, results achieved by others had allowed the club to sink to their all-time lowest League position. The Blues were third from bottom, with only Brian Horton's Huddersfield Town and Reading below them. Crewe, Bury and Stockport County were looking down with relish, no doubt. Forest, seeking to maintain a 100 per cent record, won a lot of corners, but a surprisingly impressive City display earned them victory, with two goals for Brannan, and a late third for substitute Dickov after Forest had pulled a goal back. The return of Kinkladze, not so badly injured as initially feared, was the inspiration required for a first win of the season. There was also a welcome return to the fold by right-back Richard Edghill. It was typical of the Blues to achieve their first win when it was least expected. A postponement denied them the opportunity to follow up with an equally typical home defeat to Crewe.

In the next fixture, another Sky Sports-inspired Friday night encounter offered Bury the opportunity to embarrass their illustrious neighbours. Gigg Lane was embedded in my memory as a place visited by the local radio linkman after just about every other club had been dealt with. City now paid their visit with Bury several places better off in the League table. Kinkladze won and then missed a penalty as City dominated in the second half. However, a Bury goal midway through the half meant that a late debut goal by 19-year-old defender David Morley, standing in for flu victim Ian Brightwell, was only sufficient for a point. Substitute Tony Scully captured a lot of attention with his debut performance on the left wing, but City's climb up the table was back in reverse gear.

Back at the Academy, the Blues began with conviction against Norwich, safe in the knowledge that no Norwich City team had departed victorious from Maine Road since the 1964/65 season. Admittedly, Forbes headed against the bar in the visitors' first attack, but for the rest of the first half, City piled forward, creating chances and looking strangely like a football team. Bradbury should have scored before he actually did, with a low shot, half an hour into the match. This first goal was somewhat spoilt by the fact that City's lone striker ought to have added to his tally on two further occasions. Quite how he failed early in the second half, only he will know. In the meantime, City's reliance on the whim of a referee's assistant backfired. Neil Adams took his chance well to make the half-time score 1-1. The increasingly familiar Symons blunder allowed Norwich to score a winner midway through the second half. So much for history and omens.

A week is occasionally a long time in football, and seven days after the Norwich defeat, City revealed their Dr Jekyll persona with as comprehensive a victory as they had achieved in a League fixture for many seasons. The visitors, Swindon Town, were lying third in the table prior to kick-off, and must have been anticipating a profitable afternoon. Frank Clark decided to omit Summerbee, favouring a back three including Beesley, Symons and Brightwell, with Horlock and Edghill as what the modern parlance describes as *wing-backs*. The other major change was the restoration of Dickov, who was something of a revelation, to partner Bradbury.

The tone was set early on by Kinkladze, who planted a spectacular free-kick directly into the top corner of the Swindon net, the highlight of a personal performance that bordered on cruelty. Edghill, impressive on the right, provided the cross that led to an own goal, and Horlock added a third, against his old club, before half-time. A three-goal lead, as any old hand such as I can testify, is not sufficient. It might have been more had Kinkladze not heavily disturbed the woodwork following another of his untouchable runs, and had Bradbury not once more failed to demonstrate killer instinct in front of goal. There were still, therefore, some reservations at half-time. These were dispelled by two early second-half Dickov goals and an act of incredible generosity by the same player, when he opted to set up Bradbury rather than go for a personal hat-trick. Bradbury scored, but looked like a man who knew he was receiving charity. Still, a final scoreline of 6-0 made a pleasant change and was entirely merited.

A 1-0 defeat at Ipswich, together with an uncannily bad combination of other scores, sent City plummeting to fourth from bottom, with Ipswich themselves one of the select few worse off. Still, with two consecutive home matches looming, the Blues had the opportunity to emphasise that new found Maine Road confidence. With Bradbury and Rösler both injured, a bemused Neil Heaney found himself restored to the side as centre forward in a 0-0 draw against Reading. City were at their infuriating worst, throwing in a late Kinkladze penalty miss for full effect. Against Stoke City, the Blues created and missed a number of opportunities. The visitors took one of theirs and the demonstrations directed against the Board were back to grace Maine Road once more. Miraculously, City, awaiting a Sunday game against QPR, still hovered one place above the relegation zone – until the Saturday results came in. An Ipswich win left City third from bottom of the League. That position could have been improved in the televised encounter with QPR at Loftus Road. Clark made a few changes, restoring Brown and even Jeff Whitley, albeit as substitute. The Blues simply couldn't score. QPR managed to score twice.

With Giorgiou Kinkladze suffering the consequences of a disagreement between his Ferrari and a wall, City, in need of points and inspiration, faced up to an evening mid-week encounter with Crewe. Frank Clark gave welcome starts to Brown, Jeff Whitley and, for the first time, Chris Greenacre. The latter rewarded his manager by scoring the only goal in a match where, for once, the opposition spurned chances to greater effect.

A goalless affair at Oxford meant that the Blues had followed a 6-0 win with a run of one goal in six matches. In yet another midweek Maine Road match, City scored two first-half goals against Port Vale. Yet twice they relinquished the lead within a few minutes. Tommy Wright, recently restored to goal ahead of the unfortunate Margetson, seemed intent on reviving memories of goalkeeping nightmares past. A third Vale goal early in the second half proved to be the winner. Frank Clark had abandoned his choices of Brown, Greenacre and Whitley, preferring instead to try Conlon in attack and Scully on the wing. An out of sorts Kinkladze returned to the midfield. But with Brightwell absent through injury, the central defensive pair of Symons and Vaughan seemed fit to rival any of City's previous worst. The whole team behaved as though they expected defeat. The manager's constant team alterations, with the exceptions of the likes of Brannan and Horlock, smacked of indecision. True, City were in the midst of a ludicrously demanding fixture list, but so was every other team in Division One. *They* seemed able to cope. Vale did not play particularly well, and managed only four efforts in the direction of the City goal all night, but they were well organised and that, sadly, was sufficient. City were a pathetically easy touch.

Three days later, on Friday, 7 November 1997, the Blues were back at Maine Road, playing host to Huddersfield Town. The opposition were adrift at the bottom of the table, having recently departed company with their manager, one Brian Horton. The match was the star attraction of Sky Sport's Friday night entertainment, and a golden opportunity for City to get some much needed points. There was more tampering by Frank Clark, who decided that Irishman Barry Conlon should be replaced by Irishman Ray Kelly, but changed his mind at the start of the second half. It seemed that no young player should be allowed more than the odd game before being omitted. Jeff Whitley was back in the side, and Brown returned as a substitute for Edghill, who was injured just before the end of a sterile first half that surely deprived satellite television of all neutral viewers. A crowd of 24,500 still turned up at the ground, and they were not impressed by the fact that the Blues went 42 minutes before managing a shot at goal, and that, from Dickov, never looked likely to beat the goalkeeper. At the other end there were a couple of alarms, but Huddersfield were so lacking in confidence that they probably didn't believe themselves capable of scoring.

City improved in the second half. There was, at least, some pressure of sorts on the Huddersfield goal, and one long-range effort by Jeff Whitley forced a spectacular save. However, with Kinkladze looking a sullen, peripheral figure, often isolated on the wings, there still seemed little in the way of an attacking plan. The crowd was noisy and supportive, and we all wondered whether a winner would eventually appear in the final 15 minutes. It did.

Huddersfield, who had not looked like scoring in the second half, put together the best move of the match, finished it well and, in an instant, ended all of the crowd's commendable goodwill. Amidst chants of 'You're not fit to wear the shirts,' and 'We're shit, and we're sick of it,' the players made little use of the remaining minutes. The familiar response to going behind was complete capitulation. Had it not been for several saves by Margetson, returning for the injured Wright, the scoreline would have been more embarrassing. There was one late scramble in the Huddersfield penalty area, but the Blues were incapable of scoring and quite capable, it seemed, of losing to anybody. The City players were demonstrating all the camaraderie and solidarity of rival tabloid journalists chasing a story involving a nun, a mass murderer, Princess Diana, Gazza, two Spice Girls, and a skate-boarding duck. Second Division football was becoming a real possibility. There was an urgent need to call in agent Mulder, to join Scully, and investigate the mysterious disappearance of all talent and spirit from Maine Road.

The unhappy City career of Nicky Summerbee was curtailed with a swap deal bringing Sunderland's Craig Russell to Maine Road. Summerbee scored on debut for his new team, managed by Peter Reid. Niall Quinn was on the scoresheet in the same match. All three went on to suffer torture by play-off.

Meanwhile, the Blues went to visit Sheffield United, and trailed for virtually the whole game. Creaney, returning from a successful loan spell at Burnley, was the latest City striker to be given half a match, alongside Clark's newest signing, Russell. Phone-ins on GMR were strangely infested with callers claiming that somehow the City team would be improved by omitting the best player. The man concerned, Kinkladze, rescued a point for the Blues by beating three defenders and crossing for Horlock to score with virtually the last kick of the match. Back at the Academy, City, still third from bottom, dominated their encounter with Bradford City, winning in excess of 20 corners, but stubbornly refusing to score until three minutes into injury time, when a looping header by Vaughan sent the crowd into ecstatic celebration. For the second week running, City had timed their scoring in such a way that the opposition were left with no time to take advantage of that curious inclination to concede a goal as quickly as possible after scoring.

Despite City's improved performance, and an actual win, I struggled to find any enthusiasm for the team. The problem was that, to be perfectly frank, it would not have bothered me to see most of them depart. There had always been players whom I did not like, but Frank Clark's selection policy was ensuring a comfortable majority. Clark's signings were favoured above those players who actually might have reason for playing with some feeling for the only club they had known. Jeff Whitley, Brown and Greenacre could expect no better than a few moments as substitute, whilst Vaughan, Symons, Brannan and McGoldrick were routine selections.

City were at their subservient worst at Edgely Park the following weak. Clark's favoured defensive line-up and lightweight midfield conceded two goals to Gary Megson's Stockport County in the opening six minutes, and another after half an hour. The Blues were seemingly intent on taking every conceivable opportunity to embarrass their fanatical supporters – no change there then. Brannan pulled one goal back in the second half.

A 1-0 win away to third-placed West Bromwich Albion once more emphasised City's erratic nature, and proved too much for the Albion manager Ray Harford, who upped and left for QPR a few days later. Frank Clark had decided to take pity on Symons, now the focus of much fan bile, and alter the captaincy. Kevin Horlock, as a Clark man, was the obvious successor. He lasted only a few minutes in the job, leaving the pitch with an injury. The Blues seemed to fare better without a captain.

Back at Maine Road, Gerard Wiekens, one of the better Clark signings, was installed as the latest captain. The side also featured Michael Brown, whose display at West Bromwich was widely regarded as one of the main reasons for victory. With Kinkladze also absent injured, Jeff Whitley was given a rare outing against Wolves. There was some optimism, yet again, that City might have turned the corner, but it proved, yet again, to be ill-founded. Wiekens and Symons, captains operating in unison, presented the visitors with the only goal of the game. Wiekens made the initial error, but Symons surpassed him by slicing the ball into his own net to end a memorable week in his Maine Road career. Rösler, returning from injury, made a second-half entrance to much applause. Within a few seconds he had been presented with and wasted City's best chance of the match.

The Georgian central defender, Murtaz Shelia, marked his full debut at Birmingham City with an eighty-eighth minute headed goal to give the Blues a lead. Bizarrely, the timing proved to be too early. City contrived to concede two goals during a period of injury time stretching for 10 minutes. I was spared witnessing that particular fiasco either live or on the radio. City were fourth from bottom of Division One, but only a single point separated them from the foot of the table, and a number of difficult home matches loomed. Eddie McGoldrick became the latest on a long list of well-paid players available for transfer. Nobody wanted them.

City's last match before the Christmas of 1997 was a home encounter with recent bogey-side Middlesbrough, who were sitting proudly at the top of the League. Bryan Robson's team were now without the whinging Ravanelli and the diminutive Juninho, and were also lacking the services of Emerson who, despite his best efforts, was still registered with the club. In keeping with the habits of the season, the Blues were much improved against a top-three side, threatening goals from the start. A rejuvenated Rösler, leading the attack with conviction, converted a twentieth-minute penalty following a rash challenge on Russell. With Edghill outstanding as a right wing-back, City added a second goal when Kinkladze created a chance that Dickov, despite a reasonable try, could not fail to convert. Rösler might have added to the tally before half-time. After the break, Middlesbrough attacked, but the City defence held firm, with Shelia making an impressive home debut. The time dragged a little as the Blues tempted fate with a rearguard action, but the distraction of a North Stand rumpus prompted by drunken Middlesbrough fans, who exited the ground only to re-enter via another entrance, made the final five minutes pass quite quickly.

This victory against the League leaders, and in reasonably convincing style, might have heralded a much needed revival. It might have, but it didn't. The Christmas of 1997 was as dismal as any ever suffered by followers of Manchester City. A miserly ticket allocation and lack of enthusiasm ensured that the Boxing Day trip to Crewe Alexandra was undertaken without my presence. Before the game commenced, I was expecting my team to leave Gresty Road with some material gain, but when Ceefax signalled the opening goal midway through the first half, all of my hopes dissipated. I knew that there would be no further goals. I was right.

Two days later, Nottingham Forest, second in the table behind Middlesbrough, were the visitors to Maine Road. Frank Clark's old team were seeking to prevent an embarrassing double. They had little difficulty in doing so. Pierre van Hooijdonk converted two penalties, with Kevin Campbell scoring in between, to leave City 3-0 down 10 minutes into the second half. The defence, despite the absence of Symons, were in generous Christmas mood. The midfield was wholly inadequate, with Brannan and Russell outstandingly so. The attack was virtually non-existent. The fact that City took advantage of Forest complacency to pull back two goals did little to hide the reality that, 12 months on, City were hovering precariously above the Division One relegation zone, in precisely the same pickle from which Mr Clark had been hired to extract them. Indeed, this time around they were only a single point clear of bottom spot. It was yet another occasion for regret that Manchester City are for life and not just for Christmas.

Meanwhile, the rumour mill was working overtime. Boardroom activity resulted in the appointment of Dennis Tueart. Some interpreted this as bad news for Mr Clark.

The first match of the new year was an FA Cup third-round tie at Maine Road, against Bradford City, on a blustery January day. Forecasts of gale-force winds and hazardous driving conditions would have been enough to deter most sane people from a trip over the Pennines. Regardless of the weather, many of my City supporter friends had already decided not to bother with this game, on the understandable grounds that the current team was the footballing equivalent of Eddie 'The Eagle' Edwards. I offered my wife the option of not going, but idiocy is obviously catching. We both went.

In the first half, Bradford City performed far better than in their earlier visit of the season, and Peter Beagrie played a large part in keeping City trapped in their own half for most of the time. The wind also contributed, with Tommy Wright, preferred once more to Margetson, unable to kick far enough upfield. For all that, it was City who scored twice, Rösler taking advantage of a defensive slip, and Michael Brown adding a second, with the help of a fortunate deflection. In between, Peter Beagrie had struck a shot against the inside of the post. The visitors also managed to find the crossbar and spurn several other chances as the match progressed.

City played the second half with Ian Brightwell as the stand-in captain for the injured Wiekens, and Jim Whitley playing alongside brother Jeff. The Whitleys, particularly the younger, combined well with Kinkladze, and the Blues missed almost as many chances as Bradford. Jim Whitley was particularly unfortunate to see a shot returned off the post. It was refreshing to see a youngster playing with such confidence. That would soon be knocked out of him.

The Bradford City Board reacted to a defeat by Manchester City by sacking manager Chris Kamara, despite their comfortable mid-table position. Portsmouth repeated the trick the following week by sacking Terry Fenwick and parting company with Terry Venables after a comfortable Kinkladze-inspired 3-0 City win at Fratton Park. Russell, Kinkladze and Rösler contributed the goals.

Jim Whitley was omitted for the visit of Peter Reid's Sunderland, including Niall Quinn and Nicky Summerbee, who both received the receptions they deserved; they were very different receptions. Summerbee's only flaw, in an otherwise faultless display of ineptitude, was the cross from which Kevin Phillips scored the winning goal in the second half. Despite playing quite well, particularly the inspirational Brown, City lacked the forward power to get a goal. Rösler and Dickov simply didn't look up to it.

A nationwide terrestrial television audience usually means defeat, and the FA Cup fourth-round tie at Maine Road, against Premier League West Ham, was no exception. Mind you, after being outclassed by the visitors in the opening half, City pulled back their one goal deficit, thanks to a magical solo goal by Kinkladze, who was at his breathtaking best. For a period of about 15 minutes, City played as well as any Manchester City team for many years, with Brown and Jeff Whitley clearly inspired by their Georgian midfield partner. The culmination was a penalty miss by Rösler, midway through the second half. Two minutes later, the most impressive mere mortal on the pitch, West Ham captain Steve Lomas, drove the winning goal through a crowded penalty area, and that was that: certainly not humiliation, but defeat nonetheless. Rösler and Dickov were looking even less up to it than usual. Frank Clark's decision to sell Lomas was beginning to look a poor one.

Three days later, at home to highly placed Charlton Athletic, there was an archetypal Manchester City performance. With the game only a few minutes old, Paul Dickov proved himself capable of dispatching a penalty kick. His later demonstrations of the art of finishing were far less satisfactory. Both he and the increasingly sulky Rösler failed to make the game safe, even when Charlton emerged in the second half with an outfield player in goal. Midway through that second half, the referee evened things up by sending off Murtaz Shelia for tackling successfully, a hitherto little-known offence. Ten men often pull together to greater effect. City's 10 conceded an equaliser and looked in trouble. The Boys in Blue seemed to get off the hook in the final minute, when Kit Symons, suffering a broken nose, headed a goal to regain the lead. Against the odds, and with a show of considerable determination, City managed to swim right back on to that hook. The defence had to survive only one attack. They couldn't manage it.

Symons made amends for his goal by falling over in comical fashion, and the equaliser was duly scored. Some people appeared to be surprised by this excessive show of incompetence. I, for one, could not attain a state of surprise because such things are entirely to be expected at the Academy. A quick glance at the League table was enough to confirm that the spectre of relegation was still looming large. Few could doubt that this was the performance of true candidates for the drop. Few, that is, apart from those selective memory-loss sufferers.

A dismal 0-0 draw at Prenton Park against Tranmere, the home side's fifth in succession, was not sufficient to provide much reassurance. Frank Clark decided to restore the recovered Bradbury to the City attack at the expense of Dickov. It made little difference. In fact, the Bradbury-Rösler partnership was more than a match for the Dickov-Rösler partnership as City faced a 10-man Norwich at Carrow Road for three-quarters of the match, yet still failed to score. It was another disappointing 0-0 draw. The latest Georgian, the snappily named Kakhaber Tskhadadze, made his debut. Sadly, we have thus far been denied the pleasure of Big Ron's attempts at pronunciation during a televised match.

City had already drifted into the relegation zone before the visit of Bury to Maine Road on Valentine's Day 1998. A glance at the League table suggested that our visitors were one of only two teams worse than the Blues in Nationwide League Division One. On an unseasonably mild afternoon, the England cricket team were collapsing in the Caribbean, and the football media hacks were preoccupied with Ruud Gullit's Chelsea departure and those FA Cup ties still taking place on a Saturday. Nevertheless, a crowd approaching 30,000 still turned out at Maine Road to see two of the bottom three in Division One play an appalling game of football. I have seen numerous feeble Manchester City displays during my many years following the team. This one ranks with the best.

There were some mitigating circumstances for all those responsible to cling to. Frank Clark's much-publicised attempt to provoke offers for 15 transfer-listed players had met with a deafening silence. Yet, as well as those fit but considered surplus to requirements, City were without a number of other players, including Kinkladze and Brown, but also Shelia, Horlock, Brannan, Wiekens and others of variable note. Frank Clark still only found a place on the bench for Jeff Whitley, preferring instead to play with Russell behind the Bradbury-Rösler partnership, allowing Van Blerk ample opportunity to demonstrate his limitations as a left wing-back. At least that was how I interpreted the puzzling City tactics. Jim Whitley did play, but as the defensive, holding, midfield player, leaving a somewhat bewildered Lee Crooks as the play-maker. Jim Whitley and Crooks did, at least, show enthusiasm. Jim Whitley was rewarded by being substituted.

In truth, neither side looked capable of scoring, and both gave every indication that they were expecting relegation. It is City's ability to lose such matches – to constantly *slump* to the occasion – that defines their unique character. When City's latest captain, Ian Brightwell, was injured early in the second half, substitute Paul Beesley received a recall to the side. Within a few minutes, Beesley had inadvertently directed the ball into his own net for the winning goal. The City response to going behind peaked at apathy.

The crowd didn't know whether to turn on the players, Frank Clark or Francis Lee, so they did all three. One melodramatic soul emerged from the Kippax on to the pitch, tore his season ticket into pieces, and cast it asunder on the sacred turf. My insider knowledge of the tortured psyche of the average City fan leads me to suspect it likely that the individual concerned has already been drawn, by forces unknown, to the ticket office, in order to rectify the matter. Bury, having missed out first time around, joined Crewe and Stockport in the ever-growing 'let's all laugh at City' club.

Wednesday, 18 February 1998: another day, another manager. In keeping with the great traditions of the Academy, Frank Clark heard of his demise on GMR. It was hardly a surprise. City, second from bottom of the second English division, had achieved another all-time low. What was more surprising was the speed with which a successor was named. It smacked of competence.

Joe Royle, having been reluctant on previous occasions, was now willing to accept what seemed increasingly like the most difficult job in English football. As far as I was concerned, whoever was the manager or Chairman, and regardless of the playing staff, City's decline seemed inevitable. It was looking like 'Mission Impossible'. If you stuck Ronaldo in a City shirt he would probably degenerate into a bungling wretch.

Royle was appointed in time to take charge of the team for the evening match at home to Ipswich Town. Frank Clark's parting contribution had been to take a rather too experienced Peter Beardsley on loan from Bolton. Beardsley fitted seamlessly into the obligatory unthreatening City attack, partnering Rösler. There is always hope that when a new manager arrives, the team will be out to impress, and an improvement will be induced. On the GMR phone-in prior to the game, one caller was certainly expecting instant progress, although his reluctant rider that he didn't think we could make the play-offs was only marginally the right side of that fine sanity line. When Kit Symons headed City into the lead after only five minutes, a dramatic improvement seemed plausible, but for the majority of the remaining 85 minutes, the Blues were comfortably outplayed. The Ipswich finishing was generous to a fault, and with seven minutes remaining, City still held the lead. A fortunate three points were within our grasp. What followed suggested more than a hint of deliberate incompetence. When an Ipswich free-kick was curled gently into the City penalty area, Tommy Wright dived sideways to clutch an imaginary ball, whilst the real one proceeded directly into the net. In injury time, Ipswich scored again. They deserved to win, but the timing of the two goals was unnecessarily sadistic.

Joe Royle made a number of changes to the management, leading to the exit of Jimmy Frizzell, and the entrance of ex-City stalwart Willie Donachie as Royle's assistant. Royle, Donachie, Hartford and, on the Board at least, Tueart, all members of the last Manchester City team to win a trophy, were thus re-united. Royle's first transfer move was to take Lee Briscoe, a left-back, on loan from Sheffield Wednesday. The main sale talk naturally concerned Kinkladze, virtually the only player anyone else was likely to be terribly interested in.

A 3-1 win at Swindon Town provided some scope for happier thoughts. Rösler scored twice, and even Lee Bradbury managed a goal. The optimists were already taking mid-table for granted and planning for next season. A few days later, without Kinkladze, City responded by suffering their worst defeat of the season, 3-0 at Reading. With other sides near the bottom showing signs of improvement, especially Portsmouth – three consecutive wins under the guidance of football genius Alan Ball – the Blues found themselves looking more vulnerable than at any point in the season. Games were running out and the occasional win was not going to be sufficient.

A 1-0 home win against West Bromwich Albion, thanks to a first-half Rösler goal, provided some relief. The victory should have been more comfortable, but the Blues seldom miss the chance to put their fans through purgatory.

Three days later, I sat amongst the Faithful at Huddersfield Town's Alfred McAlpine Stadium to witness the achievement of a season's first for the Blues: a second consecutive League victory. Prior to kick-off, the PA announcer made light of his inability to cope with some Georgian names. Mind you, he also struggled with Uwé (Hughie?) Rösler and even, strangely, Craig Russell. Much of the important action took place in the murky distance, in front of an unfinished and consequently empty stand. The roof was there, but little else. One startling new development was City's ability to cause a threat at corners. It was from a Beardsley corner that the Blues took an early lead. To be honest, apart from the fact that they had scored, and that a Georgian head was implicated, I couldn't make out the precise nature of the goal because of poor visibility due to mist and rain. Apparently, Tskhadadze won the initial header and Wiekens glanced the ball in from close-range. I should have had a better view of the incident leading to Huddersfield's equaliser, from the penalty spot, but apart from indecision between Wright and his defence leading to the initial danger, I was unable to decipher the reason for the referee's decision: a Symons tug, apparently. Just before half-time, I was also unable to make out much of the build-up to City's second goal, although I could see the lone figure in front of goal directing the ball into the net: Lee Briscoe converting a Beardsley cross, apparently. I told you that live football was so much better than televised football.

The second-half header dispatched gloriously by Tskhadadze – nicknamed 'King of the air' back in Georgia – from Beardsley's corner was, I am glad to say, far clearer, and allowed City the luxury of a two-goal cushion. I needed Ceefax to fill in the details of the other two goalscorers when I got home. The pressure was clearly addling the brain of some fans. There was talk of it being a good time to sell Kinkladze because there was the ideal replacement in Beardsley.

A few days later, fellow-strugglers Oxford United were the visitors to a Maine Road awash with high hopes. The team responded with a performance that combined woeful defending with laughable finishing in just the right proportions to secure yet another home defeat. The first half had been uneventful until, just before half-time, the obligatory Symons howler – on this occasion a misplaced pass on the edge of his own penalty area – was severely punished. With Horlock and Brightwell both injured, and despite the return of Wiekens, Symons was Joe Royle's choice as captain. Royle had been trying to boost the confidence of Symons, praising him in the press. As far as I could see, it didn't seem to be working. The Blues rallied at the start of the second half, their pressure culminating in a particularly favourable opportunity for Lee Bradbury, who found himself with a clear run at the Oxford goal. There were a number of options available, including the shot past the goalkeeper, the taking of the ball around the goal-keeper, and the square pass to an unmarked Rösler. City's record transfer fee striker elected to slow down, in the hope of being caught by a defender, before side-footing the ball gently and directly to the grateful Oxford goalkeeper. Bradbury was demon-strating the predatory instincts of an elderly arthritic sheep with no remaining teeth, a pronounced limp, and poor eyesight. And fleas.

I was willing Bradbury to do well. He had, at least, got youth on his side. There was a chance that he would get better. But life at the Academy was having a strange debili-tating effect on him. A few minutes after the worst miss, Joe Royle took pity on Brad-bury by substituting him. The relief was tempered somewhat by the appearance of Dickov.

The increasingly familiar 1-0 home defeat loomed large, and would have been achieved had it not been for the sheer determination of Craig Russell, who presented the ball to an Oxford striker, not once, but twice in quick succession. On the second oc-casion, a shot was squeezed below Tommy Wright for the second goal. At 2-0, it was City's worst home defeat of the season. The Blues were still very much in the mire.

Saturday, 14 March 1998 was another in a long line of miserable days as a Manches-ter City fan. In fact, in recent years, football's main function in my life seems to be to ruin an otherwise enjoyable weekend. I didn't even go to the match. A trip to Vale Park would not have been beyond me, but I simply couldn't muster the necessary enthusi-asm. Port Vale, one of the few teams below City in the League, were having a terrible run of results. For Vale, just like several other Division One teams before them, a game against the Blues was a much needed boost.

Not going to the match saved only a couple of hours of travelling-time misery. I still followed the proceedings live, as usual, on GMR. The City team was much changed. Some of the variations were enforced. Shelia, by far the more impressive of the two Georgian defenders, was injured and out for the rest of the season. Lee Bradbury, un-derstandably, was left out of the team. The 34-year-old Richard Jobson, whose serv-ices were secured on a two-year contract by Joe Royle, was immediately called upon to play alongside the inescapable Symons. With Kinkladze recovered from injury, Pe-ter Beardsley was sent back to Bolton. Briscoe also departed.

Despite the prospect of our best player returning, the announcement of City's start-ing line-up convinced me that my decision to stay at home was an astute one. Evi-dently Joe Royle had already succumbed to the unaccountable madness that afflicts all Manchester City managers. He had restored both Ged Brannan and Neil Heaney to the side ahead of Michael Brown, who had to be content with a place as substitute for the second successive match. Maybe I have learned nothing about football from all my years as a spectator, but to me, after Kinkladze, Brown was the player City could least afford to be without. I certainly was not alone in being baffled by the team selection. Both Whitleys were playing to begin with, but after a dreadful start and a goal for Port Vale, Jim Whitley was replaced with Dickov. The derision of the fans was clear enough, even via the medium of radio.

In the second half, after Brown was eventually introduced at the expense of Brannan, the Blues equalised through Wiekens. A draw would not have been such a bad result. At least Vale would be denied all three points and remain in the relegation zone instead of City. This prospect was clearly unacceptable to the Blues. The offside-trap failed, Vale scored a late winner, and City grabbed their place in the relegation zone. With only eight matches remaining, relegation was beginning to look the most likely outcome of City's worst ever season.

Two days later, Francis Lee decided to resign as Chairman and remove himself entirely from the Board. In the absence of anybody else to blame, some fans were turning their bile on Lee. Having benefited from the vitriolic hounding of Peter Swales, Franny clearly didn't relish similar treatment. There is little doubt that Lee's decisions on choice of manager, whilst often limited by a lack of suitable applicants, had proven to be unsuccessful. The accusations that insufficient funds had been forthcoming were less convincing. The money spent by those various managers may not have been enough to compete with those occupying the upper reaches of the Premier League, but surely it was sufficient to build a team competitive in Division One. It had been comprehensively squandered.

The first game of the post-Francis Lee era was a home clash with play-off contenders and FA Cup semi-finalists Sheffield United. The most notable incident, in a mundane scoreless draw, was provided by Royle's first major signing, Jamie Pollock (£1 million, from Bolton). Pollock endeared himself to the Faithful after 10 minutes in a City shirt by committing an horrendous foul and getting involved in a punch-up. Yellow cards were waved, and Pollock settled down to playing football. He played pretty well, but it was another bad day for City.

It was around this time that Newcastle United began toying with the idea of relegation from the Premier League, whilst two of their directors offered words of wisdom to the unwashed masses, concerning the merits of all females in the North-East of England and the intelligence of Newcastle United fans. It was mooted that Newcastle were becoming the laughing-stock of football. I resented that. We had clearly earned the right to be the laughing-stock of football, and no Johnny-come-latelys were going to take that away from us without a fight!

Joe Royle came up with some surprises on transfer deadline day, bringing Ian Bishop back to City on a free transfer from West Ham, and attempting to improve a woeful attack by signing Shaun Goater (£400,000 from Bristol City). Both went straight into the starting line-up at the Pulse Stadium, Valley Parade, against my new home-town team, Bradford City. I was feeling unusually chipper before this match. There were pals staying over to enjoy the occasion, it was a bright and warm afternoon, and I had just received the surprising news that someone was prepared to publish this sorry tale. Despite Joe Royle's interesting decision to omit from the team the most talented player at the club, possibly ever, City's first-half display encouraged happy thoughts. Jeff Whitley, sneaking in unnoticed at the far post, headed a Pollock cross over the Bradford goalkeeper to give the Blues a first-half lead. I was even able to forgive Goater his two spurned debut chances, one miskicked, the other only narrowly wide. Goater's pace and height at least caused the opposition defence concern. There were a few testing moments for the Faithful leading up to half-time, but nothing to suggest the turn around to come.

At the start of the second half, Edinho, sporting white boots, came on for Bradford, and Ian Bishop, not fully fit but showing some nice touches, went off. Pepper scored a good equaliser, and the Blues visibly wilted. The rotund John McGinlay struck the post twice in quick succession after profiting from a smartly taken free-kick whilst the City defence power-napped. The Blues appeared to restore some equilibrium and the inspirational Pollock, clearly the captain regardless of the whereabouts of the official armband, twice went close. There was, however, something all too familiar about the decisive moments. Kit Symons, who had been content to hoof the ball in random directions whenever it was within hoofing range, amply demonstrated why he was adopting such a tactic when, in trying to play some football, he presented possession to the opposition in a position from which they easily manoeuvred a clear run on goal for Edinho, who scored.

In this match, Symons was extraordinary. As a schoolboy, I had a football game called *Striker*. When you pressed the head of a player, his legs would shoot upwards in a kicking motion. It wasn't a particularly good game. There was little opportunity for subtlety, and the rules were too complicated. Whenever the ball was near to Symons, it was as if he was a *Striker* player with a fully depressed head; the foot just went straight up in the air. I wasn't alone in being less than impressed. He didn't have many friends in the Pulse Stadium at the end of the match, at least not from Manchester. He probably made some new ones from Bradford.

Goater had an excellent chance to equalise but scuffed his shot wide. The final touch came in injury time when Jeff Whitley was sent off. I don't know why. The Blues should not have lost but they did, and that was all that mattered. Symons was not the only one with a depressed head.

With relegation getting ever closer, Joe Royle was demonstrating admirably his intention to take seriously the role of all Manchester City managers to confuse the Faithful. He continued to ignore Kinkladze, citing mental attitude as the reason. Admittedly, Gio seemed all set to join Ajax, but after the loyalty shown by the player to City, such treatment did not look right. In any case, he was still a genius with a football, and it would not be too controversial to suggest that these were a little thin on the ground at Maine Road.

For the re-match with Gary Megson's Stockport County, Royle decided to drop Symons to substitute and recall the long-forgotten Vaughan, whose earlier form had been particularly unimpressive. The City back three of Wiekens, Jobson and

Vaughan, with Jeff Whitley and Richard Edghill on the flanks, was yet another previously untried combination. With Pollock rightly installed as captain, alongside Bishop and Jim Whitley in midfield, and Goater making a home debut in attack, on this occasion partnered by Bradbury, Joe Royle had already instigated a number of changes in the team. With only six games remaining, and the League table taking on an alarming appearance, the one change most needed was an improvement in results.

With rain and wind in equal measure, and a full house to witness the event, you could hear the traditional whoosh as the derby-game form book flew out of the window, and City registered their second most emphatic win of the season, thanks to a little help from an old friend, Eric Nixon, in the County goal. After only a few minutes, Eric parried an optimistic shot from Pollock into the path of Goater, who delighted the Faithful with a debut goal at the North Stand End. This being City, there was barely time to register an improved feeling of well-being before County had equalised. Midway through the first half, Eric had to leave the field for treatment following a head injury. City failed to test the stand-in goalkeeper, but Eric returned in time to flap at a cross, and present Richard Jobson with a chance to head his first City goal. A couple of minutes later, Lee Bradbury found himself through on goal, one-on-one with Nixon. For the first time in a City shirt, Bradbury came out on top in that type of confrontation, and City had a 3-1 lead at half-time. Bradbury, whose best City performance to date this was by some distance, even added a fourth goal, after an astonishingly neat build-up, to give the Faithful that almost-forgotten luxury of an unassailable lead (probably) with over half an hour to go. I, for one, did not recall how to respond, and took refuge in anxiety for most of the remaining minutes. The result did not improve City's League position that much, but they did at least limp fractionally out of the relegation zone.

Apparently Eddie McGoldrick, one of a number of players sent out on loan, was playing for County. I didn't even notice him.

Easter represented City's last realistic chance to avoid taking their relegation battle right to the end of the season. At Wolves, the Blues got a good start when Pollock scored. A gargantuan error by Margetson, who had been playing well in recent matches, presented the home side with an equaliser. Early in the second half, Wolves had a player sent off, and Kevin Horlock celebrated his return to the side with a spectacular goal, direct from a free-kick. Against 10 men, City made every effort to throw away their advantage. A goal five minutes from the end, also direct from a free-kick, by City old boy Paul Simpson, allowed them to achieve their apparent objective.

I was becoming increasingly perplexed by views expressed on phone-ins and elsewhere by my fellow fans, and media pundits. In times of crisis, and there are rarely any other times, some City followers seem to blame the best player for not being even better, rather than the others for being, at best, inconsistent or, at worst, useless. The idea was catching on. With the opposition down to 10 men, and the Blues in truly desperate need of all three points, who would you like to bring on in the hope that a moment of magic might snatch those points in the closing minutes: Craig Russell or Gio Kinkladze? Joe Royle sent Russell on. He had no remaining alternatives. Kinkladze was not considered good enough even for the substitutes' bench.

On Easter Monday, City made clear their intentions to give relegation very serious consideration. Against Birmingham City, the Blues were well on top in the first half, with Pollock and especially Bradbury spurning good chances, and Wiekens rattling the crossbar at the North Stand End. In the second half, the Blues were lamentable. Still, with all three of the teams beneath us in the League losing, a draw didn't seem so bad. Bearing this in mind, City contrived to concede a last-minute goal, scored by Dele Adebole, formerly of Crewe. It completed another great holiday day at Maine Road for me. For reasons best left unexplained, I had queued twice at the ticket office, only to fail in my attempts to secure tickets for the final match of the season. I was less fortunate with the game against Middlesbrough, on Friday, 17 April 1998. I got those tickets.

Despite the fact that Captain Marvel's Middlesbrough were pushing for promotion and boasting several megastars amongst their ranks; despite the fact that the match was covered live, albeit on Sky TV; and despite yet another injury crisis – Jobson and Wiekens both out – resulting in the pairing of Symons and Vaughan alongside Edghill in City's back-three; I was hopeful that our brave boys would get something from this match. The Blues have long demonstrated their ability to lose when least expected to, but they have also, on occasions, achieved surprising victories. There were, after all, wins over both Forest and Middlesbrough to look back on in this very season. With only three matches remaining, City desperately needed a result. They got one: a crap result.

It was a wet, windy and cold Friday night at the Riverside Stadium, with the gloomy ICI backdrop contributing much to Boro's claim for the ugliest location of a football ground. The teams entered to the sound of operatic screeching, a blatant attempt to copy Sunderland, who make their entrance to the same bit of Prokofiev that used to greet the on-stage arrival of The Smiths (*Romeo and Juliet*, 'Dance of the Knights'). You see, as well as an inspiring tale of sporting endeavour, this book is educational and cultural.

To begin with, City rode their luck in defence and offered some threat in attack, but whenever the opposition goal was in sight, the preferred option seemed to be a gentle pass to the Boro goalkeeper. A couple of minutes before half-time, Paul Gascoigne bamboozled several City defenders to set up Alun Armstrong for the only goal. It was greeted with a mixture of sounds over the PA system, including some thigh-slapping accordion music. A few minutes later, Steve Vickers was sent off for a head-butt on Bradbury, who seemed to take an indecently long time before deciding to go to ground. I'm not sure whether the tabloids grabbed this opportunity to run another *dirty Vickers* story.

If the Blues needed a bit of luck, this was it. Unfortunately, they needed a lot of luck. With 10 men to face for the whole of the second half, Joe Royle instigated some complex tactical changes. They were certainly too complex for me to fathom. The initial idea of introducing Rösler, to join Bradbury and Goater in attack, was short-lived. The German retreated with injury after only a few minutes on the pitch. Part of the tactics seemed to involve abandoning defence on the right side altogether. Even ITV, with their increasingly elaborate diagrams depicting positional formations, would have been flummoxed. I can only assume that whatever instructions were given, the players did not comply, unless they were under orders to perform like a cowering shambles, in which case they did an admirable job. Seldom can 10 have had such a comfortable half of football against 11, despite the fact that two of the home side's megastars, Branca and Gascoigne, were forced to retire due to injury.

This was not so much *Dogs of War* as fluffy, pampered poodles with pretty, laser-blue ribbons. It was City's twenty-second League defeat of the season, their ninth by a score of 0-1, and their seventeenth by the odd goal. Considering that the Blues had achieved only eleven wins and eleven draws, the goal difference of minus-four was astonishing. This, in itself, is typical of City, because goal difference doesn't count in the Nationwide League. After this showing, I expected relegation.

By now the chant of 'I'm City 'til I die' was becoming increasingly common. I know that it is intended to display admirable defiance in the face of adversity, but to me it's beginning to sound like a form of punishment. I can imagine a judge; a fat, bald man, not unlike a typical English referee but younger and sporting a ludicrous wig; looking me sternly in the eye and proclaiming: 'I sentence you to be taken from this place to another place, where you shall be City 'til you die, and may God have mercy on your soul.'

This may well contravene some European directive on human rights, especially after the events of Saturday, 25 April 1998, at the Academy, which almost defy description. The excruciating Vic Reeves-in-the-club-singer-style rendition of *Blue Moon*, by Vince, the master-of-ceremonies, prior to kick-off, was merely an appetiser for the horrors to come.

It was City's last home match, and with a win against QPR essential to survival, the management decided that the idea of actually playing the best player at the club in the first team might have some superficial merit. Gio Kinkladze was selected. Within a minute of the start of the match, he had won and then gloriously dispatched a 25-yard free-kick to put the Blues ahead. We were in the land of fairy tales. Maine Road was a place of wonderment. It could only be a parting gesture from the gifted Georgian, but what a gesture.

The remainder of the opening 25 minutes simply beggared belief. After eight minutes of play, Vaughan, struggling to match his opponent, eventually managed a toe-poke in the direction of Margetson. The City goalkeeper inexplicably picked the ball up. You can't do that. It's against the rules. For some reason known only to himself, Margetson did not hang on to the ball. The City defenders looked unaccountably confused and ambled in a collective daze, oblivious to the possibilities of a rapidly taken free-kick. When old boy Mike Sheron received the benefit of quicker thoughts from one of his colleagues and shot into an empty net, those sleepy Boys in Blue were awoken with a start.

That would have been bad enough, but Jamie Pollock's emphatic headed own goal could justifiably have prompted the equivalent of a steward's enquiry. Pollock first chipped the ball over a couple of other players, with considerable skill and panache, before planting his firm header over the City goalkeeper's head. It was one of the most extraordinary things I have ever seen in a game of football. It would be easy to dismiss this as a simple error but, in fact, it was quite a complicated error. There really has to be some explanation for this sort of phenomenon. It happens far more frequently than can be attributed to chance. Surely such ineptitude cannot occur naturally. I've seen the 'X-Files'. I know the sort of thing that goes on. Is there an ancient burial ground under Maine Road? Are there sinister forces conducting some obscure mind-warping experiment? Maybe it's the sheer weight of pessimistic vibes emanating from the stands; a sort of gloomy telekinesis.

A fellow-sufferer has suggested that we might consider adopting the Columbian approach to scorers of own goals. I have pointed out that if everyone who committed that particular misdemeanour whilst wearing a City shirt was shot dead, there would not be many of the squad left. Thinking about it, I'm not entirely convinced that this isn't an argument in favour. It is best not to think too much when following Manchester City.

Without really trying, Rangers led 2-1. In an attempt to make amends, Pollock smacked a shot against the underside of the crossbar. By way of variation, Horlock located the upper-side of the crossbar. Bradbury did what he seemed to be best at, missing a number of golden chances. Having said that, Kit Symons very nearly put the match completely beyond City's grasp. After giving the ball away in front of the North Stand, Symons lunged and felled his opponent in the penalty area. For once, he escaped unpunished.

City's best available defender came on at half-time. Unfortunately, Ian Brightwell, dressed in a suit, was only carrying out the half-time draw, having been utterly ignored by Joe Royle – I admit to being biased when it comes to Brightwell; he reminds me of happier days. Ian Brightwell was the last of my beloved class of '86. His departure to Coventry, at the end of the season, was a cruel irony.

Two minutes into the second half, Shaun Goater created an opportunity that even Bradbury could take, and my hopes were raised marginally above absolute zero. They remained in that relatively elevated position until, with 15 minutes remaining, Kinkladze was replaced with Dickov. At the end of the match, the City players lingered near the tunnel, unsure of whether to risk a lap around the pitch. They decided that it may not be such a good idea, despite the fact that most of the crowd remained as if expecting it. A 2-2 draw meant that City relinquished control over their own destiny. Their position as fifth-best team in Greater Manchester was already assured.

The final match of the season, at the Britannia Stadium, Stoke, brought together two sides who both needed victory to give them a realistic chance of avoiding relegation. Even then, other results also had to go in their favour. I didn't get a ticket, although I was queuing outside the Maine Road ticket office when the last were sold. I was feeling a little sheepish because, just behind me in the queue, two stalwarts were complaining loudly about these part-timers who had suddenly emerged to snap up all the tickets, denying people, such as themselves, who had been to every other away game. Only at the Academy could you witness such desperation to attend a relegation; not so much glory-seekers as misery-seekers. Maybe I hadn't earned the right to this particular bit of first-hand misery.

The cunning ploy of omitting Gio Kinkladze for several crunch matches, including two featuring long periods against 10-man teams, further backfired when City's request that Georgia release Kinkladze from an international friendly match against Tunisia was turned down. We could hardly complain. It was difficult to make a case for Kinkladze being an essential member of the team when he hadn't merited selection for several games prior to the QPR farce. Kinkladze, playing for Georgia on a Saturday, would have to be back in time for a 1.30 Sunday kick-off time. City made the relevant arrangements, at considerable expense. For once, I had reason to thank Sky TV; in fact, more than one reason. I was able to watch the game on Sky Sports 3, at a friend's place in Manchester.

Kinkladze, having scored for Georgia, arrived back in the early hours of the morning, but was considered too tired to play from the start. It didn't matter, because City played with such confidence and passion, dominating utterly from the word go, that victory was never in doubt. Shaun Goater, performing heroically, sprinted through to lob Neville Southall for the only first-half goal. Shortly after the break, Goater's header was blocked, but Dickov followed up to score. Although Peter Thorne pulled a goal back, there was hardly time to feel the angst, because Lee Bradbury headed City's third goal almost immediately. Goater again outpaced the defence to add a fourth, injuring himself in the process. It was only then that Kinkladze came on to make his farewell appearance. Another Thorne goal and a late effort by Horlock completed a resounding and emphatic 5-2 victory, and it was all completely and utterly irrelevant.

From the second minute, Port Vale had led at Huddersfield. They built on that lead at regular intervals to end up as 4-0 winners. In Bradford, the home side held out for longer against Portsmouth, but conceded a goal just before half-time, and went on to lose 3-1. The vital opening goal was presented to Portsmouth, in slapstick fashion, by ex-*Nation's Team* goalkeeper Gary Walsh. Alan Ball, football genius, was quick to claim the credit for another miracle performed. He could hardly be more hated by fans of either Manchester City or Stoke City, but you can't fault his effort in attempting the impossible. Both teams were the victims of Ginger Spite. There was, it has to be said, a certain inevitability about it all.

For the last 15 minutes at the Britannia Stadium, the whole crowd was aware that the match was meaningless. Both teams were about to be relegated. Manchester City, for the first time in their history, would play in the English third division. I was resigned to this happening before the matches even began. City have never had that little bit of fortune required in a situation like this. Whilst the likes of Coventry City and Everton survive year after year in varying and convoluted fashion, Manchester City, given the chance on the final day, always go down. It's what we are there for, so it seems.

City finished just one point below QPR, Portsmouth and Port Vale. With one more point, they would have jumped above all three of them. We had seen 38 players used, five different captains and two managers (rather restrained, that one). There are plenty of other players who didn't feature, but who were also more than happy to collect their enormous wages. Apart from the recent Royle signings, who had to be given a chance, I would have been quite happy never again to see any of the players brought into the club by our recent procession of managers. One had gone already. Before the Stoke game, Rösler had departed to the German League-leaders, Kaiserslautern, with City receiving no transfer fee.

The exception is, of course, Kinkladze, but nobody could possibly have expected him to stay; even the most die-hard of optimists. Gio's loyalty had already been above and beyond the call of duty. Some people sought to blame Kinkladze for City's dramatic decline during his three-year period at the Academy. There seems to have been some distortion of the notion of cause and effect. To me, blaming Kinkladze for City's slump was like attributing global warming to the advent of aromatherapy. During Gio's three years, the Blues were represented at first team level by 60 players. Might I be so bold as to suggest that this may have had more to do with the team's failings than the selection of one talented individual? Bizarrely, both Kinkladze and Rösler could look forward to the prospect of the Champion's League with their respective new clubs.

I like Joe Royle. He seems like a decent chap and a good manager. I don't understand his position on Kinkladze towards the end of the season, but there's nothing to be done about that now. I'm hoping that the Blues go back to relying heavily on a youth system, developing their own talent, instead of paying high wages to inadequate journeyman mercenaries. I'm hoping that this marks the lowest point and that we will be able to recover to respectability, at least. With the enormous amounts of money floating around in the Premier League, it's hard to imagine how City will be able to compete with the best in the foreseeable future, but all you can do is hope. I knew that the Blues would, as always, begin the next season as favourites for promotion. As always, that would mean nothing. After what has happened in recent years, there seemed no reason to assume that City would do any better in a lower league. I suppose that dropping down the leagues may lead eventually to some of our less able players finding a level at which they are able to contribute. All you can do is hope.

I'm hoping for a potential sequel in about 10 years time, with a snappy title such as 'Over the Royle Blue Moon: the Miraculous Recovery of Manchester City'. All you can do is hope. I don't expect, just hope.

Looking on the bright side of events, the Blues did win three of their five consecutive relegation battles. Sorry, that's the best I can do.

In the absence of anybody of sufficiently lengthy association with the club to blame – new Chairman, new manager, new players even – I recommend that we all turn on Moonchester, the mascot. It's been steadily downhill since he first appeared. All together now, 'Moonchester out!'

Conclusion

Football in this country, so we are repeatedly told, is on an upward curve. Well, not for me and others like me it isn't. There are times when I would be quite happy to see English football abolished completely. That is the state to which my allegiance to City has reduced me. At least then, I could avoid having every weekend tainted by the performances of a bunch of overpaid men impersonating professional footballers, their apparently wilful incompetence seemingly induced by the mere wearing of a City shirt. Whilst the games are still being played, I will feel compelled to place my feelings of well-being under their influence, regardless of whether I am in attendance or not. I wonder if there is some kind of treatment for this self-inflicted misery, but I fear not. At least, I am not alone. Group sessions for many thousands of us run on a biweekly basis throughout the year, pausing only for that all too brief summer respite.

My only conclusion from this sorry tale is that Manchester City fans are all being tested. Just how bad do the Blues have to be before large numbers begin to give in? In fact, throughout the desperate 1997/98 season, the Faithful continued to attend in astonishing numbers, demonstrating a thoroughly irrational loyalty that ought, in a fair world, to be rewarded. Other so-called big clubs in similar dire straits have not been so fortunate in the blind devotion of their fans. There is no shaking those loyal Blues from their determination to remain, whatever the provocation. I fear that the difficulties will come in the longer term. How do you persuade a child that their best interests lie in following Manchester City? Answers on a postcard, please.

Although Manchester City are guaranteed my continuing blind devotion, this does not necessarily extend to individual players. There was a time when merely playing for the Blues meant hero status, but that time has passed. I now operate a system of devotional apartheid. Those who are not products of the Academy youth system must earn my devotion, whereas those who have emerged from within the City ranks are entitled to it by right. Judging by the nature of some frequently audible vitriolic comments from fellow fans, particularly at home matches, I may be in a minority as far as this attitude is concerned. I don't claim to speak for City fans and no City fan can assume to speak for me. We are not a homogeneous mass, merely a disparate group thrust together by adversity, like victims of the same incurable disease, or members of alcoholics anonymous. I'm Craig and I'm a Manchester City fan.

What we do have in common is that, collectively, we are Manchester City, more than any Chairman, Directors, managers or players, all of whom come and go with alarming regularity. And even if the habit of attending matches was broken, once trapped, there is no escape. A bad result for the Blues, or yet another good result for *The Nation's Team*, will still cause that same anguish. I suppose that we could try speculative brain surgery or life on a remote desert island but, even then, some prat on a yacht is liable to float by sporting a red shirt. And knowing our luck, the brain surgery would erase all memories of the 5-1 derby win, whilst leaving us with a never-ending repetitive mind-loop replaying *those* goals by Antic, Villa, Lomas O.G., Pollock O.G., Antic, Villa, Lomas O.G., Pollock O.G., Antic, Villa, Lomas O.G., Pollock O.G . . .

I calculated recently that I have spent approximately two months of my life watching City perform live. Maybe we should be able to opt to get it all over with in one go. Imagine the purgatory of a two-month City match. You can bet that the Blues would take an early lead, and hang on to it for 60 days before conceding two goals in the last two minutes, one a comedy own goal.

It may be that my football team chose me because of my often pessimistic nature. Certainly, if you look at my music collection, melancholy tunes predominate. Recent additions include Portishead and Massive Attack – hardly foot-tapping, karaoke material. Mind you, listening to such things makes me feel uplifted; watching City rarely has a similar effect. In any case, the number of unreconstructed optimists around the Academy remains at stubbornly high levels. I prefer to think of it the other way around. I blame my occasionally bleak outlook on Manchester City Football Club.

It is fashionable to attribute blame whenever anything goes awry. I like to apportion the lion's share to Peter Swales, John Bond and Alan Ball, but am forced to acknowledge the significant contributions of Malcolm Allison, whose transfer madness was costly in more than one sense, and Francis Lee, my boyhood hero, who can hardly claim to have improved matters on the field during his stint as Chairman. In reality, such a dramatic and comprehensive decline, achieved against considerable odds, can only be ascribed to a team effort. City's decline has been a complex, multi-layered farce, with trouser-dropping contributed from numerous sources, and many different faces dripping with the remnants of custard pie. For what it's worth, I would consider the worst cock-ups to be three Peter Swales decisions: firstly, to bring back Allison; secondly, having sanctioned the spending spree, to sack Allison prematurely and appoint John Bond; finally, to dismiss Peter Reid. Since Reid's departure, every season has been a struggle.

Even as I write, with the worst ever season barely over, the optimists are predicting recovery and I hope that, for once, they are right. I am sick of having my gloomy prognostications proved correct. There is a common view that we may now be poised to turn the corner. Unfortunately, this turning of the corner has been mentioned rather frequently. Multiple turning of corners leaves you going round in circles.

Still, when all's said and done, being a City fan brings with it a certain credibility – nobody could seriously accuse us of being glory-seekers – and unlimited opportunities to laugh at yourself and your team. City are undoubtedly something of a phenomenon. And at least we don't support *The Nation's Team*. That should be some comfort to you all, because as far as football is concerned, despite all that has happened, I cannot imagine anything worse. I really can't.

And remember, it is only a game. Isn't it?